BLUE

The Architecture of UN Peacekeeping Missions

MALKIT SHOSHAN

Actar Publishers

Contents

Intro-duction

UN Peacekeeping Missions 2020

13 UN peacekeeping missions
Countries contributing uniformed personnel: 121
Personnel: 95,110
Budget 2020: US$6.5 billion
UN presence in 207 cities, towns, and rural areas with over 540 sites including various camps and super camps, airfields, headquarters, and logistics centers.

I. BLUE: The Architecture of UN Peacekeeping Missions

As of 2020, United Nations peacekeeping missions were taking place in 13 countries. Their material footprints cover large territories, with a physical presence in over 150 African cities and rural areas. These missions are deployed in some of the world's most impoverished areas, where issues of perpetual armed violence, extraction and dispossession, and extreme climate conditions converge. Their spatiality is deeply embedded in the legacy and history of modernity and the nation-state—its institutions, bureaucracy, and governance structure. Since 2000, with the end of the Cold War and the beginning of globalization, the impact and footprint of peacekeeping missions have grown markedly. Their expansion can be linked to global processes of militarization, financing, and procurement methods dependent on centralized and ever-growing global supply chains.

In the past decade, I have researched the UN missions' impact on cities and communities in conflict-affected regions. I began this work in 2007 after visiting Kosovo and witnessing the United Nations' massive presence in cities. The extensive material footprint of UN missions raised many questions about their legitimacy, their legacy, and the capacity of their architecture to contribute to or sustain peaceful environments. This long journey, which began with a spatial and even design-related question, developed into a lengthy inquiry into the powers that operate in the background of spatial production. This project inevitably expanded to include other disciplines and assembled partners in the fields of international relations, policy, economics, the social sciences, anthropology, human rights, military engineering, and environmental studies. In the process, architecture and design tools became the vehicles for highlighting the connections between these fields and how they are being consolidated, materialized, and synthesized in space. The experience as a whole demonstrates the need for designers to rethink how design, architecture, and urban planning tools can be used for research, advocacy, and empowerment, and contribute to social, political, and cultural change.

With our think-tank FAST: Foundation for Achieving Seamless Territory, working on the margins of architecture with values and priorities that reach far beyond material form, we discovered a new space for connecting with the world. As we navigated scales, complexities, and different institutional realities, we realized that we could become agents of change. We amplified progressive voices within existing institutions with the aim of shifting the status quo. The most effective tool was the ability to make connections and uncover the entanglement between financial, political, social, and cultural mechanisms and the production of space—the built and lived environments. We began tracing the associations between words in policy documents, procurement methods, and spatial production, highlighting issues of equity, institutional responsibility, and accountability. As we deployed this multi-scalar and cross-disciplinary approach, we explored how to intervene in these relationships and contingencies to produce space through words as well as through formal design: influencing policies and institutional processes to help liberate resources, empower marginalized communities, and contribute to a more just society.

Design Activism

BLUE is not just a research and design project; it is an experiment with activism. It is an unsolicited project that emerged after a visit to Kosovo, where compounds, camps, logistic hubs, headquarters, checkpoints, and all sorts of physical installations were built swiftly under the auspices of a UN peace mission, reaching a point where they began to dominate the local landscape. This material presence raised many questions: How do these foreign missions impact the local population? Who designs them? For whom? Who pays for them? How are they procured and maintained? Is the local population involved? If so, how? What will be left behind after the missions are gone?

These questions expanded into the need to situate international peace missions within broader historical, cultural, social, economic, and political contexts. This level of complexity required, among other things, rethinking the operative field of architecture not as a privately commissioned task but as a public service—encompassing research, advocacy, and activist practices. How do we claim the knowledge produced by architecture and design and their specific representation formats as agents and tools for activism? What kind of strategies, tactics, and actions can be used to intervene in political processes to instigate change? These questions led to an ongoing exercise in challenging hegemonic powers and visions through a set of accumulated actions that operate in multiple spaces simultaneously.

Striving to contribute to social, political, or cultural change is a noble goal, but it is also an extremely complex and slow process. This project started in 2007 as an open-ended exploration. The exploration of the subject of UN missions has coincided throughout with design experimentation rooted in activism.

Research in Public

Where to begin? The visit to Kosovo was the jumping-off point for a long journey of exploration, improvisation, and intervention. The inquiry had no clear institutional support, target group, or audience, and it had no defined relationship with one discipline or another. The reality in which peace missions take place and their spatial manifestations are notably invisible to people who are not directly impacted by them. The subject is under researched. Information is mostly classified, and sites are restricted. The geographical areas in which peace operations take place are hard to reach because of security concerns, remoteness, and lack of infrastructure such as roads and airports. Information on present and past missions is mostly restricted, protected, and unavailable to the general public.

In "Becoming Research," Irit Rogoff discusses the meaning of research today:

> It allows a small amount of agency within a world whose rampant neoliberal drives have taken away both agency and the ability to actually argue points in terms of content and substance. The shift from someone who expresses themselves individually to the position of being a researcher is a shift in which one doesn't simply acquaintance or protest against but allows oneself to get involved with the workings of institutions, of protocols, of memory, and of community—not in compliance, or defiance, but in efforts to rewrite these through their very working.[1]

1 Rogoff, Irit. 2018. "Becoming Research" in: Choi Jina and Helen Jungyeon Ku, eds. The Curatorial in Parallax. Seoul, Republic of Korea: National Museum of Modern and Contemporary Art, Korea, pp. 39–52.

This research, too, had to operate in all these realms, outside the neoliberal logic and contingent on institutions, protocols, memory, and community.

This new project had to be realized on multiple fronts to create alliances and partnerships that could permit access to information, institutions, and communities. Building on my previous projects in the field of architecture, politics, and activism (such as *Atlas of the Conflict*, *One Land Two Systems*, *Reconstruction of Memory*, and *Zoo*) I approached local academic and cultural institutions in the Netherlands: TU Delft, the Creative Industries Fund, and Het Nieuwe Instituut to help hosting these inquiries. It took a couple of years to consolidate a platform from which this research could be launched. I curated a series of public events and conversations at the intersection of design, activism, and security studies under the title "Drones and Honeycombs," with the intention of breaking down the research into three areas: 1. Drones, in reference to the influence of war machines and technological innovation on our lives; 2. Compounds, in reference to the growing militarization of the built environment and the production of all sorts of spaces of exception; and 3. Missions, in reference to the international organization and management of war/peace and the impact of international relations and policy on shaping our lived world.

These three areas of inquiry were translated into a sequence of public events that brought together these research interests with policy makers, cultural and knowledge institutions, and the public. It allowed me to establish a relationship with the Dutch Ministries of Foreign Affairs and Defense and other relevant actors. We used conventional formats such as symposiums, workshops, conferences, and exhibitions as platforms for a public investigation, in which we invited military engineers, diplomats, human rights lawyers, and activists to take part. While the military engineers slowly provided information about the hardware, specific drawings, materials, design parameters, and spatial considerations, the diplomats and lawyers provided information about the software, the national and international policies, and the mandates of the Dutch engagement with the UN. Slowly, we were allowed to access decision-making processes, protocols, and designs while establishing and solidifying relationships with relevant institutions.

Public Programs, Representation, and Policy Interventions

One of the consequences of this public inquiry was the invitation to participate in a wide range of public programs, including curating the Dutch pavilion for the 2016 Venice Architecture Biennale. This international cultural platform allowed us to further the visibility and impact of our research, collect evidence, and form new alliances with various institutions. We received a formal invitation from the Dutch ministries to visit a Dutch-designed base in Mali (see Camp Castor).

Public exhibitions, like the Biennale, can serve as powerful tools for advocacy and engagement. The Dutch Chief of Defense, Tom Middendorp, attended the exhibition's opening. He arrived with a delegation of soldiers wearing celebratory uniforms complete with unusual hats, pom-poms, and bells. Their march through the Venice Biennale, so out of place, resembled a Sicilian procession or an art performance.

Middendorp has a background as a military engineer. As he toured the exhibit, he spent some time next to the large light installation containing some 170 blue light bulbs. Each represented an African city with a large UN presence. Combined, these places are home to over 30 million inhabitants. Usually, UN regional maps offer an abstract overview showing the names of missions and the agencies involved. Here, liberated from institutional protocols, we could use our own aggregated data to inform the design. I decided to include the names of all the cities and a detailed relational overview: the number of local inhabitants in relation to the number of foreign peacekeepers and the host country GDP in comparison to the mission expenditure. These relations are not commonly shown, but they revealed the immense magnitude of missions. Middendorp was surprised by the scale and by our approach to data and space. He studied the rest of the exhibition and paused again next to the series of policy recommendations we put forward. Inspired, upon returning to the Netherlands Middendorp began using his agency to advocate for the need for a paradigm shift in the ministry, NATO, and the UN.

Our questions resonated deeply with civil servants, journalists, diplomats, and politicians, who shared the project and its premise with their networks. Consequently, the Dutch Ministry of Defense launched a two-day conference called "Ecosystems" and "Future Force," held in The Hague.[2] Their European partners were invited to address the topic. As this process was unfolding in the Netherlands, the Dutch permanent mission to the UN was campaigning for a seat on the UN Security Council. They were looking to promote a new approach to UN missions. They invited us to join the Dutch Minister of Foreign Affairs, Bert Koenders,[3] to present BLUE at the UN Secretariat.

The presentation included an address to the African Union member states and the exhibition "Blue: Islands in Cities" in a space adjacent to the Security Council chamber. We wrapped our findings around the UN tower's pillars and questioned the institution's impact on cities and communities across the world, and on the environment. A few months later, after the Netherlands won its bid for a seat on the Security Council, its representatives attempted to further disseminate the notion of sustainability, legacy, and responsibility for the disruptions caused by UN bases, introducing new language into the outcome of the so-called C34 negotiations. Led by a Special Committee, the negotiations ended with a resolution on peacekeeping to be adopted by the General Assembly on a yearly basis. These steps paved the way for further engagement and change. The resolution reads, as follows:

> The Special Committee emphasizes that the least disruption in transition and departure takes place when United Nations missions work closely with their national counterparts and regional partners. Mission transitions should take into account and seek to minimize potential economic impacts of the mission's departure. In this light, the Special Committee recognizes that co-use and after-mission-use of United Nations facilities by the local population and members of the UN family contributes positively to a smooth transition and to sustainability of a United Nations mission. The Special Committee acknowledges that co-use is depending on the current safety and security situation whilst after-use will only be possible if the facilities are constructed in such a way that they fit within the local culture and can be maintained, after mission's departure, through local available resources. As such, the Special Committee requests the Secretariat to develop policy on the co-use and after-use of United Nations facilities in missions by the local population and requests to be briefed on the progress well before its next substantial session. (New paragraph —Netherlands, 17.01.2017)

Each of these events led to new partnerships and changes in awareness, policy, and culture. The exhibition at the UN brought us into contact with the institution's officers and with international policy research institutes such as the Center on International Cooperation at NYU and the International Peace Institute.

2 Future Force Conference. 2017, available at: www.futureforce conference.com.

3 "Speech Koenders at 'What Design can Do'." Government of the Netherlands, available at: government.nl/documents/speeches/2016/07/01/speech-koenders-at-what-design-can-do, and "Koenders visits UN in New York."

"Mr Koenders will also open an exhibition entitled 'Blue: Islands in Cities' at UN Headquarters. It charts the research by Dutch-Israeli architect Malkit Shoshan on how UN peace mission bases can be used by local communities both during and after a mission.

Mr Koenders will also speak about the Kingdom of the Netherlands' bid for a seat on the UN Security Council for the 2017–2018 term. 'We want to shoulder our share of international responsibility and make a meaningful contribution towards a safer, fairer and more prosperous world,' commented Mr Koenders. The elections will be held in June." Government of the Netherlands. News item, 25-01-2016, 13:45, available at: www.government.nl/latest/news/2016/01/26/koenders-visits-un-in-new-york.

Both helped FAST translate the project into policy papers that have been used by various UN agencies and member states.

Our fascination with Kosovo and our background in architecture and comprehensive spatial analysis have led us not only to develop a project but to slowly form a new practice at the intersection of architecture, international relations and activism.

On the margins of architecture and in its intersectionality with other fields, we found an entire world. We have built up multiple partnerships and relationships with others who care. As we have attempted to capture, liberate, and decentralize information and resources, our research has always been made public: our maps, spatial analyses, observations, recorded stories, and evidence have been placed on decision makers' tables to challenge their policies and actions. These evolving and revolving tactics—incidents, events, and interventions—on multiple scales and in a variety of spaces, have helped us shift the discourse and multiply our allies within governmental and intergovernmental institutions, cultural institutes, and, on the ground, with communities that have been directly impacted by UN missions. As we turn away from conventional architecture, critical theory, and crisis/poverty/disaster fetish aesthetics – seen all too often in architecture—we continue to seek out and discover new avenues for the subversion of power, empowerment, and change. Rather than designing physical spaces, we have learned that interventions in policy—by introducing new language, definitions, or single words—can liberate spaces and resources, empower local communities, and contribute to changing institutional practices and cultures.

BLUE

BLUE was initially used in reference to our first comprehensive case study, the Dutch Camp for the UN in Gao, Mali: Camp Castor. The camp is situated along the Niger River at the edge of the Sahara Desert. Here, the nomads, the Tuareg—also known as the "blue people" because of their indigo clothing—and the "blue helmets" of the UN meet. BLUE represents the convergence of the desert and the Dutch approach, the nomads and the settlement.

In Camp Castor, various shades of BLUE are intertwined; each represents different cultures and institutions: blue as boundlessness in modernism, or as the engineer's blueprint, blue as protection of the human body by the spirit world, blue as a peaceful background on the UN flag, and blue as the expanse of seas and skies in the Netherlands. For us, there are various shades of BLUE too. BLUE exists at the intersection of architecture, human rights, and activism. It emerges in times of conflict as the endless space of imagination and pragmatism that can produce alternative visions. BLUE is made up of a series of narratives based on conversations with military engineers, architects, local inhabitants, anthropologists, economists, activists, artists, policymakers, journalists, and novelists. Incorporating cultural and spatial explorations, BLUE situates architecture in three distinct ways: as research, identifying and uncovering spatial challenges and opportunities; as a practice, improving people's living environments; and as a critical cultural space, reflecting on phenomenal transitions in society. With this approach, we ask whether architecture can reinvent both the built environment and itself.

Notes on Peace

What does peace actually mean? The word has many associations and connotations: peace as the absence of war, peace as an agreement and a compromise between two or more parties. Immanuel Kant's idea of "perpetual peace"[4] from 1795 departed from the assumption that

> The state of peace among men living side by side is not the natural state (*status naturalis*); the natural state is one of war. This does not always mean open hostilities, but at least an unceasing threat of war. A state of peace, therefore, must be established, for in order to be secured against hostility it is not sufficient that hostilities simply be not committed; and, unless this security is pledged to each by his neighbor (a thing that can occur only in a civil state), each may treat his neighbor, from whom he demands this security, as an enemy.

Kant's articles for perpetual peace among states were also the origin of a new paradigm of international relations, human and civil rights, and institutions like the UN and the nation-state, ushering in the triumph of modernity—that very modernity, which, in the words of Hanna Arendt, is

> an age of bureaucratic administration and anonymous labor, rather than politics and action, of elite domination and the manipulation of public opinion. It is the age where history as a "natural process" has replaced history as a fabric of actions and events, where homogeneity and conformity have replaced plurality and freedom, and where isolation and loneliness have eroded human solidarity and all spontaneous forms of living together. Modernity is the age where the past no longer carries any certainty of evaluation, where individuals, having lost their traditional standards and values, must search for new grounds of human community as such.[5]

The conversation about peace is also a conversation about war. As Walter Benjamin also wrote, "He who wants peace should speak of war. He should speak of the past one and, above all, he should speak of the coming one."[6] The end of World Wars exacerbated the creation of a new global order of governance. Old empires were disassembled into nation-states, and international relations and diplomacy became the most effective tools for the prevention of wars and their sequential devastation, and for the advancement of peace under the auspices of the United Nations,[7] an assembly of internationally recognized nation-states working in pursuit of four pillars: peace and security; human rights; the rule of law; and development.

The integration of peace and development was first conceived by President Roosevelt and Governor Herbert Lehman (one of the brothers in the Lehman brothers banking group of NYC). Lehman was appointed by Roosevelt to lead the European Recovery Program (ERP) and to set up the Office of Foreign Relief and Rehabilitation (OFRRO). In 1947, OFRRO was integrated with the United Nations Relief and Rehabilitation Administration (UNRRA). At its peak in 1946, it included 12,893 staff members and an operational budget of about US$2 billion. Roosevelt and Lehman's intervention in the recovery of European nations created the global financial institutions and mechanisms that connected the processes of making, keeping, and building peace to the world of finance.[8]

In keeping with the four pillars, the UN conceived programs and agencies to cultivate the means to promote, preserve, and tangibly build peace around the world. Today, these means continue to evolve in order to address

4 Kant, Immanuel. Perpetual Peace: A Philosophical Sketch, 1795. London: S. Sonnenschein, 1903.

5 d'Entreves, Maurizio Passerin, "Hannah Arendt", The Stanford Encyclopedia of Philosophy (Fall 2019 Edition), Edward N. Zalta (ed.), available at: https://plato.stanford.edu/archives/fall2019/entries/arendt.

6 Walter Benjamin, 'Peace Commodity' (1926), in Walter Benjamin's Archive, trans. Esther Leslie, Verso, London,2007, pp. 56–7.

7 The Charter of the United Nations was signed in San Francisco on June 26, 1945 and is the foundational document for all the United Nations' work. The United Nations was established to "save succeeding generations from the scourge of war," and one of its primary purposes is to maintain international peace and security. Although not explicitly provided for in the Charter, peacekeeping has evolved into one of the main tools used by the United Nations to achieve this purpose. The Charter gives the United Nations Security Council primary responsibility for the maintenance of international peace and security. Source: United Nations Peacekeeping Operations Principles and Guidelines, UN, 2008.

8 Williams, Andrew J. "'Reconstruction' before the Marshall Plan." Review of International Studies, vol. 31, no. 3, Cambridge University Press, 2005, pp. 541–58

past, present, and future challenges to peace and security; expand human rights, update the rule of law; and contribute to a more stable world overall. At the same time, this process is subjected to external politics, power dynamics, and other forces that affect the interpretation and implementation of these aspirations for peace.

In 1964, two decades after the end of the Second World War, the editors of the first issue of the *Journal of Peace Research*, all men, described two polar scenarios for the state of the world. The first was based on the Hobbesian war of all against all—a world characterized by an entirely individualistic structure without cooperation or the formation of groups, a world of constant conflict, unfettered in the choice of means of destruction: "everybody uses whatever kind of violence he knows to destroy whomever he wants. Hobbes had the vision; nuclear physics has perfected the means."[9] The second scenario was an "extending sphere of cooperation, integration and harmony to encompass the whole world until a state is reached where Man experiences no differential in his identification with other men, and the violence is reduced to zero."[10]

The editorial team sought to use their journal as a space for broad discussion on peace and felt that it might offer "the conditions for moving closer to a universal state of General Complete Peace, or at least not drifting closer towards General Complete War."

A few years later, in an essay titled "Violence, Peace and Peace Research," Johan Galtung, a Norwegian sociologist and the principal founder of the discipline of peace and conflict studies, addressed the relationship between violence and peace. If peace is the absence of violence, he reasoned, then we should attempt to gain a better understanding of how to define violence. He argued that "an extended concept of violence leads to an extended concept of peace"[11] and offered an in-depth definition of two types of violence: personal and structural, positing peace as the absence of both.

Regarding personal violence, Galtung wrote, "[a] clear subject-object relation is manifest because it is visible as action. It corresponds to our ideas of what drama is, and it is personal because there are persons committing the violence. It is easily captured and expressed verbally since it has the same structure as elementary sentences in (at least Indo-European) languages: subject-verb-object, with both subject and object being persons. Violence without this relation is structural, built into the structure."

He continued to expand on this description by referring to structural violence as social injustice. "The absence of structural violence is what we have referred to as social justice, which is a positively defined condition – egalitarian distribution of power and resources." Social justice is a positive peace, and peace researchers can posit various models of participation, decentralization, co-decision, and "richer concepts and forms of social action that combine absence of personal violence with fight against social injustice... There are more than enough people willing to sacrifice one for the other—it is by aiming for both that peace research can make a real contribution."

Exploring the connection between personal and structural violence on the scale of the body and the institution is critical for the achievement of peace. In *Emergent Strategy*, Adrienne Marie Brown discusses the relationship between small and large in a chapter titled "Fractals," which she defines as "infinitely complex patterns that are self-similar across different scales."[12] She applies this idea to all sorts of organizations that work toward social change and social justice, and she critiques their structure as they reflect the status quo. She quotes Albert Camus, "The only way to deal with an unfree world is to become so absolutely free that your very existence is an act of rebellion." The absence of violence and the existence of social justice should be embedded in peacekeepers' systems and protocols. And yet, rather than evolving and progressing toward peace, the

9 An Editorial. Journal of Peace Research, 1964, Vol. 1, No. 1. 1964, pp. 1–4..

10 Ibid

11 Johan Galtung. "Violence, Peace, and Peace Research". Journal of Peace Research, 1969, Vol. 6, No. 3 (1969), pp. 167–191.

12 Brown, Adrienne M. Emergent Strategy: Shaping Change, Changing Worlds. Chico, CA: AK Press, 2017.

UN and its agencies have drifted toward the perpetuation of highly hierarchical and exclusionary practices, power dynamics, and violence.

If peace is a process that is endlessly evolving and negotiating a space between utopia and a pragmatic state of conflict resolution, what does it mean to "keep the peace" in myriad specific and endlessly complex contexts?

After all, peace is not a neutral term. In fact, it has often been abused. In *Violence Taking Place*, Andrew Herscher reminds us how destruction has often been a precondition for the realization of new regimes of social and political power, and that these new regimes contribute to the erasure of past cultures. These cycles of violence are taking place not only in times of war, but also in times of peace. Similarly, in the *Shock Doctrine*, Naomi Klein investigates how wars, coups, terrorist attacks, market crashes, or natural disasters are fertile ground to push through radical pro-corporate measures, often labeled as "shock therapy." She examines the brutal tactic of using the public's disorientation following a collective shock: "After a crisis, private contractors move in and suck up funding for work done badly, if at all—then those billions get cut from government budgets",[13] and bypass the participation of the locals.

Peace is an idea that manifests itself in space, societal institutions, and human relations. It has an aspirational, rhetorical, and a material form. Keeping the peace, in this project, entails a study of the institutional hardware—bases, headquarters, airfields, and supply chains; and software—international relations, policy, regulations, training protocols, corporate procurement, financial flows, and all sorts of fluctuating guidelines and jargons used by policymakers to guide and sustain the peace apparatus.

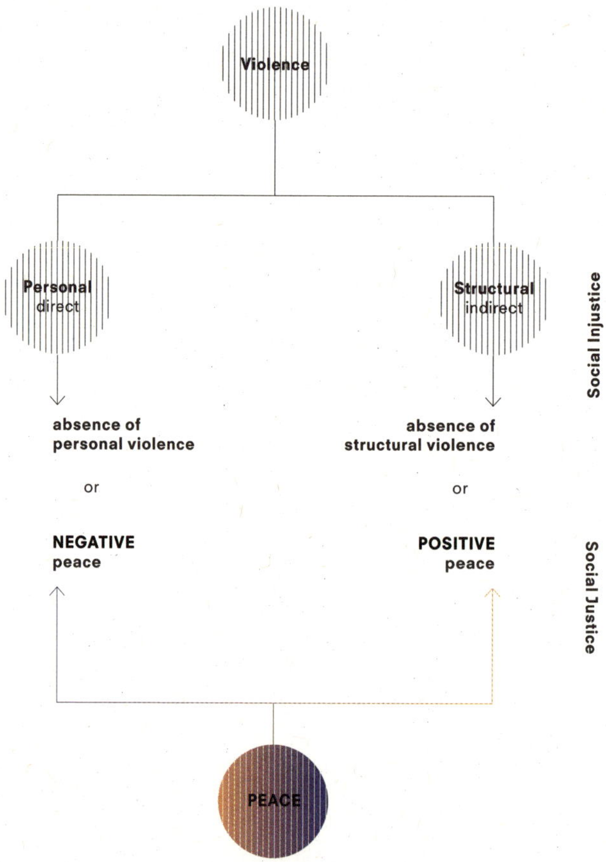

The Extended Concepts of Violence and Peace by Johan Galtung.

Peacemaking, Peacekeeping, and Peacebuilding

Peacemaking, peacekeeping, and peacebuilding are not only terms but are protocols and agencies that guide the UN's peace implementation process. After the end of the Cold War and in the early days of globalization, an unprecedented number of violent intrastate conflicts emerged, which led to an evolving and expanding international response on the part of the UN. In 1992, the Secretary-General Boutros Boutros-Ghali introduced the idea of post-conflict peacebuilding in "An Agenda for Peace."[14] It included four main areas of action: the use of *preventative diplomacy* before the eruption of violence; *peacemaking* as a way to bring hostile parties to agreement; *peacekeeping* operations deploying military personnel and civilians for the prevention of conflicts and peacemaking; and *peacebuilding*, aimed at strengthening and solidifying peace to avoid relapses into conflict. In 2000, in response to the failure of complex peacekeeping missions in Africa and the Balkans, the Brahimi Report[15] expanded the scope of peacemaking/keeping/building, and in 2005 the Peacebuilding Commission was established by the UN to draft long-term strategies for reconstruction, institution-building, and sustainable development in war-affected regions.[16]

Although in theory "the term peacebuilding has become broader to cover all activities undertaken before, during, or after a violent conflict to prevent, end, and/or transform violent conflicts and to create the necessary conditions for sustainable peace—including peacemaking and peacekeeping as part of the peacebuilding process," in practice peacekeeping and peacebuilding are situated in two separate UN departments with different mandates. The amount of resources dedicated by the UN for peacekeeping—from deployment of troops to mission budgets—far exceeds those assigned for other UN programs. Peace operations are divided into two groups: "(1) the traditional 'peacekeeping operations' that are backed by the UN Security Council, have the consent of the parties in the conflict, operate within a limited mandate (self-defense and defense of the mandate), and act with impartiality; and (2) 'peace support operations' that do not need the consent of the conflicting parties, are not necessarily neutral, are impartial to the mandate, and can make use of the full spectrum of force to fulfill tasks such as countering peace spoilers and applying pressure for the peace operation to succeed, assisting interim civil authorities, protecting humanitarian relief operations, and guaranteeing or denying movement, etc."[17]

This research focuses on the first, traditional peacekeeping operations, aiming to reveal their spatial footprint and their impacts on the built and lived environments. Their scale also compels us to question and reimagine the international, spatial, and cultural structures we put into place to support communities across the world in times of crisis.

13 Klein, Naomi. "Naomi Klein: How Power Profits From Disaster." The Guardian, 2022, https://www.theguardian.com/us-news/2017/jul/06/naomi-klein-how-power-profits-from-disaster.
14 "An Agenda for Peace: Preventive Diplomacy, Peacemaking and Peace-keeping." Report of the Secretary-General pursuant to the statement adopted by the Summit Meeting of the Security Council on 31 January 1992. Boutros Boutros-Ghali, available at: https://digitallibrary.un.org/record/145749?ln=en.
15 "Brahimi Report." Report of the Panel on United Nations Peace Operations (2000). Identical letters dated 21 August 2000 from the Secretary-General to the President of the General Assembly and the President of the Security Council. A/55/305–S/2000/809. Distr.: General 21 August 2000.
16 Reychler and A. Langer (eds.), "Luc Reychler: A Pioneer in Sustainable Peacebuilding Architecture" in Pioneers in Arts, Humanities, Science, Engineering, Practice 24. 2020, pp 271–299.
17 Ibid.

Overview of Chapters

The book is divided into four main parts. The first part offers a brief introduction to UN peacekeeping missions, their history and evolution, from their inception to this day. The overview is not situated within the boundaries of one discipline or another. It brings together various narratives and field observations while referring to scholarship in cultural history, international relations, spatial analysis, and design.

It touches on and draws links to the history and legacy of colonization in Africa, beginning with the first European expeditions, which laid the foundations for European domination, modern global practices of resource extraction (materials and bodies), trade systems, supply chains, and modular construction techniques. These early expeditions of religious and scientific explorers laid the foundations for the exploitation of the continent and are at the root of many of the conflicts that have shaped people's lives, nature, and large ecological systems across Africa and the world. These are the conflicts that the next generation of international missions are meant to address under the auspices of the international community and the UN. The first UN mission to Israel–Palestine was followed by 56 others, many of which were situated in areas of former European colonies. In the early 1990s the locations shifted to the regions impacted by the collapse of the Soviet Union and the end of the Cold War. In 2020, the UN had 13 active missions, 7 of which are in Africa.

The second part of the book focuses on the operational phase of a UN mission. It looks at the beginning of the UN mission in Mali (MINUSMA) and its immense material footprint through personal observations from field research and ongoing conversations with military engineers, diplomats, UN officers, politicians, rebels, anthropologists, economists, geographers, cultural historians, and designers. The research attempts to capture some of the complexity embedded in the production of UN missions, their institutional protocols, history, and everyday reality. Our investigation resulted in an advocacy campaign and an intervention on a policy level to introduce the notion of legacy. It stressed the need for responsibility and accountability on the part of UN agencies and the international community with regard to the impact of their missions.

The third section of the book centers on the drawdown of a UN mission. It examines the closing of the UN operation in Liberia (UNMIL) and the end phase of the mission. Similar to the previous chapter, it builds on various resources, including field observations, spatial analyses, literature, documentary films, testimonials in books, news items, and blogs, as well as ongoing conversations with UN officers, diplomats, policymakers, local inhabitants, and others. This segment of the book further examines the environmental impacts of UN missions and the waste they leave behind. Following the Mali research, this effort was intended to ramp up pressure on UN agencies and outline new parameters for referencing and input on how UN missions end and what they leave behind.

The last part, Design for Legacy, is the summary of policy recommendations for changing practices. It emphasizes the need for UN agencies to address, during deployment, issues of accountability and responsibility for the impact of missions and the legacy they leave behind. Rather than taking a dogmatic tone, this part attempts to showcase our ability to drive change by confronting large-scale institutions like the UN through engaging with their bureaucracy and processes. The chapter offers a new strategy and matrix for legacy that has been endorsed and promoted by various member-states and UN agencies, which highlights a path toward new practices in the deployment and, most critically, the transition and drawdown phases of UN missions.

UN

UN Peace-keeping Missions and Their Evolving Spatiality

UN peacekeeping missions 2020

13 UN peacekeeping missions are deployed in more than 200 cities, towns, and rural areas, with 540 sites that include bases, camps, outposts, headquaters, logistic hubs, and airfields.

II. United Nations Peacekeeping Missions

"UN peacekeeping is a unique global partnership. It brings together the General Assembly, the Security Council, the Secretariat, troop and police contributors and the host governments in a combined effort to maintain international peace and security. Its strength lies in the legitimacy of the UN Charter and in the wide range of contributing countries that participate and provide precious resources."[1]

In 2020, the United Nations conducted 13 peacekeeping missions[2] worldwide, with total spending of US$6.5 billion and a total of 95,110 personnel deployed in the field.[3] In 2016, peacekeeping operations covered an area of over a million square kilometers, having a large-scale presence in hundreds of cities, villages, and rural areas across the world. Mission bases, camps, supercamps, airfields, headquarters, and logistics hubs were planned, constructed, and deployed by the UN within and adjacent to populated areas, becoming long-term features within local environments. This vast spatial manifestation comprised about 270 sites with a yearly construction, real estate, and heating and cooling budget totaling US$448,287,372.[4]

UN peace operations are often deployed in the world's most impoverished and imperiled urban and rural environments with long histories of violence. In 2016, UN peace operations were present in more than 170 municipalities in Africa, with a combined population of 31 million. These areas are inhabited precariously, often poorly planned, and built in zones exposed to various hazards, making them vulnerable to droughts, floods, and violence. Such pressures intensify with the effects of climate change and rapid population growth. In rural areas, too, peace operations are present in environments threatened by desertification, over-exploitation of natural resources, and climate variability.

Despite the multidimensional challenges for peace and security, peace operations are driven by narrow political and security considerations and siloed mandates. Mission personnel often have little familiarity with or regard for the local context and are poorly trained in responding to such complex challenges. Furthermore, peacekeeping operations increasingly intervene in conflict settings that are highly violent and remote. This results in a growing dependency on external supply chains, fortification, and militarization of mission bases, which expands their material footprint, isolates peacekeepers from the local context, and increases their environmental waste and carbon emissions. Although UN missions are designed to function as autonomous infrastructures, and although they are perceived as self-sustaining operations and guided by the principle of "Do No Harm," they share ground with the surrounding communities. They are connected to local water resources by drilling wells and pumping water from aquifers; they consume resources from the local markets, inflating commodity prices and the massive amounts of materials, equipment, and goods they bring into mission areas generate long-term pollution and altogether contribute to global environmental degradation.[5]

And yet peacekeeping missions have not always operated at this scale. To better understand UN peacekeeping missions, their evolution, expansion, and increasing impacts on cities, communities, and the environment, it is necessary to situate them within their historical, institutional, and spatial contexts and utilize multidisciplinary and multi-scalar approaches when it comes to analyzing them.

1 United Nations Peacekeeping Webpage: "What is peacekeeping?" available at: https://peacekeeping.un.org/en/what-is-peacekeeping.
2 And UN peace operations.
3 UN Peacekeeping, "Peacekeeping Operations Fact Sheet," 2017, available at: peacekeeping.un.org/sites/default/files/pk_fact_sheet_dec_17.pdf.
4 UN Procurement Division, "Statistics", available at: un.org/Depts/ptd/statistics/2016.
5 This data was collected through interviews and observations as part of an independent research project. The spatial, socioeconomic and urban aspects and the case study on Mali draw on broad practical and analytical expertise in architecture, urbanism, anthropology, landscaping, economics, military engineering, and policy gathered through workshops, field research, and design exercises. See also Malkit Shoshan and Jane Szita, "Reimagining the Peacekeeping Mission: Legacy Scenarios for Camp Castor," Het Nieuwe Instituut, January 2015, available at: https://drones-honeycombs.hetnieuweinstituut.nl/sites/default/files/workshop_report._gao_legacy.pdf. and at: BLUE: Architecture of UN.Peacekeeping Missions. Volume 48. Archis, 2016, pp 1–48.

UN observation post, 1950s. Israel-Syria border. UN media archive.

UN observation post, 1950s. Israel-Egypt border. UN media archive.

History of Peacekeeping

The United Nations was established in 1945 after the devastation of two World Wars with the goal of preventing future wars. Succeeding the League of Nations, the UN principles and organizational structure are based on a treaty between nations, known as the UN Charter.[6] It lays out the three UN pillars: to uphold HUMAN RIGHTS; to address economic, social, and health problems to improve people's livelihoods—i.e., DEVELOPMENT; and to promote PEACE AND SECURITY. The charter also outlines the organizational structure of the UN, which includes six principal organs: the General Assembly, the Security Council, the Economic and Social Council, the Trusteeship Council, the International Court of Justice, and the UN Secretariat.

Since its founding, the UN has evolved and expanded from 26 member states to 193 today.[7] The first surge of new members had to do with global shifts following the decline of European imperialist powers and the independence of their colonies.[8] Between 1955 and 1970, the UN gained 70 new member states in territories released from the grip of European colonizers, half of which are located in Africa. After the collapse of the Soviet Union in the 1990s, the Soviet Block dissolved into 15 additional member states. The emerging new states were often entrenched in internal and external stresses, power struggles, civil struggles, and wars.

The national recognition process generated internal tensions, particularly along newly formed political borderlines. The first peacekeeping mission was deployed along the borders of the newly UN-recognized state of Israel after the withdrawal of the British Mandate from Palestine and the following 1948 war. Peacekeepers were sent to monitor ceasefires, supervise armistice agreements, and prevent isolated incidents of violence from escalating. The second mission was set up along the borders of India and Pakistan to supervise the ceasefire in the state of Jammu and Kashmir. Both missions are still active today.[9] Since the outset, peacekeeping missions have followed these three fundamental principles: 1) consent of the national sovereign parties involved in the conflict, 2) impartiality, and 3) non-use of force except in self-defense and defense of the mandate. International Human Rights Law[10] and International Humanitarian Law are central to the normative framework of United Nations peace operations.[11]

The Department of Peace Operations (DPO) holds the primary responsibility under the United Nations Charter to maintain international peace and security.[12] The Security Council decides when and where a UN peace operation should be deployed. It consists of 15 member states, 5 of which are permanent: China, France, Russia, the United Kingdom, and the United States. Permanent members hold veto power and can reject any substantive resolution; this makes the decisions concerning peace and security highly exclusive. The Security Council resolutions are political and made on a case-by-case basis. The deployment of a peace operation follows a resolution that establishes the mission's mandate and size. The Security Council continuously monitors the work of peace operations. It can vote to extend, amend, or end mission mandates as it deems appropriate. It alone has the power to make declarations regarding peace operations, which member-states are obligated to implement.

At the time of establishment, UN peace operations had a limited role and budget. Over time, their mandates, budget, and numbers of personnel expanded significantly. For comparison, in the 1970s, the UN's yearly budget was US$394 million, of which 6 percent was allocated for its peace operations. In 2018, the UN's total assessed contribution was US$11.91 billion, of which about 60 percent was allocated for its peace operations.[13] The increased budget was linked, among other things, to changes in conflict settings, missions' mandates, and financial arrangements.[14]

6 The Charter of the United Nations was signed in San Francisco on June 26, 1945 and is the foundation document for all the United Nations work. The United Nations was established to "save succeeding generations from the scourge of war", and one of its main purposes is to maintain international peace and security. United Nations Peacekeeping Operations Principles and Guidelines, UN 2008.

7 About UN Membership and Member States, available at: un.org/en/member-states.

8 The United Nations and Decolonization: www.un.org/dppa/decolonization/en.

9 UN Peacekeeping History, available at: https://peacekeeping.un.org/en/our-history.

10 United Nations peacekeeping operations should be conducted in full respect of human rights and should seek to advance human rights through the implementation of their mandates (See Chapter 2). United Nations peacekeeping personnel – whether military, police or civilian – should act in accordance with international human rights law and understand how the implementation of their tasks intersects with human rights. Peacekeeping personnel should strive to ensure that they do not become perpetrators of human rights abuses. They must be able to recognize human rights violations or abuse and be prepared to respond appropriately within the limits of their mandate and their competence. United Nations peacekeeping personnel should respect human rights in their dealings with colleagues and with local people, both in their public and in their private lives. Where they commit abuses, they should be held accountable. Source: United Nations Peacekeeping Operations Principles and Guidelines, UN 2008.

11 International humanitarian law is known also as "the law of war" or "the law of armed conflict" and restricts the means and methods of armed conflict. International humanitarian law is contained in the four Geneva Conventions of 1949 and their two Additional Protocols of 1977, as well as in rules regulating the means and methods of combat. International humanitarian law also includes conventions and treaties on the protection of cultural property and the environment during armed conflict, as well as the protection of victims of conflict. Source: United Nations Peacekeeping Operations Principles and Guidelines, UN 2008.

12 United Nations. Role of the Security Council: peacekeeping, available at: un.org/en/role-of-security-council.

13 In the 2018/2019 period the UN budget was US$5.4 billion and peacekeeping budget was US$6.51 billion, available at: 1) un.org/press/en/2019/gaab4328.doc.htm, and 2) un.org/press/en/2017/gaab4270.doc.html.

Today's deployment of peace operations depends on an entire industry of global supply chains that move consultants, builders, maintenance workers, food, prefabricated structures, water pumps, and energy stations along with any number of vehicles, machinery, and office supplies across the world. These global supply chains have reciprocal relations with UN agencies, by virtue of which they sustain and ensure each other's existence and constant growth. This results in a massive increase in their spatial footprint and greenhouse gas emissions, with the associated environmental degradation.

Yet, the security aspect and remote setting of peace operations keeps them highly confidential and hidden from public awareness, despite the immense global public resources that are put toward their financing and maintenance, and despite their massive material and environmental footprint.

UN peacekeeping post in the Golan Heights overlooking the Tiberius Lake. Yutaka Nagata, UN media archive.

A Visit to the UN Archive

It is not easy to find information about the spatial footprint of UN peacekeeping missions for multiple reasons. First, they are situated in remote conflict-affected regions that are very hard to access due to militarized violence and lack of infrastructure. Second, they are designed by highly bureaucratic institutions that are almost impossible to penetrate, and very little information is, in fact, accessible to the general public. Most of the drawings and plans of their bases and sites are highly classified. And oftentimes, during the deployment of missions, ad-hoc decisions by UN agencies and troop-contributing countries can shape spaces in ways that are impossible to track or document.

A few years ago, I decided to visit the UN archive in New York City to find out more. The visit required preparation; I had to schedule my meeting weeks in advance, fill out forms, and deliver a list of folders that I would like to examine.

Navigating the UN archive database remotely and selecting folders for review was not straightforward either. It required preliminary knowledge of UN codewords and abbreviations. A succession of email exchanges with a UN archive employee led to the decision to use a range of keywords, including #peacekeeping, #compound, #camp, #headquarter, #blueprint, and #Africa as well as mission abbreviations like MINUSMA, UNMIL, and MONUSCO. Eventually, a selection of folders cleared for public viewing was pre-assembled by archive employees in anticipation of my visit.

Arriving in midtown Manhattan, the archive building itself was somewhat secluded, located on a side street a few blocks away from the UN headquarters. When I finally found the entrance and rang the doorbell, a young employee opened the door enthusiastically. She was the archive manager. From her reaction, it was clear that the archive did not have many visitors. She accompanied me to a small and tired-looking reading room. The shabby space looked like an old-fashioned library dedicated to an obsolete discipline, filled with tables that seemed much too big for the room. The walls were covered with shelves occupied by books mostly about the Israeli-Palestinian conflict, including biographies of Ben Gurion, Moshe Dyan, and other figures. Next to these sat old atlases by the World Bank of areas labeled as "underdeveloped." On the other side of the room, on four metal carts, there was a pile of folders awaiting my attention. The papers were old, thin, and yellowing. As I browsed through them, I found myself transported to a different era.

One of the first folders included private letters, photographs, and postcards. I came across two intriguing postcards written by a UN employee back in the 1950s, exhibiting firsthand experience from Tripoli. The first of the cards enthusiastically greeted the beginning of a UN mission; the image on its front was of a building in Tripoli. The second postcard was a bit more peculiar; the same UN employee sent his office a note:

"Dear George, Have just purchased the Sahara Desert. Should I charge this to account 560 or 691? I hear they are reorganizing again. Best to truth"

These were exciting times for Africa. Many countries had begun to loosen the stranglehold of colonialism. Libya had become independent from the UK in December 1951, followed by Sudan, Tunisia, and Morocco. Mali gained its independence from France in June 1960, followed by Congo, Somalia, and Niger. The African continent was embarking on a new era—a post-World War epoch. It was a time of euphoria and wonder that saw a new world order beginning to emerge. The post colonial division of Africa, however, involved the rise and fall of many conflicts and many nation-states. The region is, to say the least, far from being stable to this day; wars, uprisings, sectarian violence, religious extremism, corruption, the climate crisis, and disease continue to tear the continent apart. UN peacekeeping operations are currently taking place in 170 cities across sub-Saharan Africa. Another folder I came across during my visit to the archive was simply titled "Congo." The UN Operation in the Congo (ONUC) was unique for its time. It was launched in 1960 as the first large-scale mission, with nearly 20,000 military personnel at its peak, making it one of the largest peacekeeping missions. ONUC demonstrated the risks involved in trying to bring stability to war-torn regions. Many have died, and stability has yet to be achieved in Congo. To this day, the UN mission in Congo is still active.[15]

At the archive, inside the Congo folder, I found a report labeled "The Future of UN bases" dating from the late 1960s. The report looked at the configuration of Camp Camina, a UN base established by peacekeepers from Belgium. The report was a unique example of contemplation and doubt regarding the legacy of UN peacekeeping missions, reminding me of many of the issues that brought me to the archive in the first place. Rather than temporary bases, overly ambitious UN structures were built in Kitona and Camina that resembled Corbusian modernist towns. Toward the end of this iteration of the Congo mission, no one knew what to do with all the buildings that had been built. Camina still exists, though perhaps as little more than a reminder of Congo's conflict-ridden past and present. I left the archive with just a few documents. It was clear that much of the research was still to be done, and it required fieldwork and creativity.

The information revealed in the old folders and the ease with which a UN bureaucrat purchased the Sahara Desert demonstrated how present missions and the history of European colonization in Africa are intertwined. It reminded me of a quote from "Arts of Living on a Damaged Planet" by Anna Tsing et al.: "Every landscape is haunted by past ways of life."[16] After visiting the UN archive, I searched further into the past, into the first explorations of Africa and the origins of modernity. It was a time when technological development allowed all sorts of explorers to set out from the shores of Europe for the first time to Africa and the world.

14 See Peacekeeping Today Table on page 49.
15 MONUSCO Facts Sheet, available at: peacekeeping.un.org/en/mission/monusco.
16 Anna Tsing, Heather Swanson, Elaine Gan, Nils Bubandt (eds.), Arts of Living on a Damaged Planet: Ghosts and Monsters of the Anthropocene. Minneapolis: University of Minnesota Press, 2017, p. G2.

Postcards found in folders corresponding to the first UN peacekeeping missions in Africa. UN archive, NYC.

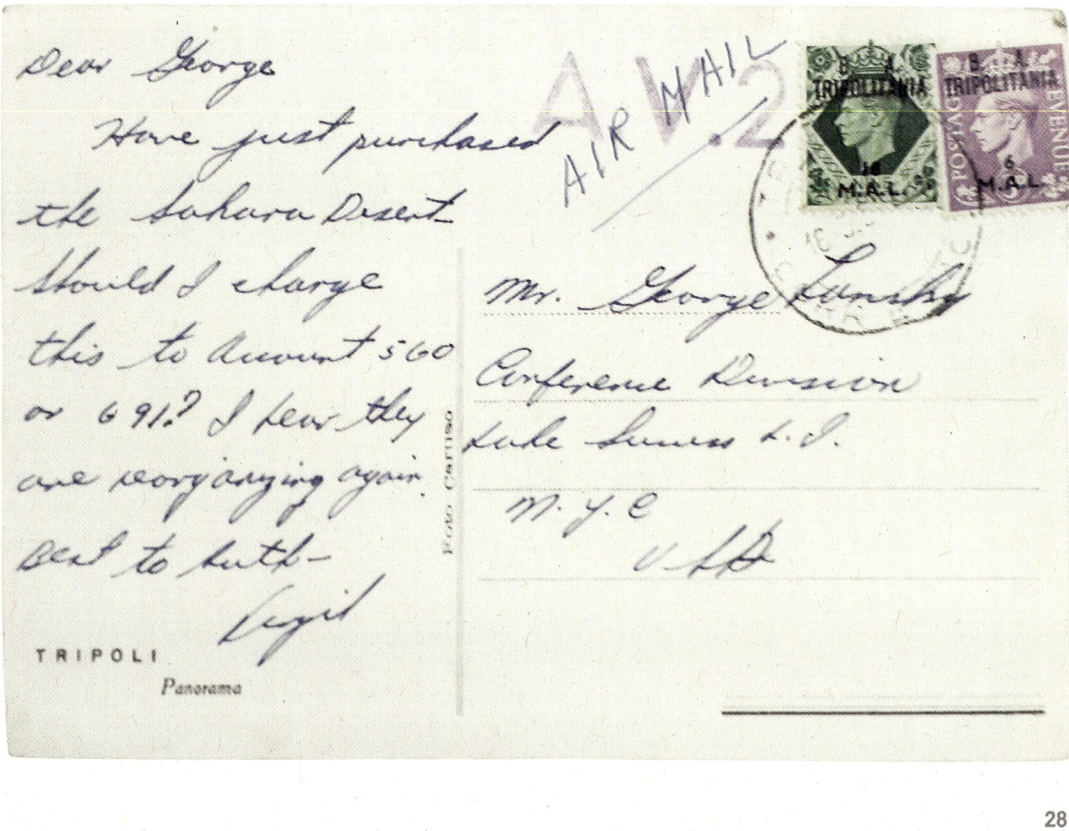

Dear George

Have just purchased the Sahara Desert. Should I charge this to Account 560 or 691? I hear they are reorganizing again. Best to Ruth—

Virgil

TRIPOLI

Panorama

Foto Caruso

AIR MAIL

B. A. TRIPOLITANIA 1d M.A.L.

B. A. TRIPOLITANIA POSTAGE REVENUE 6 M.A.L.

Mr. George [illegible]

Conference Division

Lake Success L.I.

N.Y.C

USA

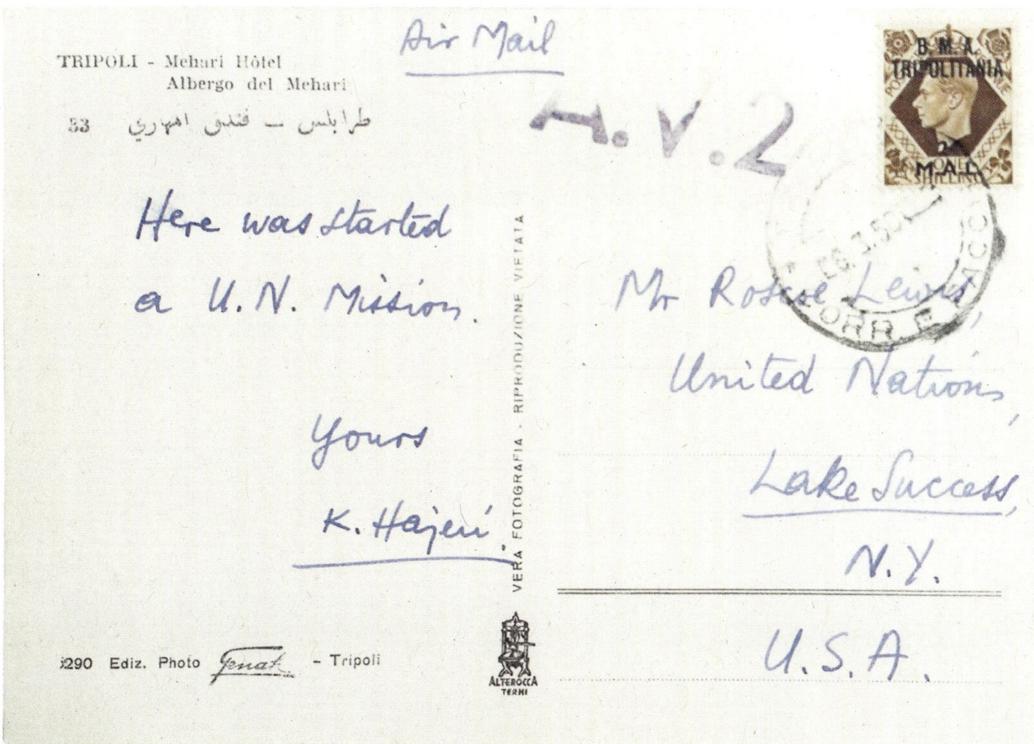
TRIPOLI - Mehari Hôtel
Albergo del Mehari
53 طرابلس ـ فندق المهري
Air Mail
A.V.2
B.M.A. TRIPOLITANIA
M.A.L.
Here was started
a U.N. Mission.
Yours
K. Hajeri
VERA FOTOGRAFIA - RIPRODUZIONE VIETATA
Mr Roscoe Lewis
United Nations,
Lake Success,
N.Y.
U.S.A.
290 Ediz. Photo Fenat - Tripoli
ALTEROCCA TERNI

Photographs by UN personnel from folders corresponding to the first UN peacekeeping missions in Africa. UN archive, NYC.

The following sequence of maps depicts a continually changing world—a flux of control over territory, nature, and people's lives starting with the first exploration of Africa by Prince Henry the Navigator and ending with the Berlin Conference.

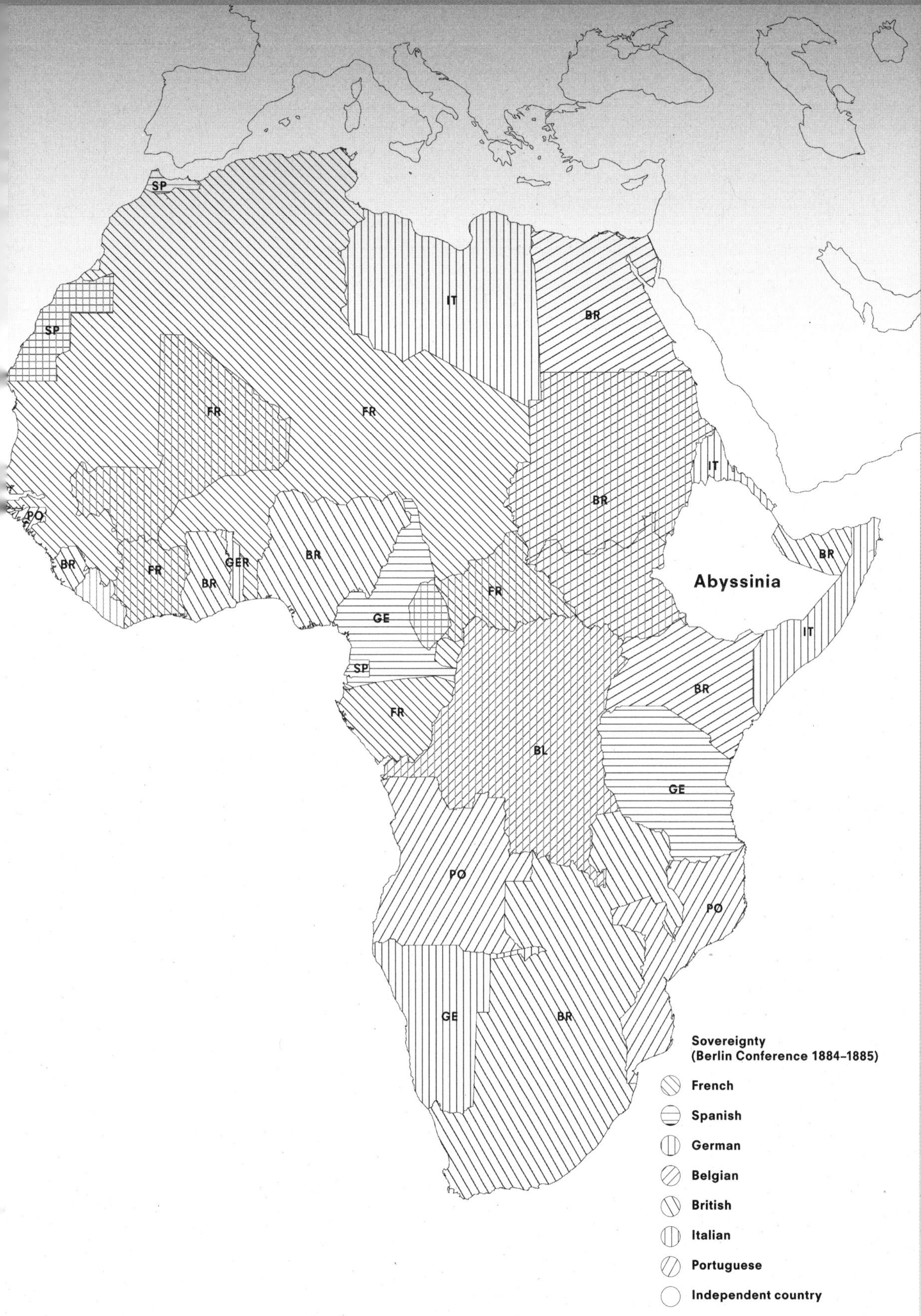
SP
SP
IT
BR
FR
FR
IT
BR
PO
BR
FR
GER
BR
BR
BR
Abyssinia
FR
GE
SP
IT
FR
BR
BL
GE
PO
PO
GE
BR
Sovereignty
(Berlin Conference 1884–1885)
French
Spanish
German
Belgian
British
Italian
Portuguese
Independent country

Portuguese expeditions to the new world 1400–1600

European explorers 1340–1600

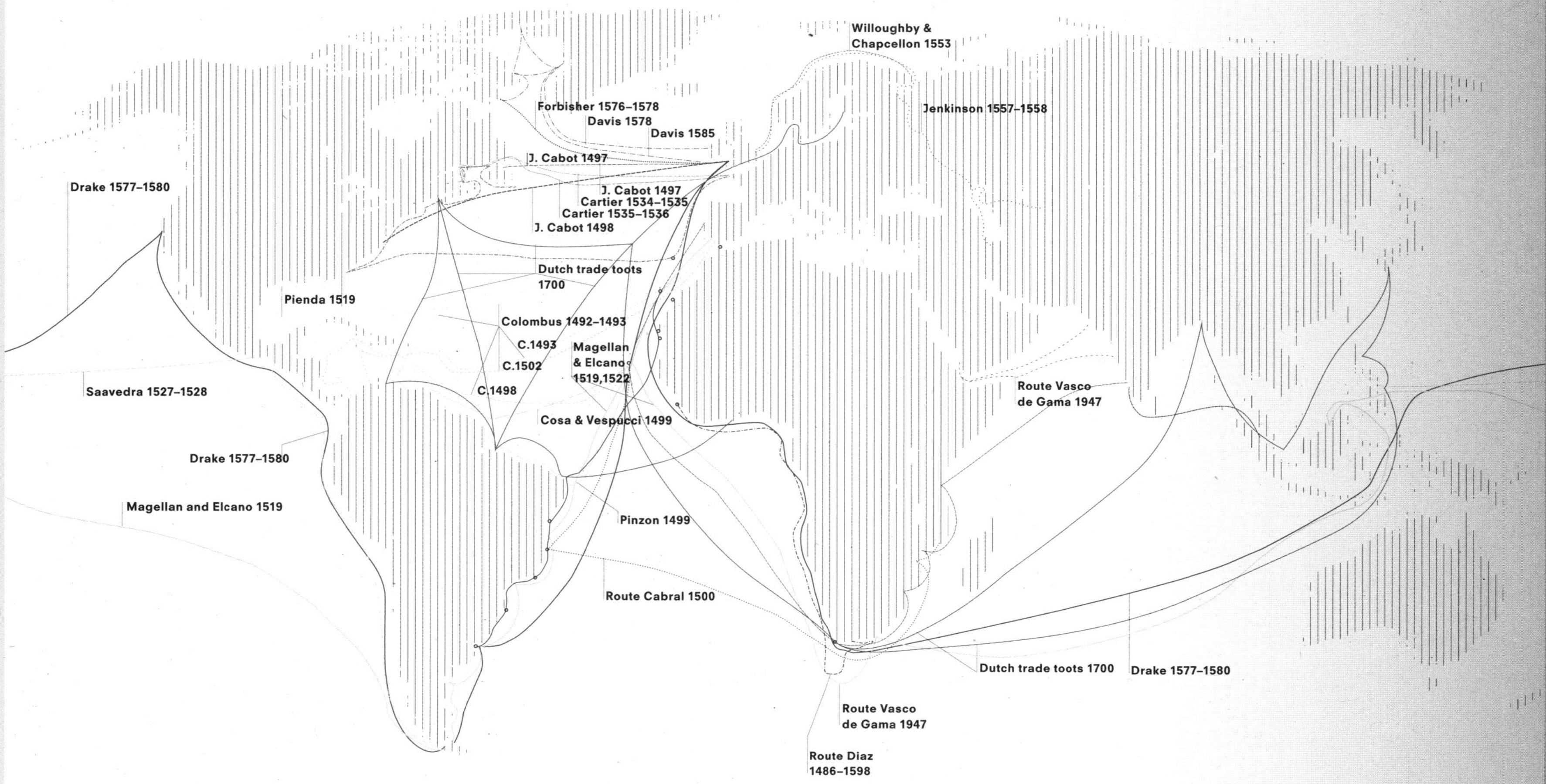

Slave trade routes 16th, 17th, and 18 centuries

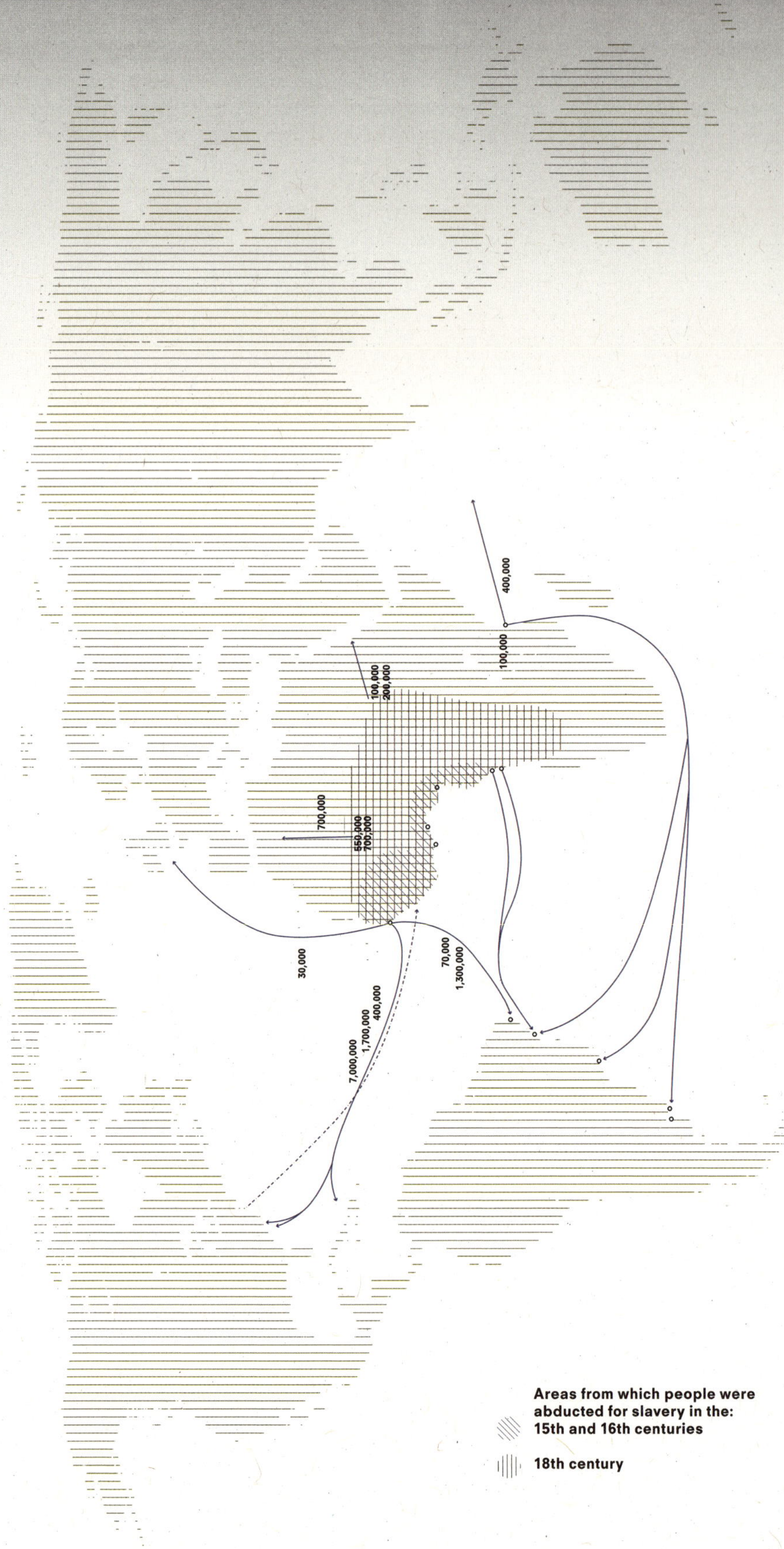

European territorial influence and colonies 1914

Missions in Africa

Past Missions and the Colonization of Africa

Prince Henry the Navigator, also known as the Grand Master of the Military Order of Christ, developed the caravel, a light ship that could sail faster than earlier boats.[17] This allowed the Portuguese to explore the shores of seas and oceans and slowly venture deeper inland, marking new international travel routes along rivers. When Prince Henry was 21, in the company of his father and brothers, he captured the Moorish port of Ceuta in northern Morocco, previously used as a base by pirates who raided the Portuguese coast, depopulating villages by capturing their inhabitants to be sold into the African slave trade.[18]

The gradual discovery of Africa by Portuguese explorers and missionaries was motivated by the desire to discover, chart, and dominate the world. Technological innovation and science were fueled and empowered by the discovery and capture of natural resources, such as precious metals. Gold contributed to the increase in military budgets, the development and production of ammunition, and the construction of forts. In these early missions, issues related to the extraction of natural resources, science, religion, and war were intertwined.

The capture of Ceuta in 1415 was followed by the exploration of the West African coast, as Portuguese explorers continued sailing south. Their routes marked Cape Bojador, Cape Blanco, Bay de Arguin (fort), Cape Verte, the Madeira Islands, Siera Leone, and the Cape of Good Hope. By 1444, Portuguese sailors had passed the Sahara Desert's southern boundaries and taken over the North African communities' ancient trade routes.[19] During their exploration of the "new world," they rapidly increased their wealth and developed more complex trade and financial infrastructures, as well as travel, construction, and warfare technologies. Upon arrival in each new place, they built a fort. Inside, they set up a trading factory and a colony. The new bases were connected to Porto and Lisbon, each adding a node to a growing network —a point of arrival and departure in the newly forming global web of extraction, production, and supply under European dominance.

The Portuguese explorers renamed their findings and marked their geographical positions on maps. The discovery of places was inextricably linked to the capture of wealth: natural resources (metals and minerals), human beings and other species, and artifacts. Wealth accelerated the pace of exploration, exploitation, and extraction. From the 14th century onward, explorers traveled across continents, seas, oceans, deserts, and mountains.

They discovered, charted, and classified places, people, cultures, and the natural world. Through military might and technological advances, European nations violently reigned over vast territories. The Portuguese expeditions were followed by English, French, Dutch, Italian, Danish, Swedish, and others. The maps in the previous pages depict the first major European explorations routes to Africa, America, Asia, and Australia.

The European colonization of Africa, which began with Portuguese, Spanish, and Italian navigators, continued expanding deep into the African continent. In 1881 only 10 percent of it was under formal European control; by 1914, it had grown to almost 90 percent. Conquering all that territory entailed the subjection of native populations and the imposition of new systems of governance, academic and religious institutions, and agricultural and technological innovations to sustain the extractive structures associated with Western colonialism.[20]

17 Lisbon Portugal Guide, available at: http://lisbonlisboaportugal.com/Lisbon-information/Henry_Navigator.html, and: https://nobility.org/2012/11/12/henry-discovery.

18 Charles E. Nowell and Felipe Fernandez-Armesto. Henry the Navigator. Encyclopædia Britannica, available at: www.britannica.com/biography/Henry-the-Navigator and Lourenço, Eduardo. The Lusiads: from national epic to universal myth. UNESCO, 1989.

19 Albuquerque, Luis de. The UNESCO Courier: a window open on the world, XLII, 4, p. 10–13, illus. UNESCO, 1989.

20 The European colonization of Africa, which began with Portuguese, Spanish, and Italian navigators, continued expanding into Asia and America and reached deep into the African continent. While in 1881 only 10% of the African continent was under formal European control, by 1914, it had spread to almost 90% of the continent. Conquering the territory included the subjection of natives and the establishment of new systems of governance, academic institutions, and agricultural and technological innovations that offset the extractive institutions commonly associated with Western colonialism.

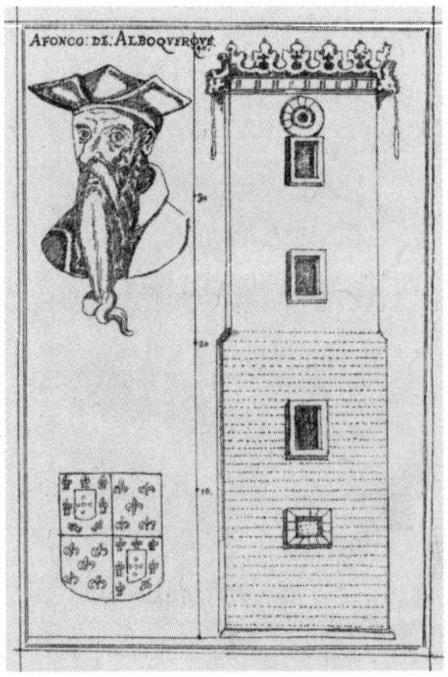

Fort Malacaa by the Luso-Malayan Manuel Godinho de Erédia. An early17th-century Portuguese illustration of the keep of the fortress and a stone relief of Afonso de Albuquerque, responsible for conquering the city in 1511.

Panel of Azulejos by Jorge Colaço (1864–1942) at the São Bento railway station, depicting Prince Henry the Navigator during the conquest of Ceuta.

Caravel. Panel of Azulejos, Porto.

Borders were undefined in old cultures. People migrated and moved across the land seasonally. They shared resources and coexisted in nature harmoniously, while maintaining family ties and depending on kinship, identity, and culture. These ancient notions of shared ground rapidly shifted from the 14th century onward. The maps in the previous pages start with the Portuguese exploration of Prince Henry the Navigator and end with the Berlin Conference. They depict a continually changing world—a flux of control over territory, nature, and people's lives.

In 1501, Vespucci sailed under the Portuguese flag. After leaving Lisbon, it took him 64 days to cross the Atlantic Ocean due to light winds. His ships followed the South American coast to within 400 miles of the southern tip of Tierra del Fuego. Along the way, the Portuguese sailors in charge of the voyage asked Vespucci to take over the command.

Amerigo Vespucci finding the Southern Cross constellation with an astrolabe Americae Retectio by Galle, Philipp. Museum Boijmans Van Beuningen.

Screenshots from "A Walk Through of the Elmina Castle – West African Slave Trade History, Ghana." YouTube, 2019.

Fort Elmina

The colonization of Africa and the world began with the exploration of seas, oceans, and shores. Diogo Gomes was a Portuguese navigator, explorer, and writer. He worked under the rule of Prince Henry the Navigator and commanded a fleet of caravels sailing south along the western shores of Africa. In 1482, his caravels sailed into Elmina's bay, situated between two different Fante kingdoms: Fetu and Eguafo. Among their ancestors were merchants and miners who had traded gold to the Mediterranean and Near Eastern lands from medieval times. The ancestors of the Akan-speakers of the forests, however, came from the north of the woods. The people on the West African coast belonged to diverse kingdoms. Family heads were united in communities under a recognized local authority. These kingdoms had a vibrant culture, trans-Saharan trade roots and markets, and fertile agricultural fields. When Gomes arrived on the Gold Coast (Ghana), he discovered a thriving gold trade among the natives and Arab and Berber merchants.[21]

Seizing the opportunity, Gomes established a trading post there at the end of 1471, naming it "A Mina" (the Mine).[22] It was the first European trading post built on the Gulf of Guinea and the oldest European fort south of the Sahara. Later, it became one of the main stops on the route of the Atlantic slave trade. The Dutch seized the fort from the Portuguese in 1637 and took over all the former Portuguese Gold Coast in 1642. The slave trade continued under the Dutch until 1814. In 1872, the Dutch Gold Coast, including the fort, became a possession of the British Empire.

First Prefabricated Building in Sub-Saharan Africa

In 1481, King João II decided to build a fort on the coast to protect Elmina's trade. He sent "all of the materials needed to build the fort on ten caravels and two transport ships. The supplies, which included everything from heavy foundation stones to roof tiles, were sent in pre-fitted form and provisions for six hundred men."[23]

The fleet arrived at Elmina, in a village called Of Two Parts. It is said that Christopher Columbus was among the fleet navigators.[24] The fort was situated in the most defensible position on the peninsula. It required the demolition of the local villagers' homes and the quarry of a sacred rock, which the animist villagers considered home to the god of the Benya River. The local opposition to the construction of the fort led the Portuguese to burn the village. Despite the local resistance, the fort tower's first floor was completed within 20 days, and the rest, including an accompanying church, was completed soon after. The fort was the first planned and constructed prefabricated European building in sub-Saharan Africa. Upon its completion, Elmina was established as a proper city with military and economic importance. At the height of the gold trade in the early 16th century, 24,000 ounces of gold were exported annually from the Gold Coast, accounting for one-tenth of the world's supply.[25] In time, Elmina became an independent state. Its people were offered Portuguese protection. If any locals attempted to trade with a nation other than Portugal, the Portuguese reacted with aggressive force, often by forming alliances with the betraying nation's enemies.[26] Hostility between groups increased, and the traditional organization of native societies suffered, especially after the Portuguese introduced them to firearms.

The European involvement disrupted traditional trade routes between coastal people and northern people by cutting out the African middlemen, and the Portuguese gradually established a West-African trade monopoly. The Portuguese authorities did not engage directly in the slave trade through Elmina to avoid disrupting the gold mining and trade routes. Instead, they shipped slaves mostly through the Slave Coast (Benin) and São Tomé. However, by the

21 Beckles, Hilary McD. Slave voyages: the transatlantic trade in enslaved Africans. Norwegian Agency for Development Cooperation, 2002.
22 Barreto, Luis Filipe. The Down of a new age. The UNESCO Courier: a window open on the world, XLII, 4, p. 4–7, illus., maps, and Massing, Andreas. "Mapping the Malagueta Coast: A history of the Lower Guinea Coast, 1460–1510 through Portuguese maps and accounts." History in Africa, vol. 36, 2009, pp. 331–365.
23 Newitt, Malyn, ed., The Portuguese In West Africa, Cambridge University Press, 1950, p. 93.
24 Hair, P. E. H., "Was Columbus' First Very Long Voyage a Voyage from Guinea?" History in Africa, vol. 22, 1995, pp. 223–237.
25 Wada, Kayomi, "El Mina São Jorge da Mina", BlackPast. January 11, 2010.
26 "Ghana History – Early Contact", available at: GlobalSecurity.org.

17th century, the situation had changed. The castle acted as a depot where slaves were brought in from different kingdoms in West Africa. The slaves, often captured in the African interior by slave catchers from coastal areas, were sold to Portuguese and later to Dutch traders in exchange for goods such as textiles and horses.

In 1637, the Dutch took over Al-Mina and turned it into the capital of the Dutch Gold Coast. During the period of Dutch control, a new, smaller fortress was built on a nearby hill to protect St. George Castle from inland attacks; this fort was called Fort Coenraadsburg. The Dutch continued the triangular Atlantic slave route until 1814 when they abolished the slave trade, in keeping with the Anglo-Dutch Slave Trade Treaty. The slaves were held captive in the castle before exiting through the castle's infamous "Door of No Return" to be transported and resold in newly colonized Brazil and other Portuguese colonies. Up to 1,000 male and 500 female slaves were shackled and crammed into the castle's dank, poorly ventilated dungeons, with no space to lie down and very little light. Once the slaves set foot in the castle, they could spend up to three months in captivity under dreadful conditions before being shipped off to the New World. An environment of harsh contrasts, the castle also had some extravagant chambers, devoid of the stench and misery of the dungeons only a few meters below. The governor's and officers' quarters were spacious and airy, with parquet floors and scenic views of the Atlantic's blue waters. There was also a chapel in the castle enclosure for the officers, traders and their families. They went about their day-to-day lives wholly detached from the unfathomable human suffering they were consciously inflicting. In 1872, the British took over the Dutch territory and the fort under the Anglo-Dutch Sumatra treaties of 1871.[27]

27 "Elmina Castle", Wikipedia, available at: en.wikipedia.org/wiki/Elmina_Castle.

Depiction of the Castle d'Elmina and the Fort St. Jago, the landed troops and a fleet on the road by Hans Propheet, 1629.

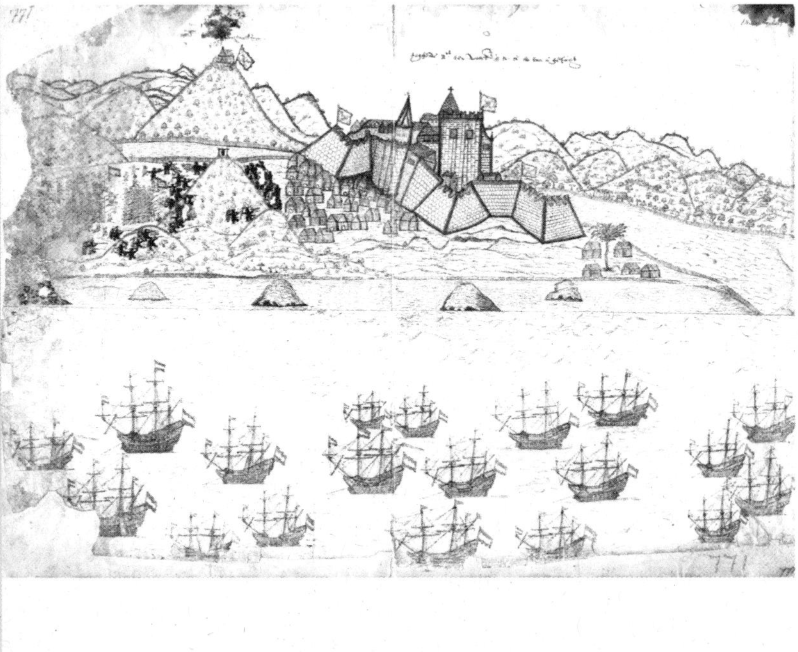

Elmina Castle, Ghana. Atlas Blaeu van der Hem, 1665–1668.

Upon arrival in each new place, they built a fort. Inside, they set up a trading factory and a colony. The new forts were connected, each adding a point of arrival and departure in the newly forming global web of extraction, production, and supply under European dominance.

Mas of the 1803 Elmina Castle and fort from the Dutch National Archives.

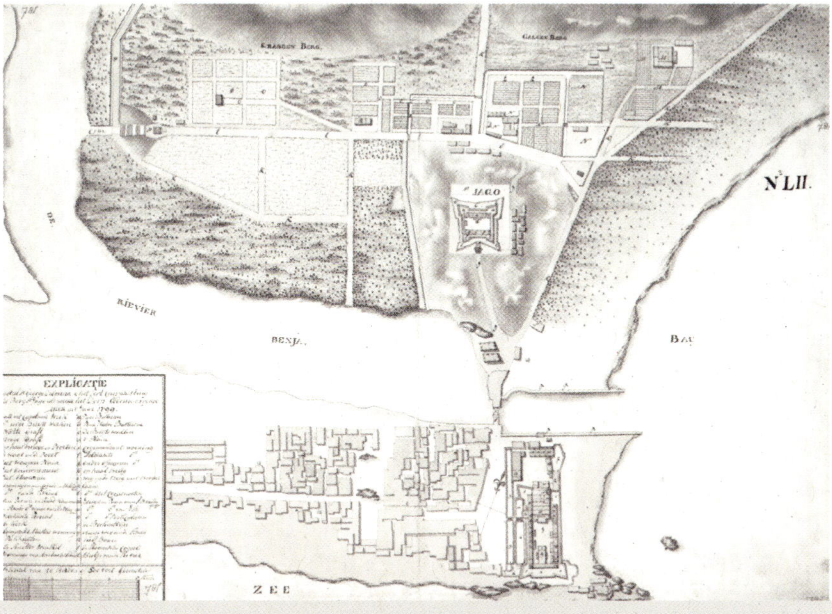

UN peacekeeping missions and current stresses in sub-Saharan Africa
2016–2020

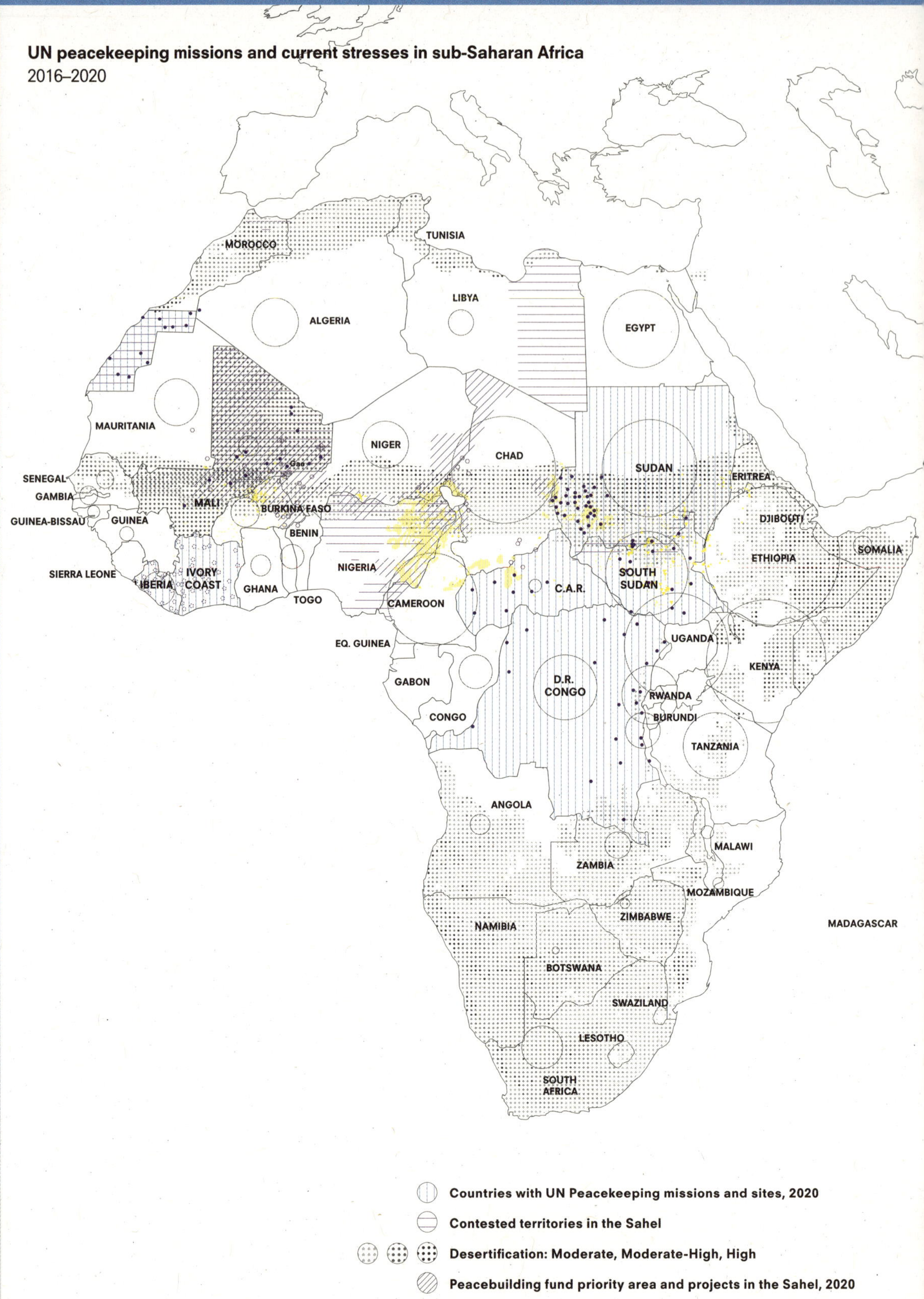

Nomadic flows and UN peacekeeping missions in sub-Saharan Africa

2016–2020

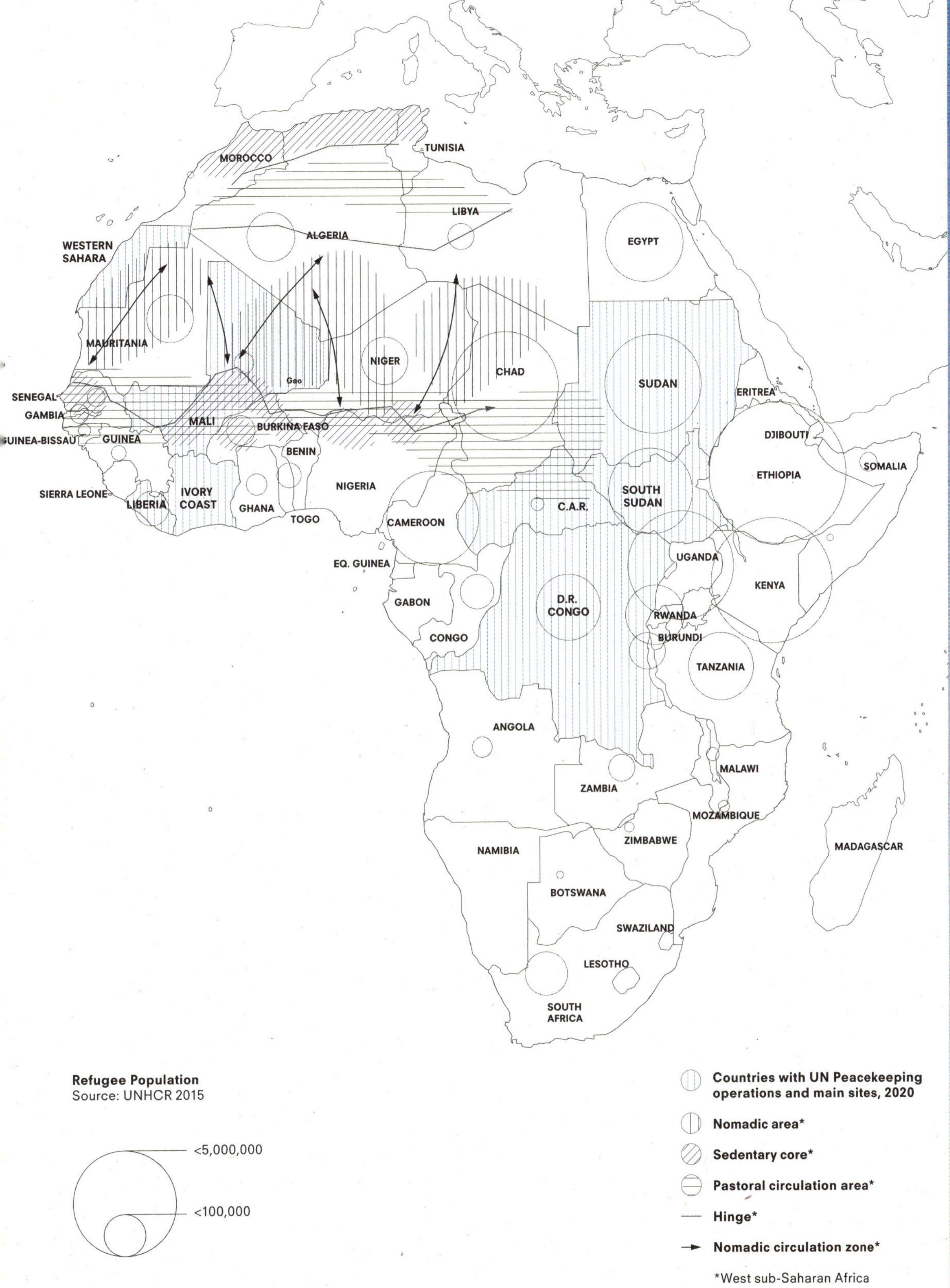

UN peacekeeping missions in Africa 1948–2020

Peacekeeping Today

The Evolution and Urbanization of Peacekeeping Missions

United Nations peacekeeping operations began in 1948[28] when a small, unarmed contingent of UN observers pitched their tents along the borders between the newly established state of Israel and its neighboring countries.[29]

The first generation of missions only began once there was peace to keep, following an end to armed conflict between nations through truce or ceasefire. Their objective was the creation of an environment conducive to peaceful conflict resolution by the adversaries' parties (nations) through measures such as mediation, negotiation, and conciliation. First-generation missions were lightly armed and left modest physical and ecological imprints. Their tasks were limited primarily to monitoring ceasefires and stabilizing situations in border regions as well as supporting political efforts to maintain the peace.[30] Particularly since the end of the Cold War, UN peacekeeping has transformed markedly as their multidimensional mandates began calling on peacekeepers not only to maintain the peace (there is often "no peace to keep") but to protect civilians; strengthen institutions and local governance; monitor human rights; provide electoral assistance; support the reform of the national security sectors; and contribute to the disarmament, demobilization, and reintegration of former combatants.[31] These newly emerging missions spreading across territories that had previously been part of the "Soviet Bloc" were similar in their approach to peace to President Roosevelt and Governor Herbert Lehman's European Recovery Program (see Notes on Peace, page 13). It connected the processes of postwar reconstruction of nations and their institutions and making, keeping, and building peace to the world of finance and the neoliberal free-market economy. Michael Kenkel has memorably described this expansion of mission mandates as advancing "from the thin blue line to painting a country blue." [32] Yet it is not only the mandates and modalities of peacekeeping that have expanded.

While international relations scholars offer various methods for examining and defining the evolution and types of missions, this study focuses on the main trends of change in relation to their spatial manifestations. Those trends of change are associated with a series of characteristics, for example the number of missions and their duration. Whereas fewer than 20 missions took place during the Cold War, more than 50 have been mandated since 1991. As of April 2021, there are 13 ongoing missions around the world. In terms of their duration, although UN missions are frequently perceived, planned, and budgeted as temporary interventions, the median time span of a mission is 6.5 years. Many operations—such as UNMIL, UNAMID, MINUSTAH, UNOCI, and UNMIK—have lasted much longer than that. The median lifespan of the 13 ongoing missions is 19 years.

Other indicators of trends of change include the size and budget of missions. As of 2016, peacekeeping operations covered over 1 million square kilometers, comprising more than 270 UN constructed bases, super camps and outposts, and 310 medical clinics.[33] In 2018, expenditures on peacekeeping totaled roughly US$6.8 billion, with US$559,090,547 budgeted for facilities and infrastructure, and a headcount of 106,338 personnel deployed in the field.

Trends of change can also be examined in terms of environmental impact and supply chains. As of 2016, UN missions were responsible for over half of the UN's total greenhouse gas emissions. Peacekeeping personnel often operate in the world's hardest-to-reach places and countries with very little infrastructure. This requires most peace operations to generate their own power and use a fleet of aircraft to manage logistics that emit greenhouse gases and cause pollution.[34] Moreover, since the 2007/8 global financial crisis, UN agencies

28 The common activities of these missions were the reduction of contact between the parties at war and diminishing the probability of the escalation of violence or accidental ruptures of the peace. The peacekeepers' activities included monitoring borders, verifying demilitarized zones, tasks related to the observance of peace resolutions, and the creation of political spaces for negotiation and mediation.

29 1) United Nations Peacekeeping, "Our History", available at: peacekeeping.un.org/en/our-history; 2) Current budgetary pressures could result in concentrated mandates that build on the comparative advantages of peacekeeping.

30 "The tasks assigned to traditional United Nations peacekeeping operations by the Security Council are essentially military in character and may involve the following: Observation, monitoring and reporting – using static posts, patrols, overflights or other technical means, with the agreement of the parties; Supervision of ceasefire and support to verification mechanisms; Interposition as a buffer and confidence-building measure." See: UN Principles and Guidelines, UN 2008.

31 "The transformation of the international environment has given rise to a new generation of 'multi-dimensional' United Nations peacekeeping operations. These operations are typically deployed in the dangerous aftermath of a violent internal conflict and may employ a mix of military, police and civilian capabilities to support the implementation of a comprehensive peace agreement." UN Principles and Guidelines, UN 2008.

32 Kenkel, Kai, Michael, "Five Generations of Peace Operations: From the 'Thin Blue Line' to 'Painting a Country Blue'", In Revista Brasileira de Política International 56, no. 1. 2013, pp. 122–143.

33 UN Procurement Division, "Statistics," available at: www.un.org/Depts/ptd/statistics/2016, and Shoshan, M. "The Architecture of UN Peacekeeping." In BLUE. Archis, 2016, pp. 6–19.

34 Environmental Risk and Performance-Management," available at: https://peacekeeping.un.org/en/environmental-risk-and-performance-management.

have become increasingly dependent on the procurement of services such as catering, technology, transport, and construction to private companies. The involvement of global supply chains in the production and maintenance of UN bases has inflated missions' expenditure. Nearly everything—from the materials used to build the bases to the air conditioning units that cool them to the food that sustains those that live within them—is imported, heightening the distance between the well-provisioned bases and their impoverished surroundings and increasing the bases' ecological impact and carbon emissions.

With regard to the integration and location of missions, the attack on the UN base in Baghdad in 2003 constituted an incisive event in their spatial evolution.[35] Since then, missions and UN bases got fortified and militarized. The growing proximity between peacekeepers and local communities has become increasingly attenuated by walls, fences, watchtowers, and barbed wire, which provide safety at the cost of social segregation. Finally, peacekeeping has increasingly become an urban phenomenon. Peacekeeping today unfolds, on a large scale, within and alongside hundreds of cities across the world. For example, in 2016, UN peacekeeping missions were present in more than 170 municipalities in Africa, with a combined population of 31 million.[36]

Bases as Fortresses

In the past decades, especially after the end of the Cold War and the launch of the "War on Terror," peacekeeping has become increasingly urbanized. Several factors explain the evolving geography of peacekeeping. At a macro-level, the politics of peacekeeping are such that it is more likely to occur in some places than in others. Divisions within the security council on specific issues, like the crises in Syria or Ukraine,[37] make it more probable for peacekeeping to occur in places like Africa, where political consensus is a possibility.

In addition, the geography and nature of conflict itself has changed. In the post-Cold War era, fewer wars have emerged between states, and more have broken out within them.[38] As a result, peacekeeping has ceased to be an activity performed mainly on the borders between countries and has instead turned inland, unfolding within and alongside inhabited areas. Sergio de Mello explained this shift:

> Contemporary armed conflict is seldom conducted on a clearly defined battlefield, by conventional armies confronting each other. Today's warfare often takes places in cities and villages, with civilians as the preferred targets, the propagation of terror as the premeditated tactic, and the physical elimination or mass displacement of certain categories of populations as the overarching strategy...As a result, even low intensity conflicts generate enormous human suffering. Humanitarian needs are disproportionate to the scale of military conflict. Meeting these needs has become more difficult, as the dividing line between soldiers and civilians has grown blurred.[39]

As conflicts turned inward, peace operations transformed too; their bases and headquarters had to be inserted locally, showing an international presence in these cities and villages where conflicts had erupted. The changes in warfare and the expanding mandate and scope of peace operations increased the number of personnel and expertise required to conduct international interventions and missions.[40]

Larger bases had to be built to accommodate the growing numbers of peacekeepers. These new facilities were erected in various urban and rural settings, including alongside local institutions such as government buildings and administrative offices. Among other effects, these physical changes have

35 United Nations. "Report of The Independent Panel on the Safety and Security of UN Personnel in Iraq, 20 October 2003", available at: www.un.org/News/dh/iraq/ safety-security-un-personnel-iraq.pdf.

36 Shoshan, M. "The Architecture of UN Peacekeeping, in BLUE, Archis, 2016, pp. 6–19.

37 International Crisis Group. "A Tale of Two Councils: Strengthening AU-UN Cooperation", available at: www.crisisgroup.org/africa/279-tale-two-councils-strengthening-au-un-cooperation.

38 N.C. Roberts, "Spanning 'bleeding' boundaries: humanitarianism, NGOs, and the civilian-military nexus in the Post- Cold war era," Public Administration Review, 2010, pp. 212–222.

39 Sérgio Vieira de Mello (Under-Secretary-General for Humanitarian Affairs and Emergency Relief Coordinator), United Nations. Security Council, S/PV.3968. January 21, 1999.

40 In addition to monitoring and observing cease-fires, multi-dimensional United Nations peacekeeping operations are frequently mandated to provide operational support to national law enforcement agencies; provide security at key government installations, ports and other vital infrastructure; establish the necessary security conditions for the free flow of people, goods and humanitarian assistance; and provide humanitarian mine action assistance. By helping to fill the security and public order vacuum that often exists in post-conflict settings, multi-dimensional United Nations peacekeeping operations play a critical role in securing the peace process and ensuring that humanitarian and development partners are able to work in a safe environment. See: UN Principles and Guidelines, UN 2008.

41 In November 2017, 66% of peacekeeping personnel were working in landlocked or hard-to-reach areas. UN Field Support, DFS Environment Strategy, "Executive Summary," November 2017, p. 3.

increased the UN's environmental footprint. The growing demand resulting from a mission's arrival challenges the capacity of local infrastructure, which is usually weak and often already overwhelmed.[41]

42 Shoshan, BLUE: The Architecture of UN Peacekeeping, pp. 6–17.
43 Greening the Blue Report, UNEP, 2017.

This, combined with security stresses and a lack of local expertise, results in a massive influx of materials and know-how into peacekeeping areas,[42] which has resulted in field missions being responsible for more than half of the total greenhouse gas emissions of the entire UN system, according to data collected by UNEP.[43]

Moreover, UN peace operations are commonly deployed in fragile urban and rural environments. Their bases are often inserted inside cities as large-scale fortified islands that negatively disrupt urban fabrics. They block roads and pathways between neighborhoods and interrupt the mobility of local inhabitants within their living environments. These inhabited areas are often poorly planned and built in zones exposed to natural hazards, making them vulnerable to droughts and floods. Such stresses intensify with the effects of climate change, which cause a rise in disease outbreaks and food and water insecurity, resulting in loss of livelihood and a displacement of the population from rural areas into cities. In rural areas, too, peace operations are often set up in fragile environments threatened by desertification, the over-exploitation of natural resources, and climate variability. Yet, despite these challenges, peace operations are driven mostly by political and security considerations rather than social or environmental ones. Peacekeepers often have little regard for the local context and are poorly trained in environmental and urban management. As missions increasingly intervene in multidimensional conflict settings, their fortified and militarized bases further isolate and separate the peacekeepers from the local context.

The scale of the spatial display of UN bases cannot be disregarded. UN camps and super camps can be larger than the towns that host them. Their footprint often absorbs local logistics hubs and transportation infrastructures such as airports and seaports. Along roads, checkpoints are set up to prioritize the movement of UN personnel over the local residents.

Within urban environments, UN bases can obstruct the mobility of pedestrians, cars, and public transportations. Moreover, host governments often allocate public buildings such as schools, football stadiums, and other communal structures for the peacekeepers' use as headquarters, police stations, or medical clinics. At the end of a mission, repurposed spaces are left with little to no regard for how local communities will be able to reuse them. Local governments are expected to convert them back to communal use, despite the fact that their resources are scarce and they struggle to offer essential civic services for their inhabitants. In addition, at the end of protracted violent conflicts, professional expertise is overwhelmed, and new efforts are needed to rebuild local capacities. UN agencies can play a significant role in ensuring the spaces they have used are returned ready for use by the local community.

In remote rural villages, the only sites that are lit at night and have constant access to water, electricity, and food are the UN bases. The disparities between the two worlds—the UN base and the local communities—are profoundly revealed in the configuration of the built environment.

Timeline of Peacekeeping Missions

The median lifespan of the 13 ongoing missions is 30 years

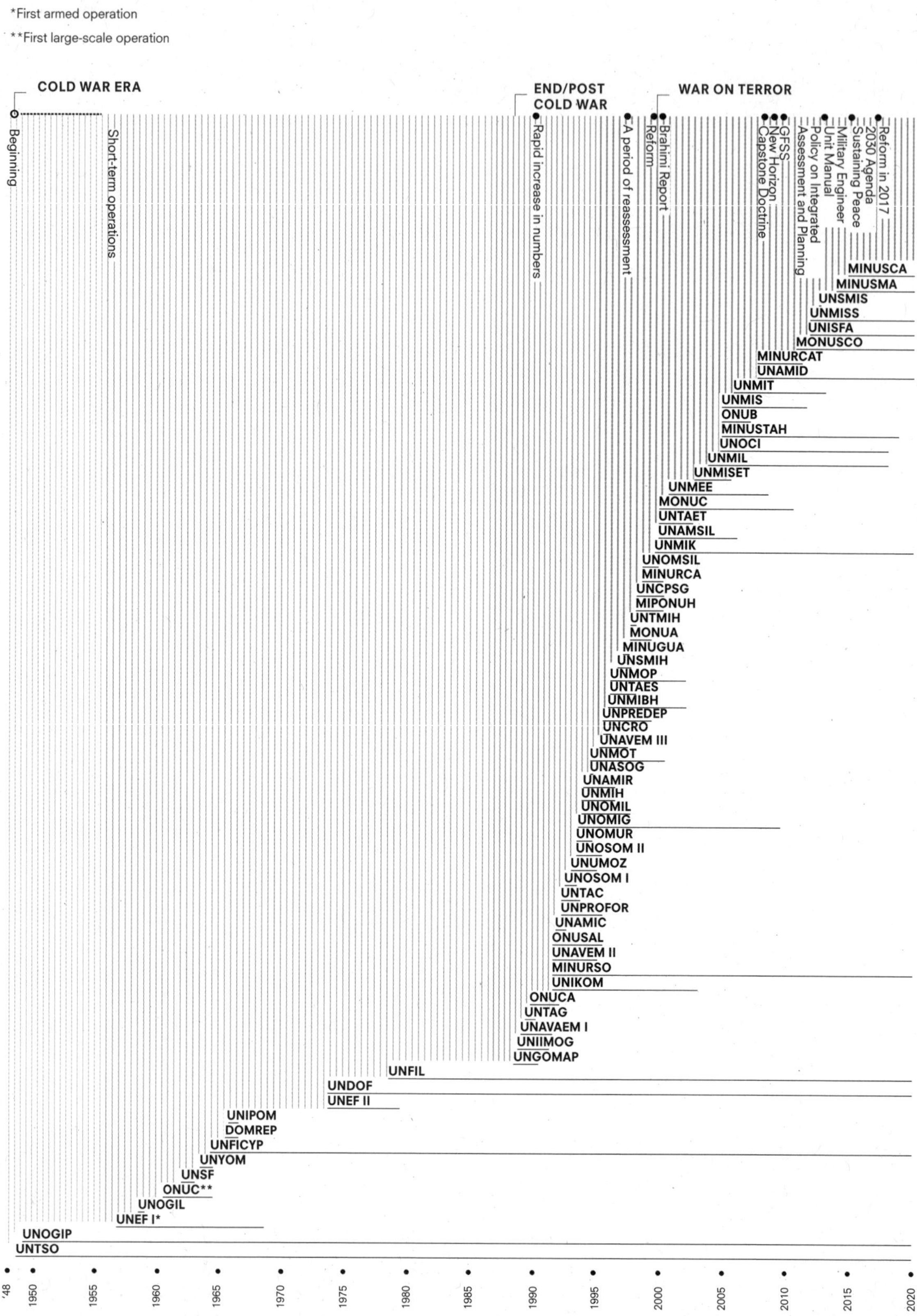

Peacekeeping Today

TREND	PEACEKEEPING
The number **of peacekeeping operations has grown.**	**While fewer than 20 missions took place during the Cold War, more than 50 missions have been mandated since 1991. As of May 2018, there are 14 ongoing missions around the world.**
The duration **of missions has increased.**	**Although UN missions are frequently perceived, planned and budgeted as temporary interventions, the median timespan of a mission is 6.5 years, and many operations—such as UNMIL, UNAMID, MINUSTAH, UNOCI and UNMIK—have lasted much longer than that. The median lifespan of the 14 ongoing missions is 19 years.**
The scale **of the footprint has expanded.**	**As of 2016, peacekeeping operations covered an area of over one million square kilometers, comprised of more than 270 UN constructed bases, super camps, and outposts, and 310 medical clinics.[44]**
The cost **of peacekeeping has grown.**	**In 2018, expenditures on peacekeeping will total roughly US$6.8 billion, with US$559,090,547 budgeted for facilities and infrastructure. The current headcount is 106,338 personnel deployed in the field.**
UN bases have grown more fortified.	**The attack on the UN base in Baghdad in 2003[45] constituted an incisive event in this spatial evolution. Since then, the growing proximity between peacekeepers and local communities has become increasingly attenuated by walls, fences, watchtowers, and barbed wire that provide safety at the cost of social segregation.**
The environmental impact **of peacekeeping has increased.**	**As of 2016, UN missions were responsible for over half of the UN's total greenhouse gas emissions. "Peacekeeping personnel often operate in the world's hardest to reach places and in countries with very little infrastructure. This requires most peace operations to generate their own power and use a fleet of air-craft to manage logistics which emit greenhouse gases and potential soil pollution."[46]**
Global supply chains **are playing a growing role, inflating budgets, making bases more homogenized and less sensitive to local climates and cultures.**	**Since the 2007/8 global financial crisis, UN agencies have become increasingly dependent on procurement of services such as catering, technology, transport, and construction. The involvement of global supply chains in UN bases' production and maintenance has inflated missions' expenditure. Nearly everything—from the materials used to build the bases to the air conditioning units that cool them to the food that sustains those that live within them—is imported, heightening the distance between the well-provisioned bases and their impoverished surroundings and increasing the bases'ecological impact and carbon emission.**
Finally, peacekeeping has become, increasingly, an urban phenomenon.	**Peacekeeping today unfolds on a large scale in hundreds of cities and towns around the world. For example, in 2016, UN peacekeeping missions were present in more than 170 municipalities in Africa, with a combined population of 31 million.[47]**

44 UN Procurement Division, "Statistics," available at: www.un.org/Depts/ptd/statistics/2016, and Shoshan, M. "The Architecture of UN Peacekeeping, in BLUE, Archis, 2016, pp. 6–19.

45 "Report of The Independent Panel on the Safety and Security of UN Personnel in Iraq, 20 October 2003," United Nations, available at: www.un.org/News/dh/iraq/ safety-security-un-personnel-iraq.pdf.

46 "Environmental Impact and sustainability", UNPK, available at: https://peacekeeping.un.org/ en/ environmental-impact-and sustainability.

47 Shoshan, M. "The Architecture of UN Peacekeeping, in BLUE, Archis, 2016, pp. 6–19.

UN Peacekeeping Expenditure and Personnel
1945–2018

In 2018, expenditure for peacekeeping totaled roughly US$6.8 billion, with US$559,090,547 budgeted for facilities and infrastructure. The current headcount is 104,043 personnel deployed in the field. These figures are considerable and directly linked to the growing material, environmental, and socio-economic impacts peacekeeping missions have on their surroundings. The UN has increasingly come under pressure to reduce costs.

Expenditure
Personnel
Missions

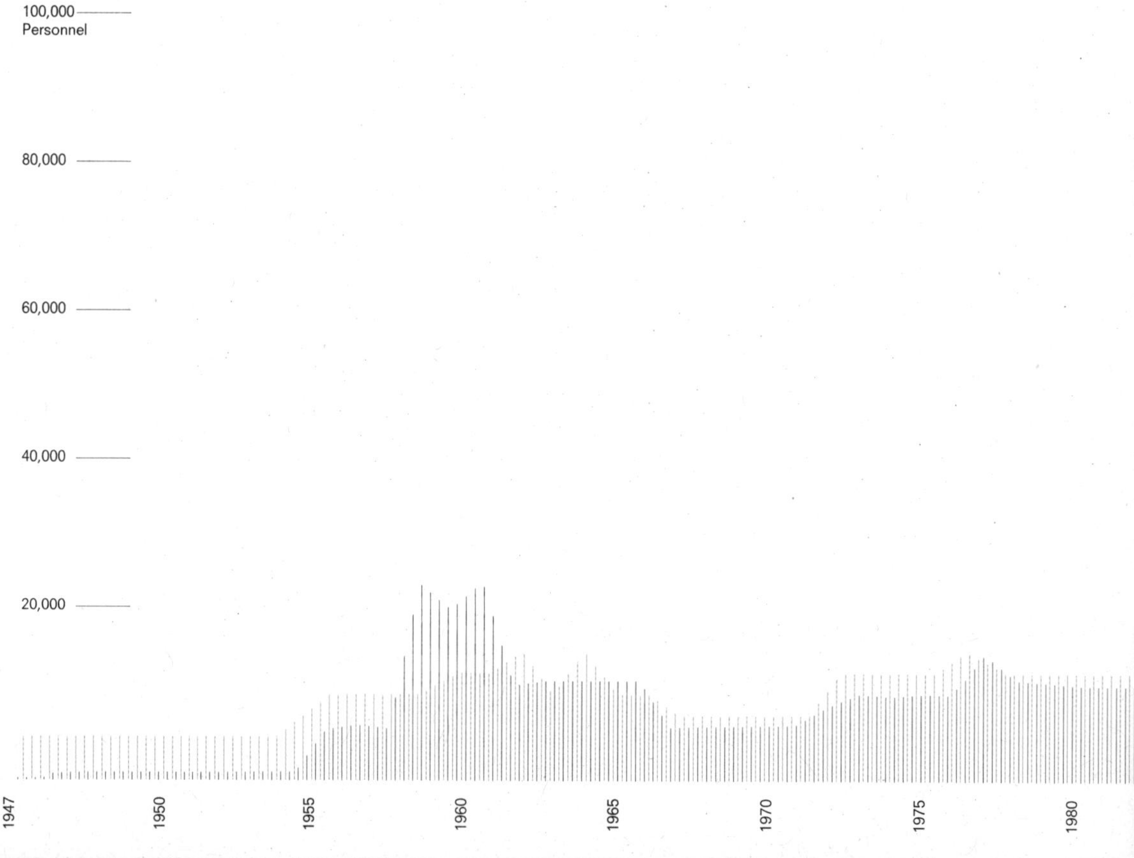

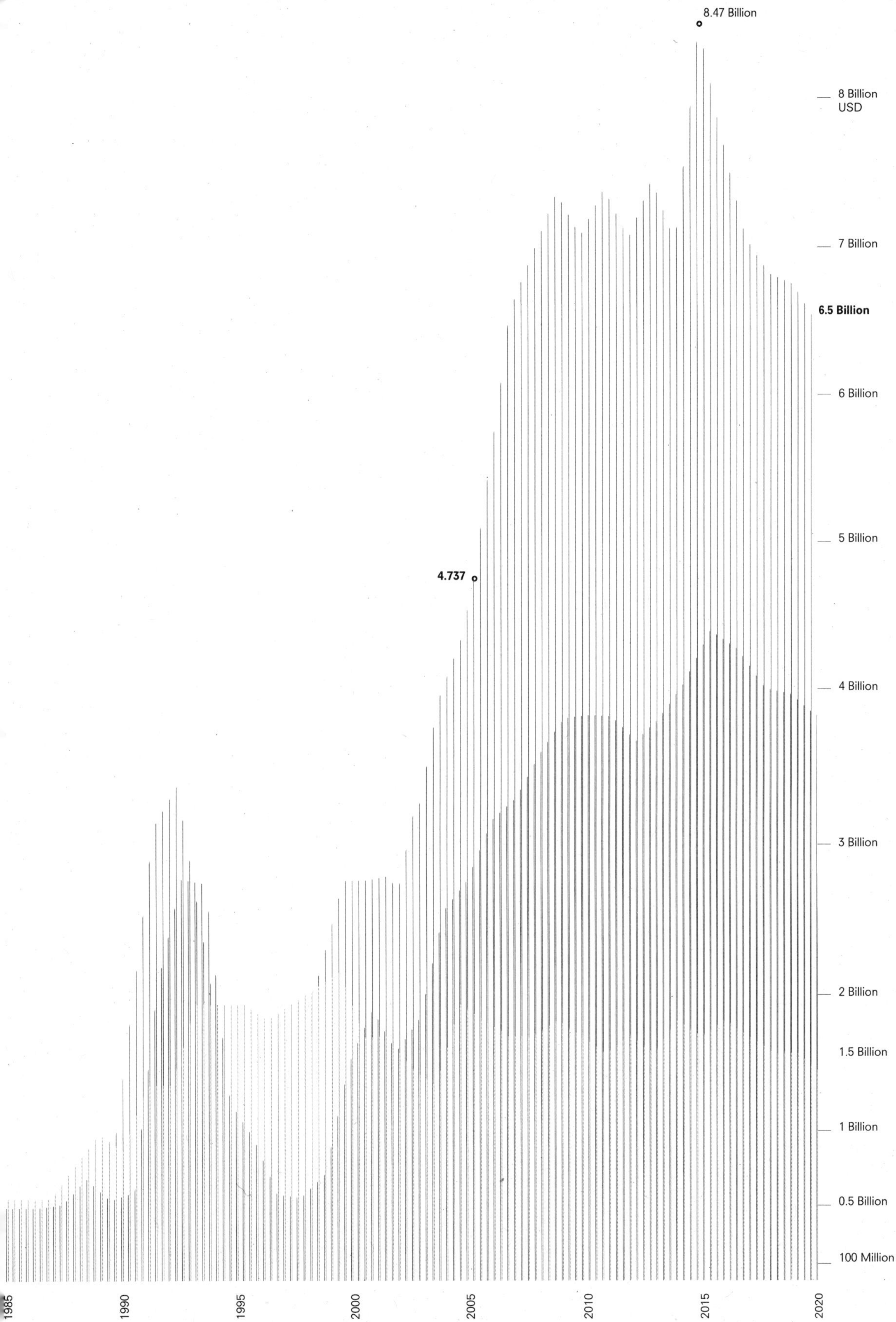
8.47 Billion
8 Billion USD
7 Billion
6.5 Billion
6 Billion
5 Billion
4.737
4 Billion
3 Billion
2 Billion
1.5 Billion
1 Billion
0.5 Billion
100 Million
1985
1990
1995
2000
2005
2010
2015
2020

Examples of Current Missions

The following maps and images illustrate the nature and scale of the peacekeeping footprint today in the Central African Republic and South Sudan. They highlight the spatial relationships between UN bases and their different locations, their presence in urban settings and their proximity to populated rural areas.

Central African Republic

The United Nations Multidimensional Integrated Stabilization Mission (MINUSCA) was authorized in April 2014 with a mandate to protect civilians; facilitate humanitarian assistance; and support processes related to justice, rule of law, disarmament, demobilization, reintegration, and repatriation. The mission includes 14,929 personnel with a yearly budget of US$976,376,000. MINUSCA bases include large-scale super camps and are deployed in 17 cities throughout the country (as of December 2020). Most of the bases are located within existing locally inhabited fabrics, as depicted in the following sequence of aerial images.

Since the 2000s, UN deployment of new large-scale peace operations has swelled drastically due to several global trends such as the increase of intrastate violence, globalization (production and finance), and the global financial crisis in 2008. The last led the UN to outsource the production of its bases to third-party companies. Their mandates of peacekeeping operations have changed (see peacekeeping today table), and they include more staff and infrastructure than previous missions. The operations now import massive amounts of materials and people into the areas where they operate, increasing their impact on their surroundings and the environment. Moreover, these missions are often situated alongside fragile rural and urban communities, exposing wide disparities between these communities and the peacekeepers in terms of their consumption and waste patterns.

CAR

Population:
5,990,855 (July 2020 est.) with low life expectancy due to AIDS, higher infant mortality, higher death rates, lower population growth rates.

Ethnicity:
Baya 28.8%, Banda 22.9%, Mandjia 9.9%, Sara 7.9%, M'Baka-Bantu 7.9%, Arab-Fulani (Peul) 6%, Mbum 6%, Ngbanki 5.5%, Zande-Nzakara 3%, other Central African Republic ethnic groups 2%, non-Central African Republic ethnic groups 1%.

Population distribution:
The majority of residents live in the western and central areas of the country, especially in and around the capital of Bangui.

Drinking Water:
Improved:
Urban: 89.6% of population
Rural: 54.4% of population
Total: 68.5% of population
Unimproved:
Urban: 10.4% of population
Rural: 45.6% of population
Total: 31.5% of population

Physicians density:
0.07 physicians/1,000 population

Hospital bed density:
Beds/1,000 population

Sanitation facility access:
Improved:
Urban: 43.6% of population
Rural: 7.2% of population
Total: 21.8% of population
Unimproved:
Urban: 56.4% of population
Rural: 92.8% of population
Total: 78.2% of population

Literacy: 37.4%

Population without electricity:
5 million (2019)
Electrification:
Total population: 3%
Urban areas: 7%
Rural areas: 0.4%

Refugees:
5,555 (Democratic Republic of Congo) (2020).

IDPs:
684,004 (clashes between army and rebel groups since 2005; tensions between ethnic groups) (2020).

Source: World Fact Book. CIA

Central African Republic · MINUSCA 2020

CAR GDP 2020 US$1.8 billion
UN mission expenditure
US$0.976 billion

150 mi

headquarters
UN base

Lifespan of the mission: 6 years
15 Sep 2014–Ongoing
Expenditure 2020: US$976,376,000
Deployed 2020: 14,926
Number of sites with bases: 18 with super camps

Inhabited areas with MINUSCA bases

Bouar. Base 1, 2013. 1/4 2000 f 500 m

Bouar. Base 1, 2015. 2/4 2000 f 500 m

Bouar. Base 1, 2016. 3/4 2000 f 500 m

Bouar, 2020. 4/4. Base 1 area: 56 hectares
City population: 40,000

Bouar. Base 2, 2008. 1/2 700 f 200 m

Base 2 area: 56 hectares
City population: 40,000

Bangui. 2014. 1/2

Bangui. 2018. 2/2 Base area (estimated): 62 hectares
City population: 734,350

Kangra Bandoro. 2007. 1/2

2000 f 500 m

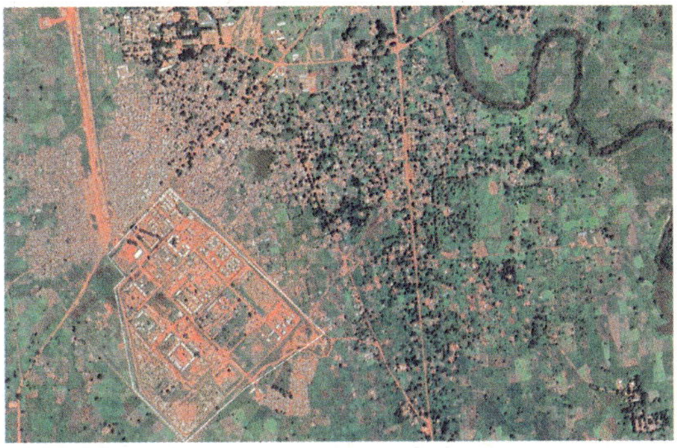

Kangra Bandoro. 2007. 2/2. Base area: 52 hectares
City population: 27,797

Bria. Base 1. 2013 1/2

2000 f 500 m

Bria. Base 1. 2020. 2/2. Base area (estimated): 47 hectares
City population: 43,000

Bria. Base 2. 2015 1/2

2000 f 500 m

Bria. Base 2. 2020 2/2. Base area (estimated): 16 hectares

Bambari. 2009. 1/2

Bambari. 2020. 2/2. Base area (estimated): 30 hectares
City population: 38,451

South Sudan

UNMISS was established in July 2011. Currently, it has 18,013 personnel stationed at multiple bases in 17 cities across the country, with the largest concentrations in Juba and Malakal. Some of the bases are surrounded by refugee camps and humanitarian missions.[48] These multiple missions increase the overall material footprint of the UN and require the establishment of sustainable and integrated legacy strategies. As the following images, maps, and charts make clear, although UN bases and the local communities share and inhabit the same ground, they are also worlds apart.

Dire security concerns and attacks against UN personnel have led to the privileging of security needs in peacekeeping settings. UN camps, super camps, and headquarters are designed as islands enclosed by barbed wire and surrounded by trenches.[49] Divorced from the local urban context, these spaces hamper the already meager development prospects in cities by blocking access, disturbing daily life, and separating communities from one another in politically charged urban settings and impoverished and precarious living environments.

South Sudan

Population: 10,561,244

Ethnicity:
Dinka (Jieng) 35.8%, Nuer (Naath) 15.6%, Shilluk (Chollo), Azande, Bari, Kakwa, Kuku, Murle, Mandari, Didinga, Ndogo, Bviri, Lndi, Anuak, Bongo, Lango, Dungotona, Acholi, Baka, Fertit.

Population distribution:
Clusters found in urban areas, particularly in the western interior and around the White Nile.

Urbanization:
Urban population: 20.2% of total population. Rate of urbanization: 4.1% annual

Drinking Water:
Improved:
urban: 85.2% of population
rural: 71.7% of population
total: 74.3% of population
Unimproved:
urban: 14.8% of population
rural: 28.3% of population
total: 25.7% of population

Sanitation facility access:
Improved:
urban: 54.1% of population
rural: 10.7% of population
total: 19.1% of population
Unimproved:
urban: 45.9% of population
rural: 89.3% of population
total: 80.9% of population

Literacy: 34.5%

Unemployment: 38.6%

Population without electricity:
11 million
Electrification – total population: 1%.
Electrification – urban areas: 4%
Electrification – rural areas: 1%

Refugees: 729,530

IDPs: 1.66 million (alleged coup attempt and ethnic conflict beginning in December 2013; information is lacking on those displaced in earlier years by: fighting in Abyei between the Sudanese Armed Forces and the Sudan People's Liberation Army (SPLA) in May 2011; clashes between the SPLA and dissident militia groups in South Sudan; inter-ethnic conflicts over resources and cattle; attacks from the Lord's Resistance Army; floods and drought.

Source: World Fact Book. CIA

48 "'UNMISS Fact Sheet", available at: https://peacekeeping.un.org/en/mission/minusca.
49 Shoshan, Malkit. "From an Island to a Catalyst," in BLUE: Architecture of UN PK Missions. Archis, 2016, p. 8.

South Sudan · UNMISS 2020

Lifespan of the mission: 6 years
9 Jul 2014 – Ongoing
Expenditure 2020: US$1.269 billion
Deployed 2020: 19,056
Number of sites with bases:
18 sites with super camps
and about 56 bases

Inhabited reas with UNMISS bases

Juba. Bases 1, 2012. 1/2

Juba. Bases 1, 2020. 2/2. Area (estimated) 100 hectares
City population: 403,000

Wau. Base 1, 2003. 1/4

Wau. Base 1, 2014. 2/4. Base area (estimated): 280 hectares
City population: 127,384

Wau. Base 1, 2018. 3/4.

Wau. Base 1, 2020. 4/4

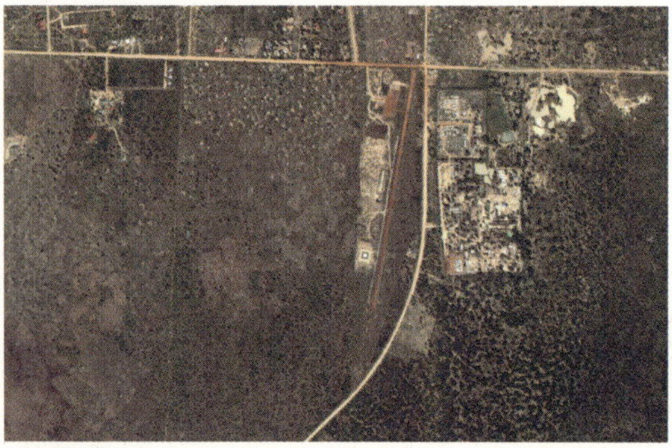

Bor, 2014. 1/2

Bor, 2020. 2/2 Base area (estimated): 90 hectares
City population: 26,782

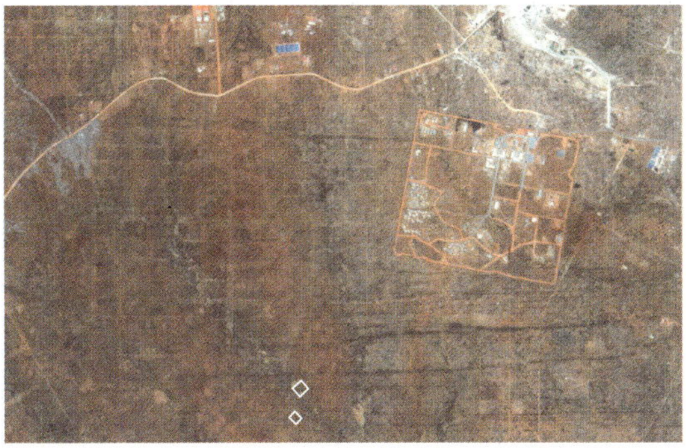

Juba. Bases 2, 2012. 1/2 **2000 f 500 m**

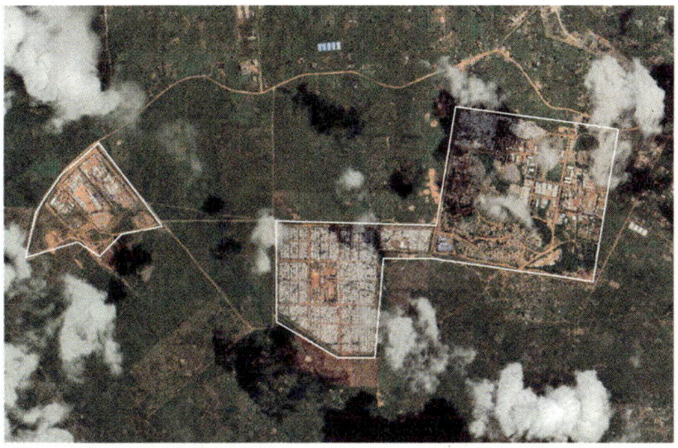

Juba. Bases 2, 2020. 2/2. Base area (estimated): 280 hectares

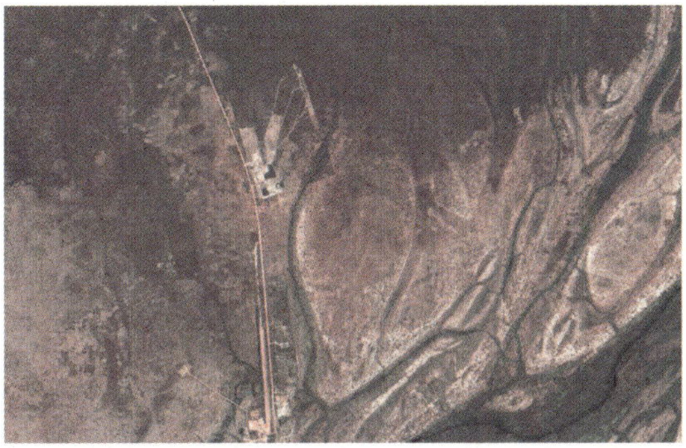

Bentiu. Base 1. 2012. 1/4

Bentiu. Base 1. 2014. 2/4

Bentiu. Base 1. 2017 3/4

Bentiu. Base 1. 2014. 4/4. Base area (estimated): 450 hectares
Population: 111,766

Malakal. 2013. 1/2

Malakal. 2020. 2/2. Base area (estimated): 225 hectares
City population: 160,765

The Changing Face of War and Peace

The expenditure on UN peacekeeping missions over time charted in relation to forced displacement, war, and drought.

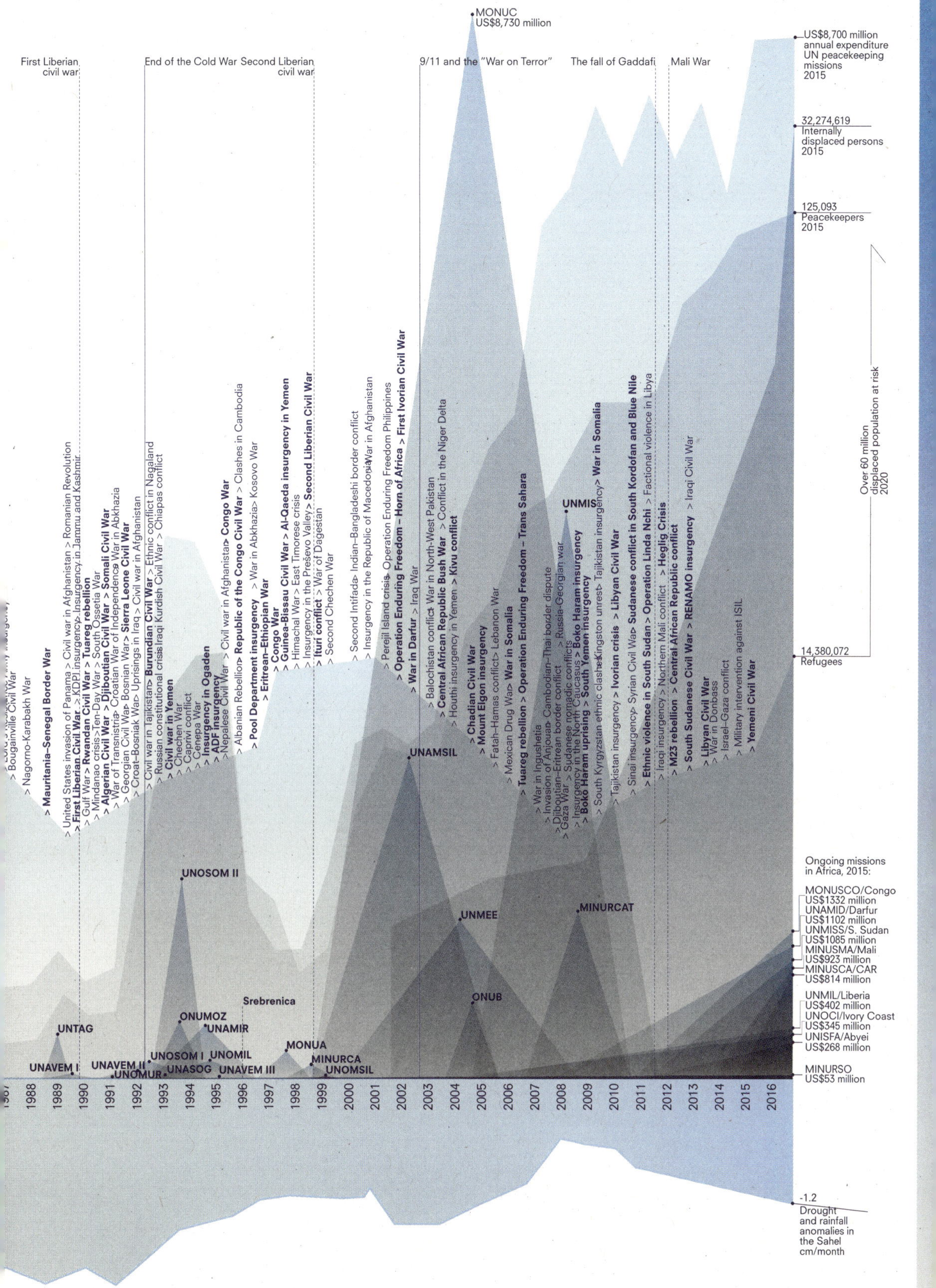

First Liberian civil war
End of the Cold War
Second Liberian civil war
9/11 and the "War on Terror"
The fall of Gaddafi
Mali War
MONUC US$8,730 million
US$8,700 million annual expenditure UN peacekeeping missions 2015
32,274,619 Internally displaced persons 2015
125,093 Peacekeepers 2015
Over 60 million displaced population at risk 2020
14,380,072 Refugees
Ongoing missions in Africa, 2015:
MONUSCO/Congo US$1332 million
UNAMID/Darfur US$1102 million
UNMISS/S. Sudan US$1085 million
MINUSMA/Mali US$923 million
MINUSCA/CAR US$814 million
UNMIL/Liberia US$402 million
UNOCI/Ivory Coast US$345 million
UNISFA/Abyei US$268 million
MINURSO US$53 million
-1.2 Drought and rainfall anomalies in the Sahel cm/month
UNTAG
UNAVEM I
UNAVEM II
UNOMUR
UNOSOM I
UNASOG
UNOSOM II
ONUMOZ
UNAMIR
UNOMIL
UNAVEM III
Srebrenica
MONUA
MINURCA
UNOMSIL
UNAMSIL
UNMEE
ONUB
UNMIS
MINURCAT
1988 1989 1990 1991 1992 1993 1994 1995 1996 1997 1998 1999 2000 2001 2002 2003 2004 2005 2006 2007 2008 2009 2010 2011 2012 2013 2014 2015 2016

Missions in Africa
2016

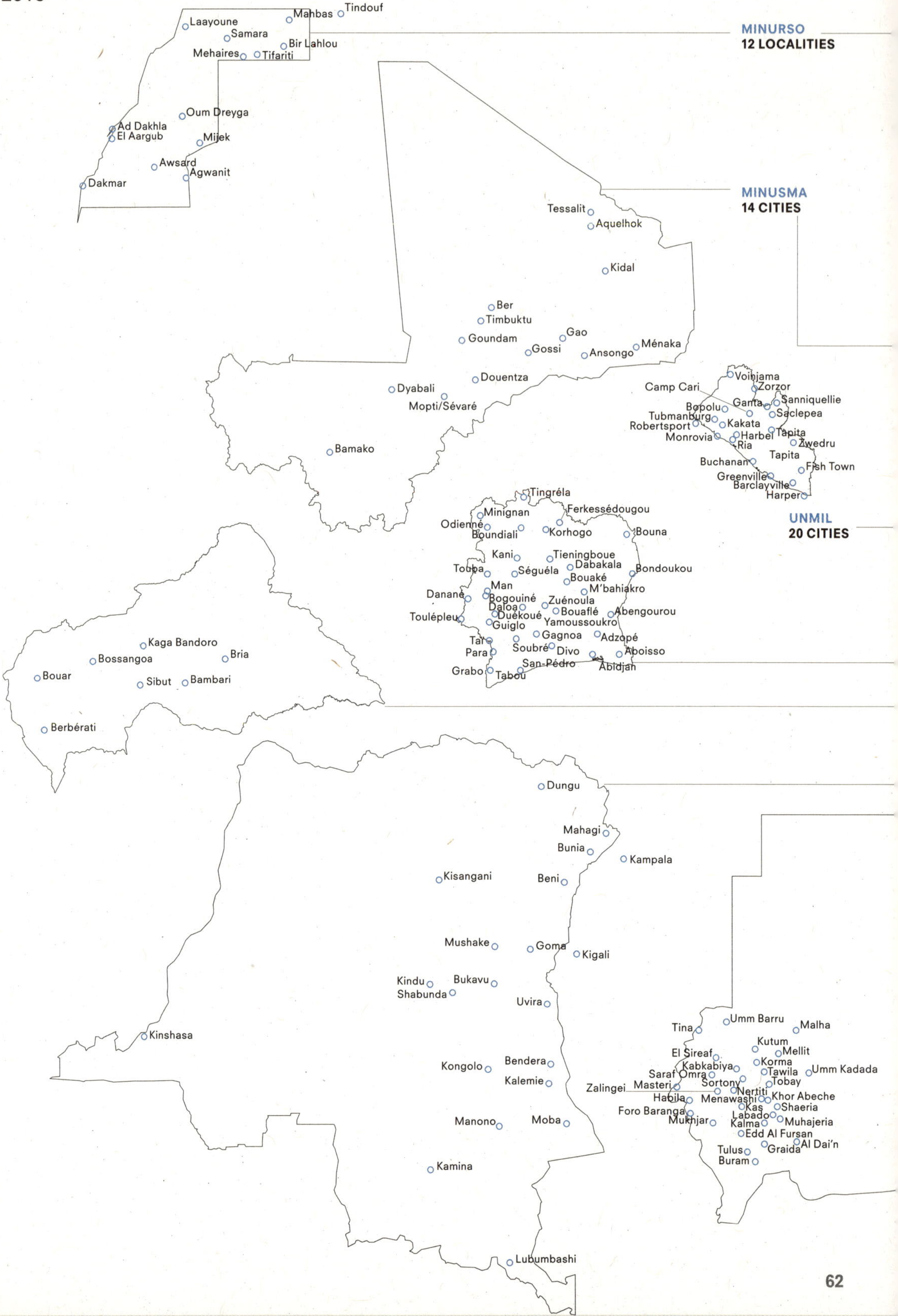

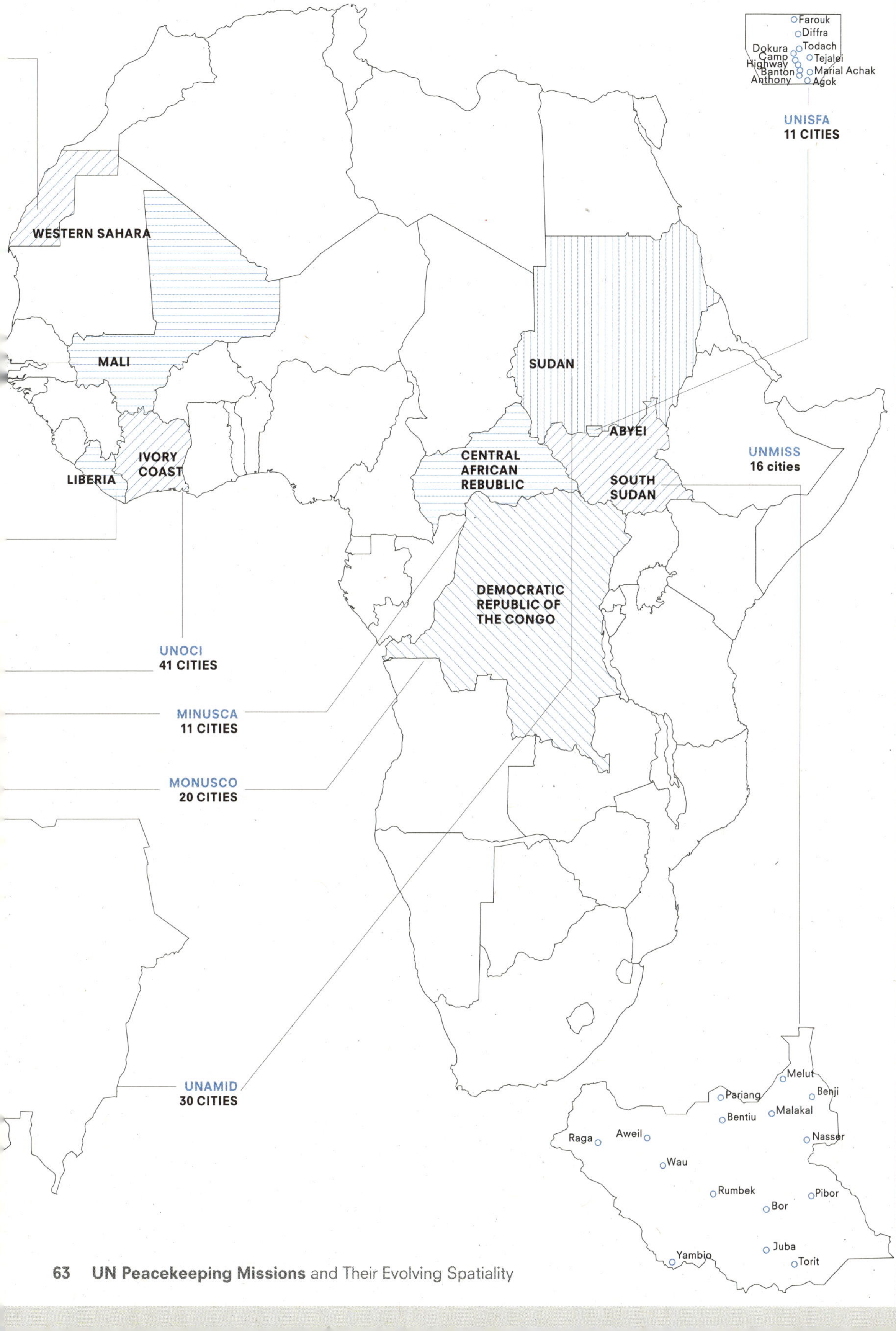
Farouk
Diffra
Dokura
Todach
Camp
Tejalei
Highway
Banton
Marial Achak
Anthony
Agok
UNISFA
11 CITIES
WESTERN SAHARA
MALI
SUDAN
ABYEI
IVORY COAST
LIBERIA
CENTRAL AFRICAN REBUBLIC
UNMISS
16 cities
SOUTH SUDAN
DEMOCRATIC REPUBLIC OF THE CONGO
UNOCI
41 CITIES
MINUSCA
11 CITIES
MONUSCO
20 CITIES
UNAMID
30 CITIES
Melut
Pariang
Benji
Malakal
Bentiu
Raga
Aweil
Nasser
Wau
Rumbek
Pibor
Bor
Juba
Yambio
Torit

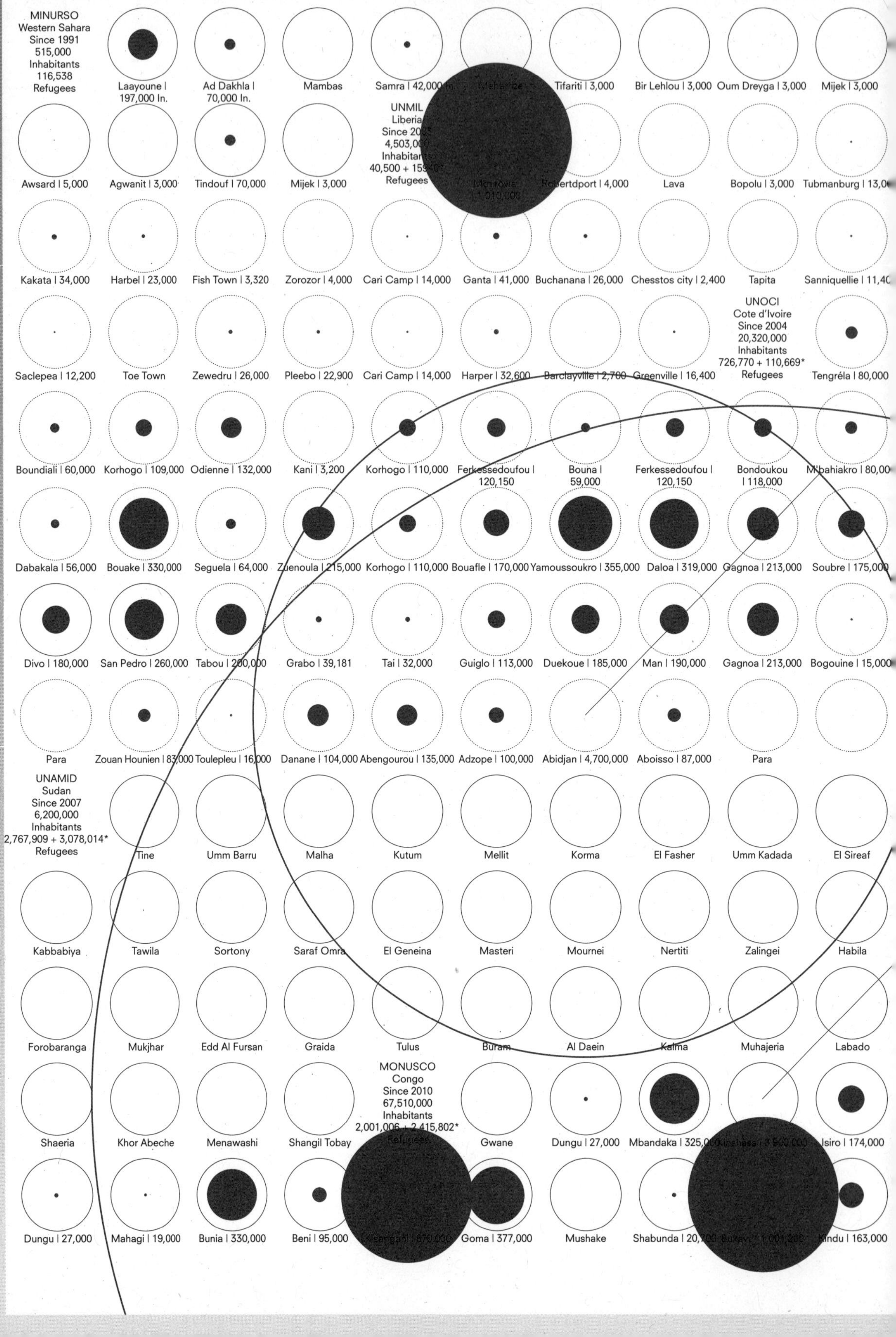
MINURSO
Western Sahara
Since 1991
515,000
Inhabitants
116,538
Refugees
Laayoune | 197,000 In.
Ad Dakhla | 70,000 In.
Mambas
Tifariti | 3,000
Bir Lehlou | 3,000
Oum Dreyga | 3,000
Mijek | 3,000
Awsard | 5,000
Agwanit | 3,000
Tindouf | 70,000
Mijek | 3,000
UNMIL
Liberia
Inhabitants
Refugees
Lava
Bopolu | 3,000
Kakata | 34,000
Harbel | 23,000
Fish Town | 3,320
Zorozor | 4,000
Cari Camp | 14,000
Ganta | 41,000
Buchanana | 26,000
Chesstos city | 2,400
Tapita
Saclepea | 12,200
Toe Town
Zewedru | 26,000
Pleebo | 22,900
Cari Camp | 14,000
Harper | 32,600
Barclayville | 2,700
Greenville | 16,400
UNOCI
Cote d'Ivoire
Since 2004
20,320,000
Inhabitants
726,770 + 110,669*
Refugees
Tengréla | 80,000
Boundiali | 60,000
Korhogo | 109,000
Odienne | 132,000
Kani | 3,200
Korhogo | 110,000
Ferkessedoufou | 120,150
Bouna | 59,000
Ferkessedoufou | 120,150
Bondoukou | 118,000
Dabakala | 56,000
Bouake | 330,000
Seguela | 64,000
Zuenoula | 215,000
Korhogo | 110,000
Bouafle | 170,000
Yamoussoukro | 355,000
Daloa | 319,000
Gagnoa | 213,000
Divo | 180,000
San Pedro | 260,000
Tabou | 200,000
Grabo | 39,181
Tai | 32,000
Guiglo | 113,000
Duekoue | 185,000
Man | 190,000
Gagnoa | 213,000
Para
Zouan Hounien | 83,000
Toulepleu | 16,000
Danane | 104,000
Abengourou | 135,000
Adzope | 100,000
Abidjan | 4,700,000
Aboisso | 87,000
Para
UNAMID
Sudan
Since 2007
6,200,000
Inhabitants
2,767,909 + 3,078,014*
Refugees
Tine
Umm Barru
Malha
Kutum
Mellit
Korma
El Fasher
Umm Kadada
El Sireaf
Kabbabiya
Tawila
Sortony
Saraf Omra
El Geneina
Masteri
Mournei
Nertiti
Zalingei
Habila
Forobaranga
Mukjhar
Edd Al Fursan
Graida
Tulus
Buram
Al Daein
Kalma
Muhajeria
Labado
MONUSCO
Congo
Since 2010
67,510,000
Inhabitants
Shaeria
Khor Abeche
Menawashi
Shangil Tobay
Gwane
Dungu | 27,000
Mbandaka | 325,000
Isiro | 174,000
Dungu | 27,000
Mahagi | 19,000
Bunia | 330,000
Beni | 95,000
Goma | 377,000
Mushake
Shabunda | 20,700
Kindu | 163,000

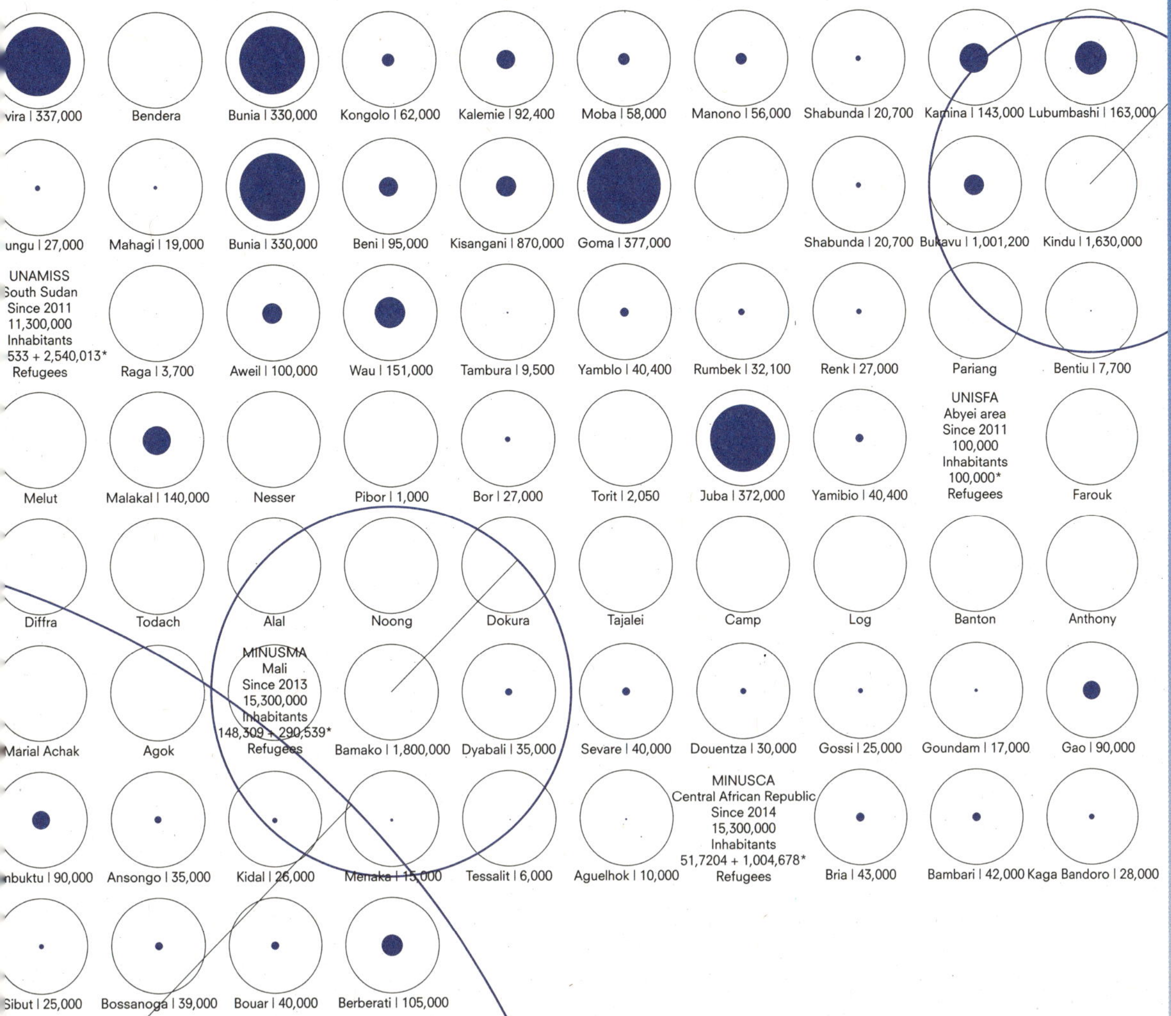

African Cities and Villages with Presence of UN Missions and Bases

Mali and the Beginning of a UN Peace-keeping Mission

Mali · MINUSMA 2020

The United Nations Multidimensional Integrated Stabilization Mission in Mali

Lifespan of the mission: 7 years
25 Apr 2013 – Ongoing
Total expenditure: US$7.32 billion
Expenditure 2020: US$1.22 billion
Total Personnel: 102,231
Personnel 2020: 15,207
Number of sites and bases: About 20

III. Mali

In the 14th century, the boundaries of the Mali Empire extended from the Sahara Desert in the east to Senegal in the west, reaching the shores of the Atlantic Ocean. Cities such as Timbuktu and Gao were known for their thriving culture and wealth. Throughout history, Mali was a trade hub due to its geographic position on a continental crossroads. Its abundance of natural resources meant it was subject to various types of foreign explorations and exploitation. Its rich history and culture thrived for millennia along the shores of the Niger River. With the Tuareg and Moor in the North and the Fula, Bambara, Malinke, and Dogons[1] in the South, people and communities from various ethnicities, religions, and lifestyles continuously shared and co-inhabited the region. At the end of the 19th century, Mali was colonized by the French and became part of French Sudan.[2] In 1960, the Republic of Mali became independent. Its arbitrarily drawn bow tie-like borders with no greater awareness of human or physical geography remain contested to this day. The northern half of the country is arid and converges with the Sahara Desert. The country's economy relies on agriculture and fishing as well as mining of gold, uranium, phosphates, kaolinite, salt, and limestone, and about half of its 14.5 million inhabitants live on less than US$1.25 per day.[3]

1 See Dutch Expedition to the Bandiagara, p151.
2 Present-day Mali is named for the Mali Empire, which at its peak in the 14th century, covered an area about twice the size of modern-day France and stretched to the west coast of Africa. In the late 19th century, France seized control of Mali. The Sudanese Republic and Senegal became independent of France in 1960 as the Mali Federation. When Senegal withdrew after only a few months, what was formerly the Sudanese Republic was renamed Mali. See: www.cia.gov/library/publications/the-world-factbook/geos/ml.html.
3 World Factbook, CIA, available at www.cia.gov/library/publications/the-world-factbook/geos/ml.html.

Urban Challenges

Mali[4] is a vast country covering 1,240,192 square kilometers, with a mostly low population density of about nine inhabitants per square kilometer on average. The distribution of its inhabitants, however, is uneven. Population pressure is mainly felt in the south of the country along the fertile valleys of the Niger and Senegal Rivers, and on the plains with good farming potential. The country has 112 cities with populations of 5,000 or more. There are only five cities with over 100,000 residents—Bamako, Ségou, Sikasso, Mopti, and Koutiala—and four cities with populations between 50,000 and 100,000: Kayes, Timbuktu, Gao, and Kati. The population of the capital city, Bamako, is estimated at between 1.2 and 1.4 million. Mali's cities form a network in which each city has a specific function. Some are fertile agricultural hinterlands (rice, cotton), which receive substantial remittances from expatriates, and tourist cities, such as Timbuktu and Djenné, which have been listed as World Heritage Sites by UNESCO.

With only 3.7 million city dwellers out of a total population of 11.7 million, Mali is less urbanized than other countries in the region. Its medium-sized and secondary cities are rapidly expanding, yet they are impoverished, with inadequate civic services and infrastructure. Improving daily life and access to primary resources in urban areas is critical to addressing poverty, especially in remote cities.[5]

Approximately 30 percent of urban dwellers live in extreme and ballooning poverty because of the disappearance of traditional support networks and challenges in accessing food, civic services, and housing. The lack of roads; drainage; and essential services such as water, sanitation, and electricity lies at the heart of Mali's urban development problems.[6] Outlying settlements have sprung up with no suitable access to infrastructures and urban services. The drinking water production is insufficient in Bamako, Kayes, Gao, Koutiala, and Kidal. The level of access to the water system varies from city to city and from one neighborhood to the next. The number of urban households connected to the sewage system is low, and Bamako is the only city with such a system. Only a few urban households have access to a latrine. Sewage, which is mainly carried through street gutters, pollutes the soil and, consequently, percolates down

4 **Mali**

Population: 19,553,397

Ethnicity:
Bambara 33.3%, Fulani (Peuhl) 13.3%, Sarakole/Soninke/Marka 9.8%, Senufo/Manianka 9.6%, Malinke 8.8%, Dogon 8.7%, Sonrai 5.9%, Bobo 2.1%, Tuareg/Bella 1.7%, other Malian 6%, from members of Economic Community of West Africa 4%, other 3%

Urbanization:
Urban population: 43.9% of total population (2020).

Rate of urbanization: 4.86% annual rate of change (2015–20 est.)

Population growth rate:
2.95%, country comparison to the world: 9

Drinking water:
Improved:
Urban: 97.1% of population
Rural: 72.8% of population
Total: 82.9% of population
Unimproved:
Urban: 2.9% of population
Rural: 27.2% of population
Total: 17.1% of population
(2017 est.)

Sanitation facility access
Improved:
Urban: 82.5% of population
Rural: 34.1% of population
Total: 54.2% of population

Unimproved:
Urban: 17.5% of population
Rural: 65.9% of population
Total: 45.8% of population
(2017 est.)

Hospital bed density:
0.1 bed/1,000 people

Energy Scarcity in Mali

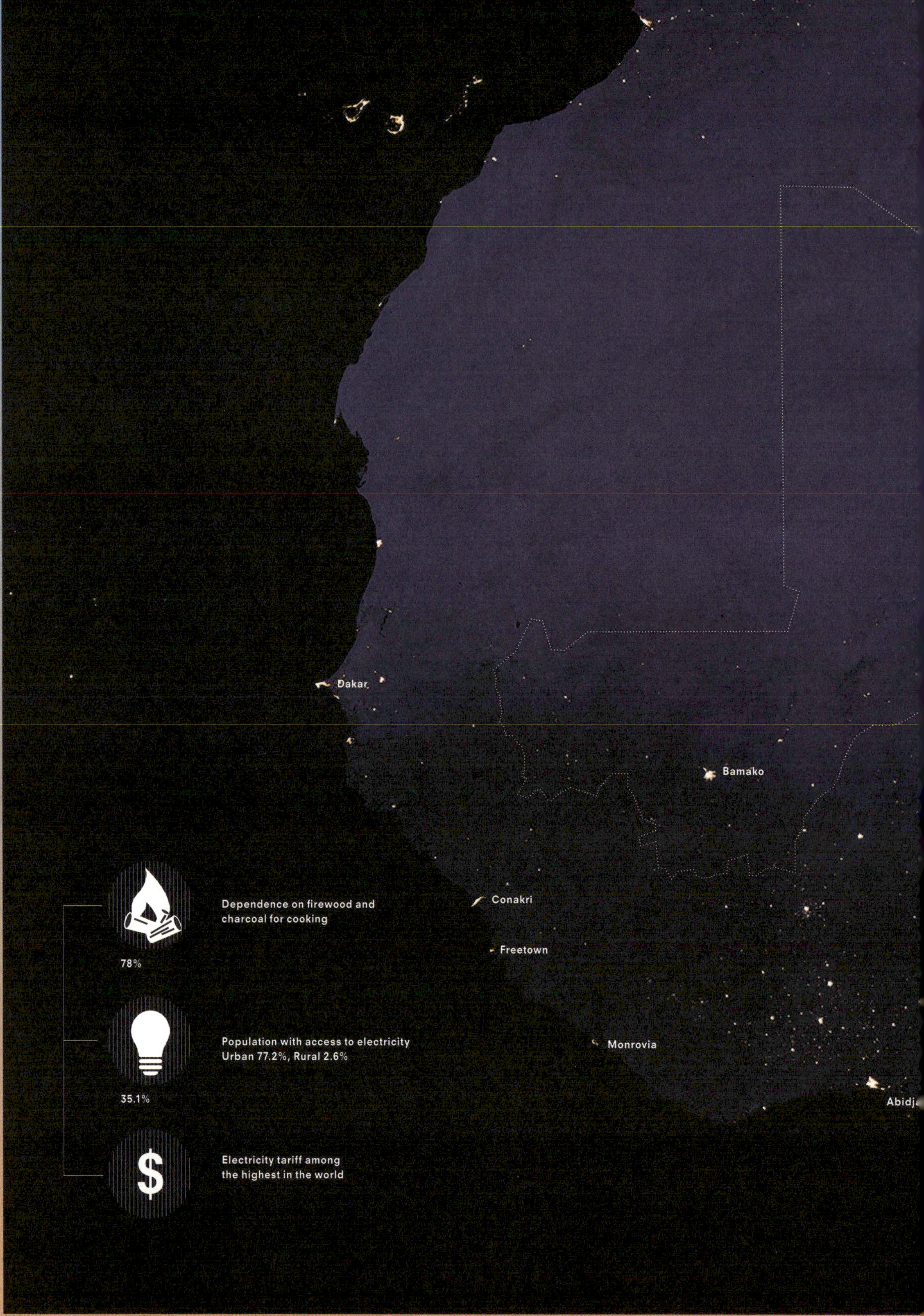

Abuja
asi
Lagos
Accra
ATLANTIC OCEAN

into the groundwater.[7] Waste collection is also inadequate and fails to meet acceptable environmental standards, which results in pollution and disease. Urban roadways are not maintained, and urban transportation is provided entirely by the informal sector, using old and poorly kept vehicles that increase pollution and the number of fatal accidents.[8]

Furthermore, opaque local land ownership and land management practices pose a problem for land tenure security, especially for poor households that depend on land for food production and self-sufficiency.

It is critical to provide facilities for harvesting, storing, and processing agricultural produce and food, in addition to supporting other economic activities, such as tourism, services, and trade in a sustainable and regenerative ways. Moreover, a better integrated network of urban centers would enhance interactions between urban and rural areas, contributing to bettering quality of life in Mali by improving access to basic infrastructure and mobility, particularly for rural areas. Equipping cities, rural areas, and households with the ability to generate basic and urban resources is key to sustaining peace in the country.[9]

In the next decade, Mali's cities are expected to double and triple in size due to natural growth, climate change, war, and armed conflict-related migrations. The circular relationship between conflict and the climate crisis continues to exacerbate Mali's urban challenges, perpetuating its struggle with poverty, disease, and human suffering.

Security Challenges

Following Colonel Gaddafi's downfall at the end of the Libyan Civil War in 2011, regional politics and power dynamics in Northern Africa, the Sahara Desert, and sub-Saharan Africa changed. At the end of his reign, militarized groups fled south into the desert.

These groups included some Tuareg men who were offered employment in Libya and fought in Colonel Gaddafi's army. The Tuareg are a seminomadic, pastoralist people, numbering from 1 to 1.5 million. They call themselves the free people and are known as the blue people due to the indigo veil men begin wearing at the age of 25. The Tuareg are grouped into independent federations that live in Algeria, Libya, Mali, and Niger (see map on page 95).[10] Tuareg camel caravans once played a central role in the trans-Saharan trade that extended from the northern Mediterranean coast of Africa to the great cities on the southern edge of the Sahara. Over the past centuries, however, the Tuareg livelihood has been subject to a continuous assault, mainly because 1) European colonization of Africa introduced new infra-structure that replaced the Tuareg trade routes;[11] 2) the decolonization processes and the creation of nation-states in Africa excluded them from international recognition and civil rights, and the newly established borders limited their movements;[12] 3) the continued extraction of natural resources by France, such as uranium mining, in areas where the Tuareg live have caused severe environmental pollution and exerted a heavy toll on people's health and wellbeing;[13]
4) rising temperature and extreme climate events, such as drought and flooding, have increased significantly over the past decades, making life in the Sahara region unbearable.[14]

The Tuareg have never been recognized by the international community as a nation, and their ongoing pleas for international recognition were ignored multiple times in the 20th century, first by the French colonial regime and then by the international community and the United Nations.[15] The most recent crisis started with Tuareg's departure from Libya and their employment and income loss. Their survival was at stake.

Electricity
Population without electricity: 10 million (2019)
Electrification – total population: 50% (2019)
Electrification – urban areas: 78% (2019)
Electrification – rural areas: 28% (2019)

Literacy: 35.5%

Unemployment: 16.9%

Refugees:
139,994 Malian refugees in Burkina Faso, Mauritania and Niger
8,457 Burkinabe refugees in Mali

IDPs: 438,935

Source: World Fact Book. CIA

5 Farvacque-Vitkovic, Catherine, Alicia Casalis, Mahine Diop, and Christian Eghoff, "Development of the Cities of Mali – Challenges and Priorities," Humanitarian Library, September 2007, available at: www.humanitarianlibrary.org/sites/default/files/2013/07/wp104_english.pdf.
6 Ibid.
7 Ibid.
8 "The World Factbook," CIA, available at: www.cia.gov/the-world-factbook/countries/mali.
9 Ibid.
10 "Art of Being Tuareg. Sahara Nomads in a Modern World," available at: africa.si.edu/exhibits/tuareg/who.html.
11 Ibid.
12 Ibid.

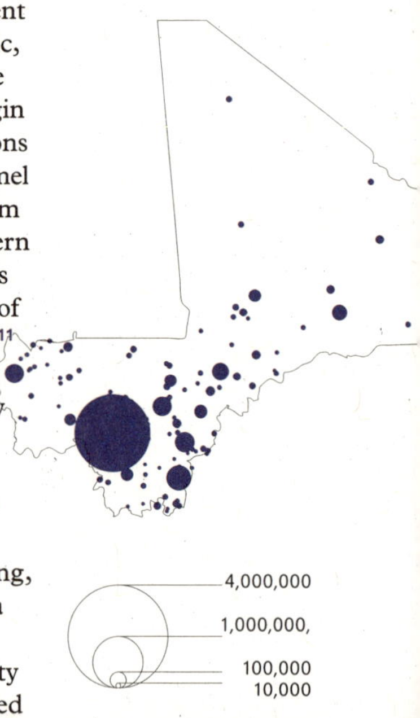

13 Carnegie Endowment for International Peace. "Uranium in Sahara Sand," available at: https://carnegieendowment.org/2013/01/22/uranium-in-saharan-sands-pub-50707.

They established the MNLA, the Movement for the Liberation of Azawad, a territory in northern Mali, which they have inhabited for thousands of years, and they began fighting for self-determination. Back in the desert, they realized that they were not alone: Al-Qaeda, IS, and other jihadist groups were also active in the Sahara, contributing to a rapid escalation in violence that threatened to destabilize the region. In 2012, the Islamist group Ansar Din joined the MNLA. Together, they succeeded in overtaking northern Mali. In 2013, the UN Multidimensional Integrated Stabilization Mission in Mali (MINUSMA) was established at the behest of the Malian government in Bamako.[16] The United Nation forces arrived to help the Malian government to gain control over the northern parts of the country and resolve the conflict. Since then, the UN has built dozens of compounds and super camps in 13 cities across Mali.

14 United Nations Climate Change. "Climate Change Is an Increasing Threat to Africa," available at: https://unfccc.int/news/climate-change-is-an-increasing-threat-to-africa.

15 The Tuareg Rebellion, available at: www.arcgis.com/apps/Cascade/index.html.

16 The United Nations Multidimensional Integrated Stabilization Mission in Mali (MINUSMA) was established by Security Council resolution 2100 of April 25, 2013 to support political processes in that country and carry out a number of security-related tasks. The Mission was asked to support the transitional authorities of Mali in the stabilization of the country and implementation of the transitional roadmap. By unanimously adopting resolution 2164 of June 25, 2014, the Council further decided that the Mission should focus on duties such as ensuring security, stabilization and protection of civilians; supporting national political dialogue and reconciliation; and assisting the reestablishment of State authority, the rebuilding of the security sector, and the promotion and protection of human rights in that country. See UN MINUSMA: https://peacekeeping.un.org/en/mission/minusma.

Security challenges in the Sahel and UN peacekeeping missions

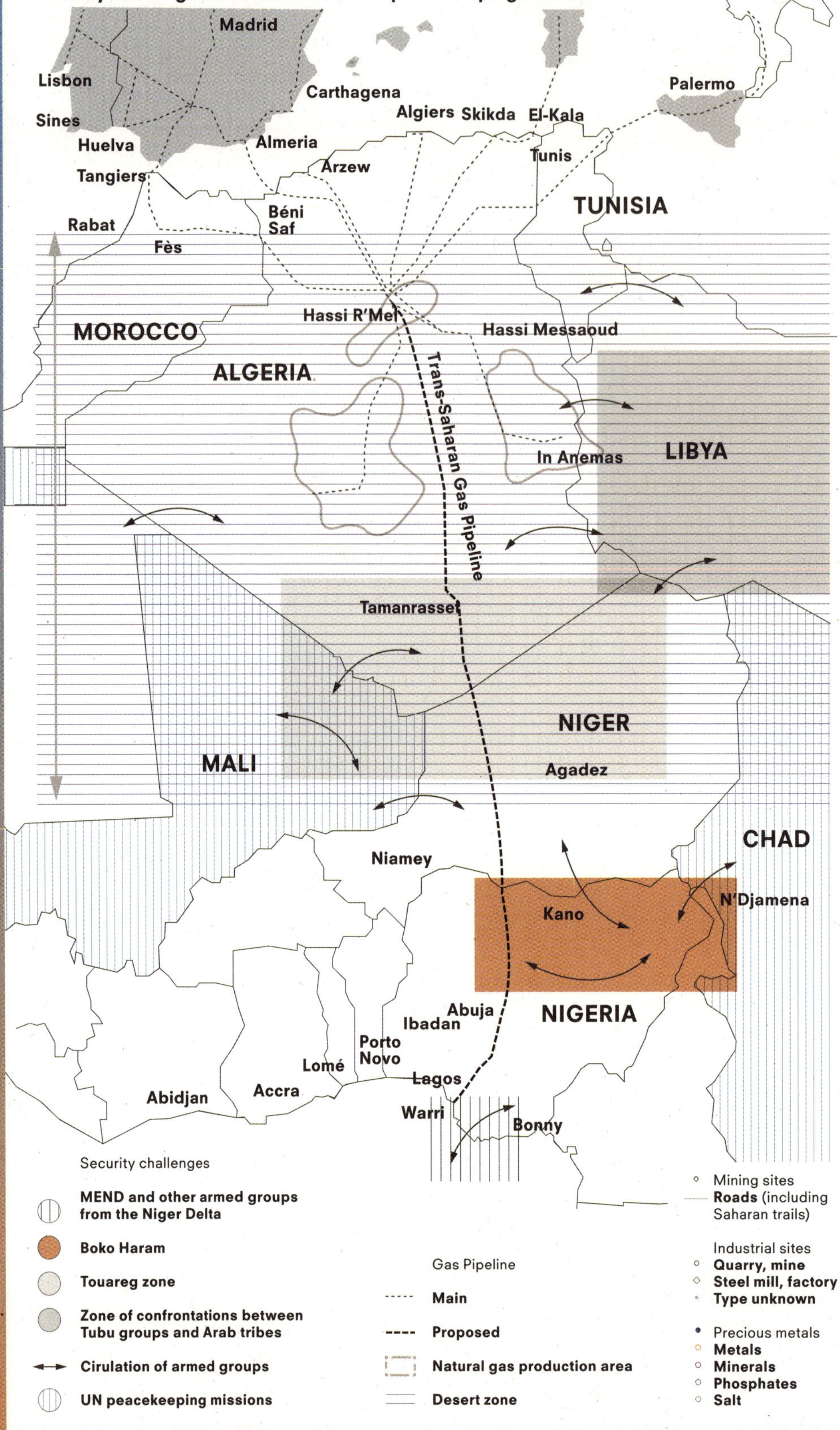

Natural resources and peacekeeping

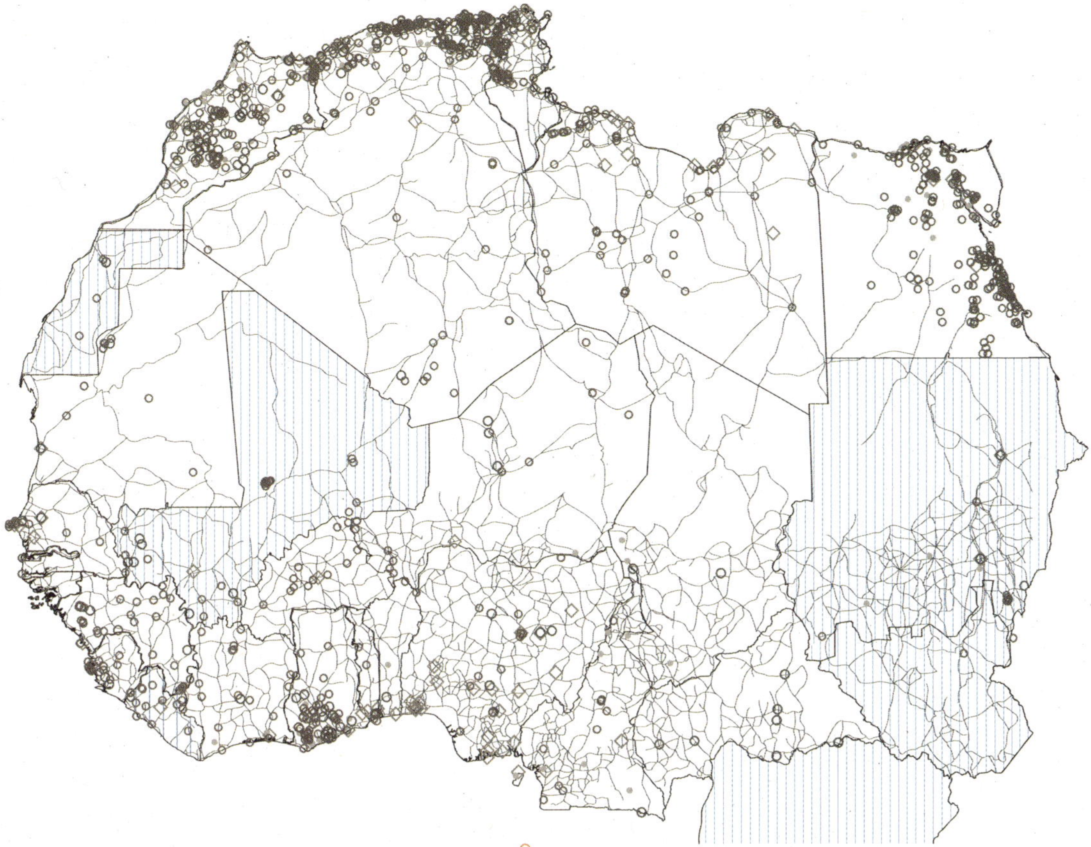

Mines and peacekeeping

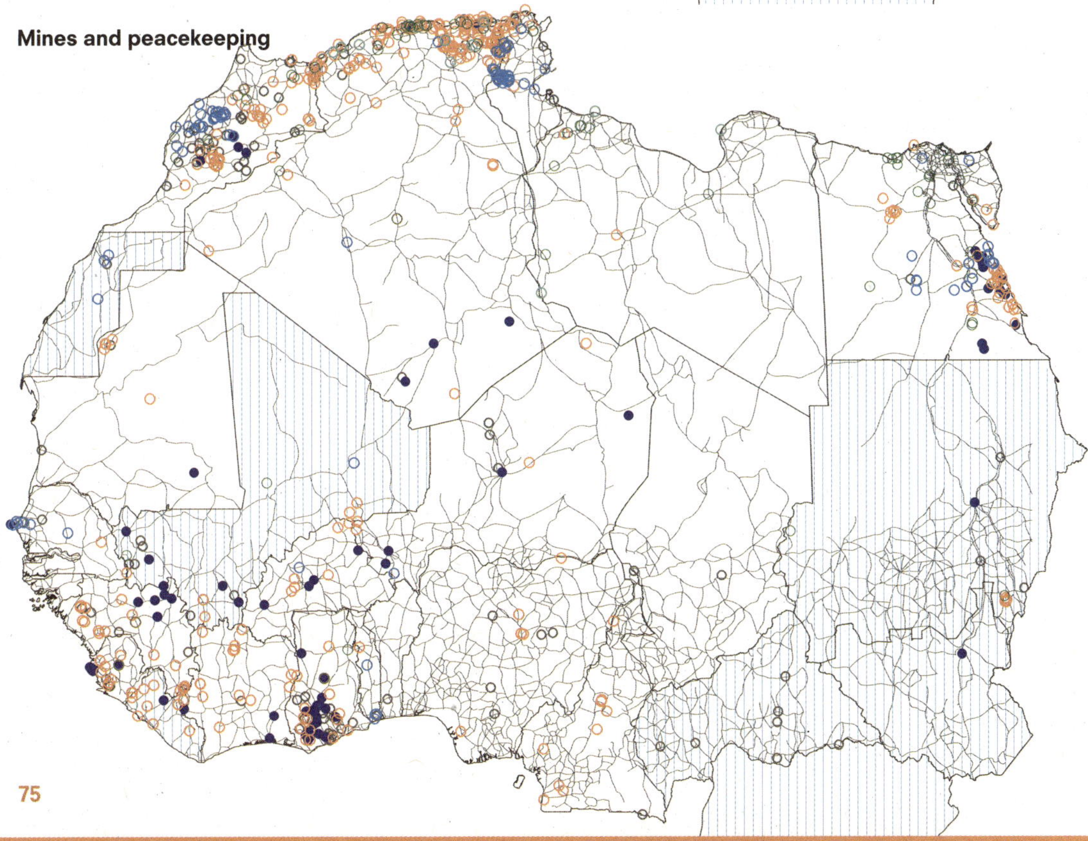

Water resources and peacekeeping

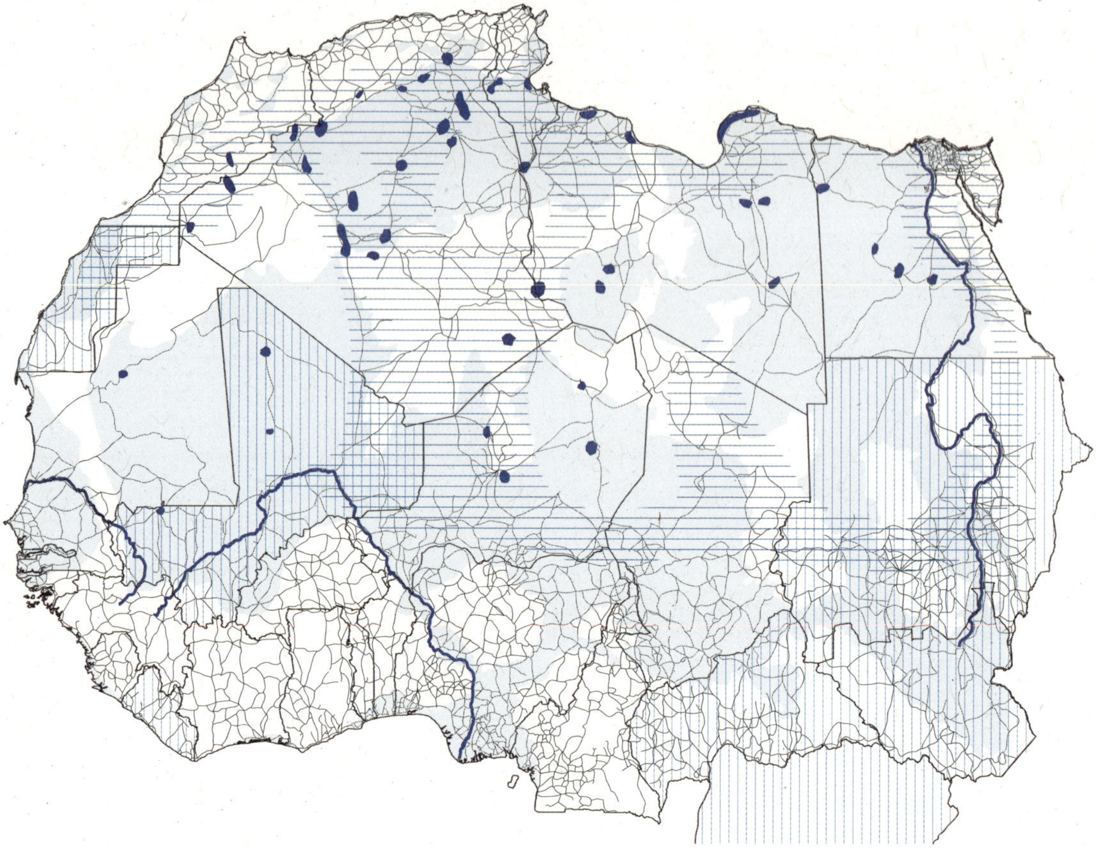

Irrigated valley

Principal oasis

Large Saharan sedimentary aquifers and their extension

Saharan and Sahelian circulation paths

Pastoral and bedouin herding

UN peacekeeping missions

Population distribution, armed conflicts, and peacekeeping

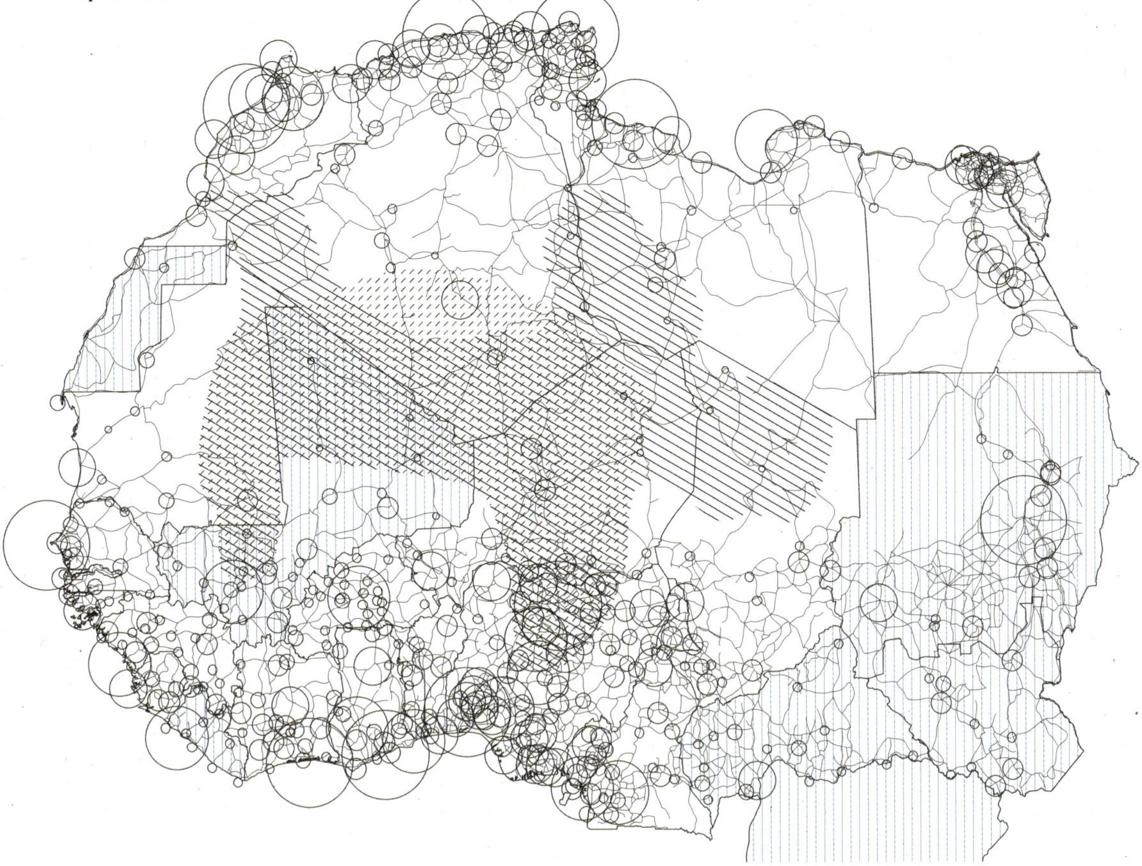

10,000–50,000

50,000–100,000

100,000–350,000

350,000–1 million

1–2 million

2–4 million

more than 4 million

Other city

"Enlarged terrorist area" according to the Trans-Saharan Counter Terrorism Initiative (TSCTI)

"Terrorist corridor" according to the Pan Sahel Initiative (PSI)

UN peacekeeping missions

The Beginning of a UN Peacekeeping Mission: MINUSMA

The peacekeeping mission in Mali was authorized in April 2013 with a mandate to support a peace agreement between the Malian government and the Tuareg.[17] The mission was asked to support Mali's interim authorities in the stabilization of the country and the implementation of the transitional roadmap. Their duties included backing the redeployment of the reformed Malian Defense and Security Forces, protecting civilians, and countering asymmetric attacks in defense of their mandate. By unanimously adopting Resolution 2164 of June 25, 2014, the Security Council further decided that the mission should focus on tasks such as stabilization and safeguarding civilians; supporting national political dialogue and reconciliation; and assisting in the reestablishment of state authority, the rebuilding of the security sector, and the promotion and protection of human rights in that country.[18]

The MINUSMA resolution indicated that the mission would comprise up to 11,200 military personnel, including reserve battalions capable of deploying rapidly within the country when required and 1,440 police personnel (comprising formed police units and individual police officers). The majority of the military, police, and civilian substantive and support components were expected to operate primarily in the north, with a possible logistics base in Gao or Sevare. A light presence, including civilians, military, and police elements would be based in Bamako. Currently, 15,209 uniformed personnel are deployed to support MINUSMA.[19] Since 2013, the UN has built dozens of compounds and super camps in 14 cities across Mali.[20] Two large UN bases are located in Gao with troops from eight different countries: Germany, the Netherlands, Cambodia, Bangladesh, China, Senegal, Egypt, and Burkina Faso. There are an estimated 4,000 UN peacekeepers in Gao.

Spatial Footprint

Since its inception in 2013, MINUSMA's troop-contributing countries (TCC), UN agencies, and their subcontractors have designed and built dozens of camps, super camps, headquarters, logistics hubs, and airfields inside and adjacent to 14 cities across Mali in support of the mission.[21] Although these spaces are mostly located within existing inhabited areas, as stipulated by the host government, the mission has rarely taken into account its multidimensional impacts on the local population and the environment when it comes to planning, procurement, construction, and deployment processes. The following description and analysis of MINUSMA corresponds to the beginning phase of the mission, from 2013 to 2018. It was based on workshops, field observations, and conversations with the local population, policymakers, diplomats, military engineers, activists, human rights lawyers, designers, anthropologists, and others. The study focuses on cases from the Malian capital of Bamako and the city of Gao in the northern part of the country.[22]

The field research in Mali took place during the early phases of the mission construction, revealing the spatial processes and various stages of a UN base's construction, the engineering logics, and in-situ implementation. The field study was conducted in March 2016 in Bamako and Gao and was hosted by the Dutch ministries of Foreign Affairs and Defense. The observations from the field study contributed to a series of events at the UN, reports, policy papers, and follow-up research.

Border fluctuations around Mali and peacekeeping

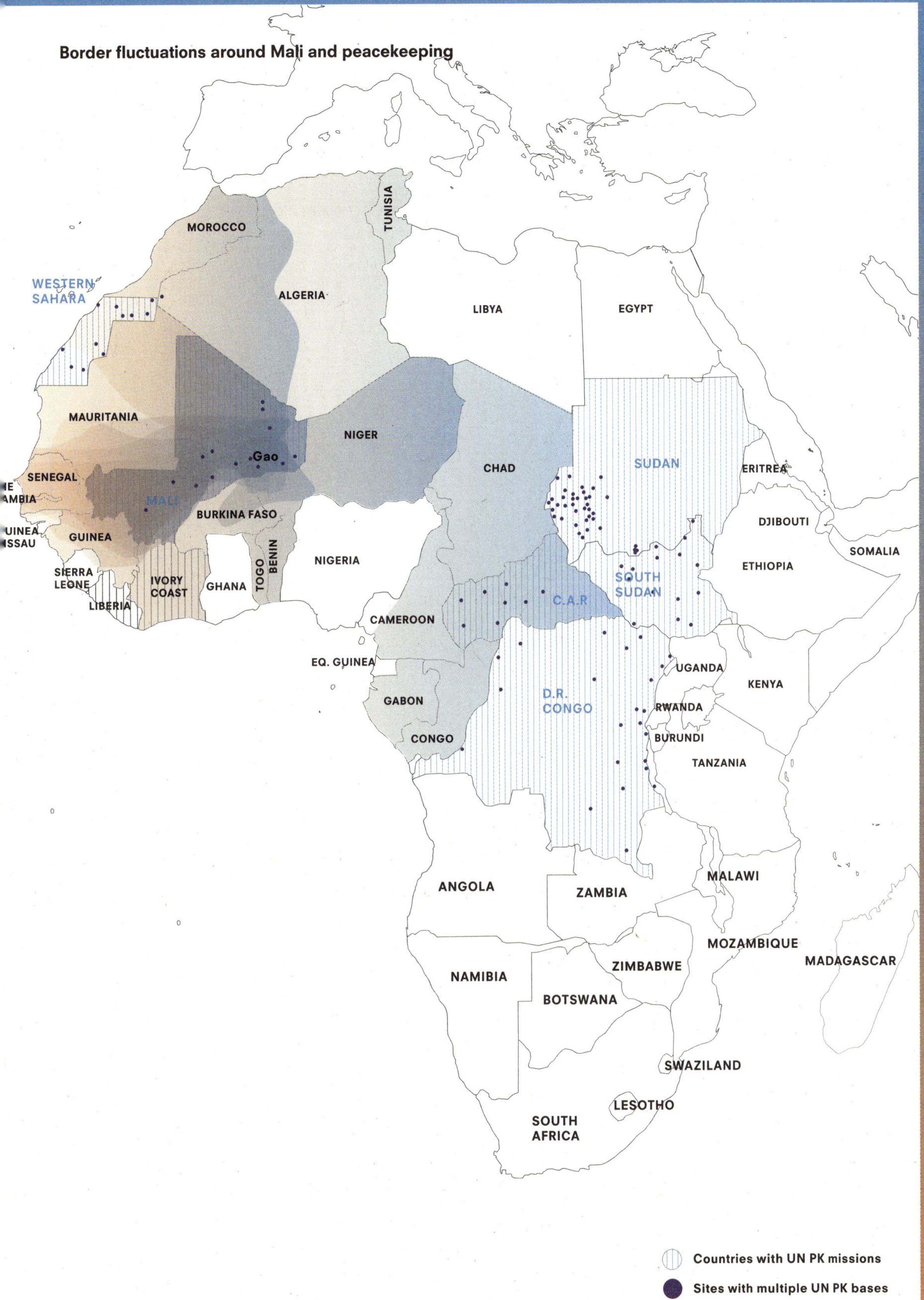

The Construction of a UN Peacekeeping Base

The UN base is the most emblematic spatial output of a peacekeeping mission. It is the site where all the UN protocols, guidelines, and bureaucracy—mitigated by financial, technological, environmental, and political factors—are distilled into material form. Its spatial production is complex; it follows strict guidelines, protocols, and a hierarchical command chain. *The United Nations Peacekeeping Missions Military Engineer Unit Manual* describes the base, in technical terms, as a site that provides the peacekeepers with basic human needs in a secure and safe environment. The bases are designed to operate as self-sustained islands: "when the UN Military Engineer Unit arrives in the Mission area, it is responsible for meeting all its own needs for rations, water, petrol, oil, etc. for up to 90 days."[23]

UN construction engineering is grouped into vertical and horizontal elements. Vertical construction capabilities include building rigid/semi-rigid and prefabricated structures, rehabilitating and repairing existing structures, well drilling, and surveying; horizontal construction encompasses the construction and maintenance of roads and bridges, airfields, and helipads. Rigid/semi-rigid or prefabricated structures (such as purpose-built container-type modular units) ensure the mission infrastructure has an adequate shelter for operational, administrative, and accommodation purposes on a continuous and extended basis. The structures must have sufficient strength to protect from local weather conditions. Given the construction's enduring intent, subtasks may include site planning, building foundations, mainframe construction work, internal finishing, and utility work.[24]

These multidimensional tasks result in a rapid spatial production that often has a vaster footprint than the surrounding inhabited areas, as shown in the sequence of aerial images on pages 84–85 and in the analysis on the following pages. Although missions and bases are considered temporary, self-sufficient systems, they have enduring consequences on their surrounding socioeconomic, cultural, and natural ecosystems.

17 "Mali: UN officials welcome accord between Government and Tuareg rebels." UN, June 2013, available at: https://news.un.org/en/story/2013/06/442632).

18 "MINUSMA Fact Sheet," UN Peacekeeping, 2017, available at: https://peacekeeping.un.org/en/mission/minusma.

19 "MINUSMA Background – United Nations Multidimensional Integrated Stabilization Mission in Mali," 2017, available at: www.un.org/en/peacekeeping/missions/minusma/background.

20 United Nations Department of Field Support, Cartographic Section and online data.

21 UN Geospatial Information Section website, available at: www.un.org/Depts/Cartographic/english/htmain.htm.

22 United Nations Peacekeeping Missions Military Engineer Unit Manual, September 2015, pp. 14–21.

23 Ibid.

24 Ibid.

MINUSMA budget, personnel, and Mali's GDP 2013–2020

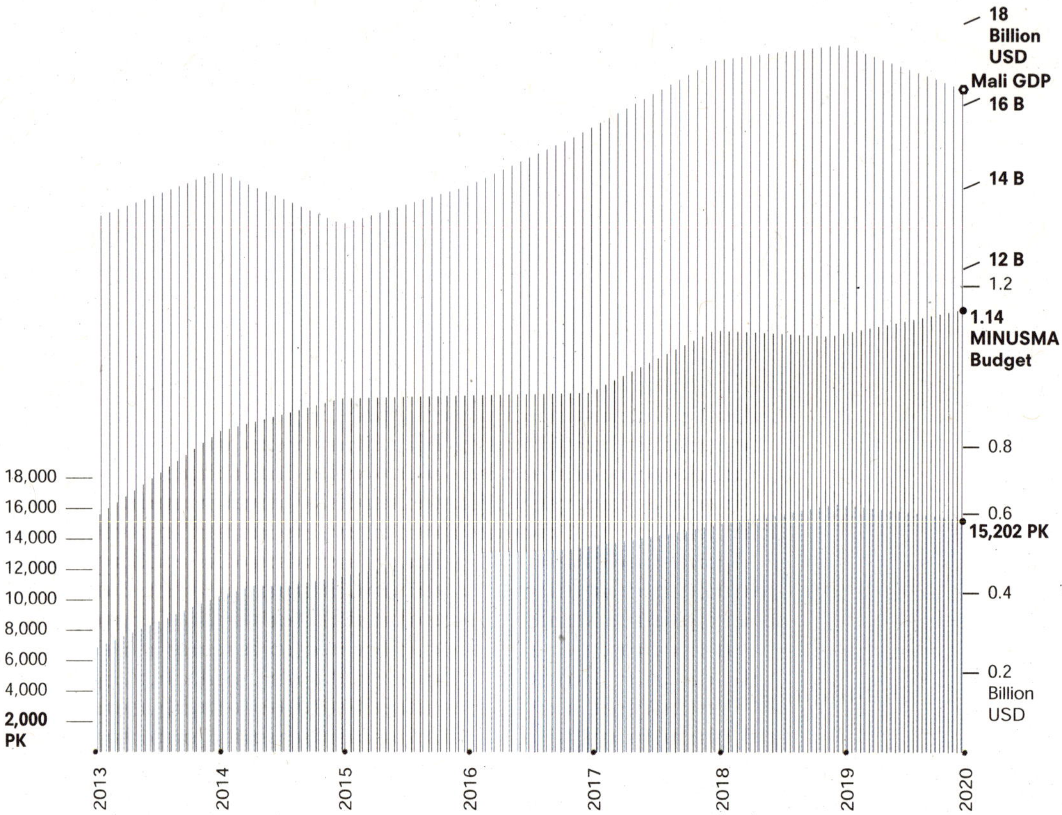

Mali's GDP
Mission's expenditure
Personnel

Peacekeeping budget 2019–2020

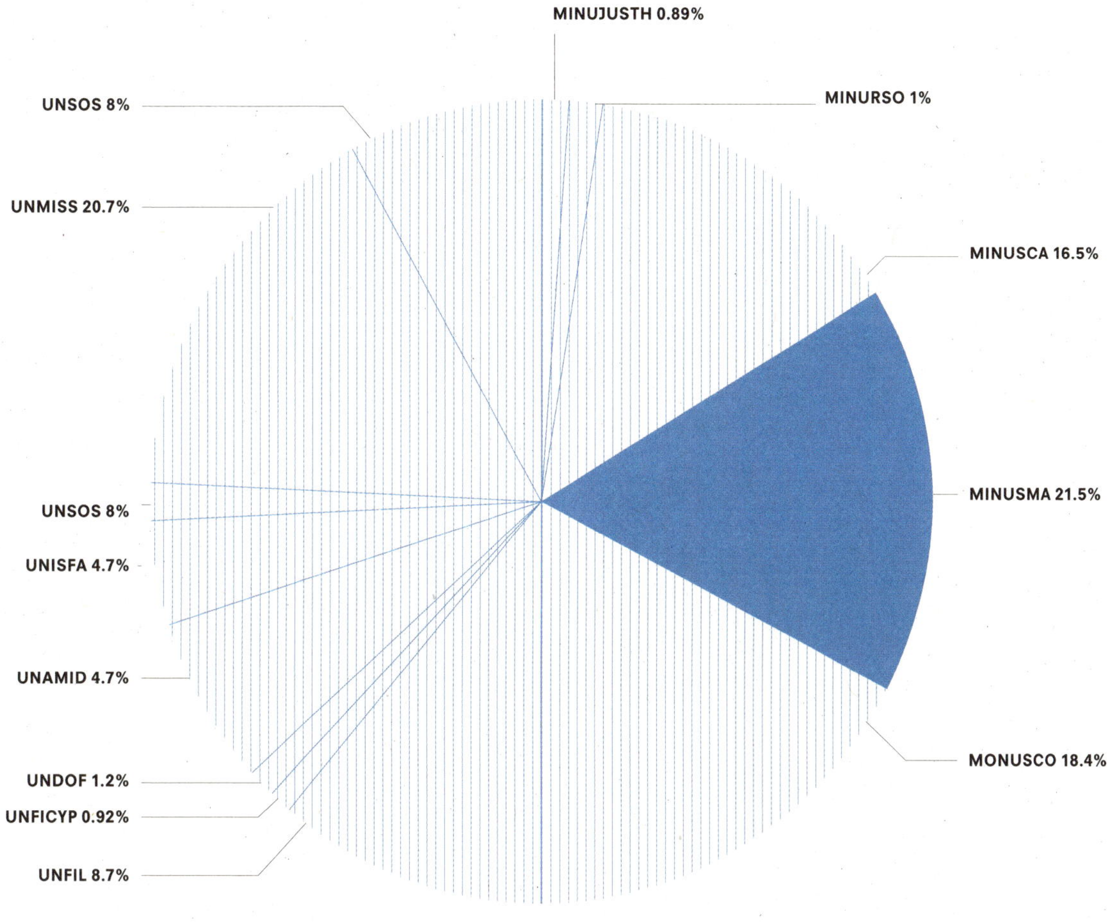

Total UN budget: 6.5 Billion USD
MINUSMA budget: 1,138,515,908 USD

Inhabited areas with MINUSMA bases

BAMAKO, 2013. 1/2 — 1000 f 250 m

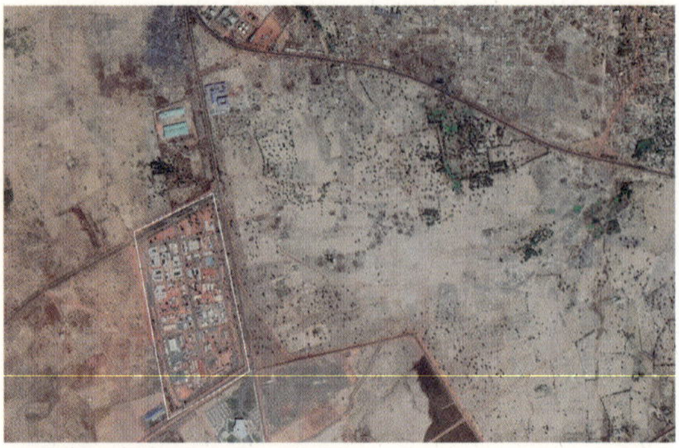

BAMAKO, 2018. Base area: 36 ha
City population: 1.809 million — 1000 f 250 m

Gao, 2011. 1/2 — 1000 f 250 m

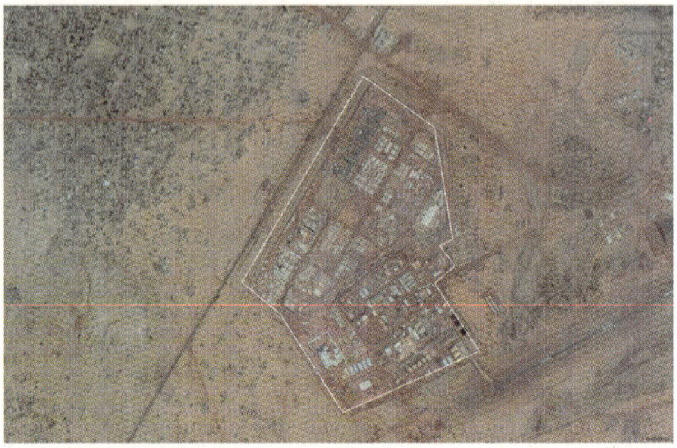

Gao, 2018. 2/2. Base area: 126 ha
City population: 86,000 — 1000 f 250 m

Kidal, 2009. 1/2 — 1000 f 250 m

Kidal, 2014. 2/2. Base area: 70 ha
City population: 25,600 — 1000 f 250 m

Timbuktu, 2013. 1/2 — 4000 f 1000m

Timbuktu, 2018. 2/2/ Base area: 60 ha
City population: 54,400 — 4000 f 1000m

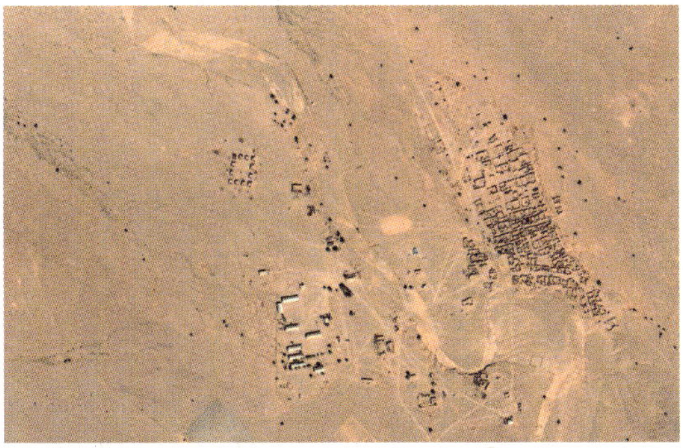

Tessalit, 2003. 1/2 — 700 f 200 m

Tessalit, 2018. 2/2. Base area: 68 ha
City population: 5,700 — 700 f 200 m

Diabaly, 2008. 1/2 — 700 f 200 m

Diabaly, 2018. 2/2. Base area: 27 ha
City population: 35,266 — 700 f 200 m

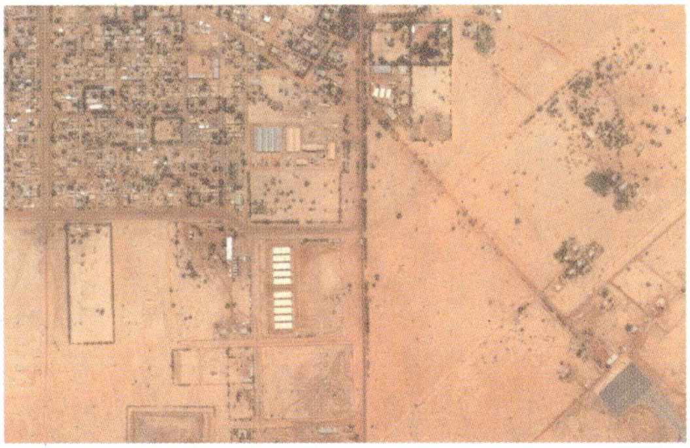

Sévaré, 2004. 1/2 — 500 f 125 m

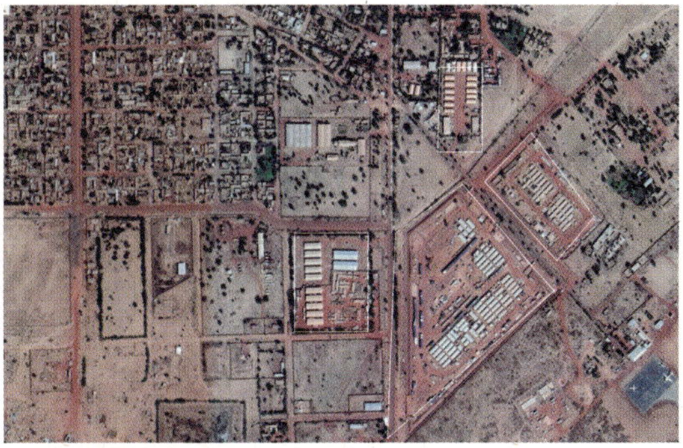

Sévaré, 2014. 2/2. Base area: 27 ha
City population: 40,000 — 500 f 125 m

Ménaka, 2009. 1/2 — 500 f 125 m

Ménaka, 2009. 2/2. Base area: 115 ha
City population: 20,000 — 1000 f 250 m

Bamako

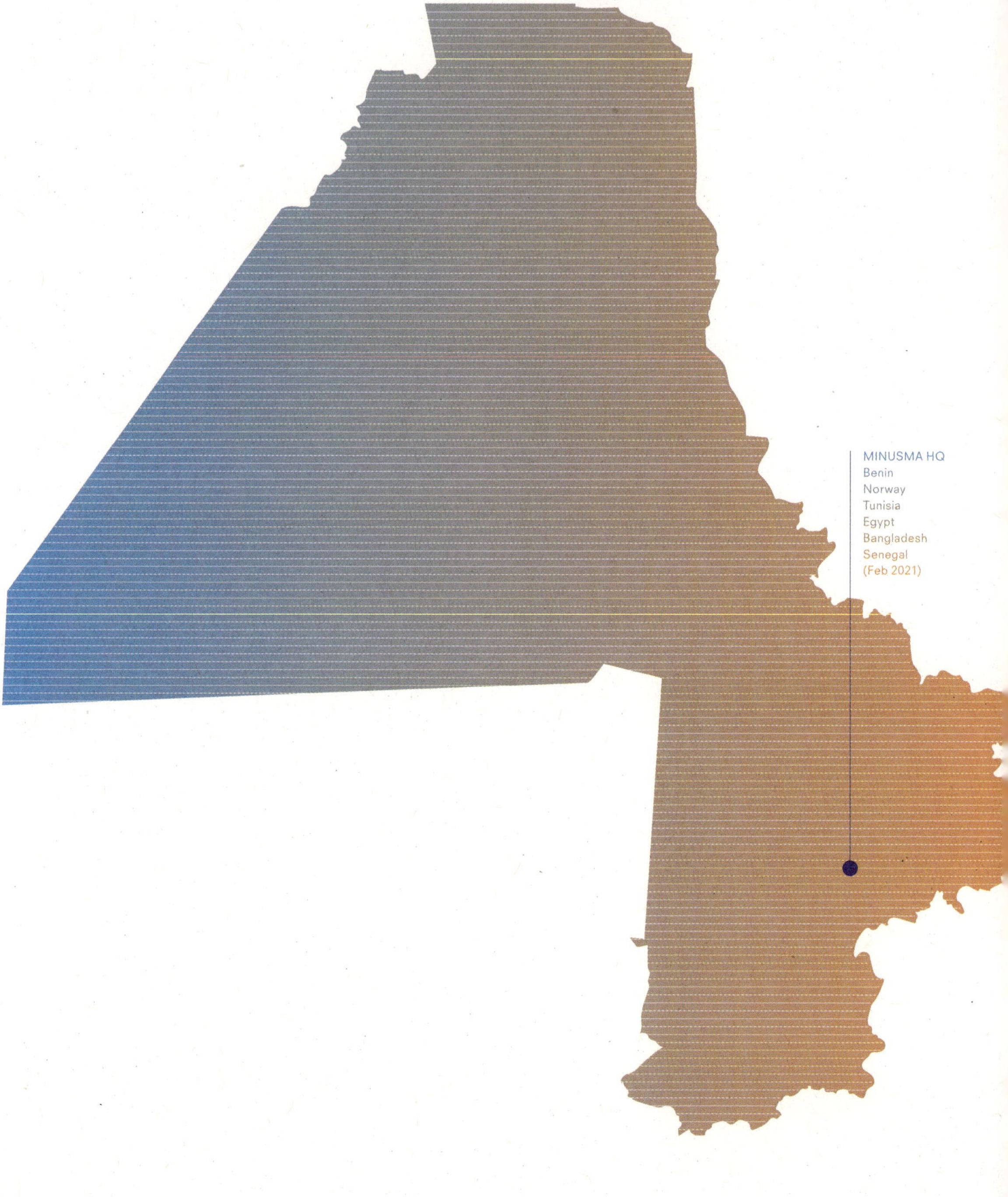
MINUSMA HQ
Benin
Norway
Tunisia
Egypt
Bangladesh
Senegal
(Feb 2021)

Bamako

Bamako is Mali's capital and its largest city, with one of the highest demographic growth rates in Africa. With almost 2 million inhabitants, it stretches over 245 square kilometers (94.6 sq mi) along the fertile Niger River Valley, which has provided its population historically with access to an ample food supply. The city has a rich history of trade, and its former inhabitants founded routes across West Africa, the Sahara, North Africa, and Europe. They traded gold, ivory, kola nuts, and salt. The expansion of European explorations and missions to Africa in the Age of Discovery led to expanding European powers and their involvement in the region through colonization, exploitation, and extraction. In the 19th century, Mali, and its capital at Bamako, became part of French Sudan under French colonial rule, which lasted until the 1960s. The city's architecture is eclectically composed of colonial French gardens, boulevards, and buildings, along with native Malian-style structures of sand, terracotta, mud, and clay. The space in between is occupied by a collection of huts, tin shacks, and tents.

25 According to the UN Peacekeeping Military Engineer Unit Manual "tentage must include flooring and the ability to heat and cool as appropriate; and netting at doors, windows and the inner/outer fly of tents. Double-layered tents with metal pipe frames are recommended due to conditions in the field. It is also recommended to mount the tents on cement or wooden foundations to ensure their stability. Deployable accommodations noted in the paragraph above are excluded from this requirement".

Arriving in Bamako

On the night of March 13, 2016, accompanied by a leading military engineer from the Netherlands, Erwin Marx, and the director of Het Nieuwe Instituut, Guus Beumer, we landed at Modibo Keita International Airport in Bamako, Mali's capital city. Although Bamako is home to 2.5 million inhabitants and has a population growth rate of 3.5%, at night, the city is surprisingly dark; it was almost invisible at the time of our arrival. We stepped out of the Air France plane into the fierce African heat. As we walked down the airstair, a group of officers from the UN mission's Movement Control Unit (MOVOCON) approached us and escorted us swiftly through the packed airport, assuring us a smooth and expedited path through immigration. They wore Dutch military uniforms with a desert camouflage pattern and a bright-yellow vests bearing the letters MOVCON. We were under their supervision from the moment we got off the plane until we left the country. They quickly grabbed our luggage and walked us to a white UN van that was waiting for us in the airport parking lot. The local driver greeted us in French, carefully stacked our bags in the back of the car, and drove us away. It was hard to see anything beyond the beaming front lights of the vehicle. The local scenery was hidden in the darkness of night.

Midgard Transit Camp, Tents, Containers, and Holes in the Ground

We headed toward Midgard, a small transit camp operated by the Dutch and Swedish peacekeepers. Although it was located just to the other side of the airport runway, the car ride took us about half an hour because the road was secured and surveilled by the Malian army. The car zigzagged its way through checkpoints and physical roadblocks; our MOVOCON guides explained away each obstacle as a necessary security measure connected to past incidents. As we drove down the pitch-dark road, our escorts pointed out their landmarks: the UN super camp, the Malian base, the Bangladeshi base, a police station. By the time we left Mali, we had become very familiar with this foreign landscape and the newly installed security infrastructure. Each of the bases was enclosed with barbed wire; they appeared, one bubble after another, all together forming secure corridors for international movement. Checkpoints, camps, guard posts, and fences were all constructed in the past two years.

When we arrived at the transit camp, Camp Midgard, the vehicle stopped, greeted the patrol unit and guards, and then passed through the gate. The head of the camp arrived to welcome us, briefly pointed out our tents, and showed us the location of showers and lavatories. We received a security briefing, our schedule for the next morning, and were then accompanied to our tents. The tents sat on a hard concrete platform. They had electricity, light, and an air conditioning unit attached high up on the tent fabric as if it were a wall. Six beds were ordered in two rows, ready for people in transit. Each metal-frame bed had a clean mattress and a mosquito-net around it shaped like a mini tent. Next to the bed, there was a small locker with sealed plastic water bottles. The tent felt solid,[25] like a concrete room. I shared it with a Dutch military doctor who was heading to Gao from the Netherlands and was expected to take the flight to Gao with us in a few days.

TCC's bases surrounding Camp Midgard. MINUSMA. Bamako, 2016.

Watching "The Enemy of the State" on Veronica, a commercial Dutch TV channel. Camp Midgard. Bamako, 2016.

Tents

Tentage must include flooring and the ability to heat and cool as appropriate; and netting at doors, windows, and the inner/outer fly of tents. Double-layered tents with metal pipe frames are recommended due to conditions in the field. It is also recommended to mount the tents on cement or wooden foundations to ensure their stability. Deployable accommodations noted in the paragraph above are excluded from this requirement.[26]

In the book *African Nomadic Architecture, Space, Place and Gender*, Labelle Prussin refers to the tent as architecture, despite its temporary nature. According to her, in order to understand the architecture of the tent, we must examine the correlation between the nature of desert life and the technology of transportation. The shape, size, and construction method of a tent are contingent on means of mobility.

She distinguishes the indigenous African tent from the missionary tent; while the first is considered home and a complex space of social reproduction and family life, the second, in her view, can be referenced as a political or religious institutional symbol that can be traced back to the Roman military, the Crusaders, the explorers of the Age of Reason, and the missionaries of modernity. Following Prussin, the typology of the Midgard tents is, too, a political and institutional symbol.

Prussin's research is situated at the intersection of history, ethnography, and gender studies. She offers another differentiation between indigenous and institutional tents: the former are designed and built by women; the latter by men. Whereas women were the architects of the nomadic built environment, men were the designers of military bases. These discrepancies can be read in the form, tactility, and production processes of each.

Prussin draws another connection between modernist architecture and the institutional tent in an allusion to "a primitive temple" referenced by Le Corbusier. His book *Towards a New Architecture* celebrates the achievement of the engineer: "The Engineer's Aesthetic and Architecture—two things that march together and follow one from the other—the one at its full height, the other in an unhappy state of retrogression"[27] As he continues to develop the logic of measures, he dedicates a section to regulating lines as an invisible architectural element. The tent is used in his narrative as an object that connects the past and the future of architecture as an engineering project. In his theories of measure and modular design, the primitive temple—created by "he who builds a shelter for his god" – constitutes the model of perfect proportions.

In Bamako, the military engineers attributed the name of their base to divine spirits too. In Norse mythology, Midgard—also called Manna-Heim ("Home of Man")—is Middle Earth, the abode of humankind, made from the body of the first being, the giant Aurgelmir (Ymir). According to legend, the gods killed Aurgelmir, rolled his body into the central void of the universe, and began fashioning the Midgard. Aurgelmir's flesh became the land, his blood the oceans, his bones the mountains, his teeth the cliffs, his hair the trees, and his brains (blown over the earth) became the clouds. Aurgelmir's skull was held up by four dwarfs: Nordri, Sudri, Austri, and Vestri (the four points of the compass) and became the dome of the heavens. The sun, moon, and stars were made of scattered sparks that were caught in the skull. Midgard is situated halfway between Niflheim on the north, the land of ice, and Muspelheim to the south, the region of fire. Midgard is joined with Asgard, the abode of the deities, by Bifrost, the rainbow bridge.[28]

26 The UN Peacekeeping Military Engineer Unit Manual, September 2015, pp 32–33.
27 Le, Corbusier, and Frederick Etchells. Towards a New Architecture. New York: Dover Publications, 1986. Print. p11.
28 Muspelheim, Norse mythology, Encyclopedia Britannica, available at: www.britannica.com/topic/Muspelheim.

It was interesting to realize how mythology offered an escape from the material world and a spirit for this carefully engineered space. Across the base, various symbolic ornaments were placed to celebrate the Swedish gods; perhaps like in Le Corbusier's tale, two stories became one, both a product of the imagination. The first was the temple, a shelter that man designed for his god; the second was the narrative of the ancient tent, attributed, too, to the skills of men. In contrast, Prussin's careful research associated the design of the nomadic tent and camp (which inspired the Roman soldiers in antiquity) with women. Women were the sole architects of the nomadic built environment; they chose the site, designed the camp, and constructed and decorated its tents.

A local Malian woman was hired as a subcontractor to manage the construction of a pergola outside the dining hall of the UN super camp in Bamako. She introduced local materials and building techniques of woven straw roofs. Bamako, 2016.

A typical tent for people in transit. Camp Midgard. Bamako, 2016.

A variety of tents. Camp Midgard. Bamako, 2016.

"Tentage must include flooring and the ability to heat and cool as appropriate; and netting at doors, windows and the inner/outer fly of tents. Double-layered tents with metal pipe frames are recommended due to conditions in the field. It is also recommended to mount the tents on cement or wooden foundations to ensure their stability. Deployable accommodations noted in the paragraph above are excluded from this requirement."

The UN Peacekeeping Military Engineer Unit Manual

"Nomadic cultures are, however, elusive, difficult to document and record. Nation states have always had problems with their nomadic population and have sought to settle them. Nomads do not observe political borders; they do not pay taxes; they are fiercely independent and live outside the cultural pale." L. Prussin

According to Prussin, 19th-century European explorers and missionaries used a military-type tent. As an example, she takes Gulliain's exploration of East Africa. He drew an illustration of his own tent next to a Somali mat and straw-covered armature.

Models of tents, designed after L. Prussin's sketches and depictions. Venice Architecture Biennale, 2016.

Among all the Tuareg, northern and southern, the tent comes into being with the marriage ceremony. Despite both ceremonial and architectural distinctions, the term for marriage (eduben or ehen) is synonymous with the term tent (ehen). The term is associated with numerous expressions related to marriage: "to set up a tent" or "to fabricate or make a tent" means to get married. To ask a woman if she is married, one asks "Have you made a tent?" To marry, for a man, is "to enter a women's tent." The womb is also called a tent, and women can collectively be referred to as "those-of-the-tents."
L. Prussin

Prussin redrew maps showing tent types in relation to ethnic origins and geographic flows; she detailed the configuration of the tents along the lines of Western disciplinary canons. She connected the tents with nomadic routes, camp layouts, their construction processes, their interiors, and their social and political role in the African nomadic cultures.

The circular shape of the tent and the round form of its roof refer to the vault of heaven. The tent is made of mats attached by cords to a heavy wooden armature; the mats are made of the leaves of young dum palm trees, cloth, or vellum. Their length, shape, and texture can indicate wealth and social status. The tent is constructed and designed by women, who are the sole architects and owners of the tents.

A typical interior of a Tuareg tent. L. Prussin.

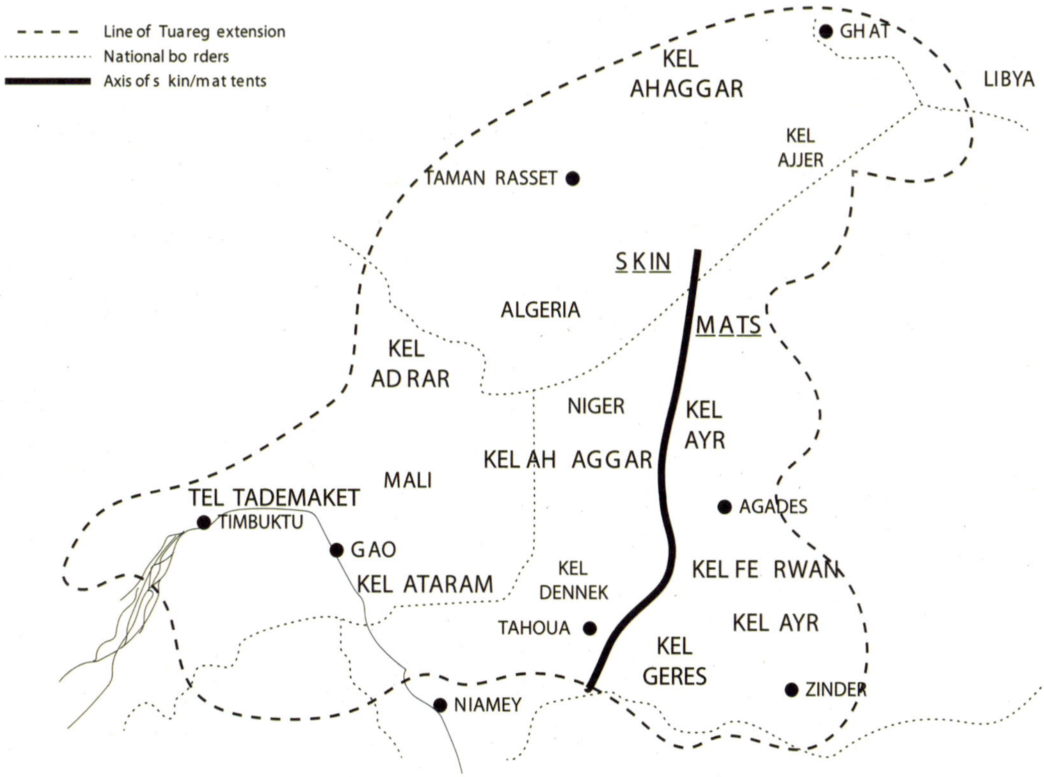

Holes in the Ground

Earthworks and site preparation are the reshaping of land by cutting, levelling, filling, and compacting earth to the desired shape using earth moving equipment. Earthworks and site preparation are fundamental to other engineer projects as they provide the basis upon which roads and bridges are built or upgraded, foundations and drainage are created for new projects, and berms put into place for force protection. [29]

29 The UN Peacekeeping Military Engineer Unit Manual. Sep 2015, available at: http://3.230.11.73/wp-content/uploads/2020/07/UN-PK-Military-Engineers-Manual.pdf.

The ground in Midgard was covered with a thick layer of gravel. The tiny gray stones separated the base from the local soil. At the time of our visit, parts of the camp were still under construction. Holes in the ground revealed the striking red color of the local soil as well as depth of the base's infrastructure, including water tubes, electricity wires, sewage, and telecommunication cables. However, on top of the gravel, a setup of containers and tents made the UN base appear foreign and ephemeral.

Containers and holes in the ground. Model. Venice Architecture Biennale, 2016.

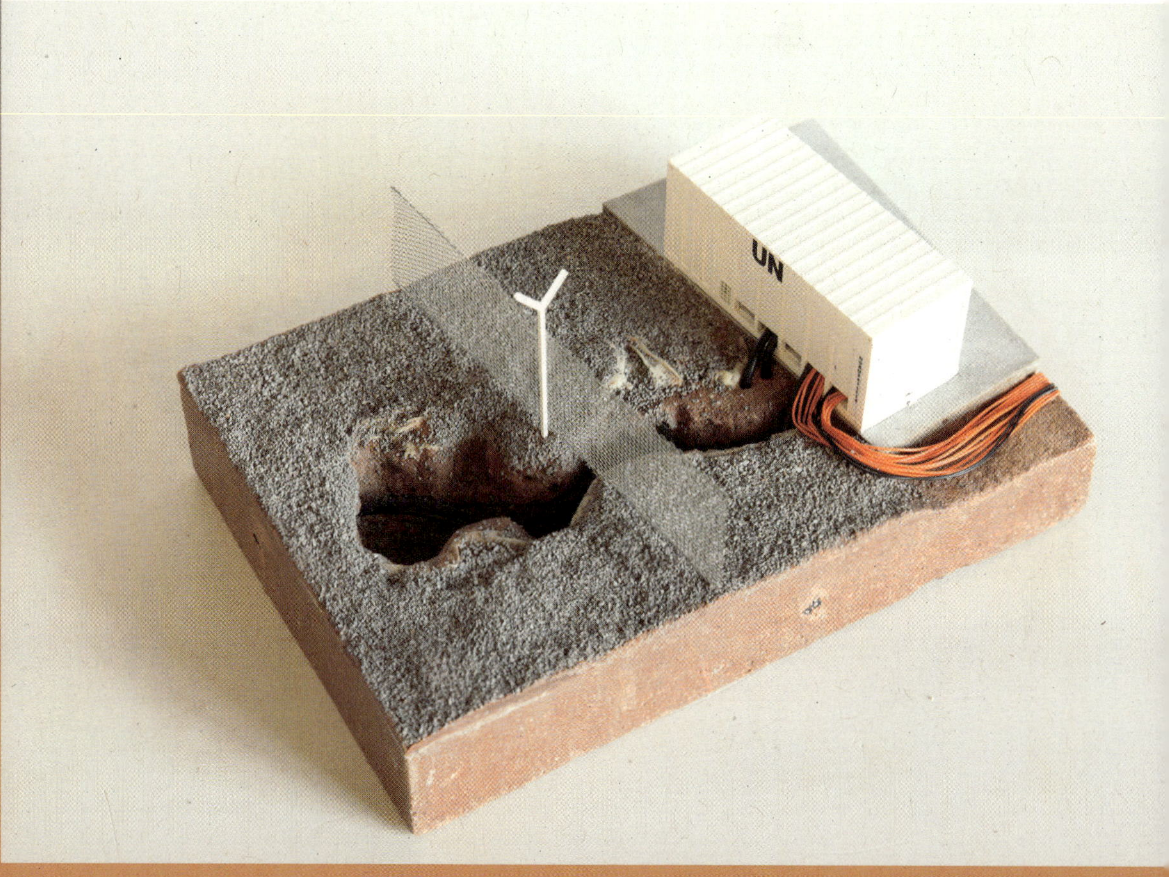

Containers

Containers are mobile shelters used for a specific purpose or service. There are three basic types of containers: truck-mounted, trailer-mounted, and sea containers. Truck-mounted containers can be dismounted and operated separately from the vehicle. Trailer-mounted containers need not be dismounted but are not reimbursed as trailers in the vehicle category. Sea containers must be maintained to international standards (i.e., certified for shipping) in order to be eligible for reimbursement.[30]

One of the most indicative objects of a UN mission is the container. Ashley Carse wrote famously about the container that "[n]o object distills an era, but it would be hard to beat the intermodal shipping container to make sense of the past half-century of economic globalization. By linking shipping, rail, and trucking networks, the container has been central to developments in logistics that have dramatically reduced the cost of moving goods over great distances. There is, to date, no environmental history of the so-called container revolution, but one might reasonably extend the well-known story summarized above to argue that this humble connective technology lubricated the operation and expansion of the vast sociotechnical infrastructure that formatted the Anthropocene—well before we knew it as such. Indeed, it is difficult to imagine a post-1950 Great Acceleration marked by rapid population growth, expanding consumption, and urbanization apart from the economic geographies of the container."[31]

UN agencies and mission-contributing forces from around the world are heavily dependent on the connective technology of the container. Each UN mission site reserves a large area for gathering shipping containers; as the mission ages, the accumulated number of containers increases exponentially, and they pile up into an odd and sad-looking landscape of material decay.

Containers are central to the logistic planning and deployment of missions; they are brought into newly occupied UN areas from around the world. At the beginning of each mission, containers are packed with construction machinery such as bulldozers, forklifts, trenchers and excavators, loaders and telescopic handlers, and all sorts of cranes. Others are filled with modular construction elements to be assembled on site, such as dry and wet walls, windows, various roofing systems, kitchens, showers, latrines, sinks, toilets, solar panels, air conditioners, and pipes. There are container units that assemble medical facilities: from operating rooms to dental clinics, pharmacies, and labs. UN bases are designed in advance by UN engineers, mostly in Europe-based logistic hubs situated in Brindisi, Italy and Valencia, Spain. These two centers incorporate the training and logistics nucleus of the UN missions' apparatus. During training sessions, engineers use abstract computerized simulators—a sort of UN SimCity of plug-and-play components obtained from a database administered by the logistics and financial team. The bases are shaped remotely on a variety of scales. Whether in response to sustainability factors, climate variation, or any number of risk factors. New and old indicators are spatialized, designed, and tested on a UN simulator in Europe and then applied physically in the actual context.

At the end of a mission, the UN base is deconstructed and sorted into small pieces. All the elements that have been shipped to sustain the mission and its forces are collected into a liquidation and disposal site. Mountains of latrines, sinks, screws, water coolers, desks, office chairs, toilets, toilet seats, computers, printers, pipes, and so on are crushed into tiny pieces. Some are stuffed back into the old containers or simply vanish. The base elements are carried away from the mission area and the critical eye of potential environmental activists or UNEP agents. My first visit to such a liquidation site was in Liberia (see page 270), although, in Mali, large piles of waste had already accumulated at the edge of UN bases in the mission's early construction phase.

30 "Manual on Policies and Procedures concerning the Reimbursement and Control of Contingent-Owned Equipment of Troop/Police Contributors Participating in Peacekeeping Missions." A/72/288. August 2017.

31 Carse, Ashley. "Dredge." Anthropocene Unseen: A Lexicon, edited by Cymene Howe and Anand Pandian, Punctum Books, 2020, pp. 121–125.

In Gao, plastic, wood, and steel crates that had efficiently stored machines, furniture, and ammunition in shipping containers had been set aside, gathered densely into vertical structures that formed a skyline of empty boxes. Next to the empty packaging material, an otherworldly landscape of detritus included a tired line-up of vehicles of all sizes that had rapidly deteriorated due to overuse or because they had been rendered inoperable by the desert wind, blowing thick dust and sand into their engines.

Containers are at the heart of the sociotechnical administration of missions. They enable their accelerating large scale and are the foundation of the rapidly spreading new typology: the super camps.

The introduction to the book *Arts of Living on a Damaged Planet* by Anna Tsing describes the tangled relationship between the past, present, and future of our planet and human actions: "Every landscape is haunted by past ways of life. We see this clearly in the presence of plants whose animal seed-dispersers are no longer with us. Some plants have seeds so big that only big animals can carry them to new places to germinate. When these animals became extinct, their plants could continue without them, but they have been unable to disperse their seeds very well. Their distribution is curtailed; their population dwindles. This is an example of what we are calling haunting."[32]

Whether they are containers or UN bases, human-designed systems and materials contribute to the emergence of new lives, ecologies, and futures. The consequences of our past decisions and actions remain with us indefinitely. Even after a liquidation, a mission exacerbates pollution, which persists in the landscapes we inhabit and occupy.

Containers—perhaps like the big animals—transport and scatter not only a material footprint; they carry ideas and values that remain in spaces and places long after missions have gone. In host communities, the containers themselves can be found at distances foreign to them, dispersed along the narrow streets of desert cities like Gao. In a human habitat cultivated organically over millennia from sand, clay, fabric, and leather, a container might appear obsolete, an alien intervention, poor and dilapidated, modern and merciless.

32 Tsing, Anna, et al., editors. Arts of Living on a Damaged Planet: Ghosts and Monsters of the Anthropocene. University of Minnesota Press, 2017, p. 2.

Indication of inground infrastructure. Camp Castor. Gao, 2016.

Inground greywater filters at the edge of Camp Castor. Gao, 2016.

Holes in the ground. Camp Midgard. Bamako, 2016.

Containers and other modular structures. UN super camp (MOB). Bamako, 2016.

Containers with generators, workshops and toilets. MINUSMA, 2016.

M G W
TARE
NET
CU.CAP

Containers with ammunition, medical equipment and solar panels. Camp Castor. Gao, 2016.

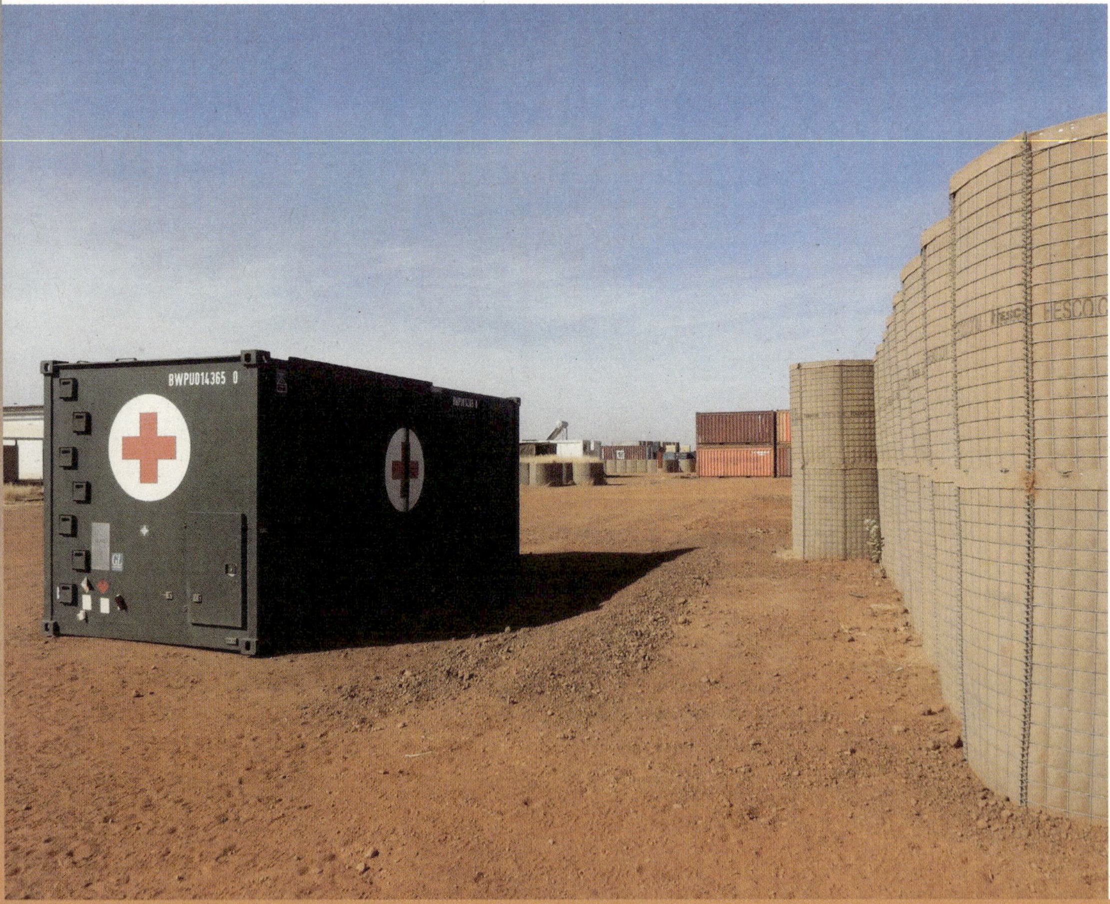

A waste site. Camp Castor. Gao, 2016.

Construction equipment and UN vehicles. Camp Castor. Gao, 2016.

UN
UN

Containers spread across Gao. Mali, 2016.

A local nomadic tent at the UN super camp. Gao, 2016.

Meetings in the City

One morning, we drove to Bamako. There, we met Mani el Ansary and Master Soumy. Mani is a Tuareg and one of the organizers of the Desert Festival in Timbuktu. He told us he had been forced into exile after the jihadists captured his city. Master Soumy is a young rapper whose lyrics describe the conflict and the situation in Mali, criticizing the corrupt Malian government. "Colonization never ended here," he said. "Decisions about our country's future and, consequently, our lives are still made in Paris. The youth that I am speaking to are a generation caught between an older fraudulent generation on the one hand and religious radicals on the other. We have no freedom to lead our lives, and hope is rapidly diminishing." The government has a monopoly on media in the country. It controls the national radio and TV stations; his music is censored on both platforms. When I asked both Mani and Master Soumy how they perceived the new UN mission that is unfolding in Mali, they were skeptical. They were suspicious of the international community's long-term intentions in remaining in the country. They saw it as yet another form of colonization, set up by the French government.

Later on, we met with a group of local architects. They had studied architecture in Tunis, Algeria, and Strasbourg. I asked them what it meant to practice architecture in a time of war and under the auspices of a UN mission. I asked if they had been approached by the UN or if they had engaged in any way with the massive construction work held by UN agencies across their city and country. Their answer was no. They had no knowledge of how the processes are managed, how the decisions are made, how the spaces are erected and designed by whom and for whom. For them, too, it was a form of colonization, a parallel world, a reality imposed on them. Their practice focused on small-scale local housing projects. They are not consulted or involved with the construction of UN sites.

Although they were pragmatic and hoped to see positive developments that would improve people's livelihoods, they felt something similar to what Mani and Master Soumy described: the UN mission disregards the locals, and their presence feels like another form of Western occupation. At the end of the meeting, we traveled to our next appointments at the UN headquarters, housed inside a former five-star hotel.

Bamako, 2016.

Bamako, 2016.

Bamako, 2016.

فندق ليبيا
SOFITEL ACCOR HOTELS & RESORTS
LIBYA HOTEL DE L'AMITIE

Techno-Political Egyptian Modernism in Mali: the Amitié Hotel Repurposed

Omar Ramzy was a prominent modernist architect who worked with Gamal Abdel Nasser to modernize and revolutionize Egyptian infrastructure and to distance the country from its colonial past. Like the new regime, his buildings attempted to promote the spirit of emancipation and development across the African continent.

After the Second World War, processes of decolonization unfolded rapidly around the world, particularly in Africa. Nation after nation claimed self-determination and denounced Western occupation and old colonialist powers.

In the first few decades after its founding, the UN recognized the sovereignty of 54 African nations. Egypt was liberated from UK occupation on June 18, 1953. Mali gained independence from French Sudan on September 28, 1960. The UN supported its new member states by offering a roadmap and tools for decolonization[33] and the shift toward self-governance.

The Egyptian revolution[34] of 1952 by the Free Officers Movement promoted a staunchly nationalist and anti-imperialist agenda. As part of the new nation's consolidation, Gamal Abdel Nasser, the post-revolution president, and his administration used techno-political tropes to generate popular support within the country and the region as part of the new regime's anti-colonialist agendas. They devised architecture and large-scale infrastructure projects to glorify their achievements. Sturdy-looking modernist-style structures, large buildings, towers, bridges, and monuments were erected first across the country and then across the continent. Materials such as exposed reinforced concrete and sophisticated engineering work were utilized as emblems of a new era, departing from the rural lifestyle toward a more urban and modernized society. Universities, bridges, dams, highways, and large-scale masterplans were conceived and built in cooperation with Cold War superpowers, the US and the Soviet Union, who offered financial, military, and technological support. They showered revolutionary African leaders with all kinds of resources in their attempt to gain their support and consequently greater control over Africa.

In 2016, I visited the Amitié/Friendship Hotel in Bamako, Mali—one of the projects initiated by Gamal Abdel Nasser and designed by his appointed architect, Omar Ramzy. A loan from the Egyptian government—funneled to Mali through the El Nasr for Import and Export Fund, which had a presence in many African countries—financed the construction of the five-star hotel in Bamako.

The materials for the construction of the Amitié/Friendship Hotel were transported from Egypt alongside a team of Egyptian engineers and contractors, who also designed and paved dozens of kilometers of road infrastructure to move the materials across the country. It has been said that Nasser used architecture as a foreign policy apparatus. Among other things, it was his counter-response to the growing involvement of Israel in the region, which had provided professional expertise to build new towns, housing, universities, and hospitals—sharing its experience in rapid nation building through large-scale spatial production.

The Amitié/Friendship Hotel, a modernist structure[35] made of reinforced exposed concrete, is the second-tallest tower in Bamako. Its lobby includes dining halls, shopping areas, and the largest cinema complex in Mali. The hotel grounds are decorated with gardens, a grand entrance, a large parking area, and a luxurious pool surrounded by a manicured garden of palm trees and grass. The hotel tower is situated just across from the Malian parliament and the government quarter of Bamako. The upper floors offer a panoramic view of the entire city.

The hotel was offered to the UN by the Malian government for use as their headquarters. The proximity to the parliament seemed valuable at that time, as

33 When the United Nations was founded in 1945, some 750 million people, nearly one-third of the world's population, lived in territories that were dependent on colonial powers. Today, fewer than 2 million people live under colonial rule in the 17 remaining non-self-governing territories. The wave of decolonization, which changed the face of the planet, was born with the UN and represents the world body's first great success.
As a result of decolonization, many countries became independent and joined the UN.
The international trusteeship system was established by the UN Charter. Affirming the principle of self-determination, the Charter describes the responsibility of States for territories under their administration as "a sacred trust" in which the interests of their inhabitants are paramount. See: www.un.org/en/sections/issues-depth/decolonization.

34 In "The wretched of the earth" Frantz Fanon argue that decolonization is always a violent phenomenon: "The naked truth of decolonization evokes for us the searing bullets and blood-stained knives which emanate from it." (pp29–30). Fanon saw decolonization as cleansing, the expunging of the colonial experience, itself achieved through violence. The disinherited or wretched in rising against the system, become 'new men', gaining authority and dignity previously denied to them by their colonial overlords. As Fanon insists, there is or will be a complete change in the social order with the earlier oppressed people now becoming free and in control of their own destinies. See: Raymond F. Betts. "Decolonization A brief history of the word" in Beyond Empire and Nation.

35 In these years, notably the 1950s and 1960s, 'modernization' and 'underdevelopment' entered the popular vocabulary. The disparity in wealth and standard of living between the former colonial powers and the colonized areas was highly criticized. After the European flags were taken down and sent home, new forms of exploitation and neocolonization took place through the establishment of economic dependency.
It was the 'worst form of imperialism' as it assumed no responsibility in the new states it was exploiting. (Nkrumah). Source: Raymond F. Betts. "Decolonization A brief history of the word" in Beyond empire and nation.

it strengthened the government's position in the event of an uprising in the north. Mali's entire tourism industry, which was thriving before the conflict, collapsed, leaving sites such as hotels and resorts empty. UN agencies often occupy them as transitional spaces during their missions. At the time of our visit, the hotel was surrounded by barbed wire fences and secured by armed UN peacekeepers. Entrance to the complex required a special permit, and the parking area was populated by white UN SUVs, minivans, and buses that shuttled peacekeepers around. Its large auditorium and theaters hosted UN conferences and various training sessions for newly arriving UN police troops.

The lobby shops and entertainment programs had all been shuttered, except for a small ATM booth, a modest improvised cafe, and a few scattered traders who sold Malian souvenirs, targeting the foreign UN personnel and the diplomats who visited the headquarters.

We arrived at the complex with a diplomat from the Netherlands Ministry of Foreign Affairs who toured the hotel with us and directed us to the 11th floor to meet with the logistics director of MINUSMA. His office was located in an ordinary hotel suite that had been converted into an operations room. The walls were decorated with logistic maps of various sizes and scales showing UN bases: some were under construction, others had yet to be deployed.

The mission's logistics was highly complex, mainly because the country is vast and landlocked and it lacks adequate roads, airports, and railways. Some 15 sites across Mali were slated to be deployed, with personnel and supplies; some were situated in remote locations with very limited accessibility. The roads were in a poor state, and airfields were mostly nonexistent; areas had to be paved to allow planes to land with troops and their equipment. Trucks transported most of the construction material and mission supplies from the port of Dakar in Senegal to northern Mali—a 2,500 km trip. Next to the Logistics Unit chief's head was a large whiteboard showing flow charts, task lists, and his mandate in bullet points, a repetitive recital offered as a response to any questions regarding his mission. His office's mandate and responsibilities had been predefined with strict limitations that could not be questioned or challenged because overstepping, he mentioned, could put the entire operation at risk.

The building was not occupied in full. The rooftop was restricted, but the floor below it was still accessible and empty. Its windows revealed a panoramic view of Bamako—from the center all the way to the periphery of the city.

Ramzy's hotel was unique amid the surrounding landscape, offering a spatial landmark, a connection with an era of great hope. Now, housing the UN mission's headquarters, with a buffer zone of militarized security—barbed wire, checkpoints, and watchtowers surrounding an administrative cluster, piles of paperwork, pamphlets, peacekeepers, and functionaries—the mission has transformed Nasser's grand architectural gesture into a bureaucratic brute.

MINUSMA HQ at the former Amitié Hotel. Bamako, 2016.

Views from the MINUSM HQ at the former Amitié Hotel. Bamako, 2016.

The MINUSMA HQ overlooking Mali's government buildings. Bamako, 2016.

The pool of the former Amitié Hotel now at MINUSM HQ. Bamako, 2016.

The Embbassy of the Netherlands in Mali. Bamako, 2016.

The Knife Cuts Both Ways

A conversation with Rob de Vos

From the MINUSMA HQ at the former Friendship Hotel, we continued to a meeting with the Dutch ambassador to Mali.

Following my field research in Mali, I met with Rob de Vos, a Dutch diplomat stationed in New York City as Consul General. His office was just next to the Dutch permanent mission to the UN, which hosted some of our workshops with UN secretariat agencies. During one of our conversations, he shared his fascination with Mali and his experiences in the country. He was responsible for setting up the first Dutch Embassy there.

MALKIT SHOSHAN (MS) **The Dutch embassy in Bamako, Mali opened relatively late. Why did the embassy open only in the 1990s?**
ROB DE VOS (RDV) The first diplomatic representation started with the office of the Dutch volunteer organization, SNV. They had a large team on the ground in Mali. The Dutch government decided to open an office because there were more and more projects being financed in Mali. In the past, we had a special Sahel Program for countries like Senegal, Mauritania, Burkina Faso, and Niger.
Dutch involvement began after the drought of the 1980s, which had made an enormous impression worldwide at the time. In Mali, we started this office of Dutch Aid, and a colleague named Arjan Hamburger did excellent groundwork. My role then was to turn the office into an Embassy, with a staff that specialized in development cooperation. We had experts focusing on women's development, environmental issues, and soil fertility. The condition of the soil has always been an important driver for the Netherlands' aid program. Our soil scientists are the best in the world. We founded a soil science institute in Mali, and you can find these institutes all over the world. Their work doesn't just focus on the quality of the soil, but also on organizing the ownership of the land, the property rights. This is one of the most crucial issues in development programs in Africa: Who owns the land? In Africa, it is traditionally communal land. No one had the sole ownership of the land.

MS **What do you mean by communal land? In most places, including in the tribal areas of Mali, people in a community know who owns what. They have their own system of governance and land allocation. What is the role of the external party in this situation?**
RDV There is a strong belief that to modernize agriculture in Africa, you need to work with clear title deeds and ownership, either on an individual, community, or land-user level. Look at the position of women, for instance. In many cases, it is not clear who inherits the land after a farmer, a husband, dies. In my opinion, development aid has done a lot to stimulate the practice that, in the end, the wife can inherit the land. This not only generates continuity of investment but will also contribute to women's empowerment and strengthening their role in the community. These days, sexual and reproductive health and rights is still one of the most important focus points of the Dutch foreign policy in Mali, together with water/food security, and the rule of law. The rule-of-law program is focused on strengthening the position and role of individual citizens and their access to the justice system, and on reducing the gap between citizens and the government.

MS **The first embassy was called an 'Aid Embassy'. What does that mean? How was it different from other types of embassies?**
RDV In principle, there is no difference between embassies. The one in Mali began with a wish for development cooperation by our Ministry of Foreign Affairs. That is the reason we started diplomatic representation in Mali. In the Netherlands' system, development cooperation is integrated as much as possible into the economic, political and cultural work. We do not have a separate aid agency, like the United States does, for instance. This demonstrates the integrated approach we take as the Netherlands. By the way, my title was Chargé d'Affaires, and I replaced the ambassador who was stationed far away in Senegal.
Today, Mali is one of the Netherlands' 15 development cooperation partner countries. In implementing its development program, we seek alignment with Mali's national strategy for economic growth and poverty reduction. The Netherlands plays a leading role in aligning the programs of the various donors in Mali. Within its bilateral development cooperation program, the Netherlands has pledged a total sum of €137 million.

MS **I read that in 1992, there were 33 large Dutch projects in Mali focused on food aid, market liberalization, debt relief and macroeconomics. Additionally, the food programs were very progressive, perhaps even visionary. They were comprehensive in their approach, including building warehouses to store food, increasing field production of rice and cotton, improving rural infrastructure, and deterring soil degradation. These are very powerful and necessary developments that carry a sense of urgency at the moment, perhaps more than ever. Can you share examples of their success and failure?**
RDV One example I particularly like is the Office of Niger. The Niger River has an inner delta, and many old civilizations in Mali were located in that area. In the colonial days, the French wanted to build up an infrastructure

of cotton production in the delta, so they started irrigation works, but the project was dependent on a quasi-forced labor system.
The locals hated it, and it was abandoned after the colonial period. The French, the Dutch, and the World Bank then picked it up again and introduced a model of small-scale farming on a large area that was inspired by Chinese rice production and the Dutch expertise on managing water flows.
The project took into account the tension that is always present in Africa between livestock keepers and agriculturalists. Many conflicts in Africa originate from tensions between the pastoralists and farmers, who compete for the same resources. In the Office of Niger project, we tried to forge a harmonious relationship between the two groups.
The livestock keepers, the Fulani people (or Peul in French), were let in with their cattle to fertilize the ground after the rice was already harvested. At the same time, their cattle consumed the stems of what was left in the field. The knife cuts both ways: one group got food, the other got fertilizer.
This project turned Mali into an exporter of rice; before that they were an importer. That's one of the best examples I have seen in Mali and in Africa, and it's also very well documented, mind you. It's important because it took place in the area between the north, where our military troops are currently stationed, and the southern part, where the situation is more stable.

MS **Did the local population participate in this project? What did they gain?**
RDV The local producers were organized in cooperatives, and the overall board of the Office was a parastatal. These corporations are often linked to the production of sugar, cocoa, and cotton, and here in the Office it worked reasonably well.
As a donor, we were strong in emphasizing up front the interests of the local farmers. I remember a fantastic event: one day we were contacted by the Malian Minister of Finance, who informed us that the army had asked for rice to be imported from Vietnam. They claimed that they liked the Vietnamese rice better, and as donors to the project we were all very upset. We were investing millions to support a successful project, and it was working; we couldn't accept the import of rice from Vietnam. The army had to use the local rice. Afterwards, the Minister told me that he needed our refusal, and our agony, in order to be able to tell the chief of the army that he could not allow the import of rice from Vietnam to the detriment of the local production.

MS **What is the key to successful development projects? And what are the risks in the northern part of Mali?**
RDV It is very difficult to intervene in these types of contexts. The ecology is very fragile, and there is animosity between various ethnic groups in Mali. Often, you encounter mistrust that is fueled by conflicts from the past. Now, Mali faces an additional problem: the jihadists, who have become more influential in the Sahel region in the past few years.
The Niger River is one the most significant resources; it allows for transport, given that movement in the desert is difficult. The limited availability of water is a challenge; local farmers' vegetable gardens are hard to maintain. The unstable situation has led to unemployment, as people can't carry out their jobs.
It's a great challenge to intervene as a donor in this region, like we did at the time of the Sahel famine. We explicitly tried to avoid only giving; instead, we wanted to cooperate with locals on the projects. Today it may seem obvious, but at that time development was more of a one-way street. For instance, we made a deal with the northern communities: we provided food for their schools on the condition that they would provide firewood for the schools' kitchens. Firewood is a precious good in the desert. We worked together to make it happen.
Today, the Netherlands funds consortiums of Dutch organizations working with local partners. To improve governance and promote democracy, the Netherlands gives financial assistance to human rights organizations, supports democratization and decentralization in Mali, and contributes to the process of improving the management of public finances.

MS **Finally, can we talk about buildings, about architecture? How do you set up an embassy? How do you choose a building? How do you lay it out and organize it?**
RDV In the case of Mali, we just bought an ordinary house. It was the result of semi-local construction; it was made of concrete, but the shape looked like a local earth mud structure. At first, it was one house, but we grew in staff and we needed more space, so we added another floor. At a certain moment, we also bought the neighboring house, and we added a corridor in between.
I liked that it was improvised, that it was part of the life around it. There was a mud road leading to it. We had our neighbors' sheep and goats in front of the embassy door. Next to it there was a huge tower that was never finished.
The residence looked like a small villa. It created a lot of action on the street. In Mali, there are many market stalls on the street with people selling chewing gum, food, cigarette lighters, etc. We had a market around us. The life in Bamako was good. Although it's a big city, it had the atmosphere of a village. The people are

The Embbassy of the Netherlands in Mali at the time of its establishment. Bamako, 1991.

wonderful. We still have friends there. I remember that the streets came to life at night; people were talking with each other all night long, and they liked to gather on the corner near our house. We felt fortunate because it was not an enclave but the real version of Africa!

Rob de Vos: Former Consul General Rob de Vos entered the Dutch Foreign Service in 1978. During his assignment he was a member of the team that opened an Embassy in North Yemen. After postings in Dar es Salaam and London, he opened a Diplomatic Mission in Bamako. Rob subsequently served in the Ministry of Foreign Affairs as Deputy Chief of Personnel Affairs. He worked as Deputy Chief of Mission in Madrid. Before his appointment as Consul General of the Netherlands in New York, Rob de Vos was the Netherlands Ambassador to South Africa. He is married to Marion and has two children.

The Embbassy of the Netherlands. Bamako, 1991.

The Road with No Name

Marion de Vos

The road with no name,
leading to a dam
in the river Niger
could have been called
River Road, Dam Road
or Road of the mango trees,
as the Delta was dotted
with mango trees
as far as the eye could see.

I don't know why,
that road stuck
in my memory,
just an ordinary road,
a road that everybody knew
who called this place home.
I knew that road too,
though it ran through
my nomad Home.

It ended abruptly
at a bank,
plunging down
where the river,
first broad and stately
at Bamako,
"the home of crocodile,"
now pushed itself forth
through ragged narrows.

A submersible bridge
sitting on rocks
in the middle of rapids
with here and there
slabs of cement in between
leading seemingly to nowhere,
had to be carefully negotiated
and was used mainly
for trade by foot.

And the river still had
thousands of miles ahead
through deserts,
along mythical cities:
Timbouctou, Mopti,
Gao, Niamey, Lokoja
before slowing down
in that other Delta
full of oil and sorrow.

Every time I drove
along that road,
I wanted to
linger in the fields,
spread a blanket,
sit under a tree
watch the white sun make
shapes and patterns,
through dark foliage

watch the people,
laboring in the fields,
curious naked children
sneaking up to
this alien white shape:
in tennis clothes, lazing,
in the heat of the day.
They would extend dirty hands
for baksheesh.

Flies thirsty for moisture
would search for
the corners of eyes
and mouth.
Termites and ants
with nasty stings
crawl all over.
Sharp stones under the blanket.
torture.

Another Sting ran through my mind:
"Many years have passed since those summer days
among the fields of barley.
See the children run as the sun goes down
among the fields of gold"
Perhaps fields of barley
sounded like fields of Mali.
Or that was what I wanted to hear
and see that sun *"in a jealous sky."*

My life was nothing like theirs,
I never sat down in those
"fields of gold"
I had another life to live:
take the short cut:
on to the American Clusb,
reach the river
before the rains came,
before the waters
would run too high.

Marion de Vos is a writer, poet,
and the wife of Rob de Vos.

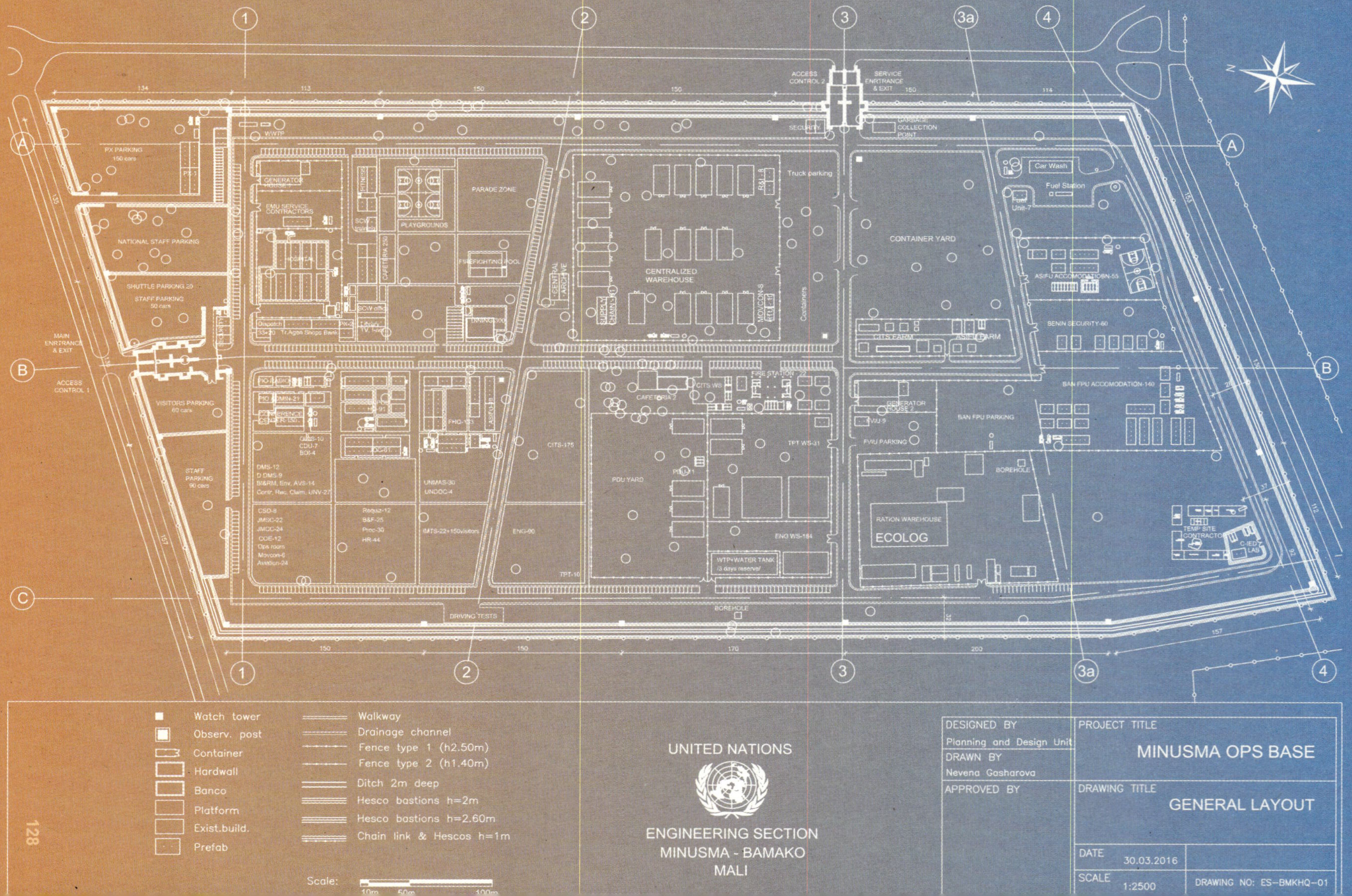
PX PARKING 150 cars
NATIONAL STAFF PARKING
SHUTTLE PARKING 20
STAFF PARKING 50 cars
MAIN ENRTRANCE & EXIT
ACCESS CONTROL 1
VISITORS PARKING 60 cars
STAFF PARKING 90 cars
WWTP
GENERATOR HOUSE 1
EMU SERVICE CONTRACTORS
HOSPITAL
PLAYGROUNDS
CAFETERIA 250
PARADE ZONE
FIREFIGHTING POOL
CENTRAL ARCHIVE
Truck parking
CENTRALIZED WAREHOUSE
SUPPLY CHAIN
MOVCON-8
Containers
ACCESS CONTROL 2
SERVICE ENRTRANCE & EXIT
SECURITY
GARBAGE COLLECTION POINT
CONTAINER YARD
Car Wash
Fuel Station
Fuel Unit-7
ASIFU ACCOMODATION-55
BENIN SECURITY-60
CITS FARM
ASIFU FARM
BAN FPU ACCOMODATION-140
BAN FPU PARKING
GENERATOR HOUSE 2
FVIU PARKING
BOREHOLE
RATION WAREHOUSE
ECOLOG
TEMP SITE CONTRACTOR
C-IED LAB
CITS-175
ENG-90
TPT-10
PDU YARD
CAFETERIA 2
FIRE STATION
TPT WS-31
ENG WS-184
WTP+WATER TANK (3 days reserve)
UNMAS-30
UNDOC-4
IMTS-22+150visitors
DMS-12
D DMS-9
B&RM, Env. AVS-14
Contr. Rec. Claim. UNV-27
CSD-8
JMSC-22
JMOC-24
COE-12
Ops room
Movcon-6
Aviation-24
Requiz-12
B&F-25
Proc-30
HR-44
DRIVING TESTS
Watch tower
Observ. post
Container
Hardwall
Banco
Platform
Exist.build.
Prefab
Walkway
Drainage channel
Fence type 1 (h2.50m)
Fence type 2 (h1.40m)
Ditch 2m deep
Hesco bastions h=2m
Hesco bastions h=2.60m
Chain link & Hescos h=1m
Scale:
UNITED NATIONS
ENGINEERING SECTION
MINUSMA - BAMAKO
MALI
DESIGNED BY
Planning and Design Unit
DRAWN BY
Nevena Gasharova
APPROVED BY
PROJECT TITLE
MINUSMA OPS BASE
DRAWING TITLE
GENERAL LAYOUT
DATE
30.03.2016
SCALE
1:2500
DRAWING NO: ES-BMKHQ-01

UN Super Camp: The Operational Base in Bamako

The MINUSMA operational base (MOB) in Bamako, also known as the UN super camp, is distinct from the mission headquarters at the former Amitié hotel, which is situated at the center of the city in the Badalabougou neighborhood. The MOB is located northeast of the Bamako-Sénou International Airport. It is surrounded by agricultural fields, farms, and small huts. The closest farm is located less than 100 meters from the base's perimeter, and the edge of the nearest urban neighborhood is about one kilometer away. Before its conversion into a UN peacekeeping base, the land served the local community as a field for agriculture and grazing.

The UN Engineering Planning and Design Unit designed the MINUSMA operational base in collaboration with a subcontracted freelance architect. The base is organized according to strict UN engineering protocols and grids. It includes water, energy, and telecommunications infrastructure as well as a hospital, a library, playgrounds, parade zones, indoor and outdoor cafeterias, a conference center, accommodations for the All Source Information Fusion unit and formed police unit, areas for security units, and offices for civilian mission support officers and police and military staff officers. The layout of the base is organized by programmatic sections that are divided by roads. The base is separated from its surroundings by a layered security belt of chain link fence and Hesco bastions (large wire-mesh sandbags)—a two-meter-deep ditch, and an additional 2.6-meter-high Hesco bastion belt. The last belt incorporates 19 watchtowers. The two entrances include a main point of access to the north along an existing local road. The principal entrance is surrounded by buffer zones and a sequence of parking lots. A smaller entrance to the west is located alongside a path newly paved by the UN in agreement with the host government.

The interior parts of the base have been gradually installed since 2015. They include a mix of prefabricated structures and containers. The base comprises an area of about 36 hectares (comparable to five typical New York City blocks) Inside the base are small areas allocated for different programs and contingent troops. To the southwest of the base, 10,000 square meters of fenced area
are assigned to Ecolog, a private global logistics company providing rations to MINUSMA. Ecolog's area includes a 5,000-square-meter warehouse, a large borehole, and over a dozen structures of a range of sizes. Contemporary urban paradigms and the UN 2030 Agenda for Sustainable Development propagate environmentally mindful practices and emissions reduction through the use of green buildings and infrastructure.[36] Yet most of the MOB's infrastructure, containers, and prefabricated structures are flown in from around the world with limited local sourcing. Moreover, the standard materials such as metal and wood generic structures have to be adapted to the local climate through excessive use of energy for cooling and heating.[37] As a result, the UN method of building and maintaining its camps has an extensive environmental and carbon footprint. MINUSMA's operational base demonstrates the missions' significant impact on the Malian environment. If the UN adopted a strategy of regenerative sustainability,[38] its missions could be regarded as resources that contribute to lasting sustainability for cities like Bamako and Gao. These cities struggle to respond to their rapidly growing populations with adequate urban expansion and infrastructure, particularly concerning access to water, food, energy, health care, education, and telecommunications networks. As mentioned above, UN bases operate for an average of about 6.5 years. In this time frame, they can gradually evolve to support the local population and bolster urban services.

36 International Policy Centre for Inclusive Growth, "A New Urban Paradigm: Pathways to Sustainable Development," UN Development Programme, Policy in Focus 13, no. 3, available at: https://ipcig.org/pub/eng/PIF37_A_new_urban_paradigm_pathways_to_sustainable_development.pdf, and United Nations, "The New Urban Agenda: Key Commitments," October 20, 2016, available at: www.un.org/sustainabledevelopment/blog/2016/10/newurbanagenda.

37 UN Environment, Greening the Blue Report 2016.

38 Regenerative sustainability is a design philosophy. It preaches a better lifestyle through the making of improvements on as many physical systems around us as humanly possible so that we leave these systems better than we found them. See: https://ecowarriorprincess.net/2020/05/regenerative-sustainability-new-frontier-sustainability-movement.

Under Construction

When we arrived at the MOB, MINUSMA's super camp in Bamako, it was under construction and partly occupied by UN agencies, TCCs, freelancers, and private subcontractors. The base was designed as an island, enclosed by barbed wire and trenches, and as the name indicates, it is enormous. Inside it, there is a hospital, restaurants, multiple offices, and a fire station. The super camp is a new typology that emerged after the UN delegated the production of its bases to the private sector. This typology is an indirect outcome of the financial crisis of 2007–2008. As the crisis increased financial pressure on member states, and consequently on UN agencies, parts of the production of mission's bases were delegated to the private sector, to companies like Ecolog.[39] Incorporating this production into the global market economy and its logic of exponential growth contributed to the spatial extension of UN bases. These new typologies are commonly found in bases built after 2010 in the Central African Republic, in South Sudan, and in Mali.

The lead designer of the MOB was a Bulgarian architect and a freelance consultant for the UN. The 2008 financial crisis hit Bulgaria hard and bankrupted many businesses; working for the UN was a way out of financial hardship. The lead contractor, from Casablanca, Morocco, provided local expertise. MINUSMA wasn't the first mission he worked on, and he seemed very resourceful in retrofitting the UN modular structures to withstand the challenging local climate, heat, and humidity. He showed us around the base and explained how he had hacked the modular system to create better air circulation and shade. For example, he provided shade and airflow by raising the roofs over the passageways between the different containers and the prefab offices and clinics. Throughout my visit to the MOB, I wondered why Malian architects were never involved with this project; after all, it is their city.

While the locals were being ignored, the ground on which the base was built, a grazing field that serviced the community and more than 300 cows, was eradicated, too. At the base, I asked if anyone knew where the cows had gone, and whether the local herders had been compensated or received another grazing field in return. No one knew the answer. Before we left the base, the architect invited us to her office. We stepped into a small white container. She looked at her desk and pulled up a map, a drawing of the base.

Bamako international airport and the UN super camp (MOB). Google Earth, 2020.

39 Ecolog was founded over two decades ago as a business providing support services for international peacekeeping forces and related global organizations' projects during their missions in remote and non-remote locations. Its founder's keen vision to identify international market needs and make strategic business decisions, brought up the centralization of a dispersed market into a united one which revolutionized the industry. **Ecolog**, which began as single support-service business, witnessed exponential growth in turnover, employee base, operations, new markets and industries, with a broad global presence and an international team of professionals ready to support clients every day, everywhere. The company have thousands of personnel and assets deployed to provide a broad variety of services, ranging from rapid deployment and construction, to camp support services including catering, supply chain & logistics and environmental services. We also provide support for retrograde operations, deconstruction, hazardous waste management, decontamination and soil remediation.Their urban environment coverage is mostly focused on municipalities, providing services and solutions for the management of urban infrastructure, waste management, traffic management and urban development procedures and ensuring implementation, including the provision and management of waste-treatment, recycling and water-purification plants. See: https://ecolog-international.com

The UN Military Engineer Manual divides the engineer's tasks into the construction, repair, and maintenance of horizontal and vertical elements. The horizontal elements include roads, bridges, airfields, paving and drainage projects, earthworks and site preparation, and boat ramps.

The images in the next pages were taken during a field study at the UN super camp in Bamako.

Earthworks

"Earthworks and site preparation are the reshaping of land by cutting, levelling, filling, and compacting earth to the desired shape using earth moving equipment. Earthworks and site preparation are fundamental to other engineer projects as they provide the basis upon which roads and bridges are built or upgraded, foundations and drainage are created for new projects, and berms put into place for Force Protection."

The UN Peacekeeping Military Engineer Unit Manual. September 2015, p20.

The UN super camp in Bamako under construction. Mali, 2016.

The UN super camp in Bamako under construction. Mali, 2016.

"UN engineers survivability tasks include construction of accommodation in camps."

UN Military Construction Engineer Units are often tasked with the construction of UN-provided rigid/ semi-rigid/prefabricated structures in campsites during the initial phase of the mission. The unit is tasked to undertake the construction of rigid/ semi-rigid/ prefabricated structures including siting of base camps."

The engineers' Vertical Construction Tasks include the construction, repair, and maintenance of rigid/semi-rigid or prefabricated structures, rehabilitation and repair of existing structures, well drilling and surveying.

The UN Peacekeeping Military Engineer Unit Manual. 2020, p83, 84.

Rigid/semi-rigid or prefabricated structures

"Rigid/semi-rigid or prefabricated structures (such as purpose-built container-type modular units) ensure the Mission infrastructure has adequate shelter for operational, administrative and accommodation purposes on a continuous and extended basis. Rigid/ semi-rigid and prefabricated structures must have sufficient strength to provide protection from local weather conditions. Given the construction's enduring intent, sub-tasks may include site planning, building foundations, main frame construction work, internal finishing and utility work."

The UN Peacekeeping Military Engineer Unit Manual. September, 2015, p18.

Construction / Dismantling of Rigid / Semi Rigid / Pre-Fabricated Structures Standards:

1. The Unit commander undertake initial survey of the task: The Commander performs engineer appreciation for the task; Calculates the time and resources required; Estimates the requirements of survey, earth work and earth moving plant requirements; Calculate store requirements for construction /maintenance; Calculate the mobilization and deployment requirements.
2. The Unit Commander issues order for construction of structures. The order includes: Details of expected task; Requirement of resources (store & manpower) to include transport requirement and earth moving plant requirements; The Unit commander estimates details of construction material requirement; Movement plan of the party; Force protection measures provided / to be adopted while on move and execution of tasks; Communication, liaison and reporting; Contingency plan and MED/CASEVAC plan; Logistical concerns/ resupply considerations.
3. The Unit is organized based on envisaged task and may include following elements: Mobilization; Task execution to include earthwork tasks as required; Store management; Protection party (if required); Logistics support.
4. The Unit is sufficiently self-sustained to operate/ undertake tasks: Generator; Welding Machine; Water pumps. Water Trucks, Concrete Mixers, Carpentry Shop, Earth movers required for levelling of campsite.
5. The Unit has proficient: Generator Operators; Earth moving plant operators; Survey tasks; Masonry works; Metalsmiths; Plumbing; Electricity works; Woodwork/carpentry; Air conditioning & heating/boiler room specialists (if tasked) Air-conditioning is a specialist task and will not be available at a basic engineer formation level.
6. Setting up of the camp site work is done by survey personnel. Survey of ground levels is carried out and GPS used to mark maps and layout sketches.
7. Drainage of the camp site is adequately addressed.
8. Earth work, including leveling with dozer, excavator, loader, dumper, motor grader, roller etc. is performed by the unit.
9. The Unit performs masonry work to include concrete casting, brickwork & foundations.
10. Safe electric connections, plumbing & metal-smith works are performed by the unit.
11. The Unit Commander exercises appropriate C2 during the move and execution of task (e.g. undertake resource management and caters for contingencies).
12. The Unit Commander is aware of the reporting procedures and reports progress of task to higher HQ.

The UN Peacekeeping Military Engineer Unit Manual. 2020, p83, 84.

Hacking the modular. MOB. Mali, 2016.

Hacking the Modular

"The camp contractor was resourceful in retrofitting the UN modular structures to the challenging local climate, heat, and humidity. He showed us around the base and explained how he had hacked the modular system to create larger rooms, better air circulation and shade. For example, by adding passages with raised roofs between the different containers and the prefab offices and medical clinics."

See "Under construction", p138.

From Global Supply Chains to Local Sourcing: Imagining a New Environmental Approach for Peacekeeping Missions

The UN's organizational culture and member states' preferences shape the way peacekeeping operations are designed and carried out. UN peacekeeping missions are planned as short-term operations. Although the median duration since 2000 has been 6.5 years, their mandates are renewed each year.[40] Missions are also carried out in keeping with a yearly budget. This budgetary cycle is among the main challenges for the implementation of environmental policies or any legacy considerations as it obstructs long-term investment, planning, and procurement, particularly since the financial crisis of 2007–2008, which increased the financial pressure on UN agencies from member states. The brief and urgent timeline of mission deployments coupled with security concerns leads to the implementation of planning procedures that leave many pressing social and environmental concerns unplanned and unresolved. These procedures, however, are hard to change and continue to be applied, especially for rapid deployments.[41]

Besides their initial design, the way missions are carried out, especially in terms of procurement and sourcing, affects their impact on the surrounding communities and the environment. The UN missions depend on global supply chains and procurement protocols that circumvent values such as local empowerment, collaboration with local experts, inhabitants, and businesses. The supply chain is global, circular, and self-fed. UN missions primarily rely on international suppliers and external logistics firms that shape the landscape where missions operate and inflate their environmental footprint. For instance, the company Ecolog has become a leading provider of catering, supplies, construction, technology, facility management, and environmental services for MINUSMA, UNSOS, and other missions.[42] As a result, capacities and resources for maintaining and supporting UN peace operations are imported from around the world, from modular construction systems to food and cooks. This global flow of commodities and expertise, which can be traced to the UN Global Marketplace[43]—the common procurement platform for the UN system—appears excessively wasteful. Misunderstandings or misconceptions about local economies as well as the lack of environmental assessments at an early stage can also lead to wasteful and damaging practices. For instance, the bricks used to build UNAMID's camp and the facilities for humanitarian aid workers in Darfur were bought from the local population in order to support the local economy and promote women's employment, but they were baked over wood fires, which contributed to deforestation. Misunderstanding of local economies and environmental practices can reverse the potential benefits of sourcing locally.

Some of the obstacles to implementing sustainable policies are associated with sourcing practices. This includes, for instance, any attempt to incorporate socioeconomic values, or aspects derived from the SDG (Sustainable Development Goals) or the UN Climate Agenda, within the scope of missions. The materials used by missions directly contribute to their environmental footprint, and these are embedded in the politics of procurement for UN peacekeeping missions. Procurement policies respond to member states' financial and political interests. Yet these interests may be contrary to the other agendas promoted by the UN, such as the Environment Strategy, which encompasses using more eco friendly materials and technologies. This constitutes a major obstacle for the implementation of environmentally sound practices. For instance, a study conducted in 2013 showed that the top troop-contributing countries were particularly suspicious of equipment standardization projects. Indeed, some member states – especially developing countries and Russia—were strongly opposed to environmental standards under the UN reimbursement system for contingent-owned

40 UN Field Support, DFS Environment Strategy, "Executive Summary," November 2017, p. 3.
41 Shoshan, Szita. "Reimagining the peacekeeping mission: Legacy Scenarios for Camp Castor", workshop report, 2013, HNI, Rotterdam.
42 Active in more than 36 countries and with 12,000 personnel in more than 150 locations, Ecolog supplies UN peace operations including MINUSMA. It provides "customized solutions to governments and defense, humanitarian organizations and commercial clients in the sectors of Oil & Gas, Mining, Energy and Infrastructure projects," available at: https://ecolog-international.com/en.

equipment (decided every three years in the General Assembly) and under the procurement principles for selecting vendors. Some governments have argued that if these principles incorporated strict environmental standards, their companies would not be competitive enough on the international market, which would violate the UN procurement objective of fair, equal, and geographically equitable treatment of potential vendors.[44] In the case of MINUSMA, the UN outsources the maintenance of many of its bases to Ecolog.[45]

The Dubai-based company provides customized solutions to governments and defense agencies, humanitarian organizations, and commercial clients in the sectors of oil and gas, mining, energy, and infrastructure projects. Ecolog is active in more than 36 countries, managing some 12,000 people in more than 150 locations, including the services it provides to UN peacekeeping missions. Each super camp in Mali has a large, designated logistics hub with accommodation units for Ecolog workers and containers filled with mission supplies.

Reducing the Footprint and Local Empowerment

Although UN agencies and member states promote a comprehensive climate agenda in keeping with the Paris Accord and the Sustainable Development Goals, and while the UN agenda promotes environmentally mindful practices and emission reduction through the use of green buildings and infrastructure, the DPKO's (Department of Peacekeeping Operations) methods of space production and maintenance generate an extensive environmental footprint.[46]

If MINUSMA outsourced its food supply to local farmers, it could reduce peacekeeping's environmental footprint, build local food production capacity, and contribute to food security. This would be especially significant in arid areas prone to protracted periods of drought, famine, and, consequently, conflicts.[47] Measures could include providing local farmers with access to better seeds, smart irrigation, and water management systems, and improving the storage infrastructure for locally produced food. The introduction of green building guidelines and technologies at UN bases would also reduce their footprint and contribute to regenerative sustainability.

Steps to support green building should draw on local expertise, construction techniques, and materials for the design of UN bases. There should be incentives to reduce the environmental footprint and support sustainable development. Incorporating local capacities and materials would mean utilizing, for example, less plastic, wood, paper, and metals that demand tremendous energy for their production through extraction, mining, deforestation, and transport and which are associated with lasting solid and liquid waste.

An integrated, non-extractive and regenerative design approach can help identify, assess, and develop incentives to include local capacity—culture, materials, and expertise. It can contribute to the reduction of the environmental footprint of missions and encourage sustainable development.

43 United Nations Global Marketplace, available at: www.ungm.org
44 Maertens, Lucile and Shoshan Malkit, "Greening Peacekeeping: The Environmental Impact of UN Peace Operations," New York: International Peace Institute, April 2018.
45 "Integrated Service Solutions," Ecolog International, 2017, available at: https://ecolog-international.com/en.
46 "Greening the Blue Report 2016. The UN system's environmental footprint and efforts to reduce it," Greening the Blue, 2017, available at: www.greeningtheblue.org/.
47 Sousa, Agnieszka, "Poor Nations Need Farm Investment or Face Importing More Food," Bloomberg.com, October 09, 2017, available at: www.bloomberg.com/news/articles/2017-10-09/poor-nations-need-farm-investment-or-face-importing-more-food-j8jssozu.

Mopti

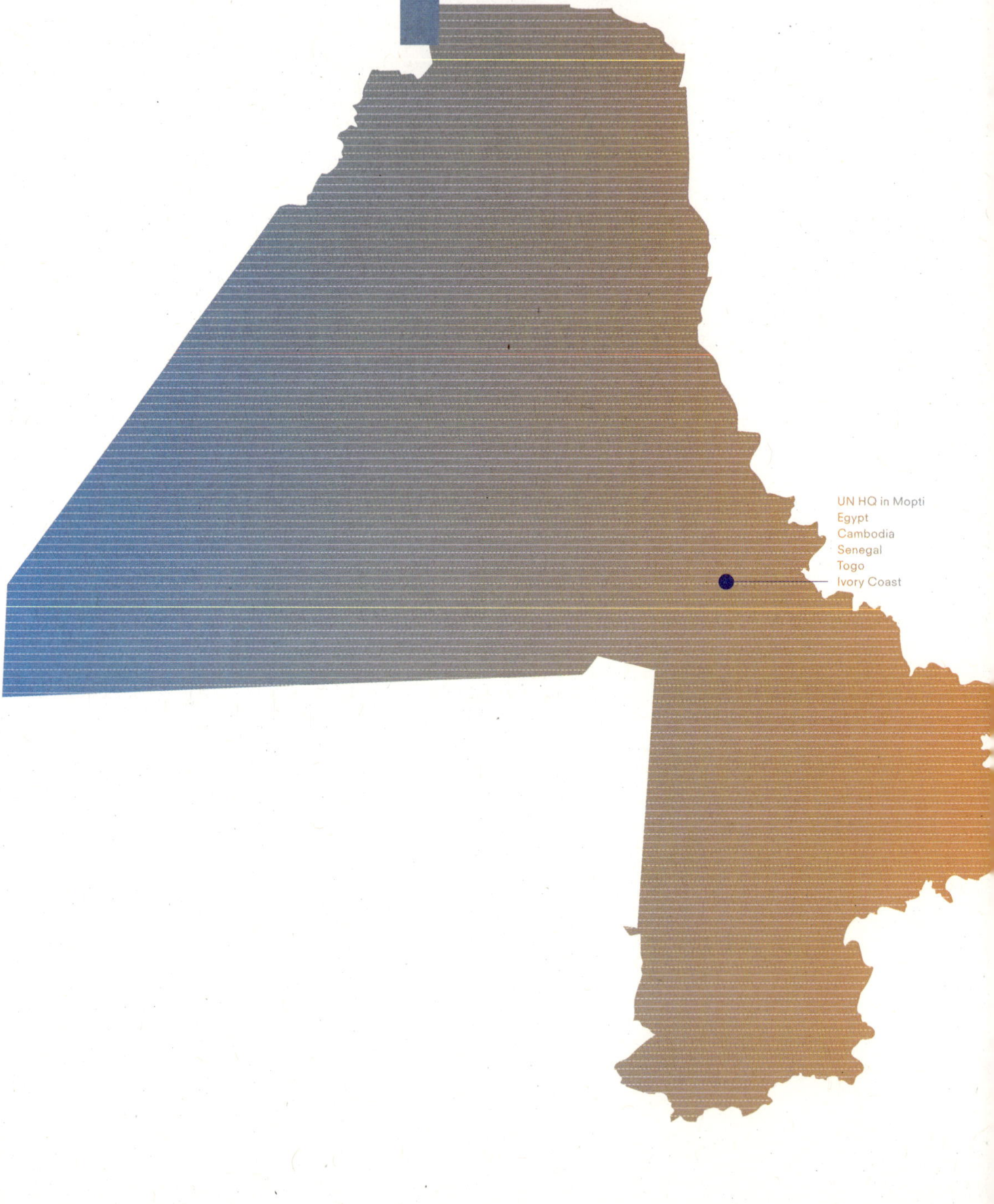

The Flight to Gao with a Stopover in Mopti

A few days after our arrival in Bamako, we were picked up again by the MOVCON unit, who escorted us back to the airport. The UN mission controlled all internal flights in Mali. The UN plane to Gao was operated by a Russian company, the sole operator of air travel, which had taken over local civilian flights. We walked from the gate to the small white UN plane and climbed the airstairs. Inside, we could pick a seat. The number of windows was limited, so I was glad I ended up sitting next to one. As we buckled our seatbelts, the flight operator welcomed us in English with a Russian accent: "Welcome on board and thank you for choosing to fly with us today." It was odd, since there was no choice to be made. It was the only way to get from Bamako to Gao by plane. The rest of the passengers were UN personnel, and only a few Malian civilians.

Along the way, we stopped over in Mopti, where new UN bases were under construction. Mopti is a town in the Inner Niger Delta region of Mali, where the Niger and the Bani Rivers converge. It is the capital of the Mopti Region and home to over 100,000 inhabitants. Elevated paths link Mopti to the town of Sevare, which hosts a few UN bases.

Another renowned ancient small town in the region is Bandiagara. The name translates roughly as "large eating bowl." It sits at the highest altitude in the country, with a population made up of several ethnic groups, including Dogons, Fulani, and Bambara. Bandiagara is bordering Azawad (see Peter Chilson's essay, pages 150–153), at the very center of the internationally recognized borders of Mali.

Azawad

Azawad is the name given to an unrecognized Tuareg state in northern Mali. Its independence was declared unilaterally by the National Movement for the Liberation of Azawad (MNLA) in 2012 after the Tuareg rebellion drove the Malian Army away from the region. As claimed by the MNLA, Azawad comprises the regions of Timbuktu, Kidal, Gao, and a part of the Mopti region, covering roughly 60 percent of Mali's total land area.[48]

> Living in a Sahara devoid of water, / Desiccated and miserable, My wish is for it to stop being subservient. This is a message for those / Who toil for the revolution.
>
> Assàwt by Tinariwen.

Mopti

The area of Mopti is well known for its Dogon inhabitants, an ethnic group with a population of about 50,000. The Dogon are known for their religious traditions, mask dances, wooden sculpture, and architecture. The Dogon have a system of written signs that numbers in the thousands, along with "their own systems of astronomy and calendrical measurements, methods of calculation, and extensive anatomical and physiological knowledge as well as a systematic pharmacopeia."[49] Their villages are built along escarpments; each contains about 44 houses inhabited by members of one main lineage traced through the male line.

The Dogon people were a source of inspiration for modernist artists and architects. In the 1970s, Aldo van Eyck, together with a group of Dutch architects and anthropologists, set up an expedition to Bandiagara.

48 MNLA. "The National Movement for the Liberation of Azawad," available at: www.mnlamov.net.

49 Griaule, Marcel (1970) [1965]. Conversations with Ogotemmêli: An Introduction to Dogon Religious Ideas.

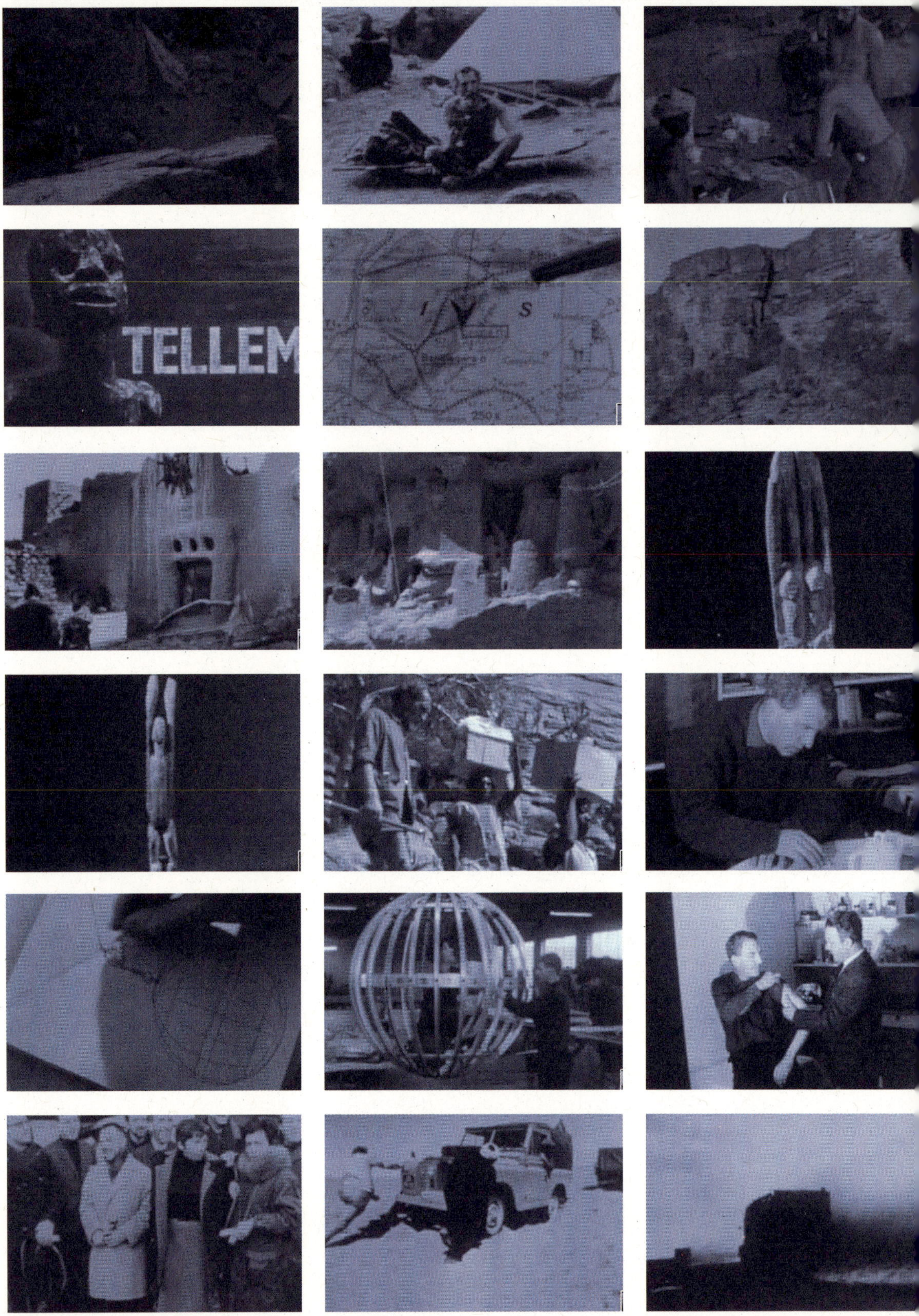

Stills from "The TELLEM-Expedition" by Herman Haan. NCRV, 1964

chef expédition
herman haan

Dutch Expedition to the Bandiagara Escarpment

In *6,000 Years of Housing,* Norbert Schoenauer describes the Dogon cluster dwelling, drawing on Aldo Van Eyck's analysis. The Dogon live in compact villages that are situated along the cliffs of the Bandiagara Plateau. Their huts are positioned close to one another and have mostly a rectangular plan. To Van Eyck, the Dogon represented a well-organized community and typified an early stage in the developmental sequence of human settlements.

Van Eyck was introduced to the Dogon culture by Herman Haan, another Dutchman fascinated by African cultures. Haan visited the Sahara and Africa over 36 times. He "had assumed the role of purveyor of images, stories, and ethnographic data on traditional African cultures and communities to the architectural community in Holland and around Team 10." During the 1950s, however, it was van Eyck who championed the new interest in non-Western countries at CIAM,[50] alongside other younger colleagues.

Van Eyck traveled to the Dogon region in sub-Saharan Africa with Haan. The encounter with the tribal culture turned him into a self-proclaimed expert who presumed to understand the tribal culture and the nature of Western/non-Western relationships, which he attempted to import into modern architecture.

Van Eyck was a collector of artifacts, objects, and meaning. He visited remote and archaic cultures, drew inspiration from them, and eventually brought elements from these spaces into the Netherlands, into Dutch cities, and into Dutch modernist architecture. His anthropological voyages to the cliffs of the Bandiagara inspired his designs. The Dogon's cluster dwellings and cosmic beliefs helped Van Eyck re-shape abstract modernist design. In some cases, his acts of reconstruction were merely acts of cultural appropriation. For example, following his travels to visit the Dogon, van Eyck coined the expression "twin-phenomenon," referencing the universal concept of twinness derived from Dogon mythology. He often used these cosmological ideas, the nature of opposites, as the gist of his architectural thought, imagination, and design—different, yet complementary.

50 The Congrès internationaux d'architecture moderne (CIAM), or International Congresses of Modern Architecture, was an organization founded in 1928 and disbanded in 1959, responsible for a series of events and congresses held across Europe by the most prominent architects of the time, with the objective of spreading the principles of the Modern Movement and focusing on all the main domains of architecture (including landscape, urbanism, industrial design, and many others). See: www.hisour.com/congres-internationaux-darchitecture-moderne-28191.

Circles

o After the Second World War, when the UN was established, and the first peacekeeping mission took place, Aldo van Eyck introduced his emblematic playgrounds to the war-torn and derelict Dutch cities. Dutch planners were facing a state of emergency. This condition proved an opportunity for Van Eyck to experiment with playfulness as an alternative approach to the top-down city.

o Van Eyck was fascinated by archaic culture. He traveled to the tribal areas of Africa and Mali, in particular to the Dogon. These cultures and spaces inspired Van Eyck to bring new forms to Dutch architecture and write architecture poems. Here his abstract modern circle absorbed new tribal meanings.

un **d**essin ne
s'**o**rdonne que
sur la **g**race;
ouvrez
les **n**ormes;

derangez
l'**o**rdre
mais avec **g**out;
outrepassez
la **n**ecessite

Aldo Van Eyck

Playground Zaanhof by Aldo van Eyck. Amsterdam, 1948.

Bricks

THE DOGON FOUNDATION

In the late 1950s, the Dutch architect Joop van Stigt joined an expedition of Aldo van Eyck and Herman Haan to the tribal areas of the Dogon and the Tellem at the Bandiagara cliffs in Mali. This was the first of many trips he took to the area. In the 1990s, together with his wife, Van Stigt set up a foundation doing small-scale interventions in Mali: the building of a dam, the digging of a well, and eventually the construction of a school. Currently, Joop's son, Jurriaan van Stigt, continues the foundation's work, producing bricks and using local materials to build schools and other projects in collaboration with the local community.

Brick production (above) Brick school in the Dogon area (below). Mali, 2015.

Bandiagara: A Town on the Border of Azawad

Peter Chilson

In early May 2012, days after a shaky alliance of Tuareg nationalists and jihadist rebels overran northern Mali, I visited the town of Bandiagara in the center of the country, an hour's drive south of where the rebels stopped. With my friend Yusuf,[51] who grew up around Bandiagara, we drove in a rented Toyota Land Cruiser to the offices of a private American rural development agency where he once worked. Yusuf told me that when Timbuktu, 170 miles to the northwest, fell at the end of March, the American staff crowded into a small fleet of SUVs and made a sudden, disorganized departure to Bamako, Mali's capital. A week later they left the country. Jihadists and Tuareg rebels declared an independent state of northern Mali, half a million square miles of sand, rock and a dwindling savanna they call Azawad. The word reflected the pastoral culture of Tuaregs in a region of different human stories and a complex mix of ethnic groups – Tuareg, Fulani, Arab, Songhai, and, like Yusuf, Dogon.

"The Americans told us they were shutting down the project but that it would only be temporary," Yusuf said. "They stopped paying our salaries and rent on the offices." He shook his head. "We'll never see them again." Now back in town with me, he steered the car onto a long dirt road near the agency's office. We found people all along the way burning their belongings in bonfires spread out every few hundred yards. The street was deeply rutted clay, wide enough for us to go around the fires. Ash and stray bits of paper blew about as the wind gusted.

People hurried in and out of mud homes and concrete villas with armloads of paper, piling it on the flames. We stopped at a villa that housed the aid agency where Yusuf had worked. Through the front gate, employees carried cardboard boxes stuffed with paper and dumped them onto a bonfire – brand new schoolbooks, records for medical clinics, grant proposals, budget reports, all burned white smoke. They burned CDs and DVDs, too, and photographs, cassette tapes, magazines, maps – all the music, movies and images they thought would get them a flogging or worse from Islamist policemen. The plastic burned black. Flames jumped and bobbed as if eager to tell what was in all that stuff, spewing sparks and ash in a cloud that rushed away on a hard-westerly wind. Twenty thousand people live in Bandiagara, which dates to 1700 when it was a hunting camp on the Yamé River. The river, dry most of the year, splits the town on a plateau in the Dogon highlands, a few miles from the sandstone Bandiagara Escarpment that drops 1,600 feet to the plain where the Sahara begins. Jihadists have captured Bandiagara twice in the last two hundred years. It briefly served as capital of the 19th century Tukulor Empire – the last great jihadist state to rule in the West African Sahel until the French crushed it in 1893 and set up a puppet sultanate in Bandiagara, which still exists. More recently, European climbers and trekkers, attracted to the high cliffs, helped the city reinvent itself as a tourist town and climbers' base camp. But on this afternoon, in my eyes, watering from the burning plastic, all of this seemed to be blowing away.

A young woman ran out of the villa that housed the aid office, clutching a shopping bag in her hands. She was barefoot and wore a traditional African flower print dress that fell to her ankles and a headscarf. When she threw the bag on the flames, three or four pairs of high-heeled shoes, red and white and black, spilled out and caught fire, bleeding inky smoke. She looked into the fire a few seconds and then jogged back inside. In the wind, her scarf flapped from a knot at her neck.

I'd never seen this before, people parting with their belongings in random panic, a ripple effect of war. I thought of a famous Vietnam War photograph of a helicopter on a Saigon rooftop, evacuating people from an outdoor stairway – CIA staffers it turned out – as the city fell to the North Vietnamese.

But this was Mali. Everything I'd known about this country I'd been visiting for 30 years was coming apart. Two months earlier, Mali was one of Africa's most peaceful and stable countries, protected by an army of volunteer farmers. Now they battled hardened Islamist groups flush with arms looted from the collapsed Libyan state of Muammar Gaddafi. For many Malians the war came all of a sudden, as if they'd awoken one day to find at their door an enemy they didn't know existed; bigger, fiercer and better armed than they were. The Malian army turned and ran, abandoning or losing in battle some eighty percent of its equipment, and regrouped across Mali's narrow waist; a 200-mile east-to-west line that ran just north of Bandiagara with jihadists on one side, the government on the other. Every kilometer or so along that line groups of soldiers camped out with light armored vehicles and pickups mounted with machine guns, Mali's best bulwark against the rebel advance.

Banks shut down along the line and trucked their cash reserves to Bamako. Schools and post offices closed. Soldiers in Bandiagara sandbagged street corners and installed heavy machine guns. A light tank on big tractor wheels occupied Martyrs Square in the city center. Soldiers patrolled the streets in crisp new camouflage and helmets, Kalashnikovs over their shoulders.

Yusuf knew the woman with the bag of shoes. He waved and shouted at her. "Fatima! Hey, Fatima!" We had pulled up just in time to see her chuck the bag on the fire. Yusuf, behind the wheel, stuck his head out the window, calling to her again but she did not hear him.

"What is all this?" Yusuf said, glancing at me. His former colleagues scurried in and out of the courtyard gate, two large swinging metal doors, feeding the bonfire in the street. They seemed giddy, like people at a neighborhood block party, shouting, occasionally laughing. This was not celebration, but blowing off tension, fear.

He threw the Land Cruiser into reverse and backed it away from the heat. We watched a pile of CDs melt in the coals. I could not tell what was on the covers. Loud popping erupted in puffs of ash and red coals sprung out on the dirt, spent batteries maybe. The sound brought more people out of the buildings, looking anxiously this way until they realized there was no gunfire. A man in sandals, a red fez and long white knee-length tunic over leggings poured a box of thick spiral bound booklets onto the fire like dishwater. Yusuf loves to talk and never let conversations lag, but he studied the scene in silence, hands on the steering wheel.

I said, "You'd think the rebels were around the corner." Yusuf looked on as if he hadn't heard me.

I got out of the car and walked to the bonfire, picking up paper as I went. I read a page from a grant proposal to the French Embassy about books for a village school, and then something concerning a women's market cooperative for selling vegetables, all of it in French, lingua franca of colonial West Africa. I crumpled the paper and threw it at the fire, which was hard to approach with the heat. I saw books in the flames, including a secondary school geography text. A Dick Francis thriller with an image of a brassiere dangling from a woman's fingers lay in the dirt just beyond the root of the flames. It was a French translation of Under Orders – a novel featuring a jockey turned private eye that I'd read years earlier. I kept glancing at it because I hated to see a good read burn. The story begins slowly but takes off when an English jockey crosses the finish line astride his horse and with a chest full of bullet holes.

The fire looked like it was spitting out of the earth. I watched, fascinated. I saw something that looked like an olive green piece of clothing that had fallen away from the flames and was smoldering. On impulse, I grabbed at the cloth, plucking out a piece of sleeve. At the top was a charred shoulder patch of the yellow, red and green Malian flag above the words, Forces Armée Malienne. It was a shred of a soldier's uniform tunic. I burned my fingers on the cloth and dropped it. Yusuf had gotten out of the car and when I looked up, sucking on the tips of two slightly burnt fingers, he was leaning against the Land Cruiser, arms folded, feet crossed at the ankles. His face was expressionless.

"Be careful," he said.

I stepped back and joined him, leaning against the car. "I think your friends are trying to erase the history of this place."

Yusuf shook his head. "Two years' work gone. I cannot participate in this. I have nothing to be ashamed of. I have nothing to hide. I have my good name."

Yusuf wanted to see old friends but instead we found the bonfire and people running around. The scene was not just about Yusuf's job at the agency – the well projects he'd developed, the rural medical dispensaries he'd built and equipped, and the literacy programs in French and Dogon he'd helped develop – but about a livelihood and years of work vanishing. Here, Mali was bleeding away and a collective national question spiraled in the smoke – What do we do now?

We stood beside the Land Cruiser as one of Yusuf's co-workers, a young man in sandals, jeans and a clean white collared shirt ran out of the villa. He was clutching a bundle of manila file folders to his chest. He threw them in an awkward flurry on the fire, which was so hot it was hard to get close. A wind gust caught a bunch of paper and blew it down the street.

"Yusuf!" he shouted, waving. He reached to shake my hand. "Who is the white man?" Yusuf explained I was a journalist. "Well you are welcome," he said to me and then laughed. "You are the last white person in all of the Mopti region."

While Yusuf and his colleague shared news, I edged toward the fire to pick up the Dick Francis novel. The book lay in the sand, charred at the edges. Dick Francis was good entertainment, even in French, and I liked the fact that he'd been a heavy drinker and a racing jockey like his detective character. I liked the rumors that his wife might have written some of his novels, a suspicion of authorship he shares with Shakespeare. Here on a 'front-line' of the war on terror – on the edge of a land where jihadists were whipping people caught drinking alcohol and unmarried couples for talking to each other in public, destroying musical instruments and burning books – the work of a writer who gave us divorced, hard drinking protagonists and himself led an unreliable life, needed rescue from the fire.

I lunged forward and snatched up the novel, jumping back when the fire, as if itself under orders, threw sparks at me.

Yusuf's colleague gave me a friendly shout. "Why do you want that book?" As I backed away from the fire, holding the book in one hand and running a hand through my hair to clear it of hot cinders, he stepped over to shake my hand again. "You will write about this, okay? You will tell the world our story." He stared earnestly into my face. "You know this is not about Tuaregs anymore. It's more serious. The jihadists are here."

I slid the book under my arm and took his hand in both of mine. "That's why I am here," I said. He grabbed the Dick Francis novel from under my armpit, maybe thinking I was about to toss it on the flames anyway or maybe because he disapproved of the brassiere on the cover, and threw it in the flames before running back into the villa. The book vanished instantly. Behind me, Yusuf laughed.

He took me inside the offices. In Bandiagara, if a building is not made of mud it's built of cinder block. Nicer buildings, like this one, are covered with handsome milk chocolate mud stucco. This building had an adobe style red clay tile roof. Inside, everything was painted white. Single room offices surrounded a small tiled courtyard with an acacia tree growing in the middle. Boxes and stacks of chairs leaned against the walls. Paper lay all over.

"Do you need to salvage anything here?" I said. "Let me help."

Yusuf shook his head. "There is nothing for us here. Let's go."

Peter Chilson is the author of the award-winning travelogue "Riding the Demon: On the Road in West Africa" and "Disturbance-Loving Species: A Novella and Stories". Chilson, a longtime visitor to Mali as a travel writer and journalist. He went back in 2012 for the Foreign Policy-Pulitzer Center Borderlands project and was one of the first western journalists to see firsthand the effects of civil war and the new breakaway jihadist state. Chilson's e-book, "We Never Knew Exactly Where: Dispatches From the Lost Country of Mali", came out in January 2013.

51 Yusuf is not his real name. It has been changed to protect him and his family, all of whom live near Bandiagara.

Bandiagara and the Dogon Plateau.

Landscape outside Bandiagara: Rocky terrain and farmland outside Bandiagara.

Bandiagara Escarpment: A section of the Bandiagara cliffs from the village of Songo, near Bandiagara.

Gao

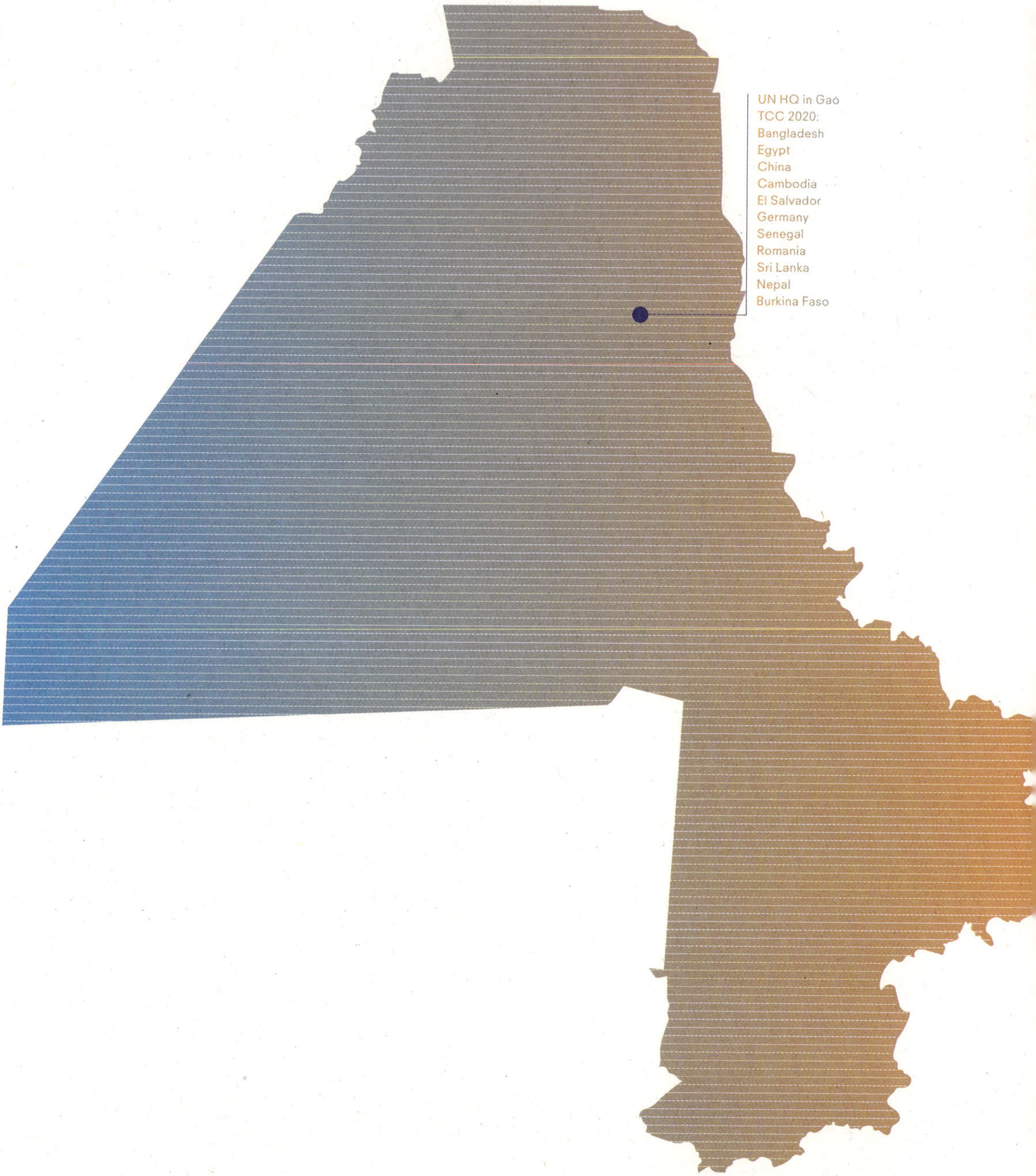
UN HQ in Gao
TCC 2020:
Bangladesh
Egypt
China
Cambodia
El Salvador
Germany
Senegal
Romania
Sri Lanka
Nepal
Burkina Faso

Approaching Gao

The layover in Mopti airport lasted a few hours. The small terminal was filled with UN personnel crossing over from the north to the south of the country. Other flights continued to Timbuktu and more remote towns, to rural areas like Menaka and Tessalit. Prior to visiting Gao, we were scheduled to visit Timbuktu, but it didn't come through due to administrative and logistical complications.

Now we were back in the air. As we approached the Sahara Desert, we noticed the landscape gradually changing from green to yellow. Just before landing, the arid yellow was interjected by a bright green and blue tone, like a paintbrush stroke: the Niger River's staggering beauty dominated the view.

The river, not only a powerful water body in the desert, is of historical significance. Its stream of water and presence brought to life and empowered ancient kingdoms and empires. Along its banks, cities like Timbuktu and Gao were formed and thrived at the continental crossroads. The gates to the Sahara Desert and the bridge between North Africa and Western Africa, it also formed a link to the southern parts of the continent, other religions, and cultures—both nomadic and sedentary.

We stepped off the plane into the bright desert sun and walked toward a small and impoverished looking terminal. The ceiling was crumbling, and bullet holes perforated the walls. The airport was surrounded by white, armed UN vehicles, mini-tanks, soldiers with machine guns, and patrols. The situation in Gao was tense, and frequent attacks targeted the UN presence.

Again, we were welcomed by new team members from the MOVCON unit, who greeted us and presented us with the program for the following days. We drove together to Camp Castor.

Flying above the Niger River. Mali, 2016.

Model of the entrance to Camp Castor (Top). Aerial images of Gao (Bottom and right): 1. Niger River, 2. Gao, 3. Gao airport controlled by the UN, 4. UN Super Camp, 5. Camp Castor, 6. Tomb of Akia. In white stroke: areas controlled by MINUSMA.
Aerial view: Google Earth.

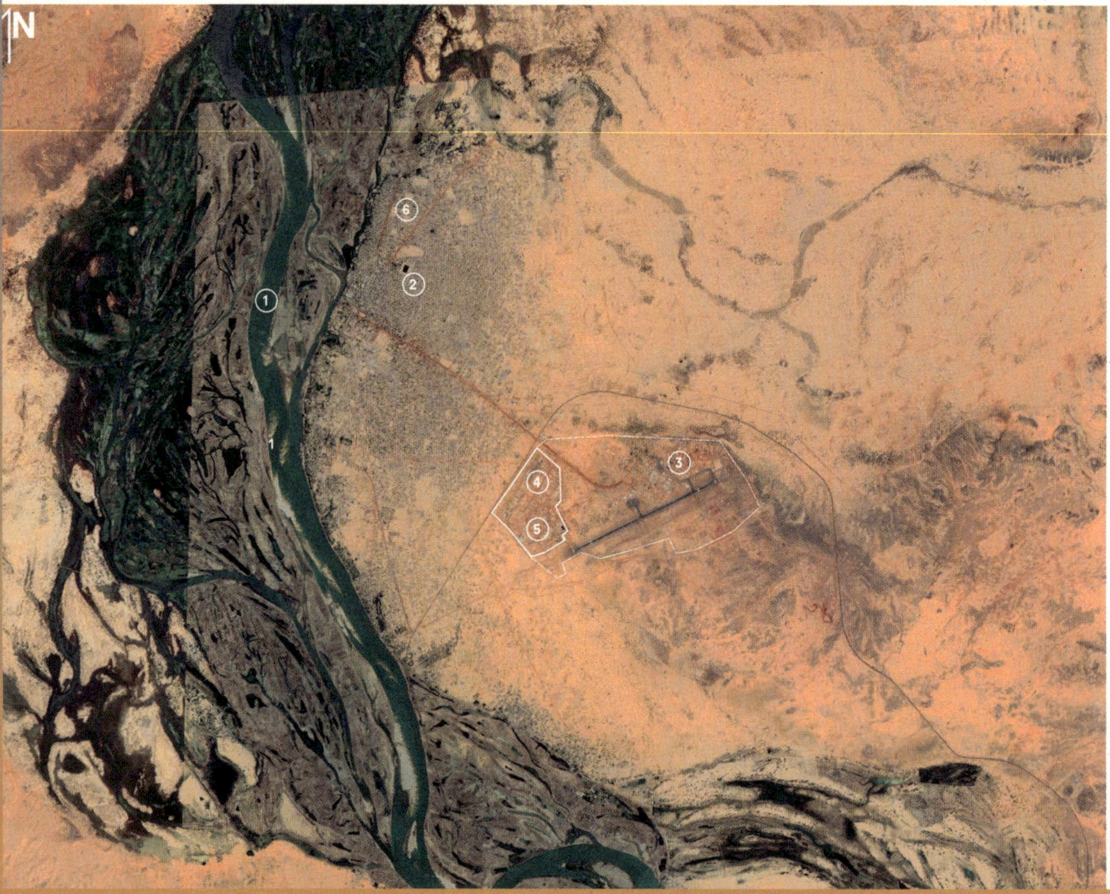

N
1
2
3
4
5

4
5

Airport terminal, Gao, 2016.

The entrance to the airport terminal. Gao, 2016.

An aerial view of MINUSMA
in Gao. Google Earth, 2020.

Dutch Military Engineering

Before visiting Mali, I had heard from UN officers at the Secretariat in NYC that Camp Castor was engineered as a state-of-the-art flawless machine. Since the inception of the UN, the Netherlands has contributed human and financial resources for its missions. Dutch army bases and mission compounds are designed by a military engineering unit that is located in a small town called Wezep in North Holland. I visited this unit a few times between 2012 and 2016 and met with the people who designed Camp Castor. On the way to Wezep from Amsterdam, I passed through Naarden, a fortified garrison town and an example of a star-fort typology. Naarden was one element of a spatial system that formed the country's military defensive line. It included inundation zones, fortified towns, forts, barracks, and other military structures. Amsterdam, the city where I was living at the time, was also engineered according to this Dutch Defense strategy. Its defensive belt consisted of circular-shaped canals and forts that protected the city. Large areas along the city's walls were designed to be flooded in times of war. Today this old formation in Amsterdam is recognized as a UNESCO World Heritage Site.

In the 15th century, Simon Stevin conceived and designed many of the forts along the Dutch Defense Line. Stevin was a "mathematician and highly influential figure in Maurice's army reforms. He introduced the decimal system, applied rigorous accountancy to the army's bookkeeping, produced standard designs for camps and fortifications, and, to ensure reliable maps for the army, in 1600, he founded a chair for land-surveying at Leiden University."[52] Together with other scientists, engineers, and visual artists, he designed fortifications and used illustrations, drawings, and paintings to demonstrate how they could be inserted at various scales into the Dutch landscape and function in times of war and in times of peace. When Stevin presented his book on the art of war to Prince Maurice, he thought it necessary to say, "I do not wish you to reckon me among the simple sham fighters," which is to say those "who only study Euclidian principles."[53] Mathematicians, scientists, and inventors like Stevin, Schooten, and Christiaan Huygens were concerned not only with theory but also with the implementation of their inventions in practice and the complexity of a lived world. Thus, his ideas and drawings were conceived to be constructed. Stevin was an expert in mechanical, hydraulic, naval, and, above all, military engineering. He designed not only fortifications but also the logistics of camps, the formations of armed soldiers, and the planning of sieges.[54]

Pieter Snyers, a war artist, depicted vast landscapes in his oil paintings occupied by forts and other forms of life, such as local inhabitants, camps, travelers, and nature. In these paintings, technology, science, geography, engineering knowledge, architecture, and wildlife were composed into one complex environment, offering a vision not only of a place or a discovery, but of the spirit of a new era, and new ways to view, relate to, and design the world. It was the origin of the order, grids, and mathematical relationships that Le Corbusier celebrated in *Toward a New Architecture*.[55] It was also the beginning of modernity: the inception of cartography and a controlled landscape inhabited by nodes of supply chains and infrastructure and extracted accordingly. There was a direct relationship and contingency, here and in the future

to come, between military engineering, technological innovation, global extraction, and finance. It was the beginning not only of modernity but of globalization. While in the 16th century, science was conceived as an integrated system that transcended (contemporary) disciplinary boundaries and scales, in the modern era and today, those comprehensive approaches have been fragmented into strictly defined siloed bodies of knowledge and practices.

When I arrived at the Engineers' unit in Wezep, I met Camp Castor's lead designers; they shared their evolving experiences and some of their main challenges over the past decades. Following the end of the Cold War, the unit had to reinvent its approach to missions and its deployment methods in order to address new global agendas and urgencies.

At the time of our visit to Mali in March 2016, Camp Castor was staffed by about 450 Dutch soldiers, it was being enlarged to accommodate the newly arriving German troops, who would replace the Dutch some years later.

52 Stevin, Simon. "Weapon and Warfare," available at: https://weaponsandwarfare.com/2019/03/23/simon-stevin-c-1548-1620.
53 Kemp, Martin. "Simon Stevin and Pieter Saenredam: A Study of Mathematics and Vision in Dutch Science and Art." The Art Bulletin, vol. 68, no. 2, 1986, pp. 237–252. Ulrike Gehring and Peter Weibel (Eds.) Mapping Spaces. Networks of Knowledge in 17th Century Landscape Painting.
54 Stevin, Simon. "Weapon and Warfare," available at: https://weaponsandwarfare.com/2019/03/23/simon-stevin-c-1548-1620.
55 See Tents on page 89.

Imagery of MINUSMA's bases in Gao. FAST/Laura van Santen, 2016.

MINUSMA's imagery. FAST/Laura van Santen, 2016.

Aerial imagery of MINUSMA's bases in Gao. FAST/Laura van Santen, 2016.

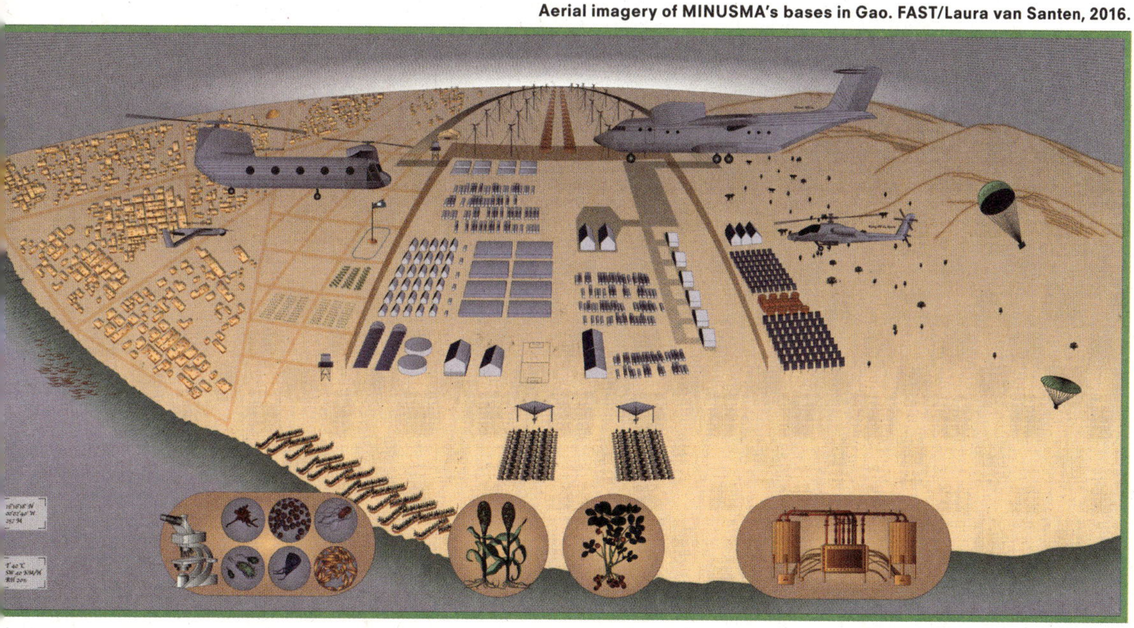

Age of Experimentation

Marcel Rot

During the Cold War, the Netherlands' army had little to no experience in constructing military bases in mission areas. After the Berlin wall fell, the focus shifted to peacekeeping and peace-enforcing operations across the world, starting in Bosnia. The Dutch Army had to learn how to do this. Only a few people who had been in Lebanon (1979–1985) had some experience. Other missions, like the ones in Indonesia and Korea, were too far in the past. The only civil engineering experience available was in laying or clearing minefields, destroying bridges or building them.

In Bosnia, the Dutch army had to learn to construct bases and maintain them. There was so little knowledge that, literally, folders were picked up at the local hardware shop with tips and tools on a wide range of topics. It was an age of experimentation, in which the army had to reinvent itself. After a while, the army realized that it needed more educated people and a kind of center of excellence in military constructions. This realization evolved into the Engineer Works Force as it is today, where most of the people have a civil diploma in construction or energy management.

Currently, new missions and the development of bases around the world are well planned and prepared. There are units with a focus on building, maintaining, and tearing down military infrastructure. If knowledge and/or capacity is lacking, the army uses local contractors to assist.

Marcel Rot is one of Camp Castor's lead military engineers.

Model. Venice Architecture Biennale, 2016.

The first Dutch base after the end of the Cold War with a flag of Gamma, a Dutch retailer from the home improvement sector for construction products and services.

An improvised toilet at a Dutch peacekeeping base in Bosnia.

An improvised observation post at a Dutch peacekeeping base in Bosnia.

An improvised watch tower at a Dutch peacekeeping base in Bosnia.

Among Soldiers

Arnon Grunberg

"The future we saw as belonging to us, a thing contested by no one, the war as a tempestuous prelude to happiness, and happiness itself as a part of our character," wrote Isaac Babel in one of his stories about the Soviet-Polish War of 1920. War, that tempestuous prelude to happiness, had eluded me so far. The wrong time, the wrong place, the same old story.

Yet fate is pliable.

At one thirty on a midsummer Tuesday afternoon I made my way to the Eindhoven airbase, from where I would fly to Kabul. Then to Kandahar. And perhaps on to Tarin Kowt, depending on the security situation, as the defense department put it. The 'security situation', a term open to interpretation. I was not going as a soldier, not even as a spiritual adviser; after having been declared unfit for duty at the age of eighteen, that would have been too much to hope for. A psychiatrist had written a letter, and a few weeks later I was notified that the Kingdom of the Netherlands would not call upon me, not even in times of war.

I was traveling as an 'embedded journalist'. What 'embedded' meant was as yet unclear, and calling me a 'journalist' was rather dubious. But, like 'security situation', 'journalist' is a term open to interpretation.

...

After half an hour the outbound soldiers – army, air force and military police – separated themselves from those who were to be left behind. The men and women in desert-colored uniforms walked with me to the check-in desk. Those military personnel in uniforms more suited for service in the rainforest remained behind.

I was the only person in line not in uniform. Wait, no, not the only one. A young man in civilian dress, a journalist for the regional broadcaster in Overijssel Province, was going to Afghanistan as well. "I'm planning to talk mostly to soldiers from Overijssel," he told me. "What's your angle?"

My angle. That I was going along to experience that tempestuous prelude to happiness seemed better left unsaid. "The person behind the soldier," I mumbled. That always worked, the person behind.

The boarding area where we found ourselves was no different from boarding areas at other airports. Normal airports, from which people left on holiday. War, though, is a kind of holiday as well. As one soldier in Afghanistan would tell me later: "It sounds weird, but I relax here."

"With us it's just like with Ryanair," Captain Cynthia said. "The first one in gets the best seat."

...

I ended up at last beside a real Dutch solider, Tinus, who after an hour's silence asked: "What are you going to do in Afghanistan?"

"I'm going to try to understand the mission," I whispered, whereupon Sergeant Jordy, sitting in the row in front of us, joined in the conversation.

The sergeant held up a wedge of cheese, as though it were the spoils of war.

"Why are you taking cheese to Afghanistan?" I asked.

"Because I love cheese," the sergeant said.

"I've got enough with me for the first few weeks, and after that they're going to send me more from Holland. I told everyone, my girlfriend, my family, my friends: "Just send cheese." In Afghanistan it melts, but that doesn't matter; it's vacuum-packed anyway. You just put it in a refrigerator and it gets hard again. After that all it needs is a good whack and it's back in shape."

"Have you been to Afghanistan before?" I inquired.

"Twice," the sergeant said, "but this time I brought a cheese-slicer." He grinned triumphantly. Then, as though relating confidential information, he said: "Once they find out you have cheese, everyone wants a piece. But if you let them cut the cheese with a pocketknife, it's gone before you know it. This time I brought a cheese-slicer, so everyone gets a thin slice, you know what I mean? So, this time they won't eat all my cheese right in front of me."
I felt a fondness for this Sergeant Jordy, who would not be entering Afghanistan unprepared. For the first time on this trip I sensed that my hunch had been right. I was going to find out something about the happiness that had eluded me all these years.

A few hours later, Captain Cynthia arranged for me to sit beside Lieutenant-Colonel Nico. An army marches on more than cheese-slicers alone. Lieutenant-Colonel Nico is a tall, athletically built man of around 40, but you could only mistake him for a gym teacher if you didn't look carefully. He commands a tank battalion. He was going to Afghanistan, however, without his tanks. The men of the 'PRTs' are recruited from within the tank battalions. PRT stands for Provincial Reconstruction Team. The army exists by virtue of abbreviation. Rarely have I picked up as many abbreviations as during my stay in Afghanistan. 'Lupa' is a lunch packet, 'detco' a detachment commander. The amount of time that saves is staggering. From now on, happiness would be just plain 'hap'.

Lieutenant-Colonel Nico had always been an

idealist, and that hadn't changed. He had originally joined the army because the Russians were coming. Within two hours, he and his tanks could be at the former East German border. He had aerial photos to show where each tank was to be positioned. Everything was laid out, down to the last square inch. But the Russians never showed up.

Lieutenant-Colonel Nico speaks of tanks with such sincere affection that I began loving them as well. I discovered that a tank can be as much a thing of beauty as a well-written novel.

Nico said: "If it hadn't been for that cabinet crisis, maybe we'd be going to Iraq right now. When you've been training all the time, at some point you want to find out how good you are at the real thing. When you write all the time, at some point you want to find out what your book does to an audience, right?"

I nodded in complete understanding. That was certainly something I wanted to find out, and I could imagine that he wanted to find that out as well. No more practicing anymore, time for the real thing at last. Maybe that's the problem with literature: it never becomes the real thing.

At least not entirely.

"But don't you find it a pity that you're being sent to Afghanistan to talk?"
I asked.

Lieutenant-Colonel Nico had told me that the PRTs would mostly talk to the Afghanis. Talk till they were blue in the face. Reconstruction is a matter of endless conversation. Of gaining the people's confidence, or, as the official phrase goes: "winning hearts and minds".

For a person who has seen the beauty in a tank, who had actually convinced me that a tank is more beautiful than the Virgin Mary, that could not be an easy assignment. But the lieutenant-colonel kept a stiff upper lip. He and his men were looking forward to the mission, even without their tanks.

"And what about Srebrenica?" I asked, because I didn't want the conversation to peter out, not yet. I wanted to go on, on with the tanks across the plains of Germany. "Is that still a trauma?"

The lieutenant-colonel shook his head. "Not for these boys," he said. "If there's one thing they have no intention of being, it's cowards. Back before seatbelts were mandatory, scads of people were killed in traffic accidents. Everyone thought that was normal.

Would a fireman refuse to go into a burning building just because there's a chance that he might not come out alive?"

Now I knew why he didn't look like a gym teacher. Everywhere the lieutenant-colonel turned, he saw death creeping up on him. He was braced for the ambush. That's how he'd looked at me as well, like an ambush.

"Did your wife take you to the airport?" I asked. "No," the lieutenant-colonel said. "That's always a bad idea. I have a buddy who's in the army too. When he goes, I take him to the airport. When I go, he takes me. I say goodbye to my family at home. It's not fair to them to do that, to drag them along to the airport like that."

I nodded, thinking about the little boy dressed up like a soldier who had been running around the departure hall.

"It's getting dark," Nico said. "That goes pretty quickly now. I'm going to catch a few winks."

I wondered whether the lieutenant-colonel really would catch a few winks, and if he did whether he would dream about Afghanistan, or still about the plains of Germany. And about his tanks, which would be at the former East German border within two hours. Not as a maneuver this time, but the real thing. Maybe the Russians would show up anyway. You can never tell. Anything is possible. The world may smell of the abattoir, but the air force KDC-10 smelled of cheese.

"I'm going to try to catch a little sleep too," I whispered. I went back to my seat. Sergeant Jordy had his eyes closed. In his left hand he was clutching an iPod.

Arnon Grunberg is a Dutch writer of novels, essays, and columns, as well as a journalist. He wrote some of his work under the heteronym Marek van der Jagt. The text above includes excerpts from the Literary Journalism Studies, originally published in NRC Handelsblad, May 1, 2010

The Legacy of Compounds Workshop. HNI. Rotterdam, 2014.

Setting up Camp Castor. Courtesy the Dutch Ministry of Defense, 2014.

Camp Castor

Camp Castor is situated next to Gao's airport. In 2016, it was staffed mainly by Dutch peacekeepers, who were also soldiers in the Dutch army. Many of them had been deployed previously on NATO missions in Afghanistan, Iraq, and the Balkans.

Castor is designed almost as a self-sustained island.[56] Although Gao's neighborhoods are fewer than 100 meters away from its edges, their proximity was not taken into account in the design of the base. To the peacekeepers, Gao's localities appear very remote, as they rarely leave the base during their deployment, if at all. Thus, they seldomly see or engage with the city and its inhabitants.[57]

Design

During the research phase of this project, in 2012–2014, we held a series of conversations and workshops to discuss the legacy of UN bases with the Dutch military engineers. They suggested taking Camp Castor in Gao, which they were designing at that time, as a case study. For one of the workshops, I asked the military engineers to bring drawings of the base at various scales—from 1:200 to 1:10,000—to examine its relationship with the surrounding urban context. I also invited an economist, a landscape designer, an architect, an urban planner, an anthropologist, a human rights activist, and diplomats from the Ministry of Foreign Affairs to the session, with the aim of exploring the base from a comprehensive perspective. I wondered whether urban spatial analysis and design methods could foster a better alignment between the UN base and its socioeconomic, spatial, and ecological impacts on its surrounding environment. The engineers provided the group with the drawings, but the city was absent from all of them; it remained blank on all scales and had not been taken into account at any point in the design phase. One of the participating engineers explained their considerations:

> The engineering corps workforce designs bases from the macro to the micro level—the entire compound and all of its elements. The design and construction of the base are carried out under inevitable time pressure and in terms of what is practical and fast. A lot of the equipment and regulations used are still based on the Cold War era. However, we realized that an automatic fast and efficient response doesn't tick all the mission boxes. These days, missions are more complex, and the infrastructure is further tailor-made. As a result, we are increasingly relying on outside expertise.[58]

While the Dutch army researches a mission before the operation starts, it relies on third parties. The Civic Military Cooperation (CMIC) organization has undertaken local inventories for all operations since Afghanistan. It advises on local power structures and crime rates, food availability, essential contacts, and so on. Camp Castor's design began after the Dutch government made a political decision to contribute to MINUSMA in December 2013. One of the engineers said, "The camp had to accommodate special forces, helicopters, and intelligence operations; each has a specific functionality. We have to reduce the requirements to essential needs because of time concerns and budget restrictions." The engineer continued,

> The UN finances the camp, and in fact, it should have provided us with a ready-made camp, but since the UN could not produce it on time, the Dutch government proposed that we should take the initiative and build the camp faster. The UN peace operation department agreed that we'll

56 The base's water supply is extracted from the local aquifer, wastewater is released into the local soil, certain materials are precured locally too.

57 And yet, peacekeepers on missions have been accused time and again of sexual abuse. Since the inception of MINUSMA in 2013 "The United Nations mission in Mali has received allegations of serious misconduct by its peacekeeping troops last week, including an alleged incident of sexual abuse", see: https://news.un.org/en/story/2013/09/449892." And: "Sexual abuse by UN peacekeepers is shocking and shameful. Why does it persist?", see: www.abc.net.au/news/2020-06-15/united-nations-un-peacekeeping-sexual-exploitation-abuse/12286664.

58 "Reimagining Peacekeeping Missions: Legacy Scenarios for Camp Castor", Het Nieuwe Instituut, January 2015, available at: https://drones-honeycombs.hetnieuweinstituut.nl/sites/default/files/workshop_report._gao_legacy.pdf.

> build and they will reimburse for what it would have otherwise provided itself. The allocation of land is usually decided by the local government and provided by an urban planning council. We get a square on a map and that's it—this is where we build.[59]

59 Ibid.
60 Ibid.
61 Ibid.

On the ground, the first stage involves working on security, the perimeter, and communication. In the past, the site would have been cleared, but at Camp Castor, "for the first time, we deliberately chose to leave the trees and vegetation as much as possible."[60] Work on stage one of the camps began with locally available materials and equipment. The prices of local construction materials, such as wood and metal wire became inflated very quickly, as the bases consumed it all. Although much had to be imported from the Netherlands, the transit time was simply too long to wait for it to arrive (the route is Rotterdam to Dakar by sea, and then Bamako to Gao by road, as the Niger River is navigable only after the rains in July and August).

The base design system acknowledges different tiers (reflecting levels of comfort): from Tier 1, a temporary camp, to Tier 4, a permanent base (a great rarity). Camp Castor, operational as a mission from April 2014, is Tier 3 (which carries a lifespan, generally, from 6 to 18 months). Usually, a mission is a one-year commitment, although this period is often extended. With longer stays, "any planning dialogue would probably be conducted with the city by the UN," according to one of the engineers, rather than by the base itself.

The first camp, complete with tents and a small R&R facility, was ready for the 400 first arrivals in April. This led to a whole raft of new influences on the design, as "all the unit commanders try to get the best they can for their unit, claiming operational necessity." However, while the design of the camp was ongoing, it also remained isolated and unconnected to the local infrastructure: "The camp is an island."

Over time, the base evolved, adding accommodation (containers with an armored shell on top) and large tents for sports activities and maintenance. One engineer said: "The thinking is only in terms of military functionalities; these lead the design. We're talking about a time-driven, 'convenient' design. Actually, it's design during build." The materials used to construct the base are redeployed where possible and economically feasible. If this is not possible, they are resold locally or otherwise deconstructed and disposed of. It is assumed that the tents and containers of Camp Castor will be shipped back to the Netherlands, but "we'll probably leave the sewage and power systems and the fence and roads—the decision whether to leave or break up the remains of the camp is a decision made by the military in The Hague, but we advise on this." "Then," commented one of the designers, "you should construct the sewers as they do locally, in Mali," to ensure that they can be taken over and maintained at the end of the mission. The cost impact of this would likely be small; however, a complicating factor is that "different organizations donate deployment and exploitation costs," said the engineer. Building to a higher, or local, standard would not cost much more, but there is an issue of controllability and motivation. "For example, when the UN pays for diesel, what incentive is there to invest in solar power?"[61] The engagement with the engineers made it clear that the base was designed and perceived as a self-contained machine, rather than a large-scale space being inserted into an existing inhabited fabric. The complexity remained only internal, with references to UN, NATO security protocols, bureaucracy, finance, and procurement constraints; all the external indicators, the city, its inhabitants, and the natural environment were blanked out.

Entrance. Camp Castor. Gao, 2016.

Expansion of Camp Castor. Gao, 2016.

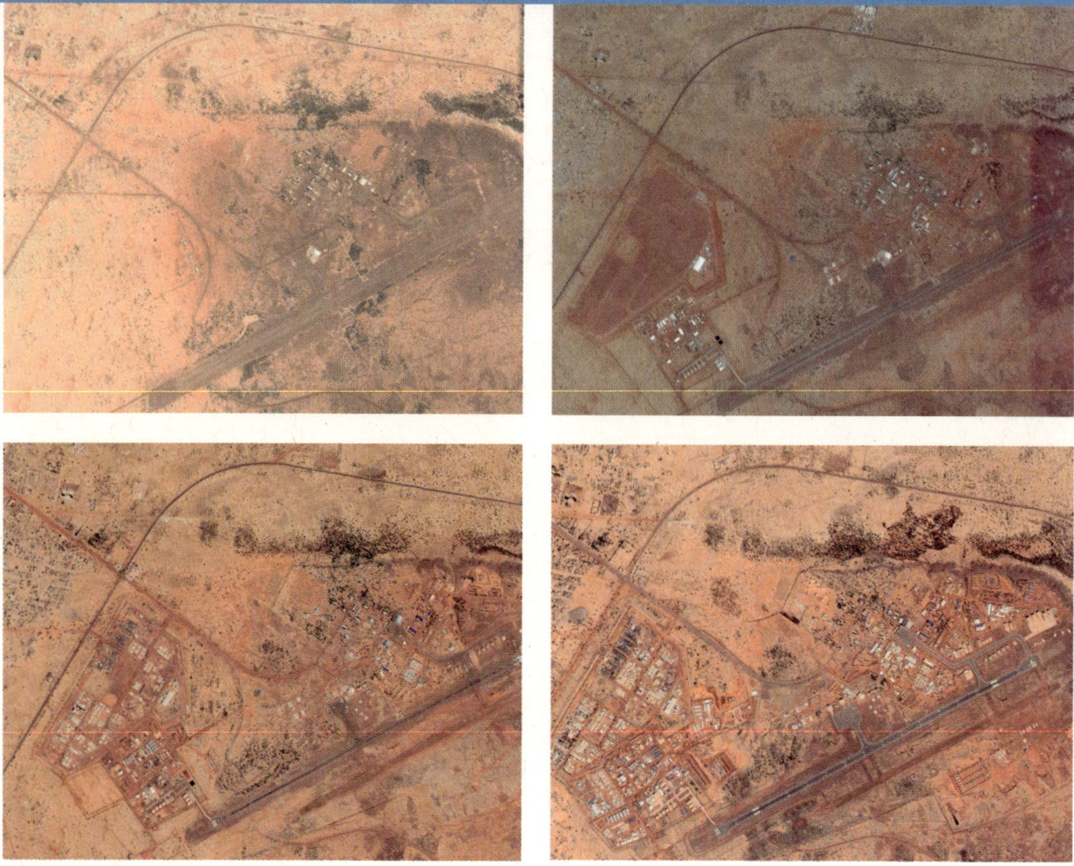

Right to left: MINUSMA Presence in Gao over the years 2012, 2014, 2016, 2019. Aerial view: Google Earth.

Meeting with a military engineer. Camp Castor. Gao, 2016.

Deployment

According to the engineers, during its initial deployment phase, Camp Castor was composed of tents and improvised office space comprised of "plug-and-play containers" with no foundations. Everything was planned to be taken back to the Netherlands at the end of the mission. Dutch engineers used soil and local techniques to compress laterite roads. However, the helipad was constructed of concrete imported from the Netherlands. The fencing around the base's perimeter was built of locally available materials such as concrete, wood, and metal wires, which inflated local prices of construction supplies. The camp's first iteration included tents and a small rest-and-recuperation facility to accommodate the arrival of the first 400 peacekeepers.

Camp Castor's electricity was at first provided only by the UN's gas and oil generators. Yet it was slowly complemented by a set of solar panels as the Dutch contingent attempted to increase the use of renewable energy (see page 180). While electricity within the base was available continuously, Gao's local system was capable of providing power for its citizens for just a few hours a day. At an early stage of the mission, wells were dug by the UN and by Dutch engineers to allow immediate access to water. Sewage, water, electricity, and telecommunications pipes and cables were installed between 1.7 and 2.5 meters underground. An assortment of filters was installed at the base's edge to treat wastewater, and three large pools were dug to collect the treated water. Within the camp, a system of flood protection channels was dug.

The base's infrastructure evolved over time, and accommodation containers replaced the tents with armored shells on top for protection against rockets. Parts of these structures were transported to Mali from Afghanistan, where the Dutch contingent was deployed in the NATO-led International Security Assistance Force. The metal prefabricated frames and sheets have limited thermal insulation, and the hot summer at the edge of the desert requires extensive use of air conditioning. Locally produced compressed red bricks could reduce the mission's environmental footprint by improving thermal insulation in the various structures, reducing the use of air conditioning and contributing to local employment and capacity building.

Through the colder months, the base's average electrical power consumption is about 450 megawatt-hours/month. In summer, this doubles to almost 900. In 2017, the average number of peacekeepers in Camp Castor was about 1,100. They used about 8,500 megawatt-hours yearly, of which 370 are generated by solar panels and the rest by generators. Water consumption in Camp Castor comprises drinking water that is bottled and brought into the base by its supply chain; other water usage for showers, cooking, and cleaning is restricted to 100 liters per person per day—20 liters over the limit prescribed by the UN. This is about 1,100,000 liters of water extracted daily from the aquifer.[62]

Although the UN sets the design and regulatory framework in advance, technological know-how and equipment quality and materials among the different TCCs are uneven. The Dutch military engineers work within the scope and design regulations of the UN. Yet their base looked different from other camps deployed by UN TCCs such as the Bangladeshi, Senegalese, or Nepalese because they added infrastructure and items to meet Dutch deployment standards. As a result, UN bases are distinct from one another in their appearance, approach, and legacy as well as in their environmental footprint.

62 Data provided by the Dutch Military Corp of Engineers.

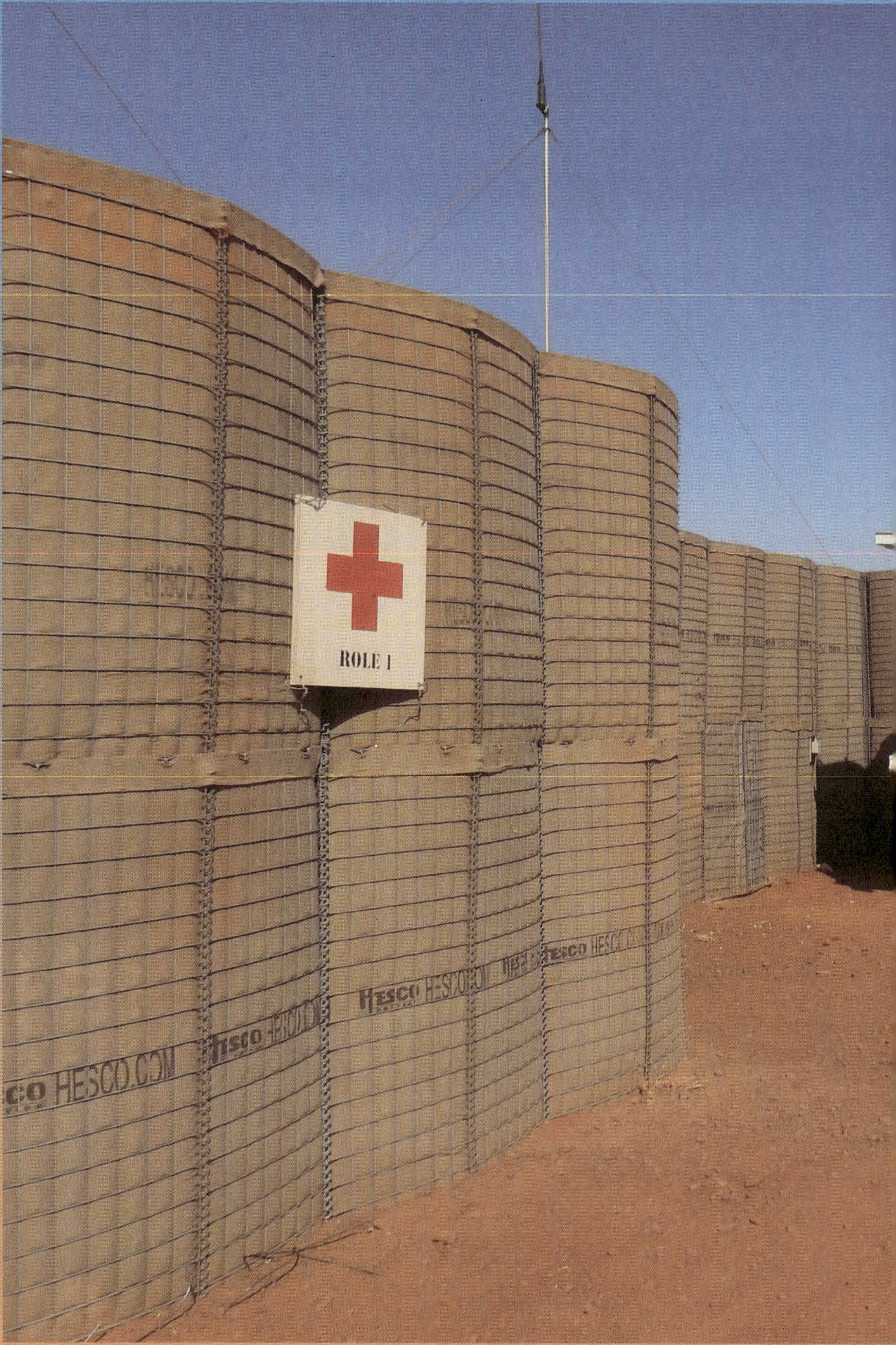
ROLE 1
HESCO HESCO.COM

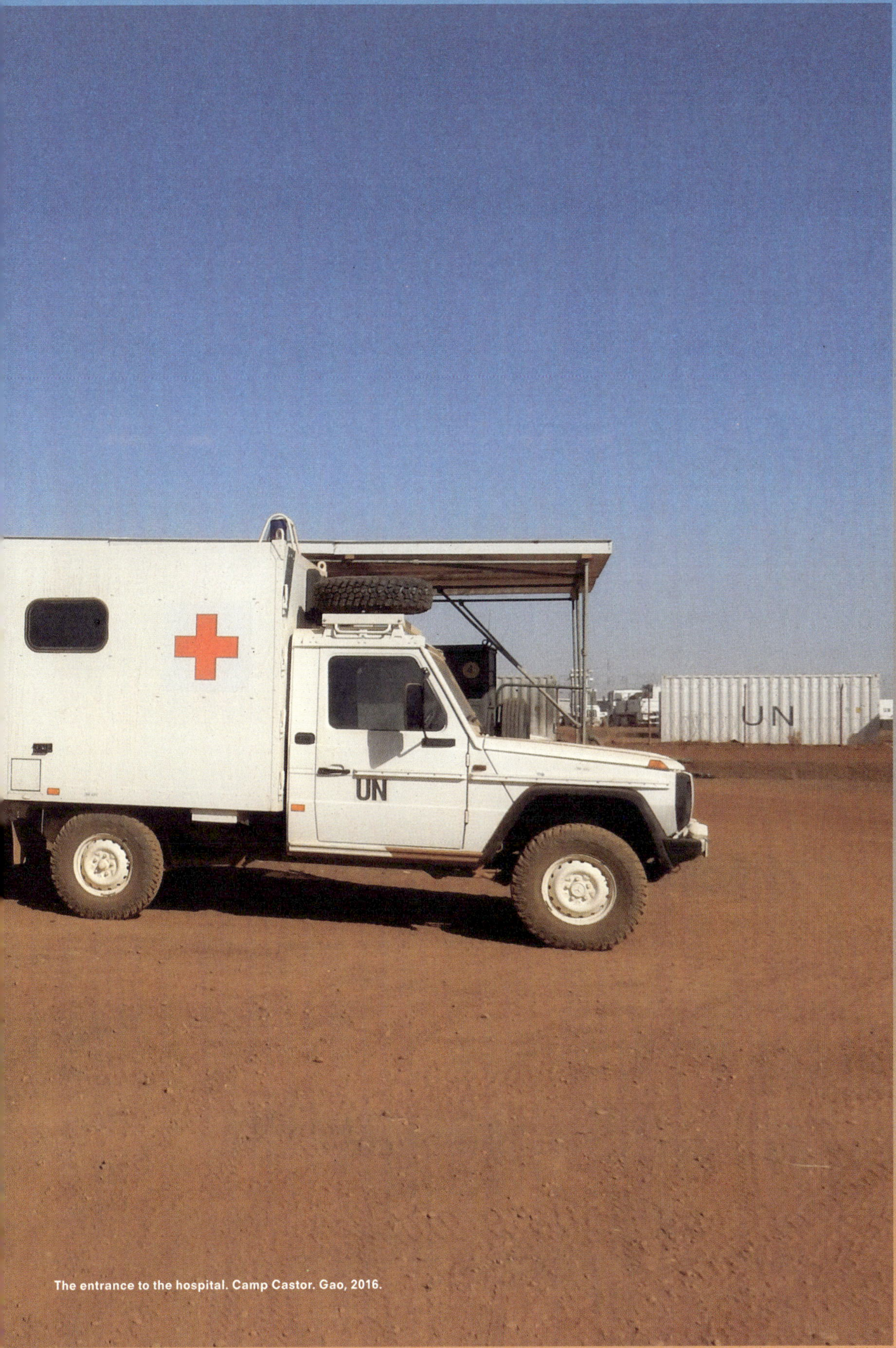

The entrance to the hospital. Camp Castor. Gao, 2016.

A hybrid solar and oil generator. Camp Castor, 2016

A flood protection drainage system. Camp Castor, 2016.

Generators. Camp Castor, 2016.

Wastewater treatment. Camp Castor, 2016

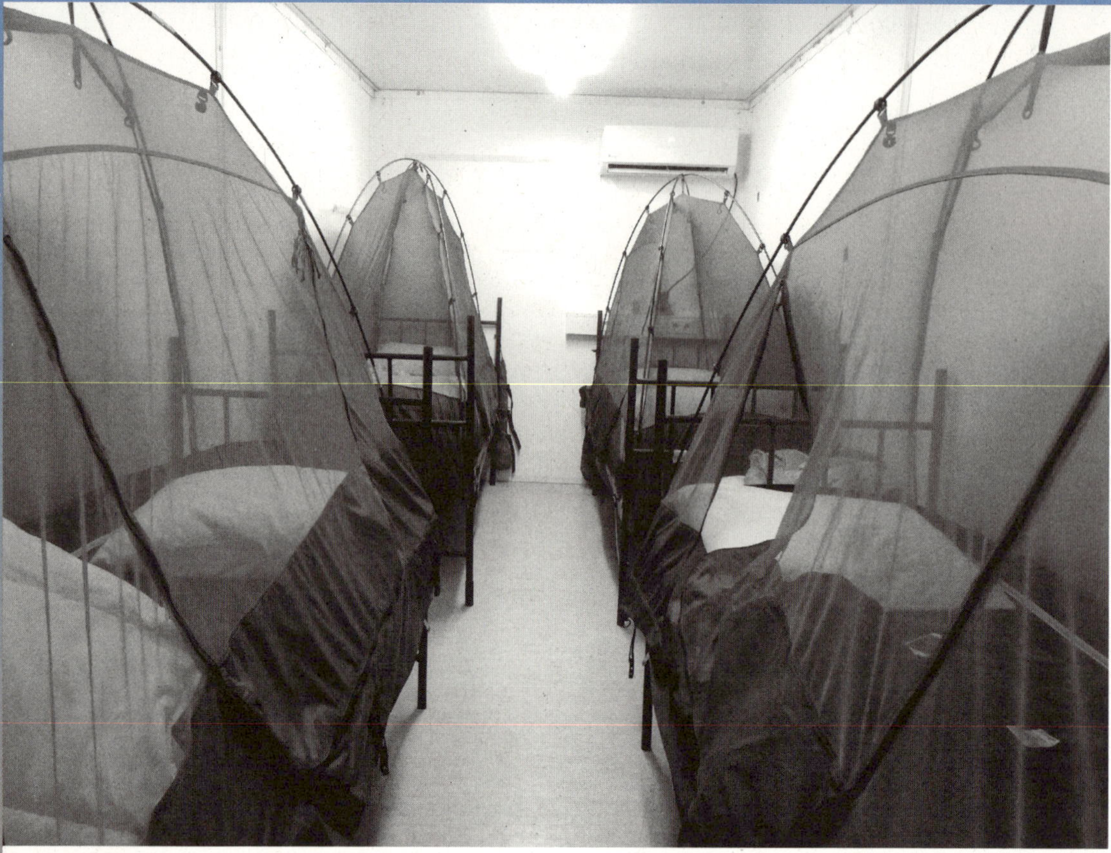

Sheltered rooms were formerly used by the Dutch army in Afghanistan. Camp Castor, 2016.

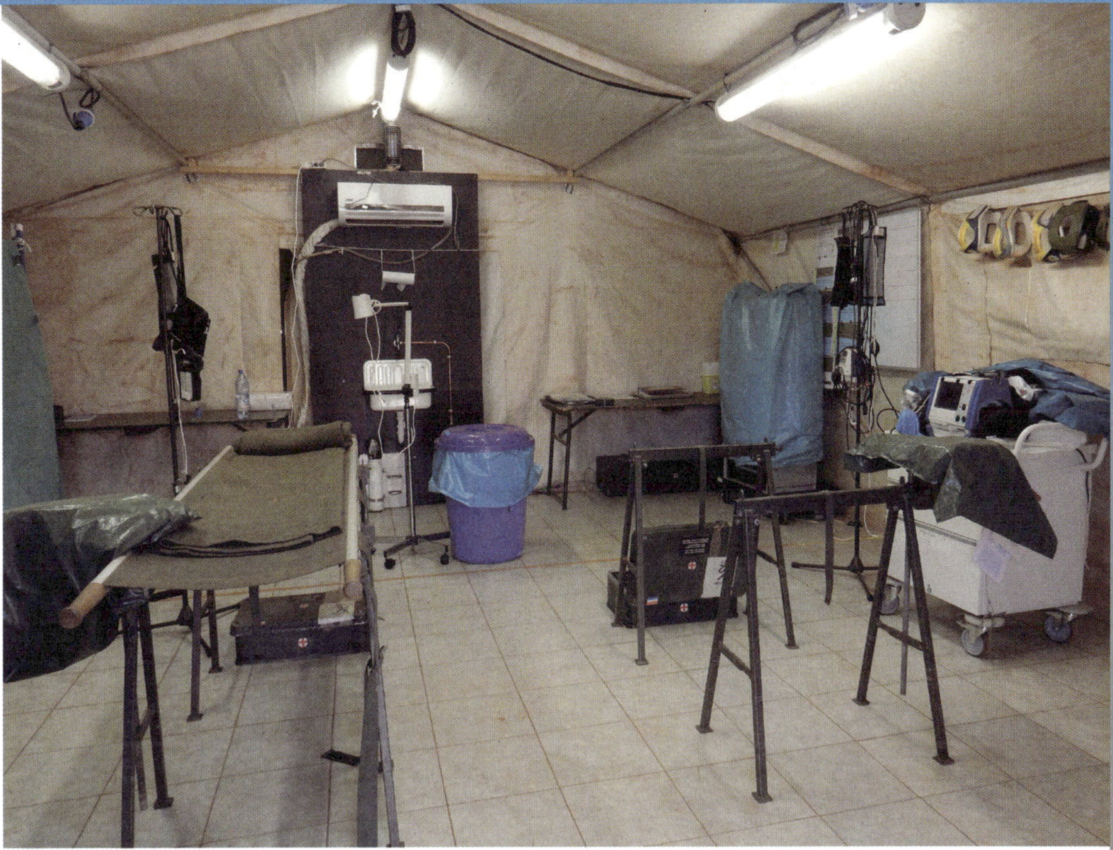

A field clinic and operating room. Camp Castor, 2016.

Workshop. Camp Castor, 2016.

The Jewels of Castor. Model. Venice Architecture Biennale, 2016.

The "Jewels of Castor"

Toward the end of our stay in Camp Castor, the Colonel who commanded the base invited us to join him for a walk. As we toured around, he pointed out the fence that separated Castor from the UN super camp. He showed us an area within the base that incorporated former local houses that had been damaged during the war, highlighting the legacy potential of these spaces. He wondered aloud, "What if we turn them into schools or community centers for the locals and hand it over to them in better shape?" He took us to areas at the fence between Camp Castor and the UN super camp, pointing out the UN engineers' design mistakes and musing about how the Dutch could have done better.

Proudly attesting to the Dutch soldiers' enormous creativity, he took us into a restricted zone, a secured island within the base, where the air force unit resided. This area was hidden from the engineers' eyes, controls, and protocols. The Colonel smiled at us and said, "You are about to see the 'Jewels of Castor.'" The air force unit had found a creative way to spend their extended solitary time in the desert. We passed the gate and entered the restricted zone. The Colonel led us toward a narrow and out-of-place stone path that we followed curiously. We began to hear the sound of running water as we passed a few large bright green plants and entered into a carefully decorated patio. At its center was a garden, complete with tropical plants and an artificial waterfall. The trail continued past the patio, heading to another installation—a wide wooden cabin with large sheets of white canvas attached to its unglazed open façade. As the fabric blew softly in the desert wind, it resembled a yoga retreat hut. We wandered past the cabin and back onto the narrow path; there was yet another peculiar-looking garden. The tropical style was replaced by a different atmosphere, like somewhere in the Arizona desert or a Western movie set. There was a wooden horse, accompanied by a large DIY totem and two fake palm trees adorned with finely detailed leaves and coconuts. The final spectacle of the *sprookjesbos* (Dutch for fairytale forest, and the name given to this area by the Dutch soldiers) was a shaded gathering space furnished as a beach bar. The front was painted in red, white, and blue stripes (the colors of the Dutch flag); fake orange trees, with oranges, were fastened to a large front opening; and at the top of the façade was a bit of irony: a "free Wi-Fi" sign (it was, of course, the most classified and restricted zone on the base) from where UN's drone espionage missions were launched.

It was a long trip, and we spent many hours under the sun. The desert can be elusive; we weren't certain if we were hallucinating—caught by a Fata Morgana, a mirage, or a Flying Dutchman. Strolling through these artifacts made the distance between body and thought, city and wilderness, reality and imagination, disappear. We were surrounded by machine guns, tanks, drones, Apache helicopters, and an intoxicating smell of diesel. It was an encounter between different orders: the Dutch approach and the desert, war and peace. It revealed humanity, with all its creativity, beauty, and violence.

Staging of an exotic garden. Airforce unit. Camp Castor, 2016.

Staging of a totem, windmill, and Old West horse. Airforce unit. Camp Castor, 2016.

Staging of a cafe, a beach bar, and two fake palms. Camp Castor, 2016.

Stills from "Overview Construction Camp Castor" by Mediacenter Ministry of Defense. 2014

Luitenant-kolonel Nicole De Wolf
Commandant Joint Support Detachment
LUCHTMACHT
ROYAL NETHERLANDS AIR FORCE

Traffic island and UN flag in front of MINUSMA's offices at the super camp. Gao, 2016.

UN Super Camp and Global Supply Chains

When in Gao, we visited another UN super camp that shared a fence with Camp Castor. The two bases surrounded Gao's airport, and together they formed an extensive UN-controlled island that was equal in size to about a third of the city. The super camp was vast and mostly under construction, like the one in Bamako. The base's entrance was a long corridor formed by a sequence of fences, gates, and armed patrols. Once passing this surveilled passage, another more symbolic ingress appeared: a roundabout—a traffic island confined by civic looking curbstones painted blue and white. At its center was a high pole with a large blue UN flag. A sandy landscape, scattered modular offices, and a singular nomadic tent surrounded the roundabout. The latter looked out of place. Perhaps local workers found the container less attractive than the desert tent. Around the traffic island, one direction led to a vast parking lot and another to an endless field of blue and white containers. It resembled a seaport. The innumerable containers had transported materials and equipment from across the world to Dakar's seaport in Senegal. From there, they were carried by trucks to Gao.

The super camp and its scale are a product of the free market economy and its global supply chain; its typology is an emblem of an economy of growth. Its design codes and protocols are similar to other mega spaces: extrastatecraft,[63] or "meta-infrastructures administered by public and private cohorts, and driven by profound irrationalities," as Keller Easterling refers to it when describing special economic zones and the international logistic hubs and networks that enable their existence. The super camp is a type of exception zone. It is isolated and fenced off. Its presence is a cultural distinction. It follows a model and method that resonate far beyond its porous boundaries. It embodies the scale and aesthetic of global procurement. It has nothing to do with the local situation, let alone a beautiful ancient desert city: the gateway to the Sahara Desert.

The spatiality of globalization defies the linear distinction between place and space, as argued by Ash Amin.[64] Globalization defined the spatially of contemporary social organization, the meaning of place, and space is more associated with the constant flow of people, goods, ideas, and information, aided by rapid transport and communication technologies. In fact, one of the UN agencies is actually a global service center (UNGSC),[65] founded 15 years ago, just after the big financial crisis of 2008. With two large hubs in Brindisi (Italy) and Valencia (Spain), it provides critical logistics, geospatial information, telecommunications technologies services, and training to all UN Secretariat entities, agencies, funds, and programs worldwide. Its three core services are 1) supply chain service (SCS); 2) service for geospatial, information, and telecommunication technologies (SGITT); and 3) central service (CS). It manages a budget of US$63 million. It includes 446 posts and maintains 76 buildings on two main sites. The UNGSC website presents a comprehensive catalog of thousands of items worth US$826 million, including containers, hangars, water pumps, vehicles, showers, kitchens, desks, coolers, beds, generators, helmets, megaphones, office supplies, and computers.

According to Mary Kaldor, globalization contributes to the shaping of new wars, their politics, economy, logistics, and multitude of impacts:

> Processes known as globalization are breaking up the cultural and socioeconomic divisions that defined the patterns of politics which characterized the modern period. The new type of warfare has to be understood in terms of this global dislocation. New forms of power struggle may take the guise of traditional nationalism, tribalism, or religious fundamentalism, but they are, nevertheless, contemporary phenomena arising from

63 Easterling, Keller, Extrastatecraft: The Power of Infrastructure Space, London: Verso Books, 2016.

64 Amin, Ash. "Spatialities of Globalisation" Environment and Planning A: Economy and Space, vol. 34, no. 3, Mar. 2002, pp. 385–399.

65 The Supply Chain Service of the UNGSC works with the Missions and UNHQ to provide an agile and responsive supply chain. From sourcing, planning to delivery and return. The center equips and enables rapid deployment of start-up missions; it helps existing missions with planning, technical, engineering and environmental expertise, and assets management. It provides ground support and contributes to the global environmental and supply chain strategies in Peacekeeping and the Secretariat. The Supply Chain Service (SCS) offers a wide variety of services not only to the Peacekeeping and Political Missions, but also to other UN entities, including Funds, Programmes, and Agencies.
SGITT is the operational hub for the support and delivery of ICT services and solutions to field operations and it operates from two locations: UNSGC in Brindisi, Italy, and UNICTFV in Valencia, Spain. SGITT supports Peacekeeping operations, Special Political Missions, UN Agencies, Funds and Programmes with round-the-clock, high-availability and resilient information and communications technology, and geospatial information services. [...]
The Central Service is a hub that provides support services for UNGSC internal operations, such as finance, human resources, procurement, property management, conference and learning services, facilities management, security and other campus support activities, while operationalizing special programmes for the Secretariat and United Nations field missions in the area of occupational health and safety. [...] It acts in an enabling role, to allow the two service delivery pillars, namely Service for Geospatial, Information and Telecommunications Technologies (SGITT) and Supply Chain Service (SCS), as well as the several tenant units, to deliver their operational mandates. Available at: www.unlb.org.

contemporary causes and displaying new characteristics. Moreover, they are paralleled by a growing global consciousness and sense of global responsibility among an array of governmental and non-governmental institutions as well as individuals.[66]

Globalization is a process that is embodied in the spatiality it produces. According to David Held "it is formed by a multitude of relations and transactions... of transcontinental and interregional flows and networks of activity";[67] these are similarly visible in the UN base. The super camp is the result of a complex matrix of flow. Mobilized by United Nations agencies, it has a large-scale impact on many places that extend far beyond the base and the specific mission. It impacts the member states that contribute their forces to missions and the communities from which the peacekeepers arrive; it affects the economies in their countries of origins, which depend on the peacekeepers' income and remittance. The transnational labor is brought into mission areas by a network of subcontractors, which has a direct impact on local communities. These circular relations are vast and complex.

Global relations are also social connections. Their territorial location, distance, and borders do not have a consistent influence. In global space, "place" is not territorially fixed, physical distance is covered in virtually no time, and territorial frontiers present no particular impediment. A place is rooted in history, community, and geography—in contrast to space that is situated in a network of flow. A place is substantive; it is politically enabling and a lived realm, involving intimate experiences and feelings of belonging. While space has no tangible scale, "It is the realm of abstract principles, rules, rationality—science, administration, bureaucracy and institutions," Peter Taylor argued.[68] That said, the reality is much more complex; when an abstract protocol is materialized
in space, it becomes a place. It inhabits multiple systems and realities at once, perhaps as the Tuareg tent in the center of the super camp or the UN container that ended up replacing a tent and was used as a shelter for a local family in the center of Gao.

The super camp is made possible by the UNGSC. A vast-looking archipelago inhabited by the presence of various UN agencies, TCCs, and their sprawling sea of prefab structures, containers, and all sorts of machines. Yet the super camp looked more civic in its design than Camp Castor, which was conceptualized as a military compound. The super camp had some aesthetic touches, like traffic islands and sidewalks marked with edge stones painted blue and white. These were nowhere to be found in Castor or the Swedish transit camp back in Bamako. Upon our arrival, we were directed to meet the super camp logistics director, a UN employee with a lot of dreams and ambitions that had been quashed by the constraining institutional bureaucracy. Originally from the region, he felt that a connection with local community organizers and women's groups was imperative to the mission's success. Unfortunately, this was not part of his mandate, and the resources available to cultivate such relations and projects in the city were insignificant. He mentioned that, under the auspices of Quick Impact Projects (QIPs),[69] he had attempted to promote initiatives like financing the construction of small community playgrounds, which had proven difficult to sustain.

QIPs are small-scale, low-cost projects, funded by the missions. They are mostly ad-hoc with no long-term or strategic objectives besides building confidence in the mission, its mandate, and the peace process among the local population. They often respond to local communities' needs and cover a wide

66 Kaldor, Mary. New and Old Wars: Organised Violence in a Global Era. Polity Press, 2012. p73. and Amin, Ash. "Spatialities of Globalisation." Environment and Planning A: Economy and Space, vol. 34, no. 3, Mar. 2002, pp. 385–399.

67 Ibid.

68 Taylor, Peter J., "Places, Spaces, and Macy's: Place Space Tensions in the Political Geographies of Modernities", Progress in Human Geography 23 (1): 7–26.

69 Quick Impact Projects (QIPs) explained:

1. What are QIPs?
Financed by MINUSMA, Quick Impact Projects (QIPs) are community projects, for a maximum cost of US$ 50,000 and a maximum 6-months duration. These projects must meet priority needs of the population and have both a quick and long lasting effect while building confidence towards the peace process, the Mission and its mandate.

2. **What are the areas of interventions covered by QIPs?**
Services and small public infrastructures rehabilitation; Training and awareness-raising activities; Employment and revenue creation.

3. **Who can submit a funding request and implement a QIP?**
Every entity legally registered and operating in the country, not pursuing profit-making purposes but social or public interests, can submit a proposal for funding of a QIP project, namely: National and Local NGOs; Associations; Governmental institutions; International agencies; International organizations. These entities can become MINUSMA partners within the QIPs progamme. Private companies cannot submit a QIP, although they may implement a project as sub-contractor for one of the partner organizations. The Mission itself, including military contingents, can also realize QIPs.

4. **What are the prerequisites for an implementing partner?**
Proven competencies; Qualified personnel; Have the logistical means necessary for the project's implementation; Demonstrate transparency and efficiency in the use of resources provided; Legal recognition. Available at: https://peacekeeping.un.org/en/quick-impact-projects-communities.

range of programmatic activities, from refurbishing schools to providing women with safe water access points. QIPS are mainly implemented through local actors, including local authorities and nongovernmental and grassroots organizations. As a result, the implementation of QIPs helps build their management capacities while broadening the mission's outreach at the local level. The conversation with the director of logistics and other UN officers made it explicit that many of the QIPS were challenging to implement, maintain, and sustain once they were realized. They are bound to fail because of the exhaustive bureaucracy and the lack of long-term planning. Lastly, their socio-economic, spatial, and environmental impact is overpowered by the scale, material footprint, and waste of the mission. The logistics director was frustrated. He recognized the power of local community groups and was eager to support their efforts to improve labor opportunities, food access, and the education system, but his hands were tied by the mission's mandate and bureaucracy. "We can collaborate with them to change the city," he said, "but it is difficult to break through the system and make the necessary resources available." He also expressed his disappointment with the engineering flaws across the super camp. The water drainage system of the base was inadequate. Recent rainfall had overflowed the base, and water had flooded into the containers and modular offices and caused extensive damage. They had lost computers, appliances, and documents. The local rainy season is massive. The abundant precipitation combined with flooding from the river and a lack of adequate drainage systems repeatedly devastates the city and pollutes the water bodies. Across the city, trenches are dug alongside the roads to collect and drain water, but these channels fill up with trash, which flows into the river, contaminating it and the aquifer. The logistics director shared some photographs he had taken during the last flood, demonstrating the damage to the base. The lead engineer for Camp Castor was at this meeting. His unit had experimented with different typologies and canal depths ahead of the rainy season. They had figured out how to best gutter water and prevent inundation. Whereas, in Camp Castor, the rainfall was absorbed by the soil, the adjacent super camp flooded. The Dutch engineer briefly explained the system to the UN super camp logistics director.

This encounter and the associated incident were illustrative of the silo mentality of the UN. Knowledge doesn't cross the base's perimeter – not from one UN camp to another, let alone to the city.

The lead engineer of Camp Castor in conversation with the logistics director of the UN super camp discussing the recent flood damages. Gao, 2016.

MINUSMA super camp. Gao, 2016.

MINUSMA's offices. Super camp. Gao, 2016.

Troop-contributing countries' (TCCs) bases within MINUSMA super camp. Gao, 2016.

Water. MINUSMA super camp. Gao, 2016.

Ecolog section. MINUSMA super camp. Gao, 2016.

Ecolog section. MINUSMA super camp. Gao, 2016.

Water and energy stations. MINUSMA super camp. Gao, 2016.

Gardening at the Nepalese TCC's base. MINUSMA super camp. Gao, 2016.

Mines and Missions: Nepalese Care Gardens in Northern Mali

The super camps in Mali stretch over a vast territory, often replacing former grazing areas, fields for crops, and other open areas. This land would have always been in use because it is part of an extensive ecosystem that supports local daily life through agriculture, grazing ground for livestock, and other forms of non-human habitation. In 2016, the super camp was partly under construction and partly occupied by UN agencies and several TCC.

Before the ground of a UN base is occupied, it is sterilized. It is reduced to bare material, engineered to become a controllable pavement. Oftentimes, after trees, huts, vegetation, and rocks are cleared, a thick layer of gravel is used to carpet the base, creating a physical buffer, a barrier between the local soil and the international presence.

In Mali, the earth has a staggering red pigment that contrasts with the white UN-imported structures—particularly in the more rural and remote areas, where traditional construction and the human habitat are organically extended as soft elevations of the soil. Buildings are made of mud and clay. They sculpt and band the earth into walls to form a built environment. It looks like a vast horizontal landscape of communal living, where materials, knowledge, and culture are entangled with the land and everything it has to offer.

In this landscape of what looks like an extensive vernacular drapery of sandcastles, the UN base sticks out. Its rigid grid is engineered and populated by rows of modular structures. The construction and system logic of the shipping container allows the tin structure to accommodate virtually infinite programs, including kitchens, showers, bedrooms, conference centers, surveillance hubs, reinforced ammunition storage, checkpoints, offices, and gyms.

When exploring the super camp in Gao, passing the Nepalese base was a memorable moment. The Nepalese TCC contributed about 114 soldiers to the UN peacekeeping force. The small unit was deployed throughout Mali for the purpose of explosive ordinance disposal (EOD), clearing of improvised explosive devices and mines that are responsible for some 15,000 deaths every year, and the most affected age group is children. One of the tasks of UN peacekeepers is to demine formerly active war zones.[70]

70 "Nepal to deploy 140 soldiers to Mali for peacekeeping", available at: https://kathmandupost.com/valley/2014/01/29/na-to-deploy-140-soldiers-to-mali-for-peacekeeping.

The small area occupied by the Nepalese soldiers at the super camp was covered by a bright green layer of edible gardens, standing in glaring contrast with the local scenery, which was a combination of the red sandy ground and the modular structures. Herbs and vegetables were planted between the white UN containers. The gardens were lush, irrigated by gray water from the showers and discharge from the air conditioners, tended with love and care by the Nepalese soldiers.

In Nepal, kitchen gardens are present in 72 percent of households and cover from 2 to 11 percent of the home's lot area. They are characterized by a complex biodiversity, with anywhere from 21 to 50 different species per household, including vegetables, fruits, spices, fodder, and medicinal and ornamental plants. The gardens constitute an essential source of quality food and nutrition. They are carefully maintained and harvested daily by women and children.

In the country's impoverished rural regions, domestic gardens contribute to food security. Some sources indicate that they provide 60 percent of the Nepalese total fruit and vegetable households consumption.[71] At the time of our visit to the base, one of the peacekeepers was caring for the garden. She was hard to make out because of her soft movement and green uniform, camouflaging her in the garden. She was kneeling silently and gently nurturing the plants. Seeing the Nepalese soldiers engaged in this act of communion with the soil, she surpassed the foreign engineering logic of the base and its modular aesthetics.

Perhaps, as Maria Puig de la Bellacasa wrote so aptly in *Matters of Care*,[72] the moment "represented matters of fact and sociotechnical assemblages as matters of care and intervention." It stood in contrast to the redacted way of living inside a UN camp, where complexity is abridged by the risk-averse institutional reasoning.

Peacekeepers' daily existence is highly dependent on external global supply chains; food is flown into UN bases from across the world, resulting in a generic menu. The Nepalese knowledge and relationship to the land succeeded in bypassing these international contractual procedures and protocols. The peacekeepers tended to the land by demining it. They replaced the bombs with seeds that they nurtured and cared for and which grew into plants, fruits, herbs, spices, and food to replenish the UN's menu. The waste from the containers, the carbon emissions, and the AC runoff were all directed back into the ground to generate something new. Here in Northern Mali, at the edge of the Sahara Desert, where the aridity is intensifying due to global warming and where rising hunger levels lead to grievances that escalates violence and overwhelms the entire region, a Nepalese soldier became an agent of care as she wove together different forms of life through an intimate knowledge and connection with the land.

71 Gautam, R, BR Sthapit and PK Shrestha (eds.), "Home Gardens" in "Enhancing the contribution of home garden to on-farm management of plant genetic resources and to improve the livelihoods of Nepalese farmers: Lessons learned and policy implications", 2004, Pokhara, Nepal. LI-BIRD, Bioversity International and SDC.

Nepalese food gardens. MINUSMA super camp. Gao, 2016.

Gao, 2016.

Houses and tents. Gao, 2016.

Visiting the City

After a security briefing in Camp Castor, we drove to the city in two armored vehicles with four armed guards, and we were forced to wear bulletproof vests and helmets. The distance between the base's perimeter and the city was about 50 meters. In less than five minutes we passed the first neighborhood. We continued driving for a few more minutes until the cars pulled over. We stopped along a dirt road. Both sides of the street were delineated by street gutters and mud homes surrounded by mud walls. Occasional gaps between the walls had been occupied by traditional Tuareg tents; next to it, goats were wandering about.

Our guide, a woman who worked for the Dutch Ministry of Foreign Affairs, had been living in Camp Castor for a few months. She was forging connections between the Dutch peacekeepers and civil society organizations operating in the region. She made a quick call, and two pastoralists with a local NGO opened one of the wall gates and welcomed us in. We passed an inner courtyard and entered the mud house. The interior looked like an ordinary office space: peach-colored walls, a mahogany desk that was too large for the room, and leather office chairs. The herders told us about their daily challenges and the overall crisis in the region. Water scarcity is a severe problem in the Sahel as a whole, and in Gao in particular. It threatens the livelihoods of millions—people, animals, and vegetation. There are increasingly prolonged and severe periods of drought, and people are struggling to survive. The herders in this small NGO had an idea for a pilot project to help shepherds discover water more easily. They had noticed that animals could sense water better than human beings, so they proposed fastening satellite tracking devices, small microchips, to their sheep. Whenever an animal found water, herders in the region would receive a notification on their cell phones. It was fascinating to learn during our conversation how nomadic culture and smart technologies can be compatible.

The herders were knowledgeable and well informed about the political situation and high tensions in the region. They still traveled across it, visiting and working with various communities—tribes of pastoralists, herders, and farmers more than anyone else. At the time of our conversation, they emphasized the poverty and famine in the east region of Menaka; they warned us it was on the verge of a catastrophe. Half a year before our arrival, a cease-fire agreement had been signed between the Malian government and the Northern tribes. However, not everyone living in those isolated areas was aware of it, and they continued fighting with one another. The two men admitted that they were worried about the UN's presence and its intentions. Without the involvement of the international community in 2013, they said, it would have been complete chaos. But now there was a cease-fire agreement in place and there was no need for the UN to stay, especially if they were not offering any support to the community.

If the international community wanted to contribute to peace, they should help the children, the men said. There are many children of all ages roaming the streets. Many of them are not sent to school because their families cannot afford it. There is no work for those who graduate from school; the job market is extremely limited. Extremist and violent groups are well aware of this situation. They prey on youth and recruit them at a very young age. By now, they have established an alternative social infrastructure that replaces the failed state institutions. They offer free schools, while state schools remain empty because they are not affordable. The community's future—the children—are being radicalized. Additionally, life expectancy in this region is extremely short. People die at a very young age because of poverty, disease, conflict, and a lack of access to health care. As a result, in this society, no one plans for the future; they live in the present. The pastoralists proceeded, "There is much more the UN could do if they wanted us to live in peace here." The constant pressures will keep the region insecure, embroiled in continuing and escalating conflict.

The meeting ended on this heavy note. It was clear that the peace mission would be ongoing because there was no end of the conflict in sight. We left the pastoralists and headed to the city center.

The Tomb of Askia. Gao, 2016.

The Tomb of Askia

Gao looks very different from Western cities. Its horizontality, uniformity of materials, and colors are beautiful. The mud buildings were interspersed occasionally with tents that merged organically with the other built structures and the natural surroundings. The spatiality of the nomadic and sedentary cultures coexist peacefully here.

At the center of the city, close to the Niger River banks, is the Tomb of Askia. It is a staggering monument to Gao's glorious past—an ancient clay structure surrounded by a mud wall, which looks as if the ground has surged upward into a 17-meter-high pyramidal sculpture. The 500-year-old structure is one of the finest monumental mud buildings typical of the West African Sahel. Its complex includes two mosques, a cemetery, and an assembly area, and it has been recognized as a UNESCO World Heritage Site. According to UNESCO the tomb is believed to be the burial place of Askia Mohammad I, one of the Songhai Empire's most prolific emperors. In 2019, UNESCO issued an 80-page report[73] listing important endangered world heritage sites. Three of the four African sites on this list were in Mali: in Timbuktu, in the old town of D'jenne, and the Tomb of Askia. Threats to the tomb include Gao's occupation by armed groups, the inability to ensure daily management to protect and preserve the site, and the risk of collapse. The tomb structure was spectacular; behind the wall gate, an inner courtyard surrounded a pyramid. The wall was, in fact, an extended belt facing the main court. The entire complex was sculpted homogenously with the same material as the soil. At the edge of the courtyard stood a telecommunications pole with a small solar board carefully placed at its top. The mud pyramid was punctured by wooden sticks that displayed the local building knowledge and preservation technique. Within one of the pyramid's faces, vernacular mud stairs were discretely placed, climbing all the way to its apex, where a panoramic scenery of the city was unveiled. Along the stairs, electricity plugs were submersed carefully within the pyramid walls. The electrical wiring was concealed by a layer of mud. The modernist order of infrastructural lines and grids of the UN base was nowhere to be seen. At the top, large megaphones were also attached onto the structure, delivering the Imam's sermons to the city's inhabitants. The effortless application of contemporary engineering knowledge, renewable energy, and regenerative resources to the ancient mud sculpture was an encouraging sight. The freestanding vernacular sublime, testimony to a rich culture and history, was a welcome break from the rigid grid of the UN base and its container aesthetics.

72 de la Bellacasa, María, Puig. Matters of Care: Speculative Ethics in More than Human Worlds. University of Minnesota Press, 2017, p18.

The Tomb of Askia. Gao, 2016.

The Revolution is Without Frontiers . Border indication of the new state of Azawad. Moussa Ag Assarid, 2014.

Cities in the Desert

A Conversation with Moussa Ag Assarid

Moussa Ag Assarid is the spokesperson for the MNLA, the National Movement for the Liberation of Azawad (the northern part of Mali) in Europe. I met him at a cafe in Utrecht together with Jonas Staal, a Dutch artist and activist who initiated the *New World Summit* platform, which gives voice to nations without political representation at the UN. Moussa was in Utrecht to participate in the summit. The story below summarizes our conversation.

Since the beginning of the 20th century, the Tuareg people have rebelled four times. The first rebellion, known as the *Kaocen Revolt*, took place in 1916–1917 against French colonial rule. This revolt was, among others in the region, the result of a long period of drought that threatened the existence and livelihood of the Tuareg. The next rebellion took place from 1962 to 1964, just after Mali's independence. One of the reasons behind this uprising was dissatisfaction with the new divisions of the Sahara by the French and other world powers, which left the Tuareg scattered between different nations – mostly Mali and Niger. The newly formed Malian army suppressed the rebellion. The next Tuareg revolt took place from 1990 to 1995. Once again, the Tuareg claimed autonomy, and once again, this uprising took place after a long drought, famine, and the economic crisis of the 1980s. This rebellion ended in a peace agreement with the governments of Mali and Niger. During that uprising, the Libyan government sided with the Tuareg and provided them with employment and economic support. In 2012, after the fall of the Gaddafi regime, they escaped Libya to avoid prosecution by the locals. Afraid for their lives and their future, they drove south to the Sahara with an arsenal of Gadaffi's weapons and established the MNLA.

In the Sahara, they weren't alone Islamist groups, from Al-Qaeda to Daesh, were gaining strength and preparing to wage a religious war throughout the entire region. In 2012, a combined force of MNLA and jihadist groups began capturing cities in Northern Mali and rapidly progressing toward the capital of Bamako. They were halted by the French army and then by MINUSMA, the UN mission.

Moussa represents a critical interest group that has been marginalized for centuries in this region. The MNLA aspires to redraw the map of Mali and claim the north as their own autonomous country, called Azawad, where Gao is marked as the capital city. Gao is located alongside the Niger River and is one of the last stops before stepping into the Sahara. Currently, MINUSMA aids the Malian government to control the city. I ask him how he envisions the future of the city. Moussa first explains the strategic value of Gao: "Gao is located along the Niger River. The river crossing is an important resource, it makes the city accessible from Algeria, Bamako or Timbuktu."

As a spokesperson for the MNLA, his priority is to clarify his view of the current conflict: "The Malian regime in Bamako started the current problems in Gao. They were responsible for training some of the Songhai people into a militia." He continued that the problem lies not only with Bamako, but that "the jihadist movement in Africa—the Azar Din or Al-Qaeda—are also a huge problem. They are terrorists, and they live among us."

"In 2012, the Malian government sent thousands of people to create small militarized groups to fight the MNLA. They did the same in 2014. They created a new militia called Ganda Koy. Without this mounting complexity and war, Gao could have been a perfect city, a model city." Moussa clarifies that they have not declared Gao as the capital of Azawad, because he does not want to be caught stating something that might inflame the conflict. He is not interested in escalation or additional controversies. He desires peace. "The situation must first calm down before further strategic decisions are taken," he emphasizes. "Kidal is another city that could serve as the capital of Azawad. Kidal is located north of the Niger River and north of Gao. This city is affiliated with the Tuareg and with the MNLA. The main obstacle to proceeding with the implementation of the Azawadian State lies 1,200 km away, in Bamako, and perhaps even further away, in Paris."

He highlights again that, among the Tuaregs, there are small extremist terrorist groups. "They live among us, and they make it very hard to reach stability." After clarifying his position, he begins speculating on the Capital of Azawad:

"The Azawadian capital is a multi-ethnic city. It is an independent city that is both vigorous and resilient. It is a city that can overcome climatic difficulties and can support its citizens economically, providing various sources of employment".

"In our city, we don't fear the other. We live in a multi-ethnic and open society and strive for cultural openness. This notion of openness is not only in mind but is also spatial. We want to live in a vast open space, with no borders. The city should be designed as a flexible space that can easily expand, shrink, and grow as needed. Particularly here, the desert is not a closed place. It has no doors. Our city should be defined by nature and emerge from the features of the desert.

We want our society to strive for ideals of respect and coexistence, appreciate not only similarities but also differences. After our independence, we want to invite others to live with us. Our cities will be open; people will be always welcome to join, and those who have left can return. We receive our friends well. We, the Tuaregs, have always been foreigners; we were outsiders to cities and society. We were the nomads. We don't wish to impose this feeling of exclusion and foreignness on anyone.

Cities in the desert have no limits. The desert is a flat construct. We want to embrace this vastness and flatness. I believe that wealthy cities and European cities are mostly vertical, dense with tall buildings. In their physicality, they depict a state of inequality. Just cities, however, expand over vast territories and their horizontality represents equality, accessibility, and environmental resilience.

We want to build our cities based on accessibility and equality. We want to build low, adjust ourselves to our surrounding. We want to enjoy the fresh air and the climate. We want to build with natural materials. Electricity-dependent ventilation is too expensive for us. For instance, Moussa continued, "my my house is made of patchwork. In the summer, the patchwork is made of textile and in the winter from the skin of sheep or goats.

I was born and raised in a tent that was made of old clothes. A tent is part of nature, and the outdoors is my home. Once we visited a family that had a house in the city. The house was, in fact, a wall that enclosed a substantial yard. Inside of the walled space, there was a small structure with a roof. It had two rooms and a small balcony. We used the covered spaces as storage; we stored our belongings there, and we slept in a tent in the yard."

At the end of the conversation, I ask Moussa what he thinks of the UN mission in Mali. He replied, "the Dutch constituent made a good impression on the local people. But other countries that contribute peacekeeping forces to the UN have another mentality; especially in the manner they are treating the locals and the MNLA. When the Dutch are present, the communication with the locals is good."

Moussa remembers his meeting with the Dutch Minister of Foreign Affairs, Bert Koenders. They talked briefly and Moussa gave him the book he had put together with Jonas Staal in the context of *The New World Summit*. The book aimed to generate public discourse on the inequality and marginality of groups that are unrepresented in institutional structures like the UN. People and communities with no institutionally lack political power, like the MNLA, have their civic and human rights violated daily.

"In 2012, the MNLA was fighting terrorists, and the UN bombed us. We had to fight two fronts, the UN and the jihadists. The UN came to protect the Malian army, not to create peace. They are now settled, and if you look at their infrastructure, I don't believe they will leave in the coming decade. It seems that they are planning to stay for ten, perhaps twenty or even thirty years. It's hard for me to think about a peaceful mix between military and civil life. In the eyes of the Azawadians, the UN, after bombing us, is military. Their intentions are not peaceful, and their legacy cannot be civil. Koenders and MINUSMA came to protect the Malians. The Malians don't need protection from us. The UN and the jihadists shot civilians, not us."

Moussa concludes by saying that "the UN should strive for peace. It should protect everybody and treat everyone the same. I hope in the future that will be the case. We want to be treated equally. We want to be respected. We don't wish to be outsiders and foreigners in the society around us. We want peace."

Sketch of a house in the desert (Azawad) by Moussa Ag Assarid. Utrecht, 2015.

Tinariwen – Elwan Ténéré Tàqqàl

Ténéré tàqqàl
Eghàrghàr wa n-fissar
Dàgh iknasàn elwan
Azzadàn dàgh-s alimmoz
Chorus
Awwànàn ichinkad Adagh
Ibas tidwin igdad iskak
Aherahàghnàt timizzagh
Tiwàr tekenzart idim n-àlyad
Chorus
A-wa àzzàman àssoheen
Dàgh idja amsistagh
Azzaràn wi àssohàtnen
Idjmadàn inibdan
Chorus
Ammun dàgh-nàgh meddàn
Tàssiknàs tayitte n-nibrar
Tigla tisrawt fàlanàgh
Istàqqàt anmàghdar
Chorus

The Ténéré has become*
an upland of thorns
Where elephants
fight each other
Crushing tender grass
under foot.
The gazelles have found refuge
high in the mountains
The birds no longer return
to their nests at night
The camps have all fled.
You can read the bitterness
on the faces
of the innocents
During this difficult
and bruising time
In which all solidarity
has gone.
The strongest impose their will
And leave the weakest behind
Many have died battling
for twisted ends.
And joy has abandoned us
Exhausted by all this duplicity.

Assàwt

Assàwt n- chàt-Tamashàq
Itlab-nen àlhorriya
D-inizdjam n-timgharen
Izzaghnen dagh-issàhra
Chorus
Wàr àhen aman tàcherràd
Tàsnin ihet mànna
Chorus
Innàr did àffo tàffijàr
Nizdjar àlghabudiyya
Chorus
Wen ehlan i-meddàn
Wi axdàmnen i-àssàwra
Chorus

That's the voice
of the Tamashek women
Searching for their freedom.
Those are the thoughts
of the old women
Living in a Sahara devoid of water,
Desiccated and miserable,
My wish is for it
to stop being subservient.
This is a message for those
Who toil for the revolution.

*Ténéré is a Tamashek word meaning empty land or desert. The plural of the word is tinariwen.

Stills from "Desert Rebel" by Abdallah Oumbadougou. Directed by François Bergeron, 2009.

Liberia and the End of a UN Peace-keeping Mission

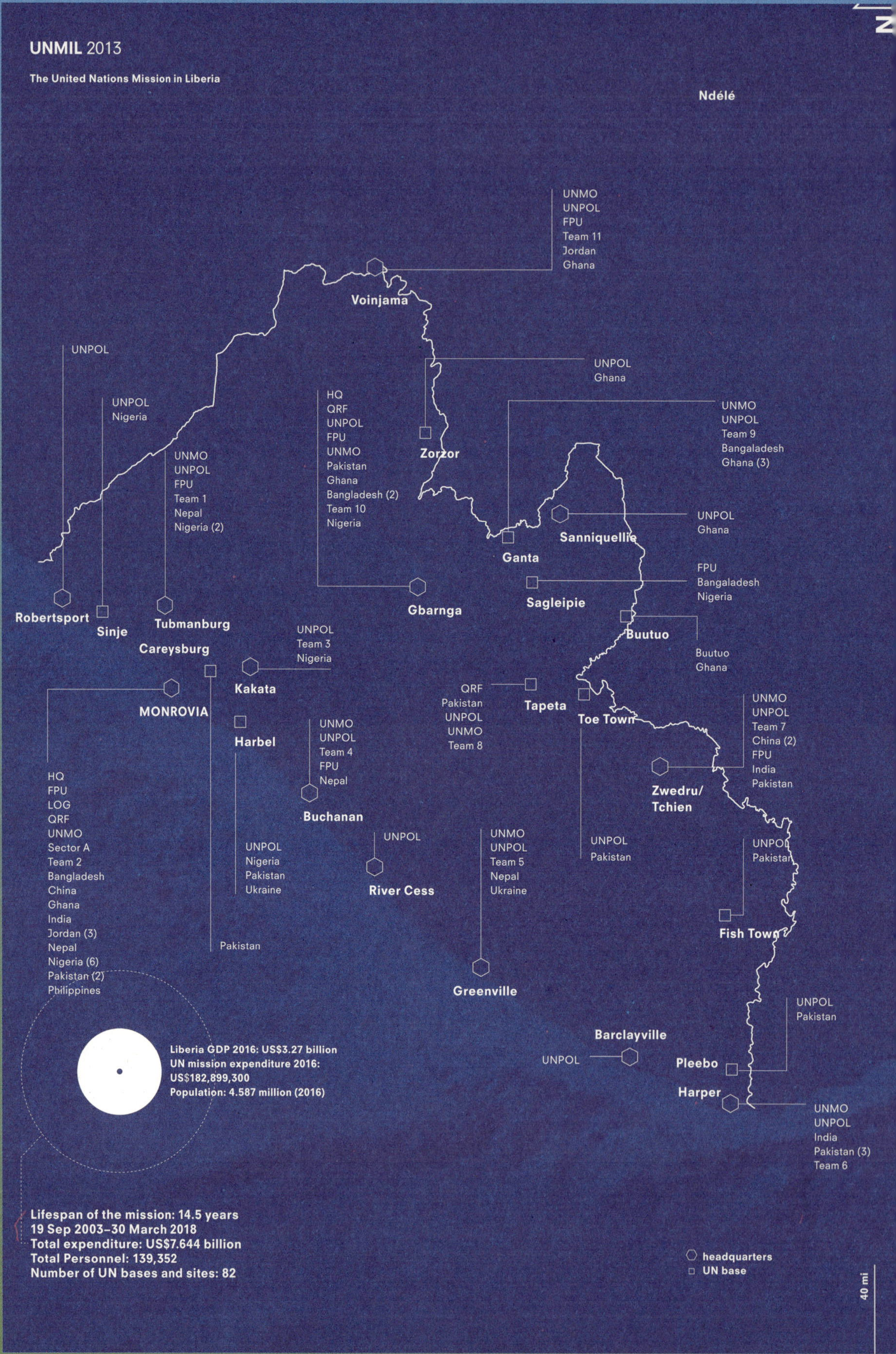

UNMIL 2013
The United Nations Mission in Liberia
Ndélé
Voinjama
UNMO UNPOL FPU Team 11 Jordan Ghana
Zorzor
UNPOL Ghana
HQ QRF UNPOL FPU UNMO Pakistan Ghana Bangladesh (2) Team 10 Nigeria
Gbarnga
Ganta
UNMO UNPOL Team 9 Bangaladesh Ghana (3)
Sanniquellie
UNPOL Ghana
Sagleipie
FPU Bangaladesh Nigeria
Buutuo
Buutuo Ghana
Robertsport
UNPOL
Sinje
UNPOL Nigeria
Tubmanburg
UNMO UNPOL FPU Team 1 Nepal Nigeria (2)
Careysburg
Pakistan
Kakata
UNPOL Team 3 Nigeria
MONROVIA
HQ FPU LOG QRF UNMO Sector A Team 2 Bangladesh China Ghana India Jordan (3) Nepal Nigeria (6) Pakistan (2) Philippines
Harbel
UNPOL Nigeria Pakistan Ukraine
Buchanan
UNMO UNPOL Team 4 FPU Nepal
River Cess
UNPOL
Tapeta
QRF Pakistan UNPOL UNMO Team 8
Toe Town
UNPOL Pakistan
Zwedru/ Tchien
UNMO UNPOL Team 7 China (2) FPU India Pakistan
Fish Town
UNPOL Pakistan
Greenville
UNMO UNPOL Team 5 Nepal Ukraine
Barclayville
UNPOL
Pleebo
UNPOL Pakistan
Harper
UNMO UNPOL India Pakistan (3) Team 6
Liberia GDP 2016: US$3.27 billion
UN mission expenditure 2016: US$182,899,300
Population: 4.587 million (2016)
Lifespan of the mission: 14.5 years
19 Sep 2003–30 March 2018
Total expenditure: US$7.644 billion
Total Personnel: 139,352
Number of UN bases and sites: 82
headquarters
UN base
40 mi
N

iV. Liberia

"Let the great heart of Christian benevolence in the North and the South unite in selecting ...the proper subjects to be sent upon the mission of redemption to the land of their ancestors, until the last slave shall have departed." Allan Yarema[1]

Liberia, the first sovereign African republic, proclaimed independence on July 25, 1847. The country was initially conceived by the American Colonization Society (ACS) in 1816, as Robert Finely, an American clergyman and educator and the founder of ACS, called to support the migration of free African Americans to their distant ancestral land: the continent of Africa. Prompted by concern over the growing number of free people of color after the American Revolutionary War, which reached 300,000 by 1830, white Americans, motivated by white supremacy, found the integration of African Americans with white culture impossible and undesirable; they started looking for a place to relocate the freed African Americans. The ACS members included mostly Quakers and slaveholders; both agreed, for different reasons, that African Americans should be repatriated to Africa.

The African American community and the Abolitionist movement resisted the idea. As recalled by Ousmane Power-Greene in the book *Against Wind and Tide: The African American Struggle against the Colonization Movement:*

> In February of 1833, Maria Stewart stood before a group of people gathered at the African Masonic Hall in Boston to condemn the ACS for its goal of "influencing us to go to Liberia." [She continued] "The unfriendly whites first drove the native American from his much-loved land," and then brought them to America, "made them bond-men and bond-women," and now sought to "drive us to a strange land." It is for this reason that "African rights and liberty is a subject that ought to fire the breast of every free man of color in these United States."[2]

Yet, the ACS movement grew, persuading former slaves and freed people, voluntarily or by force, to travel back to Africa. In 1820, the first group of immigrants was sent to Sherbro Island in Sierra Leone. Many of them died of malaria, yellow fever, and impoverished unhealthy living conditions. Between 1820 and 1821, Eli Ayres, a physician and the first colonial agent of the ACS in what later became Liberia, joined an expedition to West Africa with Robert Field Stockton, a naval innovator who captured California during the Mexican-American War. Their mission was to suppress the slave trade and look for land to settle the recently freed African American people.[3]

Along their journey, they came across a plot of land around Cape Mesurado, which was inhabited by the Dey and Bassa peoples. They negotiated a deal with the tribes' leaders and purchased a 130-mile long and 40-mile wide swathe of coastline for $300 worth of goods on behalf of the ACS. This land would later form the basis of Liberia—or the ACS's colony for the liberated African slaves. It was said that Stockton threatened the local headman, King Peter, at gunpoint to force the deal and secure the land acquisition.[4]

Thereafter, the survivors of Sherbro Island were moved to Cape Mesurado and became the first settlers of Liberia. As the community of immigrants grew, so did the resistance among the local indigenous population. The friction between the emerging colony and the locals continued to dim the idea of "*the land of the free*" and eventually culminated with two sequentially devastating civil wars.

In the early days of the colony, all sorts of disputes mounted regarding the ACS's style of governance and its unequal distribution of resources among the various groups of settlers. On July 26, 1847, the Liberian Constitutional Convention was convened. It declared that the Commonwealth of Liberia,

1 Yarema, Allan. The American Colonization Society: An Avenue to Freedom? (Lanham, MD: University Press of America, 2006). p. 38.

2 Power-Greene, Ousmane. "'One of the Wildest Projects Ever': Abolitionists and the Anticolonizationist Impulse, 1830–1840." In Against Wind and Tide: The African American Struggle Against the Colonization Movement. NYU Press, 2014. p. 46.

3 Liberia. From Colony to Republic. 1820 to 1847, available at:www.loc.gov/collections/maps-of-liberia-1830-to-1870/articles-and-essays/history-of-liberia/1820-to-1847.

4 Hollander, Craig. "Navigating Slavery: Robert F. Stockton and the Limits of Antislavery Thought", available at: https://slavery.princeton.edu/stories/navigating-slavery.

a colony founded and controlled by the private ACS, was an independent state with a system of local administration and laws. Slavery and participation in the slave trade were forbidden. Finally, the initial settlement was renamed Monrovia, instead of Christopolis, after the American president, James Monroe. The colony was formally named Liberia.[5] The sovereign power, however, continued to rest with ACS agents.

As the colony grew, the tensions with the local population continued. It is said that the new settlers "recreated American society, building churches and homes that resembled Southern plantations. And they continued to speak English. They also entered into a complex relationship with the indigenous people – marrying them in some cases, discriminating against them in others, but all the time attempting to 'civilize' them and impose Western values on the traditional communities."[6] The repatriated former slaves established "an oppressive regime similar to the one they had escaped from, and even enslaved the indigenous population, which they considered 'uncivilized.'"[7]

In 1875, a war broke out among the settlers and the confederation of Grebo peoples; it was mediated and temporarily resolved after a US-led intervention.

Liberia's population, economy, territory, and control over indigenous land and people grew exponentially in the decades to come. The colony built homes, schools, churches, and a university. The agriculture, shipbuilding, and trade sectors thrived. As the only free republic in the region, it became a model for African colonized people struggling to achieve independence.

In 1944, a new president, William V.S. Tubman, was elected and remained in power until he died in 1971. Under his mandate, he modernized Liberia's industries and infrastructure. He opened the republic to international trade and strengthened the country's relations with the West and other African nations while working closely with the US. The country's revenues kept climbing, especially after the discovery of natural resources and minerals such as iron ore, timber, diamonds, and gold. Yet not all the inhabitants of the country flourished. The inequality between the ruling elite and the indigenous populations had greatly increased by the end of Tubman's time in power. After his death in 1971, Tubman was succeeded by William R. Tolbert.

Tolbert inherited a divided country. Liberia's majority lived in poverty, and the president's attempts to liberalize and heal the divisions failed. His efforts to support local food production in 1979 resulted in a commodity price surge that provided the spark for a prolonged period of violence.

In 1980, Samuel K. Doe, an indigenous master sergeant from the Krahn people, a minority group from the area of Zwedru, led a coup. Together with a militant group, he stormed the presidential mansion in Monrovia, shot Tolbert, executed members of the Cabinet, and imprisoned many others. After seizing the government, Doe installed the People's Redemption Council (PRC) and ruled the country with other 14 officers. It was the first time that the indigenous population was in power.

Doe's violently established government lasted for 10 years until Charles Taylor, who initially supported Doe and worked as director of the General Services Agency (GSA), was accused of embezzlement. He fled to the US, where he was captured and detained. After escaping prison, Taylor relocated to Libya, where he was trained as a guerrilla fighter. Upon his return to Liberia in 1989, he led the National Patriotic Front of Liberia (NPFL), backed and financed by Muammar Gaddafi, to topple Doe's government. Taylor started the First Liberian Civil War (1989–1996), gained control of a large portion of the country, and became one of the most prominent warlords in Africa.[8] In 1990, Prince Johnson,[9] a senior commander of Taylor's NPFL, broke off and formed the Independent National Patriotic Front of Liberia (INPFL).[10] Despite the

5 "From Colony to Republic. 1820 to 1847", available at: www.loc.gov/collections/maps-of-liberia-1830-to-1870/articles-and-essays/history-of-liberia/1820-to-1847.
6 "The Lone Star: The Story of Liberia", available at www.pbs.org/wgbh/globalconnections/liberia/essays/history/
7 Ibid.
8 See Hotel Africa, page 253.
9 Johnson is still a Liberian politician and the current Senior Senator from Nimba County.
10 "Justice at last?" *The Economist*. May 31, 2007. Retrieved August 5, 2007.

presence of the Economic Community of West African States Monitoring Group (ECOMOG), Johnson captured most of Monrovia, tortured and executed Doe, and had his body thrown off the 4th-floor balcony of Hotel Africa. Johnson, however, was not able to form a government. He escaped Liberia, clearing the way for Charles Taylor's government to form.[11] The first civil war ended in 1996, as Taylor ran for president with the slogan "He killed my ma, he killed my pa, but I will vote for him."[12]

The election was supervised by the first peacekeeping mission to Liberia, UNOMIL, which certified that 75 percent of the vote went to Charles Taylor. His ruthless administration lasted for about five years. After his attempt to murder his political opponent, Roosevelt Johnson, and the massacre of hundreds of members of the Krahn ethnic group, he drove Liberia into its Second Civil War (1999–2003). Liberians United for Reconciliation and Democracy (LURD), the rebel group, struck from the north, and the Movement for Democracy in Liberia (MODEL) attacked from the south. The Accra Comprehensive Peace Agreement was signed by the warring parties on August 18, 2003, marking the political end of the conflict.[13] On April 26, 2012, Charles Taylor became the first former head of state since the Nuremberg trials to be convicted for war crimes and crimes against humanity by an international or hybrid tribunal.[14]

11 Nyanseor Siahyonkron, Elder. and J. Kpanneh Doe. Better Late than Never: The Execution of Michael J. Doe by Gen. Prince Y. Johnson, available at: www.theperspective.org/2018/0410201803.php.

12 Left, Sarah. "War in Liberia". The Guardian. London. Retrieved January 18, 2008.

13 Liberia Comprehensive Peace Agreement, available at: www.usip.org/sites/default/files/file/resources/collections/peace_agreements/liberia_08182003.pdf

14 Charles Taylor. Human Rights Watch, available at: www.hrw.org/topic/international-justice/charles-taylor.

Liberia and the End of a UN Peacekeeping Mission

Liberia experienced two civil wars between 1989 and 2003 that claimed the lives of almost 250,000 people and left the country's economy and infrastructure in ruins. Homes, community centers, schools, airports, and public buildings were destroyed, as were basic services and grids such as electricity, sewage, and waste management.

United Nations Mission in Liberia (UNMIL) succeeded several other international peacekeeping and peacebuilding efforts in Liberia. The Economic Community of West African States (ECOWAS) from 1990–1997; the United Nations Observer Mission in Liberia (UNOMIL) from 1993–2003, and the United Nations Peacebuilding Support Office in Liberia (UNOL) made several interventions during the conflict to bring peace from 1997–2003.

UNMIL itself was deployed in October 2003 in accordance with the United Nations Security Council resolution 1509 (2003). It was among the first "integrated" missions, bringing together peace and development actors under a single coordination structure. Peacekeepers included key civilian personnel responsible for peacebuilding tasks such as security sector reform and ensuring the observance of the rule of law. By 2005, thousands of peacekeepers were deployed in more than 20 cities and villages across the country. At its peak, UNMIL had more than 70 bases throughout the country in a variety of shapes and sizes; some were located in existing structures such as the former CIA base or the former Hotel Africa. Others were built on private land leased to the UN or were constructed on public land provided by the local government. Starting in 2015, UNMIL began to wind down. It was present in only five sites in 2016, and by 2017 the remaining UN troops were mostly stationed in Monrovia and Zwedru. During the last year of the mission, more than 75 sites went through a liquidation and handover process, while all lasting UN actors relocated to operate from the Star Base, a large complex at the Monrovia seaport. The mission ended on June 30, 2018.

This chapter explores the completion of UNMIL, including the end phase of the mission, its liquidation, the handover of assets and security control to the local government and its agencies, and finally, the withdrawal of all peacekeepers and removal of their bases. This section attempts to examine the spatiality and legacy of UNMIL while focusing on Liberia's capital city, Monrovia, and the more remote town of Zwedru, located along the border with Ivory Coast. Both cities, like the country as a whole and the region at large, were ravaged by long civil wars in past decades.

This chapter comprises three main elements:
1. the distribution of UNMIL bases and their state at the end of the mission, 2. Liberia's urban challenges, and 3. identification of legacy potentiality of the UN mission and its bases.

The "Liberia and the End of a UN Peacekeeping Mission" chapter is based on a series of meetings, workshops, field research, policy analysis, and advocacy and dissemination events carried out by FAST from 2017 to 2020 with the support of the Center on International Cooperation at New York University, the Permanent Mission of Australia, and the Permanent Mission of the UK to the United Nations.

UNMIL Spatial Evolution

2003–2017

UNMIL constructed and deployed 79 bases in about 20 cities and villages throughout the country, achieving significant physical coverage. During this period, the number of personnel and expenditure of the mission fluctuated.

2003

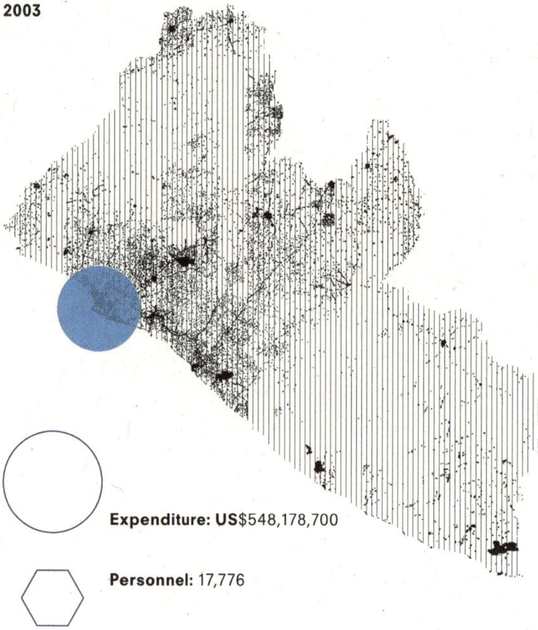

2004

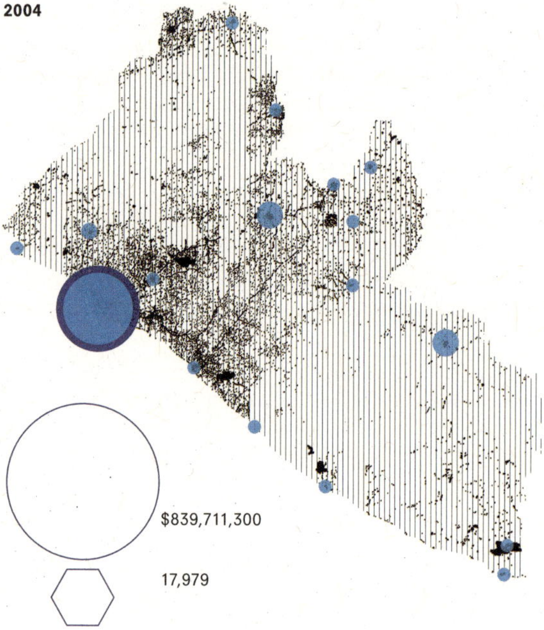

2013

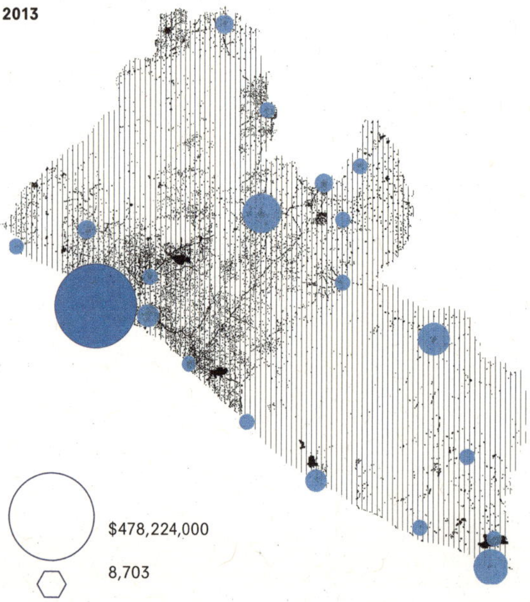

2015

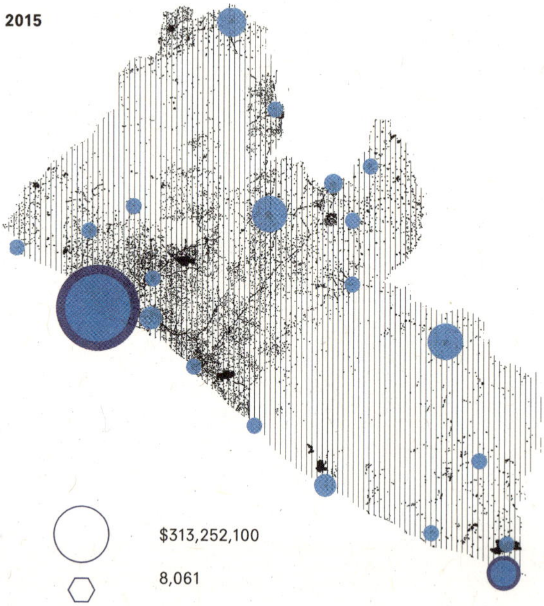

Lifespan of the mission: 14.5 years
September 19, 2003–March 30, 2018

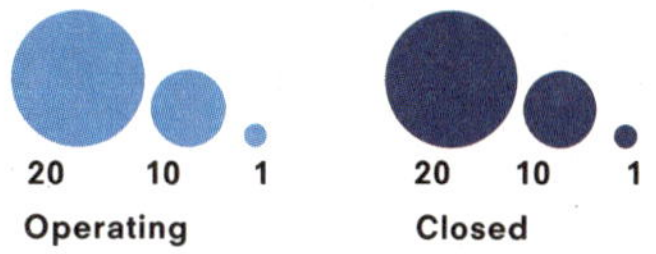

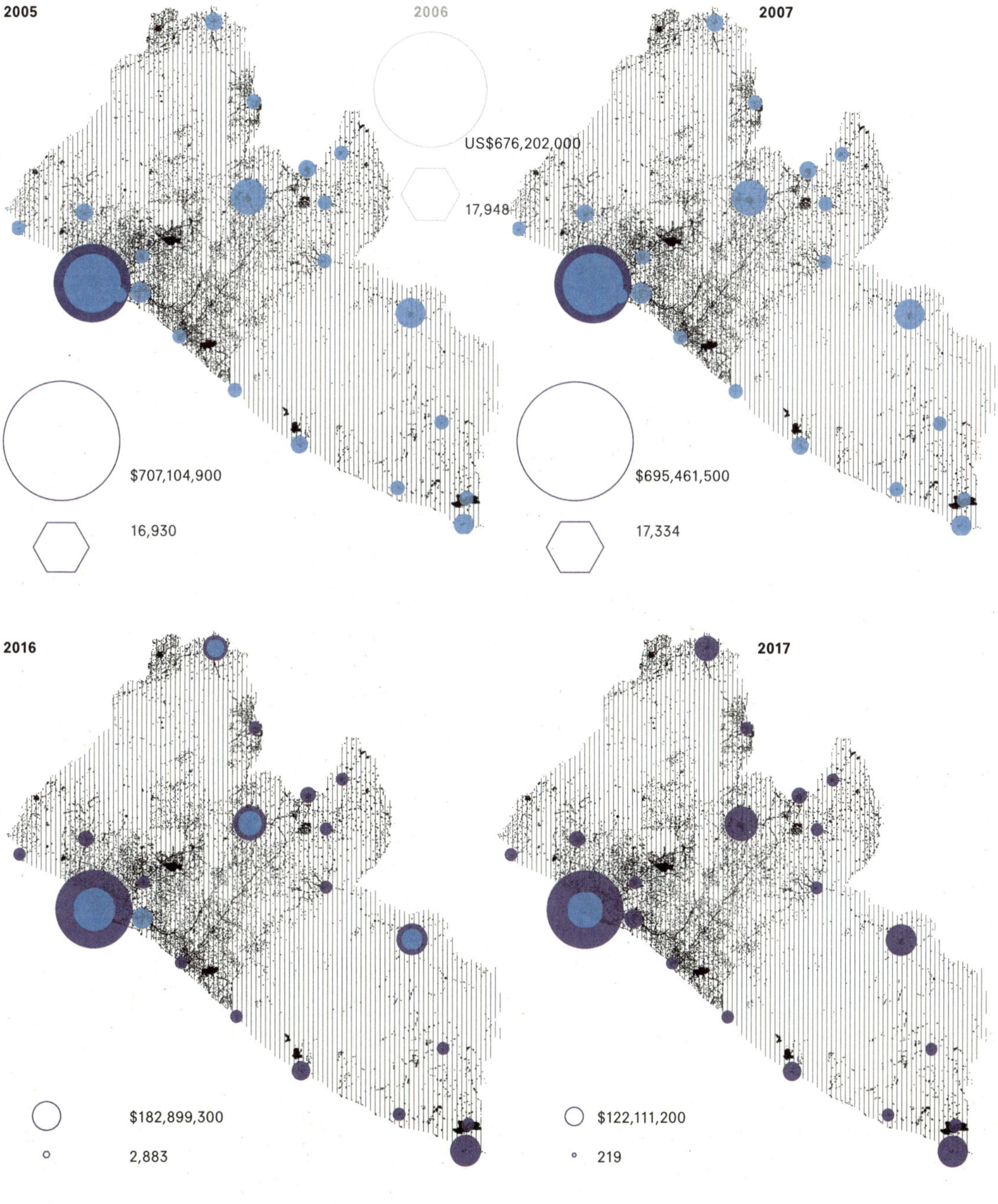

UNMIL expenditure and personnel

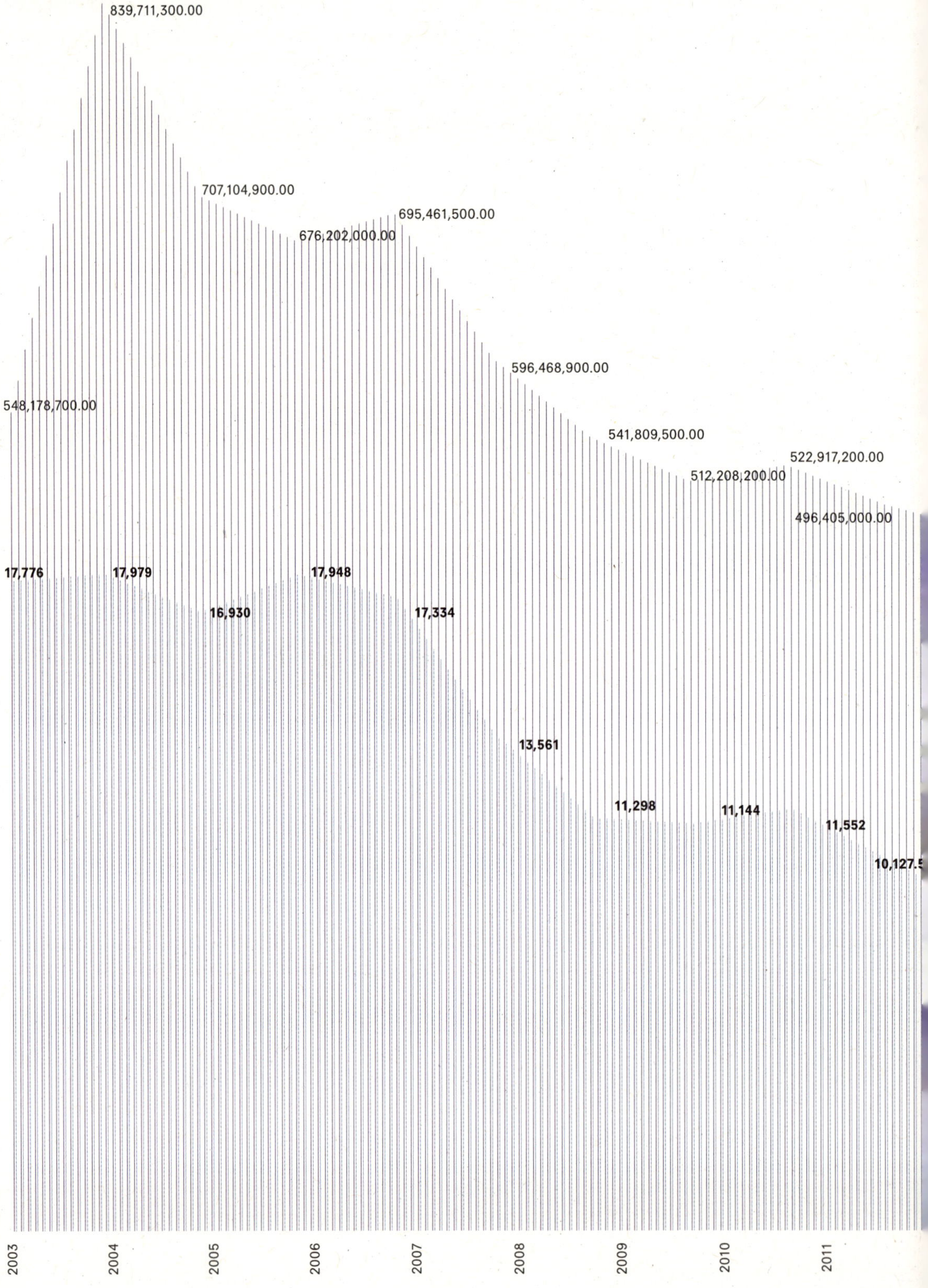

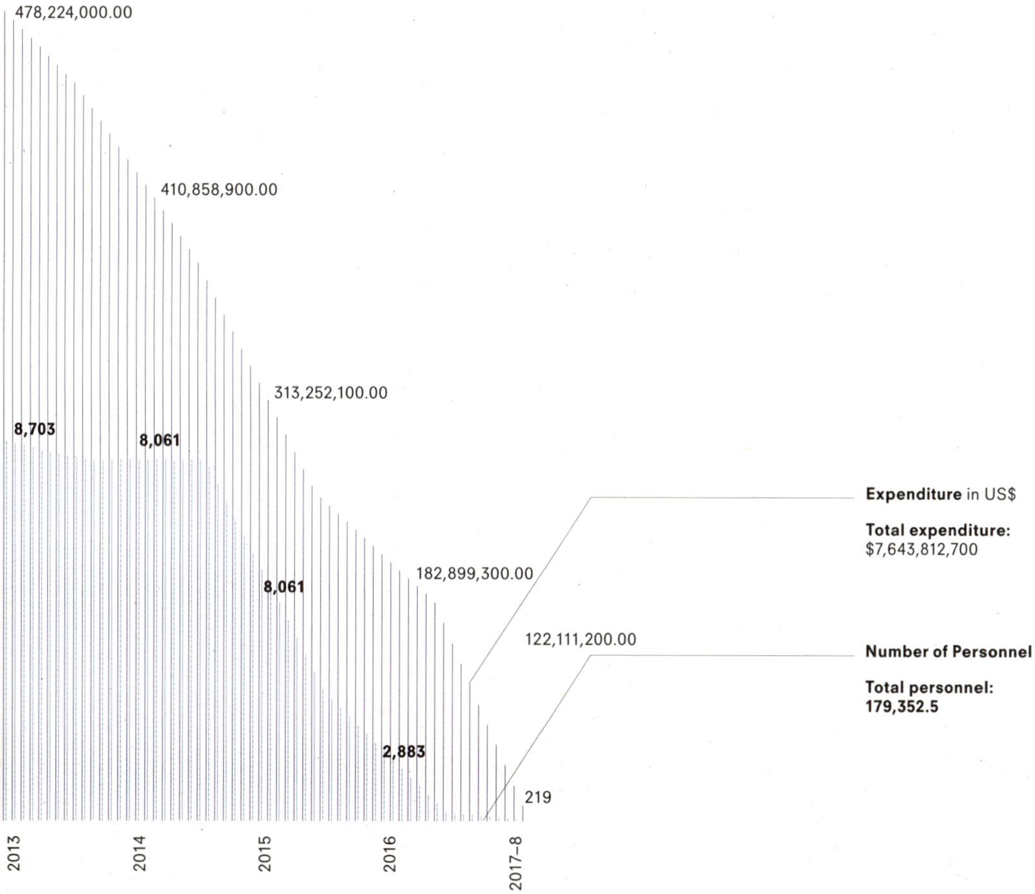
478,224,000.00
410,858,900.00
313,252,100.00
182,899,300.00
122,111,200.00
8,703
8,061
8,061
2,883
219
2013
2014
2015
2016
2017–8
Expenditure in US$
Total expenditure:
$7,643,812,700
Number of Personnel
Total personnel:
179,352.5

UNMIL expenditure exceeded Liberia's GDP from 2003–2006 and exceeded the government's revenue from 2006–2013

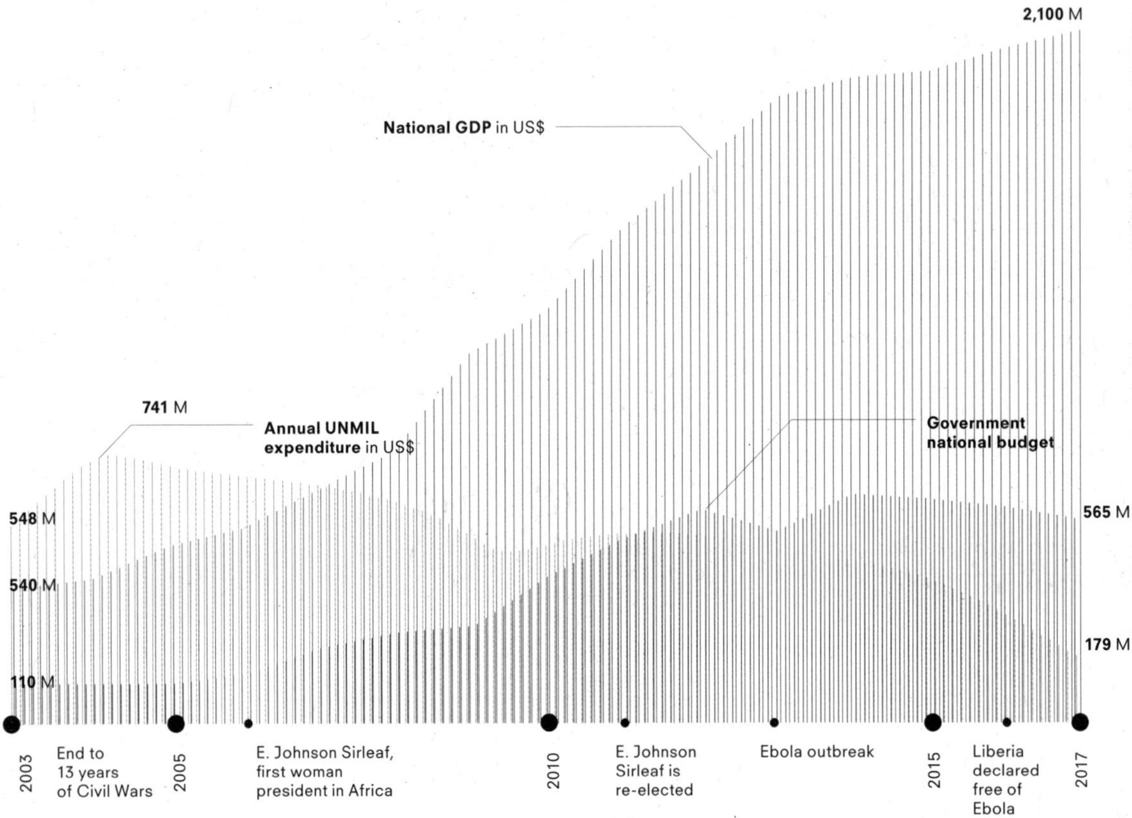

UNMIL expenditure in relation to Liberia's national budget and GDP.

Urban Challenges in Liberia

After 14.5 years, the UN peacekeeping mission in Liberia came to an end on March 30, 2018. It claimed to have achieved most of its goals and departed Liberia just months after a contested election ended in a peaceful transfer of power.[15] Yet the challenges facing Liberia are enormous.

Liberian cities and rural inhabited areas have yet to repair the public and social infrastructure that was destroyed during the civil wars. From 2003–2016, UNMIL was the largest development catalyst in the country due to its personnel number, expenditure patterns, and material footprint. The mission attracted contractors and service providers from the entire region and the world. Its services, however, never turned into a meaningful investment for the local communities and country.

Often, a mission's presence in a war-torn place requires the UN to ensure access to roads, airfields, logging, and provisions for the daily needs of its personnel. When the UN has a significant presence in one country for years, those services expand. New hotels are built, and shops are set up to cater to UN personnel. In 2016, at the time of our visit to Liberia, the prices for hotel rooms and apartment rentals for foreigners were surprisingly high, with rates similar to those in New York or Paris. The foreign investors who owned those spaces did not leave their revenues in the country, nor did they translate into a long-term investment in the cities that hosted them. The quality of the water and energy grids servicing these international presence was poor and in a dilapidated state by the time the UN had to leave.

During its lifespan, UNMIL expenditure exceeded Liberia's GDP from 2003 to 2006 and surpassed the government's revenue from 2006–2013.[16] Its departure has been met with a considerable amount of anxiety and unease, including concerns about the "financial cliff" that its absence portends.

Although the UN Country Team[17] has been actively engaged in the transition, it lacks both the resources and the coverage that UNMIL achieved at its peak. The transition has also coincided with a period of profound economic hardship. In 2014, the country was hit with twin crises—in the form of the Ebola pandemic and the fall in commodity prices—from which it has not yet recovered. Its GDP growth fell to 0.7 percent in 2014. It has since risen to 2.5 percent but remains substantially below the pre-Ebola average of more than 7 percent. The country faces high inflation and is increasingly on the verge of debt distress, with total debt stocks as of June 2017 exceeding US$730 million. A human development crisis underlies these economic challenges. Most of the population still lacks access to basic services such as water and electricity. Almost half of Liberians are food insecure. Health care is either inaccessible or unaffordable for the vast majority.

As Secretary General Antonio Guterres put it recently: "As the mandate of UNMIL ends on 30 March 2018, Liberia enjoys peace and stability...However, serious challenges remain. The overwhelming majority of the population has yet to see the anticipated dividends of peace, while many of the root causes of the conflict have not been addressed."[18]

The following charts and images highlight these and other key peacebuilding and development challenges facing a post-UNMIL Liberia and form the basis for the ideas and proposals that follow.

15 UNMIL factsheet. UN, available at: https://peacekeeping.un.org/en/mission/unmil.

16 United Nations Digital Library. Budget of the United Nations Mission in Liberia for the periods from 1 August 2003–30 June 2018, available at: https://digitallibrary.un.org.

17 The UNCT includes all the UN entities working on sustainable development, emergency, recovery and transition in programme countries. The UNCT is led by the UN Resident Coordinator, who is the representative of the UN Secretary-General in a given country, available at: https://unsdg.un.org/about/how-we-work.

18 1) UNMIL Documents. UN, available at: https://unmil.unmissions.org/Documents and www.cabri-sbo.org/uploads/files/Documents/liberia_2017_formulation_external_budget_framework_ministry_of_finance_ecowas_english_1.pdf; and 2) Budget Framework Paper 2017/18. Presented to the National Legislature of the Republic of Liberia on 30th April 2017 at the Capitol Hill, Monrovia, Liberia, available at: www.cabri-sbo.org/uploads/bia/liberia_2017_formulation_external_budget_framework_ministry_of_finance_ecowas_english_.pdf.

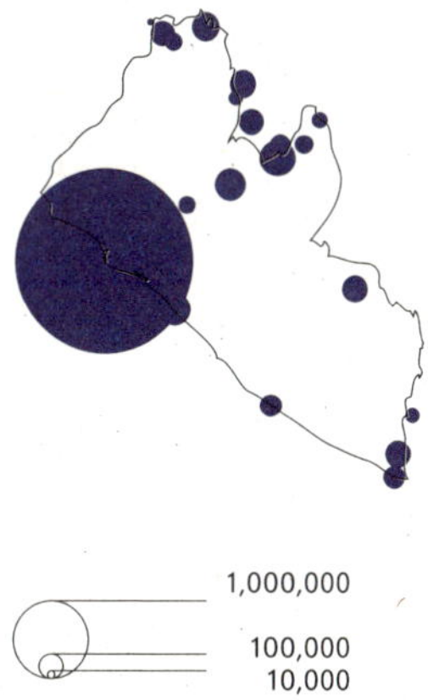

Rainfall Flooding

Population lacks access to clean safe drinking water

Legal and illegal water wells are the most common source of contaminated ground water

Cost of 50lt of bottled water (54% population lives w/ less than US$2,00 a day)

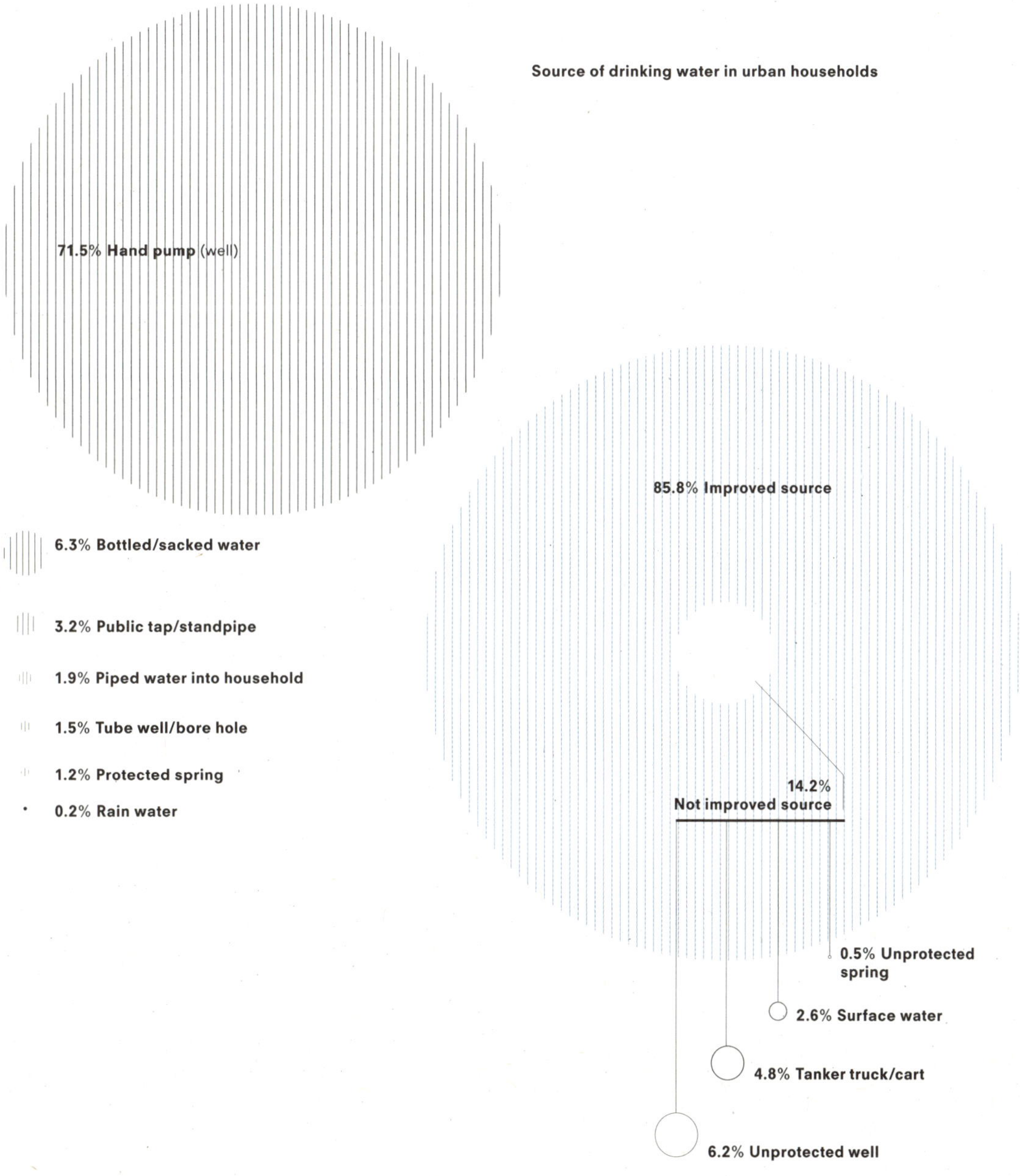

Annual rainfall and rainwater harvesting potentiality

Annual Rainfall (mm)

<2000 >2800

Annual rainy days

Annual rainfall

Monthly rainy days

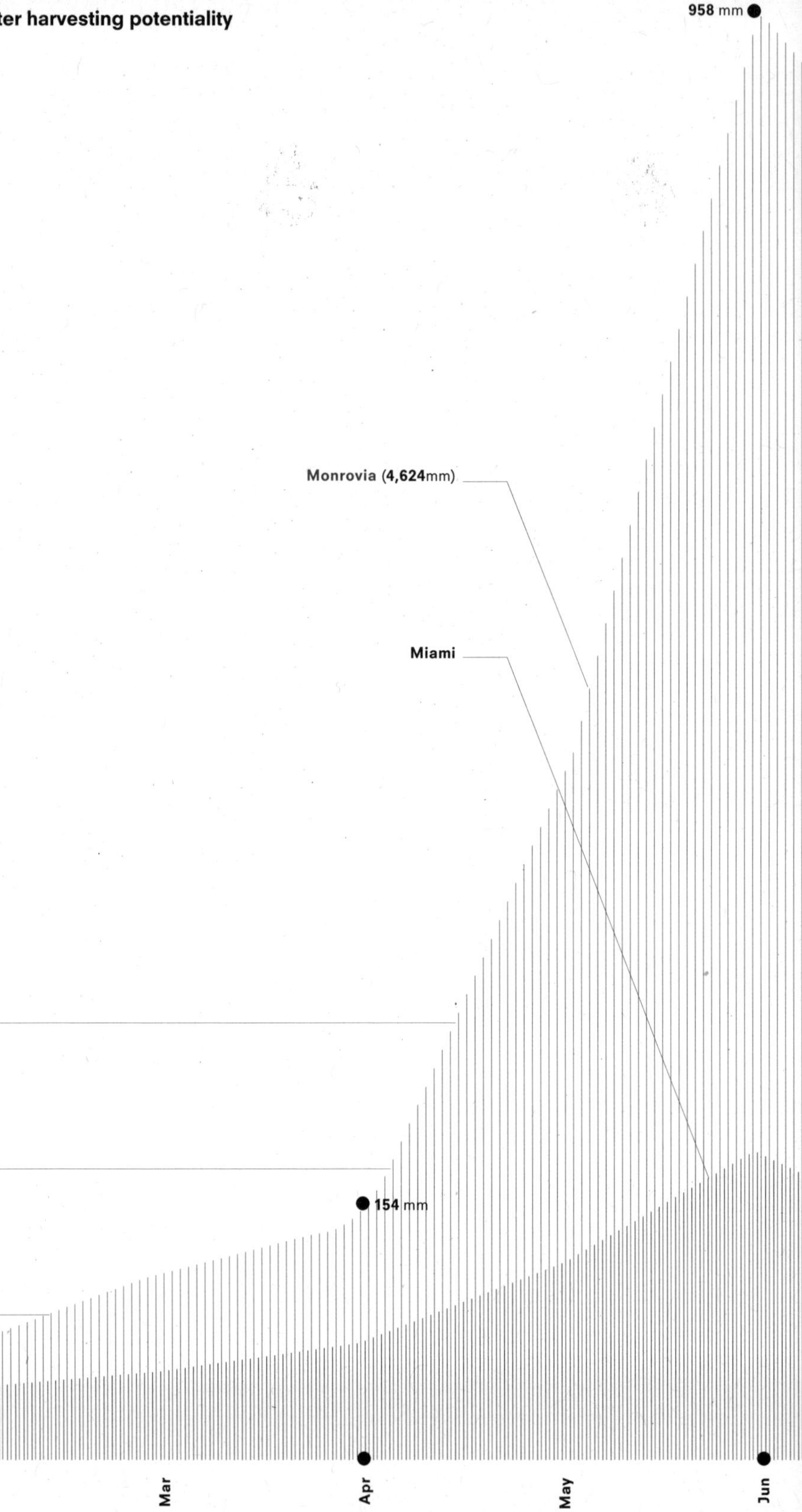

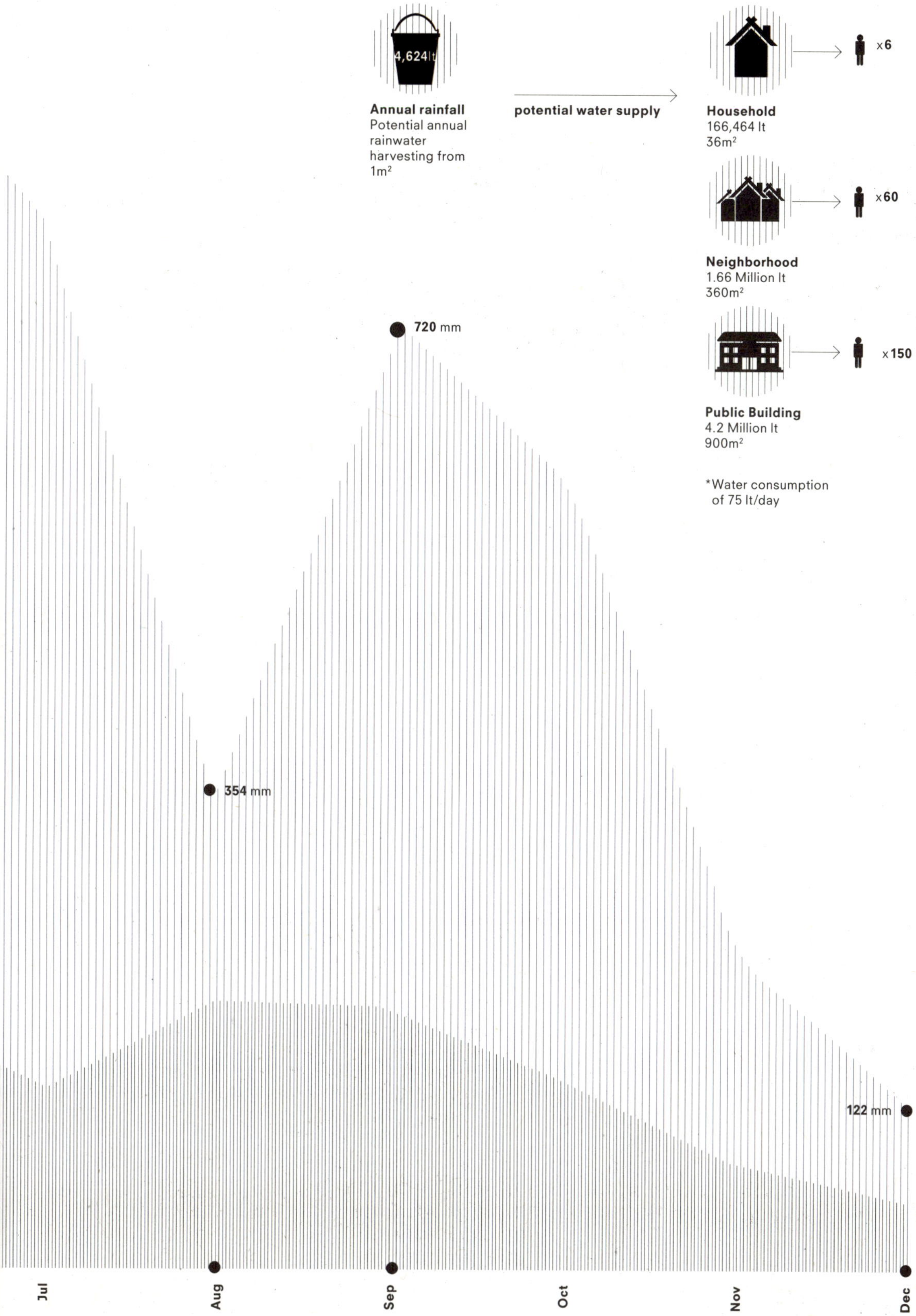
4,624lt
Annual rainfall
Potential annual rainwater harvesting from 1m²
potential water supply
Household
166,464 lt
36m²
x6
Neighborhood
1.66 Million lt
360m²
x60
Public Building
4.2 Million lt
900m²
x150
*Water consumption of 75 lt/day
720 mm
354 mm
122 mm
Jul
Aug
Sep
Oct
Nov
Dec

Floods

"Monrovia is the wettest capital city in the world in terms of annual precipitation."
The Economist, Sep. 11, 2012.

Pollution

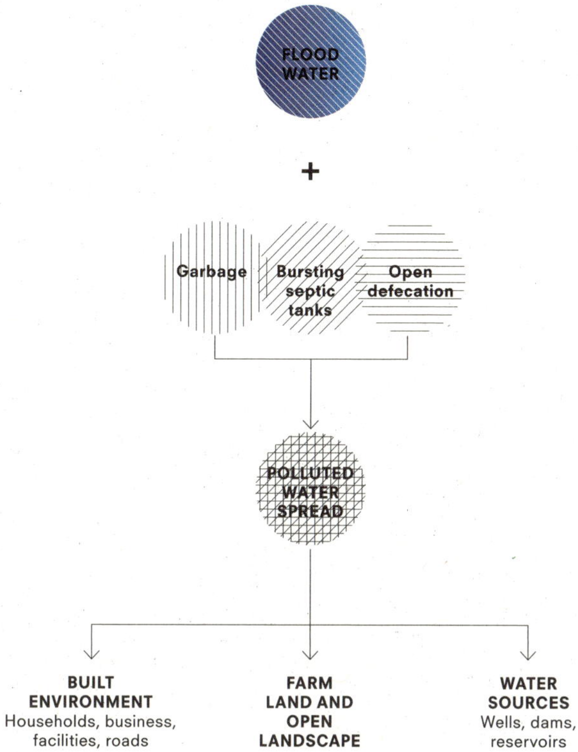

Drinking water sources

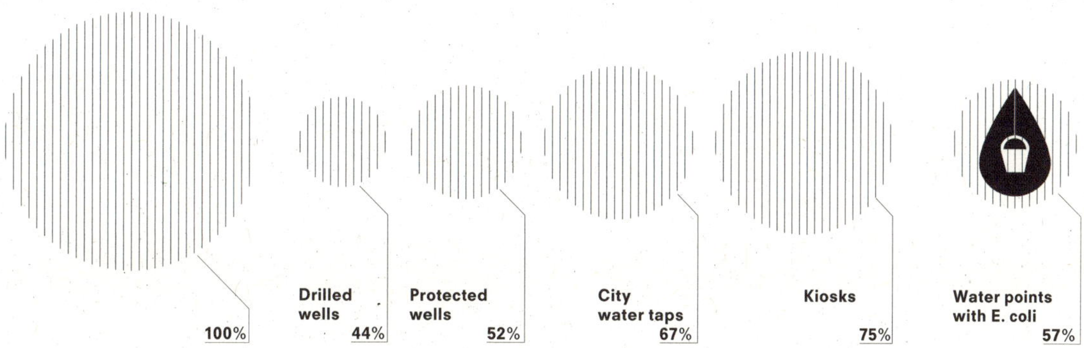

Urban Expansion and Sea Level Rise

Saint Paul River

Mesurado River

Population Growth:

80,000 (1960)
572,000 (1986)
1,144,000 (2008)
1,413,000 (2017)

Altitude
of most of the city

10–65 f.a.s.l.

Depth
of ground water

15–50ft.

Map of urbanized areas:

1960

1986

2016

Swamps
Coastline 14.2mi
Atlantic Ocean

Waste and Sanitation Infrastructure

Urban 49% — **Rural 7%**

Population with **access to sanitation**

<**20%**

Population with access to a toilet

30%

Collection of daily waste in Monrovia

>**500**/year

Deaths of children <5 due to poor sanitation in Liberia

Distribution of households by human waste disposal

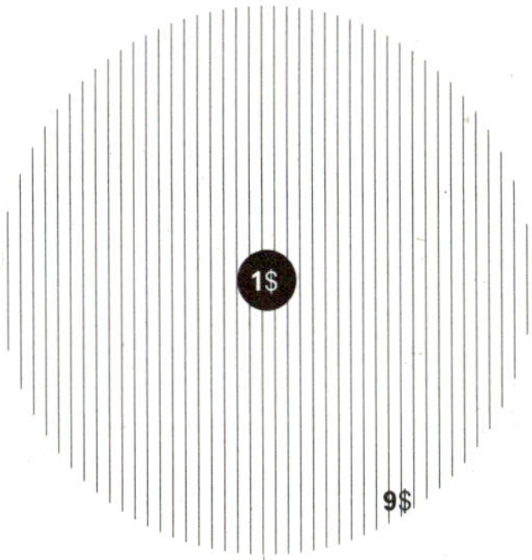

1 USD spent on sanitation improvements is equal to US$9 of savings on health, education, social, and economic development costs

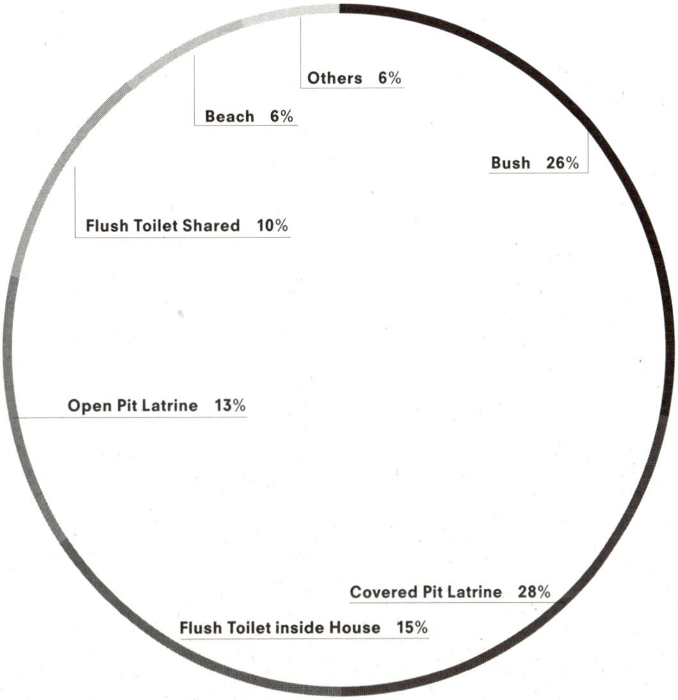

Population practicing safe hygiene behavior 5%

Morbidity in children under five years old
Malaria **18%**
Diarrhea **22%**

Deaths
related to water, sanitation, and hygiene
+ 18%

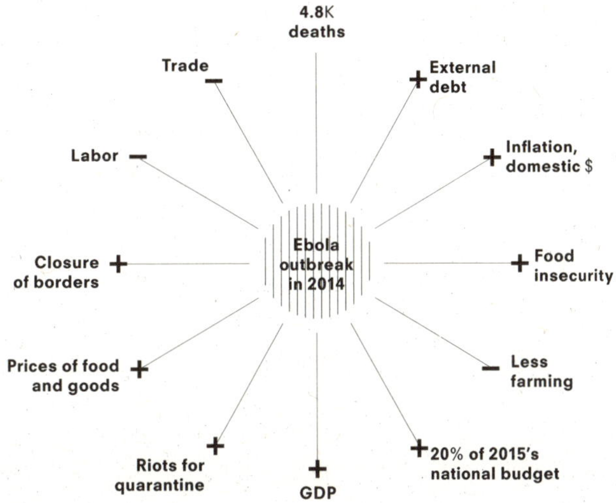

Energy Scarcity

mako
Uagadugu
Kumasi
Accra
Abidjan
San Pedro
Atlantic Ocean

Proportion
of the population
under 18 years old

51%

37%

Households with
orphans or foster children
under 18

Education and Unemployment

Education and employment are at the core of the country's recovery and independence. Liberia is facing many challenges, including the shattered state of the education system, the limited access to schools, and the lack of professional expertise. The continuous violence, civil wars, and the recent Ebola pandemic exacerbated the economic hardship in the country. According to Human Rights Watch, many people lost their lives due to these dire stresses, leaving 51 percent of the population under 18 and 37 percent of the households consisting of orphaned children. Moreover, the wars subjected thousands of children to extreme violence, killing, rape, sexual assault, abduction, torture, forced labor, and displacement. Children who fought are among the most hurt by the war. Not only did they witness numerous human rights violations, but they were also forced to commit abuses themselves.

United Nations agencies estimate that approximately 15,000 children were involved in the fighting. Generations of children who have been acculturated into a world of violence and destruction have been expected to go through a peaceful transition back into society without the necessary skills, support systems, and opportunities to do so, leaving them vulnerable to relapse, re-recruitment efforts, and criminal activity. The situation has left the country with a lack of expertise at all levels and subjected the entire population to dependency on external aid.

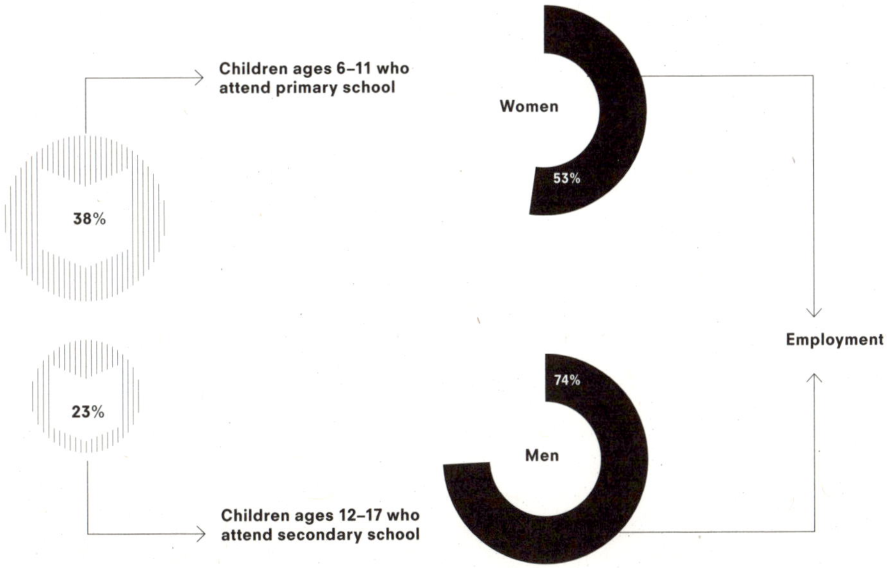

Food Insecurity

While Liberia's population has shown steady growth since the 1980s, its GDP per capita remains low, 49 percent of its households experience food insecurity, and 25 percent of the population has no access to improved water sources.

Households with moderate or severe **food insecurity**
49%

Infants born with **low birth weight**
14%

Household **expenditure on food**
65%

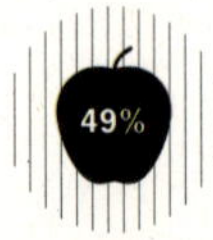

Households with **moderate or severe food insecurity**

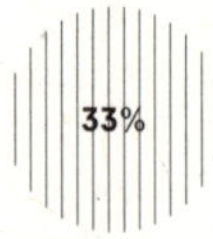

National Illiteracy
52%women
29% men

Population with **no access to an improved water source**

Population with **access to electricity**

80% importation

"**Liberia (is) importing more than 80% of its staple food,** making the country vulnerable to global food price volatility. Poorly integrated, the sector lacks basic infrastructure such as machines, farming equipment, farm-to-market roads, fertilizers and pesticides, and food storage capacity." Source: USA International Trade Administration.

Bushmeat crisis
Population growth and commercial trading of bushmeat increase the pressure on wildlife. Modern hunting practices are not regulated, and the butchering processes are associated with the spread of diseases. This could evolve into a long-term food security issue.

Unsustainable harvest of bushmeat health risk

Displacement and Refugees

Liberia's civil wars claimed about 10 percent of the country's population and forcibly displaced about half of its inhabitants. These protracted crises have left the economy of the country and the daily livelihood of its remaining population in a dire state to this day.

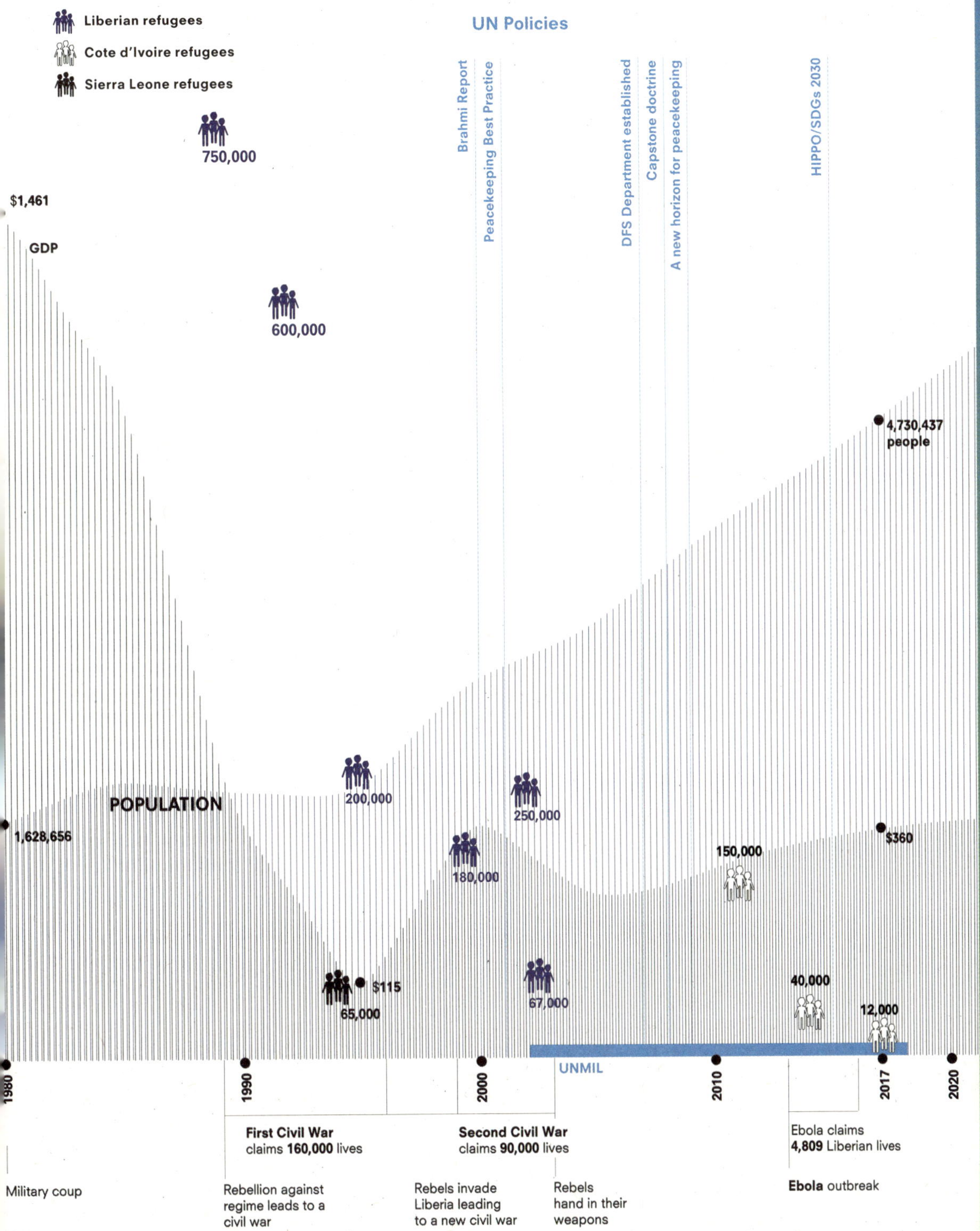

Monrovia

Field Research

The following analysis is the result of field research conducted in Liberia in November 2017, which includes a detailed record of UNMIL bases and observation of their urban surroundings. Additional data was gathered through a series of locally conducted interviews at the different UN bases. Based on this research, subsequent study and conversations took place at the United Nations Headquarters in New York. Integrated spatial and data-handling programs such as GIS and Google Earth were used to complement the field research, produce spatial analysis, and overview UNMIL bases. The final part of this chapter offers a series of examples for legacy considerations and a summary of findings.

Operating bases and units · December 2017: **8**

Number of personnel: **741**
Closed bases and units: **64**

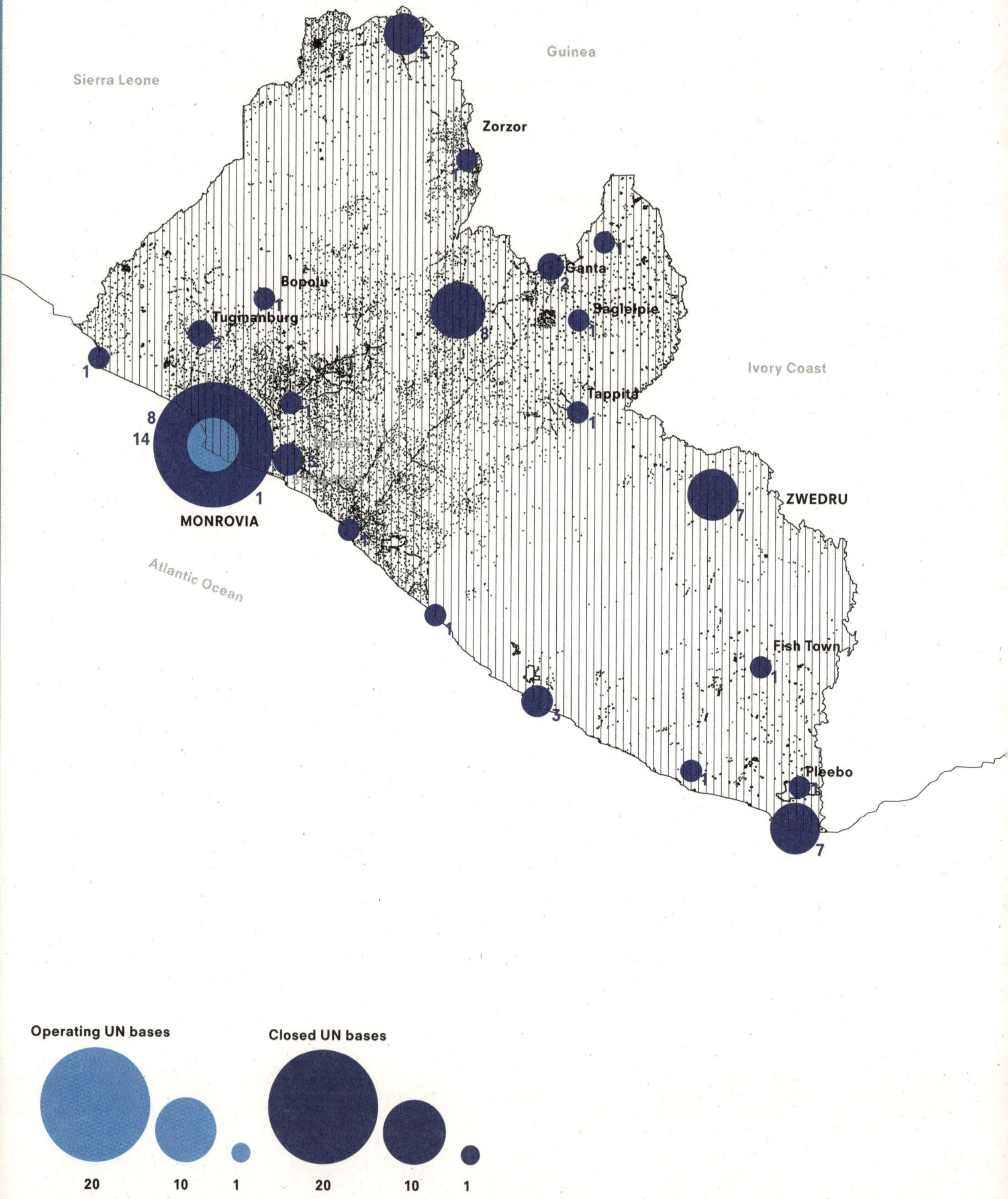

UN Bases Monrovia Area

NAME	DEPLOYMENT status at the time of the visit	STATE	SIZE	OWNERSHIP
 UN HQ	Deployed Closure date: 21 March 2018	Refurbished 12-story tower includes offices, café/restaurant and a supermarket. UN modular structures such as containers and corrugated tin cabins distributed around the building parking lot. These were used as small offices for UN guards and local security personnel.	About 2.4 hectares	Private
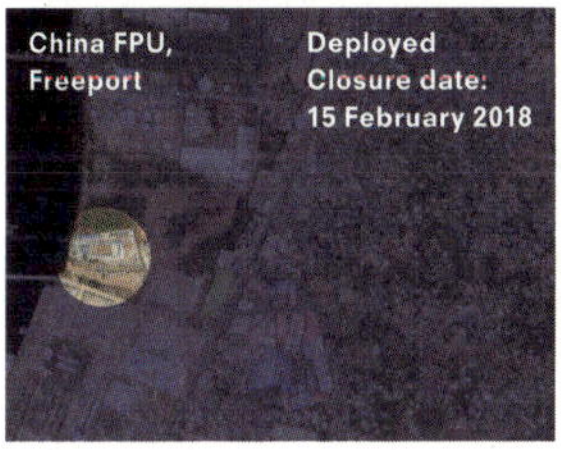 China FPU, Freeport	Deployed Closure date: 15 February 2018	The layout of the base consisted of a large square framed by U-shaped one-story modular structures. These housed offices, lodging and recreation areas, medical clinics, a large dining room, indoor and outdoor kitchen, showers and toilets. The base included water treatment, water supply, and diesel-based energy plants. The base was situated along the Monrovia coastline, with direct access to an old pier and the ocean. To the east and within the base, two hydroponic greenhouses produced enough vegetables to feed 140 people for three weeks. Their installation and maintenance cost was about USD 4,000. On the base there was a small pig farm and a fenced fishing area in the sea. The base was self-sufficient in terms of food production.	About 2.4 hectares	Government
 Star Base	Deployed Closure date: June 2018	A large base included a variety of buildings such as former Liberian factories that were converted by the UN mission into warehouses, office buildings, car repair facilities, a large supermarket and gyms. In addition to the transformation of the factories, the UN installed new modular structures to function as offices for the engineering and the cartography units. At the edge of the base a large waste site collected discarded equipment from all the UN bases in Liberia. Next to it, there was a system of underground filters linked to a small wastewater treatment plant.	About 26 hectares	Government
 RHQ Cari Gbarnga	Decommissioned Closure date: 16 June 2017	A large site that resembled a holiday village used to function as a CIA base before the war. In it, there was a swimming pool, tennis courts, small villas surrounded by gardens and private parking lots. The site was privately owned by a Lebanese company that leased it to the UN for the duration of the mission.	About 8.5 hectares	Private

UN Bases Monrovia Area

NAME	DEPLOYMENT status at the time of the visit	STATE	SIZE	OWNERSHIP
 Camp Abuja	Deployed Closure date: 31 January 2018	This UN base was made of small modular structures and containers connected through open-air corridors. A large area with dilapidated former Liberian buildings, such as an old church, an office building and a garage, were situated within the boundaries of at the base.	About 4 hectares	Government
 Pak. Med	Deployed Closure date: 30 April 2018	A set of modular buildings around an open-air yard formed a tier-3 field hospital. It included multiple clinics and medical experts. The hospital capacity was 40 beds a day. However, it had no patients at the time of our visit. The doctors stated the average number of patients per week to be 10–15.	About 1.5 hectares	Government
 Camp Clara* The site of former Hotel Africa	Decommissioned Closure date: 24 March 2017	This UN base was located adjacent to the former Hotel Africa. The site included scattered decrepit skeletons of former UN structures, such as metal wireframes of large warehouses and parts of wooden pavilions of a UN restaurant and large plastic sheets. Along the coastline, inactive UN watchtowers were still intact. The hotel was stripped, burned and the remaining walls were penetrated by bullet holes, as the site was heavily damaged during the civil wars. At the time of our visit the hotel ruins were guarded by a security company and a homeless family.	About 40 hectares	Private

*See Hotel Africa and the Crumbling of Modernity.

Monrovia is the capital and the most populous city in Liberia, with 939,524 inhabitants. It is situated along the Cape Mesurado peninsula, and its boundaries are shaped by the Atlantic Ocean coast, the Mesurado River, and the Saint Paul River.

The city was named in 1924 after US President James Monroe, a prominent supporter of establishing a colony for freed Black slaves from the US and the Caribbean islands in Liberia.

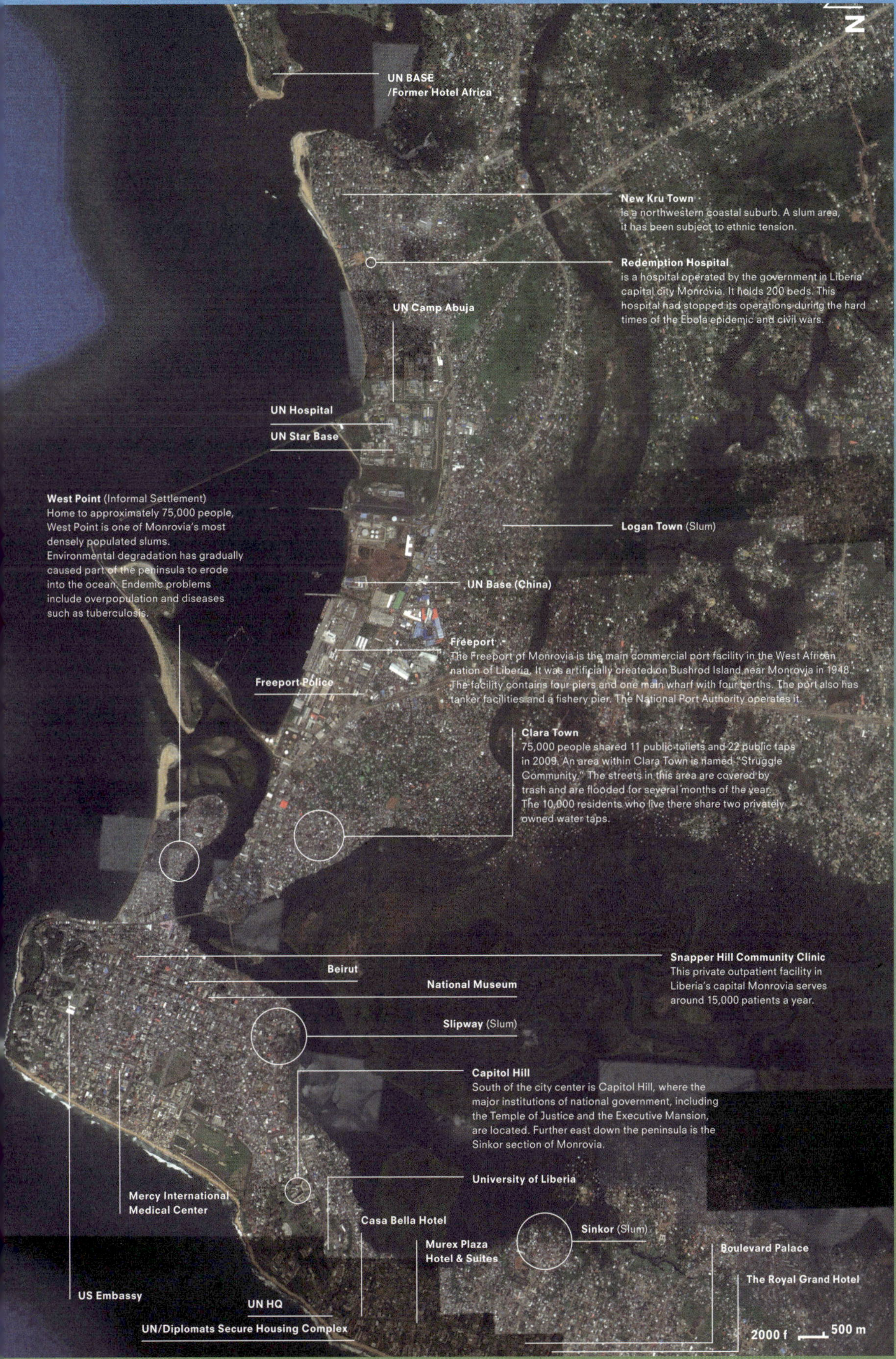
N
UN BASE
/Former Hotel Africa
New Kru Town
is a northwestern coastal suburb. A slum area, it has been subject to ethnic tension.
Redemption Hospital
is a hospital operated by the government in Liberia' capital city Monrovia. It holds 200 beds. This hospital had stopped its operations during the hard times of the Ebola epidemic and civil wars.
UN Camp Abuja
UN Hospital
UN Star Base
West Point (Informal Settlement)
Home to approximately 75,000 people, West Point is one of Monrovia's most densely populated slums. Environmental degradation has gradually caused part of the peninsula to erode into the ocean. Endemic problems include overpopulation and diseases such as tuberculosis.
Logan Town (Slum)
UN Base (China)
Freeport
The Freeport of Monrovia is the main commercial port facility in the West African nation of Liberia. It was artificially created on Bushrod Island near Monrovia in 1948. The facility contains four piers and one main wharf with four berths. The port also has tanker facilities and a fishery pier. The National Port Authority operates it.
Freeport Police
Clara Town
75,000 people shared 11 public toilets and 22 public taps in 2009. An area within Clara Town is named "Struggle Community." The streets in this area are covered by trash and are flooded for several months of the year. The 10,000 residents who live there share two privately owned water taps.
Snapper Hill Community Clinic
This private outpatient facility in Liberia's capital Monrovia serves around 15,000 patients a year.
Beirut
National Museum
Slipway (Slum)
Capitol Hill
South of the city center is Capitol Hill, where the major institutions of national government, including the Temple of Justice and the Executive Mansion, are located. Further east down the peninsula is the Sinkor section of Monrovia.
University of Liberia
Mercy International Medical Center
Casa Bella Hotel
Sinkor (Slum)
Murex Plaza Hotel & Suites
Boulevard Palace
The Royal Grand Hotel
US Embassy
UN HQ
UN/Diplomats Secure Housing Complex
2000 f
500 m

Remains of the hotel and the mission, 2017.

Hotel Africa and the Crumbling of Modernity

A Visit to Camp Clara

On the coast of Monrovia, along the shores of the Atlantic, a former luxury resort stands dilapidated, embodying the shattered dreams of emancipation and a long history of violence. The visit to the former five-star Hotel Africa in 2017 was part of a field study of the drawdown phase of UNMIL.

Upon our arrival, we were scheduled to visit Camp Clara, a recently evacuated UN base situated within the Hotel Africa complex and one of the first deployment sites of troops from the United Nations Mission to Liberia (UNMIL). We met our hosts – an Egyptian peacekeeper and a logistics director from El Salvador – at the UN headquarters' secured parking lot, crowded with white SUVs, and headed to the camp, some 16 kilometers away on the northern outskirts of Monrovia.

As we drove toward the Virginia District – originally called New Virginia by the largely African-American population that settled there – Monrovia began to appear. We passed compounds, ministry buildings, a university campus, local markets, schools, and informal neighborhoods. Since the deployment of UNMIL in 2003, the road leading to the headquarters had been populated by small businesses, hotels, restaurants, shops, and small compounds catering to the large community of foreign diplomats and aid and development workers. Many of these venues, we were told, were owned and managed by a group of Lebanese businessmen involved in the region since the 1960s.

Our hosts from the UN shared their experiences with us, at times mentioning their isolated lives in Liberia, the long distances from home, their disconnect from the local community. They faced difficulties finding suitable lodging: the local housing quality was poor and rents were skyrocketing. The real-estate and tourism industries, they said, were run by business-savvy landlords who hiked their rates for international aid and development workers, so the rental price of an apartment in Monrovia could end up being equal to those in New York or London's prime neighborhoods. Although market rates were inflated, profits that could have been used to improve the quality of the built environment or to facilitate better access to essential services were not invested back into the city or the community. Everything was made to be transitory, exploitive, and unsustainable.

This lack of long-term investment was particularly evident during the Ebola epidemic that struck Liberia from 2014 to 2016, when, as the peacekeepers described, the dread of death was everywhere and mandatory isolation hit local communities hard. UNMIL itself had been deployed after the second of two civil wars that left the country in ruin. but by 2015, it had begun to wind down. Its departure, coinciding with a dip in global commodity prices and the Ebola crisis, resulted in a steep economic decline from which Liberia has yet to recover. Much of the population still lacks access to basic services such as clean water and electricity. Almost half of Liberians are food-insecure, and healthcare is either inaccessible or unaffordable for the vast majority.[19]

Eventually, we passed the city center and seaport and made our way through a sprawl of informal tin huts. Bright green palms and mango trees unevenly covered the exposed soil, and we drove off-road, leaving clouds of red dust behind. Camp Clara had been decommissioned and handed over to the Liberian government half a year before our arrival. By the time we reached the site, the UN troops and most of their equipment were gone. The Egyptian peacekeeper parked the SUV at the edge of a barbed-wire fence and an armed guard in civilian clothing came toward us. We were told that the land had been purchased from the government by a South Africa-based private investment company, which would spend more than USD 100 million on rebuilding the hotel. In the meantime, the company had hired security to protect the asset and keep away trespassers.

After a short chat, he allowed us on site, where Camp Clara and the Hotel Africa building shared the same lush tropical soil. Alternating in time, each had a distinct function, legacy and ghostly imprint. The first visible trace of the hotel was a seven-story, modernist-looking block with strip balconies along its façade overlooking the Atlantic. On the ground floor, there were the remnants of a grand lobby, two circular halls surrounded by greenery – now a mix of invasive tropical plants that had taken over once-manicured gardens – and a pool shaped like the African continent.In The House at Sugar Beach, Helene Cooper[20] describes the glory days of the hotel. The luxury beachfront resort was funded by a group of Congolese businessmen and Lebanese merchants to host the 1979 meeting of the Organization of African Unity (OAU). In expectation of the OAU meeting, the chairing Liberian government set up a series of billboards along Tubman Boulevard. depicting African leaders. Many were left blank, as Cooper writes, because governments across the continent were facing coups and revolutions. Soon after its construction, Hotel Africa became known for its extravagant parties. The round dance halls of its famous Bacardi Disco hosted wedding receptions and pool parties.

When we arrived, the building was bare, stripped of its furniture, window frames, doors. The remaining skeleton revealed only the structure, pillars, and stairs. It was quite literally a postwar ruin in the shape of Le Corbusier's Dom-Ino House. Looted and partially burned, its walls were covered in bullet holes. The building's height, offering a panoramic view of the entire area and coastline, had made it a strategic location during the wars. Rebels had used the building to launch attacks on Monrovia in 2003.

For a moment, while walking past the pool toward the beach, I felt a breeze from the sea that reminded me of home – I grew up in Haifa, a city in Israel along the Mediterranean coast. Later, I saw a series of national flags on poles at the far edge of the site that seemed oddly new. One had blue and white stripes – to my surprise, it was Israel's.

It's strange to realize how personal associations and other histories can intertwine in a thought at moments like this. The links between Liberia and Israel, their successes and tragic failures, go back to the nineteenth century, to movements and ideologies of liberation from oppression and violence and to the idea of a return. For the Jewish people, it was Zionism, the return to the promised land, which inspired Black Zionism, the movement for emancipated slaves' return to Africa.

In 1822, American settlers arrived in this area with ships of emancipated slaves under the auspices of the American Colonization Society. With the support of President James Monroe, they purchased a small piece of land from local chiefs, later naming it Monrovia in the president's honour. As the number of settlers grew, the native population dwindled; the emancipation of one group resulted in the dispossession of another. Liberia's late-twentieth-century civil wars can be traced back to this act of liberation – not dissimilar to the story of Israel and Palestine.

Between the pool and the hotel were the derelict metal frames of two modular military hangars left behind by UNMIL. From where I stood, what I saw were bodies crumbling into other bodies. The remnants of a former modernist beach resort with its pool, disco club, and casino all in ruin, the skeletal frames of the modular military structures, and fragments of canvas bearing the UN logo. The ferocity of the damage inflicted on the hotel building and the tenuous skeletons of the UN modules stood together in deafening silence as reminders of tragic failure, a collapse of collective hope, national dreams, and modernity itself.

It was a lot to take in, but the peacekeepers prompted us to continue toward the beach cabanas and villas, some of the various lodgings Hotel Africa had offered. We walked down an unpaved path toward the far end of the site facing the Saint Paul River. This part had round, single-story bungalows with gazebo roofs. Designed as apartment suites, each included a living room, a kitchen, a couple of bedrooms, and a garden. Scattered, small, and seemingly insignificant, the cabanas seemed to have remained in better shape than the hotel block. Some of the units had been repurposed and used by UN peacekeepers for storage, office space, and as bars.

The largest bungalow, overlooking the estuary where the Saint Paul River and the Atlantic come together, was also where Charles Taylor, president of Liberia from 1998 to 2003 and for a time the most prominent warlord in Africa, liked to hang out at the hotel. Taylor, who earned a degree at Bentley College in the US and trained as a guerilla fighter in Libya, returned to Liberia in 1989 to overthrow Samuel Doe's government, beginning the First Liberian Civil War.[21] For a while thereafter, he lived at Hotel Africa, using it as a hub for global smuggling networks and trading illicit diamonds for arms.

At that time, one of the hotel's permanent residents was Guus van Kouwenhoven, a Dutchman who had been caught and imprisoned by the FBI in the 1970s for attempting to sell stolen artwork, including a Rembrandt. In the 1980s, van Kouwenhoven ended up in Liberia managing Hotel Africa, and then headed up the Liberian Oriental Timber Cooperation, a cover for his gunrunning. At the hotel, Van Kouwenhoven and Taylor traded illicit diamonds for weapons, later expanding their operations to Guinea and Sierra Leone. Likewise, Viktor Bout, a former KGB officer and military translator who used Hotel Africa as a base for his pilots, smuggled weapons from Eastern Europe to Africa and the Middle East after the collapse of the Soviet Union.[22] The history of violence entrenched in these three inhabitants stills reads in the skeletal hotel complex today.

When UNMIL was launched in 2003, shortly after Taylor's exile, the first UN troops deployed at Camp Clara were Irish peacekeepers who turned Taylor's cabanas into a recreation room and an "Irish bar." During our visit, we followed our hosts to the front door of the cabanas and exited through the back door into the former garden. We could see the estuary, a stunning view, and our hosts stood in awe of the transition. They had loved visiting this base during their deployment for the bar and restaurant along the riverbanks. The site offered a place for coming together and for rare moments of escapism from the day-to-day pragmatism of peace missions – and from what can, at times, feel like their utter futility.

The hosts had good memories of outdoor gatherings, enjoying the backdrop of the ocean and the river, and were elated to see that a wooden deck the UN troops had installed along the riverbanks was still partially intact. For us, the deck was a ruin, a vacant remnant of the UN's presence. The big cabana looked like the last spot the UN had evacuated, as if they had left in a rush. There were large sheets of plastic hanging from a temporary wall, pieces of outdoor rubber flooring, and UN food packaging scattered around.

Here, one reality tumbled into another: a layered history of colonization, hedonism, greed, war, international relations, diplomacy, and the global apparatus of humanitarian aid all left their marks. The remains – whether defaced by graffiti and bullet holes, torn away by looters, or left behind by the UN mission – inhabit the former resort complex not as ghosts but as lived artifacts. In one way or another, Hotel Africa and Camp Clara seemed still alive, coexisting in symbiosis with the surrounding ocean and plants. The ocean waves had reclaimed a few cabanas, and the humidity and salt had worked their way into the material, carving new shapes in the wood, concrete, metal and plastic. Tropical plants and their exposed roots had entered the buildings, covering floors and walls and taking over some of the domesticated plants that had been brought in by the landscapers from around the world to decorate the hotel gardens.

The day we walked around the site was beautiful. The sea was calm, the breeze was gentle. Children around us went on playing. What was once a storied hotel was, for them, not a broken ruin but a new home.

19 ReliefWeb. Event Summary: Launch of UN Peacekeeping Missions in Urban Environments: The Legacy of UNMIL – Liberia. 2019. Available at: https://reliefweb.int/report/liberia/event-summary-launch-un-peacekeeping-missions-urban-environments-legacy-unmil.
20 Cooper, H. The House at Sugar Beach. Prince Frederick, MD: Recorded Books, 2008.
21 "How a tyrant's 'logs of war' bring terror to West Africa." The Guardian, May 27, 2001. Available at: www.theguardian.com/world/2001/may/27/theobserver.
22 "Dispatch from Camp Clara." NewsScoops.Org – Irish Newspaper Investigations.Available at: www.newsscoops.org/?p=443.

Modular hangar left by UNMIL, 2017.

Remains of the hotel and the mission, 2017.

Family of a private security guard at the hotel pool, 2017.

Former pool and bar overlooking the ocean, 2017.

Skeletal frame of what was once Charles Taylor's villa, 2017.

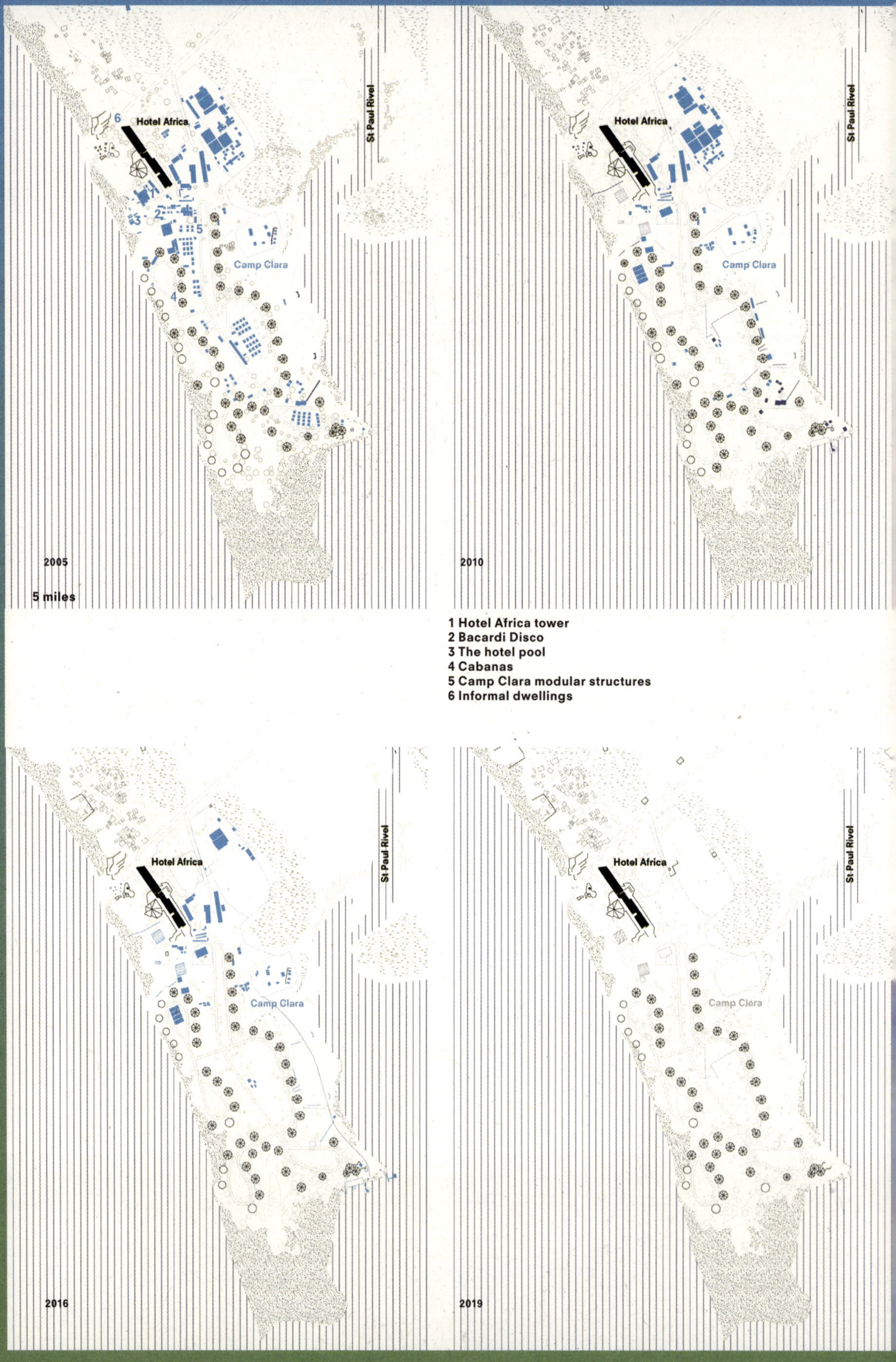
Hotel Africa
St Paul Rivel
Camp Clara
1
2
3
4
5
6
2005
5 miles
2010
2016
2019
1 Hotel Africa tower
2 Bacardi Disco
3 The hotel pool
4 Cabanas
5 Camp Clara modular structures
6 Informal dwellings

Atlantic Ocean

Cabanas with blue stripes painted during UNMIL's deployment, 2017.

Remains of the hotel and the UN camp, 2017.

The former hotel pool.

Camp Clara at the former hotel during the UNMIL deployment. Monrovia, 2003–2015 (Flicker).

A Visit to a Liquidation and Disposal Site 1

The UN *Department of Field Support Liquidation Manual* defines liquidation as the process of closing down a mission. It generally occurs in two tracks: the technical liquidation process that focuses on the physical closure of the mission, and the administrative liquidation process that can only be completed when a final performance report has been submitted to the General Assembly by the mission.[23]

For Liberia, the liquidation plan detailed various components, including a) staff downsizing, b) asset disposal and handover of premises, c) liquidation steering committee and liquidation working group, d) financial closure, e) records disposition, f) camp sites closure, g) communication with UN HQs, h) interaction with non-UN authorities, i) liquidation activities reporting.[24]

According to the liquidation manual, asset disposal is an important part of the technical liquidation. It includes a disposal plan (ADP) that divides assets into five categories: Group I includes equipment in good condition that will be redeployed to other peacekeeping operations or placed in reserve for use by future missions; Group II comprises equipment to be redeployed to other United Nations activities (e.g., special political missions), provided there is a demonstrated need for the equipment; Group III is equipment to be sold to other United Nations agencies, international organizations, or non-governmental organizations; Group IV consists of equipment that cannot be disposed of in groups I–III and therefore is subject to commercial disposal; and the final group, Group V, encompasses assets installed in a country that would set back its rehabilitation if dismantled, such as airfield installations and equipment, buildings, bridges and mine clearing equipment. Such assets are to be turned over to the government in return for compensation or—with the prior approval of the General Assembly—contributed free of charge.[25]

During our field research in Liberia in 2017, UNMIL was undergoing its liquidation phase. Technically, most of its camp sites had been closed. Some had been handed over to the local government, and only a handful of bases remained deployed. At that time, several disposal sites were active, including a large open area surrounded by fencing that was allocated for the collection and disposal of much of the material left in the UN bases after the troops had left. A hilly landscape of latrines, coolers, office equipment, toilet seats, large water barrels, computers, keyboards, and all sorts of appliances were laid out in piles. It was astounding to see the abundance of supplies destined to be destroyed in a city and country that lacked all those resources.

We walked around the site with the UN environmental officers, who were content with their ecological achievements and at having collected so much equipment in such an orderly way. In the past, that wasn't the case, the environmental officer said. This was a precedent and an example of best environmental practice for UN agencies. Changes at the UN are incremental, and the incorporation of an environmental approach in missions' mandates was the result of a long and tiring struggle on the part of UNEP and other environmental advocacy groups.

After decades of negative reports about the carbon emissions and waste produced by UN peacekeeping missions, a new initiative to develop an environmental strategy for peacekeeping was launched in 2017. Its application is still a source of confusion for the peacekeepers, and its straightforward implementation is still caught up in the institution's politics.

23 Liquidation, UN, available at: https://casquebleu.org/index.php?title=Liquidation.
24 Audit of liquidation planning in the United Nations Mission in Liberia, OIOS Office of Internal Oversight Services Internat Audit Division Report 2018/067.
25 Ibid.

UNMIL disposal site. Monrovia, 2017.

UN Peacekeeping Missions and the Environment

Climate change is a "crisis multiplier" that has profound implications for international peace and stability. [It requires] deep partnerships within and beyond the United Nations system to blunt its acute effects on food security, natural resources, and migration patterns fueling tensions across countries and regions.[26]
Secretary-General António Guterres

The environment is not only a silent casualty of war and armed conflict but of peacekeeping missions too.[27] The UN Environment Programme (UNEP) has repeatedly reported that UN peacekeeping operations produce over half of the overall UN system's greenhouse gas emissions, which adds up to "approximately 1.75 million tons of CO2 per year—about the same size as the climate footprint of the city of London."[28]

The physical landscape of UN peacekeeping missions can be most aptly characterized as an assemblage of large-scale fortified islands that takes on a variety of spatial typologies. In 2018, the United Nations conducted 15 peacekeeping operations worldwide with a total spending of US$6.8 billion and 106,338 personnel deployed in the field. In 2016, peacekeeping operations covered an area of over a million square kilometers, and the yearly expenditure on buildings and construction, real estate, and heating and cooling totaled US$448,287,372. The various peacekeeping missions incorporate more than 270 constructed sites, including, among others, camps, super camps, airfields, and 310 medical clinics.[29] This material conglomeration is predominantly constructed and maintained by the peacekeepers in coordination with private companies, global supply chains, and logistics systems. Their spatial production is disproportionately large in scale and foreign in shape and technology when compared to their local context. The result is an excessively extractive, wasteful, and environmentally destructive practice.[30]

UN peacekeeping missions impose short- and long-term stresses on local populations, natural resources, and the environment. They burden local inhabitants by exerting pressure on their scarce resources, and their massive material presence[31] generates negative environmental impacts that remain long after the missions are gone.

Geographically, peacekeeping missions take place in the world's most impoverished and imperiled areas, situated in places that are suffering some of the worst effects of climate change.[32] In 2016, peacekeeping missions were present in more than 170 inhabited African sites with a combined population of 31 million, and with an average population growth rate of 3.2 percent per year, the highest in the world. These areas are experiencing rapidly rising temperatures[33] and cumulative high-impact climate events, such as heat waves, droughts, sea level rise, storm surges, and floods. The shifting climate conditions intensify famine, poverty, destruction of habitat, displacement, disease, and conflicts.[34] The confluence of the changing climate, rapid population growth, weak institutions, and violent conflicts is taking an ever-swelling toll on human lives.[35] The climate crisis is expected to instigate "the biggest threat to security that modern humans have ever faced."[36] However, it is not only the inhabitants of sub-Saharan Africa who are living on the front lines of the climate crisis; tens of thousands of peacekeepers, representatives of 121 countries, are there too. UN agencies must lead by example in an international effort focused on environmental stewardship, which should be cross-pillar and central to all their mandates and missions, rather than offering a case-by-case response, an ad-hoc solution, or yet another intricate bureaucratic procedure.

26 "Climate Change 'Biggest Threat Modern Humans Have Ever Faced', World-Renowned Naturalist Tells Security Council, Calls for Greater Global Cooperation." SC/14445 23 FEBRUARY 2021 www.un.org/press/en/2021/sc14445.doc.htm
27 "Good Environmental Stewardship Integral to Peacebuilding, Secretary-General Says in Message for International Day"SG/SM/16316-OBV/1396. 4 NOVEMBER 2014. www.un.org/press/en/2014/sgsm16316.doc.htm.
28 UNEP. "Greening the Blue Helmets. Environment, Natural Resources and UN Peacekeeping Operations." 2012. https://wedocs.unep.org/bitstream/handle/20.500.11822/8840/UNEP_greening_blue_helmets.pdf?sequence=3&amp%3BisAllowed=
29 See UN Procurement Division, "Statistics," available at www.un.org/Depts/ptd/statistics/2016; and Shoshan, *BLUE: The Architecture of UN Peacekeeping.*
30 See UN Super Camps and Global Supply Chains on page xx. and Politics of Sourcing and Procurement on page xx.
31 See UN Super Camps and Global Supply Chains on page xx.
32 "Climate Change Is an Increasing Threat to Africa" https://unfccc.int/news/climate-change-is-an-increasing-threat-to-africa
33 State of the Climate in Africa, 2019. World Meteorological Organization. https://library.wmo.int/doc_num.php?explnum_id=10421
34 Ibid.
35 "Climate Change and Urban Vulnerability in Africa," CLUVA, accessed October 24, 2017, www.cluva.eu/.
36 "Climate Change 'Biggest Threat Modern Humans Have Ever Faced', World-Renowned Naturalist Tells Security Council, Calls for Greater Global Cooperation." www.un.org/press/en/2021/sc14445.doc.htm

Environmental concerns in peacekeeping need to shift the paradigm from waste reduction mitigation to holistic and regenerative systemic approaches.

The Environmental Impact of UN Peace Operations

In recent years, the Foundation for Achieving Seamless Territory (FAST) has collaborated with the International Peace Institute (IPI) and the NYU Center on International Cooperation (CIC-NYU) to advocate for broadening the responsibility and accountability of UN peacekeeping missions when it comes to their growing environmental impact. Our progress so far has been incremental. During conversations, workshops, and public events, we have faced institutional resistance to change, obscure politics, and bureaucratic fatigue, which has translated into a profound lack of imagination on the part of policymakers in the UN Peacekeeping Department.

One of our efforts to influence an institutional shift was the report "Greening Peacekeeping: The Environmental Impact of UN Peace Operations,"[37] published in April 2018 in collaboration with the IPI. The following section includes selected elements from the report that demonstrate this challenging institutional setting, its environmental approaches, and their constraints. The essay below ends with a list of recommendations that were developed in collaboration with the Peacekeeping Department of Field Support (DFS) and their environmental section.

The first part of the report addresses the challenging contexts in which UN peace operations are active. Their presence results in multiple environmental concerns that have been receiving growing institutional attention. The second part is dedicated to DFS's environmental approach, including policies, guidelines, and small-scale projects. The third part assesses the challenges DFS faces in the implementation of its Environment Strategy, launched in 2016 and in effect since January 2017. The mainstreaming and fulfillment of the different objectives set up in the strategy are slowed down by disparities among missions, which leads to uneven implementation of the environmental policy along with difficulties in ensuring oversight from UN headquarters. The final part suggests a series of recommendations to improve current practices and prevent short- and long-term environmental damage in the context of UN peace operations. Differentiating between short-, medium-, and long-term recommendations, it offers suggestions on how to strengthen financial and human resources dedicated to addressing environmental issues in missions; how to mainstream eco friendly practices through training and best practices; and how to advocate for stronger oversight, carefully build local capacity through local sourcing, and improve current indicators. A UN presence in fragile and conflict-prone areas should not be a source of added stress; it should improve local environmental sustainability and build resilience, especially because such actions are inexorably linked to conflict prevention.

37 Lucile Maertens and Malkit Shoshan, "Greening Peacekeeping: The Environmental Impact of UN Peace Operations," New York: International Peace Institute, April 2018.

38 This part of the essay is based on a report published in collaboration with the International Peace Institute in 2018. See: Lucile Maertens and Malkit Shoshan, "Greening Peacekeeping: The Environmental Impact of UN Peace Operations," New York: International Peace Institute, April 2018.

Challenging Environments

Institutional Attention to the Environmental Impacts of UN Missions[38]

In the 1960s and 1970s, major environmental incidents and concerns about their effects on human health brought ecological issues onto the international agenda. Two decades after the first environment-focused conference in Stockholm, the 1992 UN Conference on Environment and Development in Rio de Janeiro led to the adoption of three significant international treaties (on climate change, biodiversity, and desertification) and international recognition of the concept of sustainable development (elaborated in the 1987 Brundtland Report). Considering growing environmental concerns at the international level, the UN Advance Mission in Cambodia (UNAMIC, 1991–1992) marked the beginning of UN peacekeepers' concern with natural resources. As far as environmental issues are concerned, the mission's main focus was the role of timber in financing the conflict in Cambodia.[39]

UN peacekeepers only really started to pay attention to their own environmental impact beginning in the 2000s. The UN Secretariat realized the environmental challenge of peace operations around 2004 and 2005, with the deployment of new large-scale operations in Darfur (2004–present), Haiti (2004–2017), Sudan/South Sudan (2005–present), and Chad/the Central African Republic (2007–2010). The number of staff and amount of infrastructure drastically increased in these missions in comparison with previous ones. Moreover, these peace operations were deployed in countries without basic infrastructure, which is necessary for tasks like waste management. This increasing attention on environmental concerns was part of a global movement in the field of humanitarian action. The UN High Commissioner for Refugees (UNHCR) began paying attention to the environmental impact of its activities within and outside of its refugee camps from the late 1980s, and especially after the 1992 Rio Summit.[40]

Humanitarian actors more strongly acknowledged the issue in the 2005 Humanitarian Reform Agenda, which introduced the cluster approach. Because of its cross-cutting dimension, the environment was not institutionalized as a separate cluster; however, a number of key documents and guidelines recognized the importance of environmental concerns in international interventions.

In addition, the Joint UNEP/Office for the Coordination of Humanitarian Affairs (OCHA) Environmental Unit has also worked "to promote that environmental issues are an integral part of all elements of humanitarian response... This means that environmental concerns are addressed and considered in needs assessment and analysis, strategic response planning, resource mobilization, performance monitoring and evaluation."[41] Even though the unit still indicated in its 2014 study that there was an urgent need to systematically address a range of issues related to leadership and accountability, there is growing interest in addressing the environmental impacts of humanitarian action, including from governments.[42]

In the outcome declaration of the 2012 Earth Summit, UN member states "call[ed] upon the United Nations system to improve the management of facilities and operations, by taking into account sustainable development practices."[43] Concerns about the environmental impact of UN peace operations also echo a growing institutional attention to the environmental footprint of the UN system. On June 5, 2007, Secretary-General Ban Ki-moon publicly requested that UN institutions lead by example and "go green." The UN Climate Neutral Strategy was approved in October 2007 by the Chief Executives Board.

As a result of this decision, the "Greening the Blue" program was launched to fulfill three commitments: to measure; to reduce; and to offset when feasible. Heads of agencies committed to expanding measurement of their environmental impact for the Greening the Blue annual reports by adding data on waste management by 2016, on the use of drinking water resources by 2018, and on staff training by 2019. Although the program is not compulsory, since 2009 the UN has presented an annual report on its environmental footprint and efforts to reduce it: 67 UN entities participated in the calculation of UN carbon emissions for the 2017 edition, and 56 provided data on waste management.[44] In parallel, the UN Environmental Management Group, established in 2001, has sought to gather all UN programs, funds, and agencies to enhance "UN system-wide collaboration and coherent responses on environmental matters."[45]

After participating in the group's meetings since 2008, DFS's proactive request to join the group was accepted. It is in the context of these efforts that UNEP produced a report dedicated to UN peace operations in 2012. This report, entitled *Greening the Blue Helmets: Environment, Natural Resources and UN Peacekeeping Operations*, was developed in close cooperation with DFS and DPKO.

39 UNEP, Greening the Blue Helmets: Environment, Natural Resources and UN Peacekeeping Operations, 2012, p. 43, available at www.un.org/en/peacekeeping/publications/UNEP_greening_blue_helmets.pdf.

40 Lucile Maertens, "Le HCR et l'appropriation progressive de l'agenda environnemental," in *Mobilité humaine et environnement: Du global au local*, Christel Cournil and Chloé Vlassopoulos, eds. (Paris: Éditions Quæ, 2015).

41 See OCHA, "Environmental Emergencies," available at www.unocha.org/themes/environmental-emergencies.

42 Joint UNEP/OCHA Environment Unit, Environment and Humanitarian Action: Increasing Effectiveness, Sustainability and Accountability, August 2014, available at www.unocha.org/sites/unocha/files/EHA%20Study%20webfinal_1.pdf

43 UN General Assembly Resolution 66/288, The Future We Want (July 27, 2012), UN Doc. A/RES/66/288, September 11, 2012, para. 96.

44 UNEP, Greening the Blue Report 2017: The UN System's Environmental Footprint and Efforts to Reduce It, 2017, available at www.greeningtheblue.org/resources/climate-neutrality.

45 See http://unemg.org/.

The report was divided into two parts: the first dealt with the environmental footprint of operations, while the second touched on natural resources, conflicts, and peacekeeping. The first part proposed evaluating the implementation of the 2009 Environmental Policy and listed "good practices" for energy efficiency and other eco-friendly practices.[46] Based on this study, UNEP developed an online training course on the environment and peacekeeping in partnership with the UN Institute for Training and Research (UNITAR) and the International Institute for Sustainable Development (IISD), and with the support of DPKO and DFS. It also intended to set up a five-year partnership with DFS to facilitate the implementation of the 2009 Environmental Policy. With a strong commitment to address these issues from Under-Secretary-General for Field Support Atul Khare, in 2016 DFS and UNEP established a project for UNEP to provide technical assistance to DFS.[47] UNEP's support for addressing the environmental impact of peacekeeping was further strengthened by the 2030 Agenda for Sustainable Development, adopted in September 2015, and the Paris Agreement on climate change, adopted in December 2015. These agreements set goals and targets for all countries, further incentivizing the UN to improve environmental management of its activities and fully implement the "do no harm" principle.

Environmental Concerns and Issues at Stake for UN Peace Operations

International relations researcher Kai Kenkel described the UN's transition to larger multidimensional missions as advancing "from the thin blue line to painting a country blue."[48] Although he was referring to the expanding scope of peace operations at large and the broadening tasks of peacekeepers, this shift is also reflected in the spatial manifestation and footprint of peace operations. More bases and headquarters had to be constructed locally to accommodate the growing numbers of peacekeepers. These new facilities were erected in various urban and rural settings, including alongside local institutions such as government buildings and administrative offices. These physical changes have increased the UN's environmental footprint. The growing demand resulting from a mission's arrival challenges the capacity of local infrastructure, which is usually weak and often already overwhelmed. At the same time, major supply routes can be hard for missions to access, as they often operate in hard-to-reach areas and in landlocked countries.[49] This, combined with stresses such as protracted conflicts, long periods of drought, and rapid population growth, as well as a lack of local expertise, result in a massive influx of materials and know-how into peacekeeping areas.[50] According to data collected in 2016, field missions were responsible for more than half of the total greenhouse gas emissions of the entire UN system (see diagrams on page 286).[51]

Military bases, camps, super camps, airfields, headquarters, and logistics hubs are planned, constructed, and deployed by the UN inside and next to populated areas, with a large presence in territories that are often poorly planned and built-in zones exposed to natural hazards such as droughts and floods.[52] These pressures intensify with the effects of the climate crisis. In rural areas, too, peace operations often intervene in fragile environments threatened by desertification, over-exploitation of natural resources, and climate variability. Yet despite these challenges, peace operations are driven by immediate political and Security considerations rather than protracted environmental ones. Furthermore, peacekeeping operations increasingly intervene in multidimensional conflict settings that lead them to militarize and to fortify their bases, further expanding their physical footprint and isolating them from the local context. This approach means that mission personnel often have little regard for the local context and are poorly trained in environmental and urban management. Concerns regarding the growing environmental footprint of UN missions have been highlighted in debriefing reports from environmental officers, the UN per-

46 UNEP, Greening the Blue Helmets.
47 UN Field Support, DFS Environment Strategy, "Executive Summary," April 2017, p. 1, available at www.un.org/en/peacekeeping/publications/UNDFS_Environment_Strategy_ExecSum_vF.pdf.
48 Kai Michael Kenkel, "Five Generations of Peace Operations: From the 'Thin Blue Line' to 'Painting a Country Blue,'" *Revista Brasileira de Política Internacional* 56, no. 1 (2013).
49 In November 2017, 66 percent of peacekeeping personnel were working in landlocked or hard-to-reach areas. UN Field Support, DFS Environment Strategy, "Executive Summary," November 2017 p. 3, available at https://peacekeeping.un.org/sites/default/files/171116_dfs_exec_summary_environment_0.pdf.
50 Shoshan, *BLUE: The Architecture of UN Peacekeeping,* pp. 6–17.
51 This is the latest available data, from the UN's annual measurement in 2017. UNEP, Greening the Blue Report 2017.
52 Shoshan, *BLUE: The Architecture of UN Peacekeeping,* pp. 6–17. See also the UN Geospatial Information Section website www.un.org/Depts/Cartographic/english/htmain.htm.

sonnel in charge of environmental issues within DFS and on field missions. For example, a former environmental officer in the UN Stabilization Mission in the Democratic Republic of the Congo (MONUSCO) emphasized the severe risks to the organization's image if it did not adequately manage its environmental impact.[53] Additionally, UN peacekeeping operations often face criticism from host countries, and their waste and wastewater management is under scrutiny, especially since the cholera outbreak in Haiti.[54]

UN bases are designed as self-sufficient islands, providing secure access to water, electricity and food for peacekeepers, and there are often extreme differences between UN bases and local populations in terms of consumption and waste production patterns. For example, the average Malian generates 237.3 kilograms of waste per year, while a UN peacekeeper produces 677 kilograms per year.[55] In other words, a peacekeeper produces about three times more waste than a Malian, which can significantly impact the local environment. It also means that a mission of 15,000 peacekeepers produces about 11,000 tons of solid waste a year, not including waste resulting from the use of ammunition. Moreover, peacekeepers are often blamed for their use of resources. For example, the UN–African Union Mission in Darfur (UNAMID) and humanitarian actors dramatically increased demand for water and wood in the region, leading to deforestation, which became "a source of tension with local communities."[56] In fragile environments, resources are often already scarce, and governance systems may be weak and unresponsive to local needs. This scarcity of and unequal access to resources and land often lie at the very center of the conflicts UN peacekeepers are mandated to manage. The deployment and presence of UN peace operations put stress on and obstruct local ecosystems, burdening the surrounding communities, forcing them to share their limited resources with the peacekeepers.[57]

If UN missions are not environmentally responsible, they face three main consequences. First, the ecological degradation resulting from UN activities affects their reception by local communities and jeopardizes the organization's legitimacy. Second, environmental damage caused by UN missions has a safety and Security dimension, since it can be a source of tension between the UN and the host community, as well as within local communities, which can hamper the implementation of the overall mandate of the mission. Third, ecological damage can have long-term consequences for ecosystems and communities, even years after a mission closes down, from waste resulting from the use of plastic bottles or ammunition to the depletion of subterranean water reserves in arid areas and the overall carbon footprint of missions due to air travel and transport.

Environmental Issues and the Security Council

The Security Council has regularly discussed environmental issues since the late 1990s. It has repeatedly examined the link between the environment and conflict, first approaching this issue through the lens of the exploitation of natural resources. It adopted a series of sanctions on certain commodities, such as timber and diamonds, and mandated peacekeepers to directly or indirectly address natural resources (e.g., supervision of the logging moratorium in Cambodia, support for policies to prevent illegal trade in natural resources in the Democratic Republic of the Congo, oversight of oil infrastructure in Sudan and South Sudan). In 2001, in Resolution 1343, it linked the exploitation of natural resources to conflict financing and recommended "to further investigate possible links between the exploitation of natural resources and other forms of economic activity in Liberia, and the fueling of conflict in Sierra Leone and neighboring countries."[58] In 2005, it adopted Resolution 1625, which recognized the potential contribution of high-value natural resources "to the outbreak, escalation or continuation of armed conflict."[59] In 2007, UN member states agreed on a presidential state-

53 Maertens, "Quand les Casques bleus passent au vert," pp. 61–62.
54 Gladstone, Rick. "Cholera 'Forever Destroyed' U.N.'s Image in Haiti, Ban Ki-moon Says", *NY Times*. www.nytimes.com/2021/06/06/world/americas/cholera-haiti-ban-ki-moon-memoir.html.
55 See Global Footprint Network, available at http://data.footprintnetwork.org/#/compareCountries?type=EFCpc&cn=undefined&yr=2013; UNEP Greening the Blue Report 2017: The UN System's Environmental Footprint and Efforts to Reduce It, 2016, available at www.greeningtheblue.org/sites/default/files/Greening%20the%20Blue%20report%202017%20-%20Brochure%20(web%20-%20low%20res).pdf.
56 UNEP, Greening the Blue Helmets, p. 21.
57 Shoshan and Szita, "Reimagining the Peacekeeping Mission."
58 UN Security Council Resolution 1343 (7 March 2001), UN Doc. S/RES/1343.
59 UN Security Council Resolution 1625 (September 14, 2005), UN Doc. S/RES/1625.

ment concluding the first debate on natural resources and conflicts. In this statement, they highlighted the role of UN peacekeeping operations in the restoration of natural resource management systems.[60] According to UNEP's 2012 report, member states also requested several missions to invest in issues related to natural resources, including the missions in Angola, Cambodia, Ivory Coast, the Democratic Republic of the Congo, Iraq-Kuwait, Liberia, Sierra Leone, Sudan, Abyei, Darfur, South Sudan, and Timor-Leste.[61] In 2013, natural resources were again on the agenda, but member states did not reach consensus for a general resolution on natural resources and conflict.[62] As a result, instead of a systematic approach, member states have opted for a case-by-case approach to environmental issues. However, putting climate change on the agenda of the Security Council is extremely controversial. Strong divisions have emerged among Security Council members, most clearly in 2007 and 2011, when they discussed the Security implications of climate change. They have also mainly only considered these issues during informal meetings (Arria formula) or indirectly as a topic related to the main discussion (e.g., on water and peace, small island developing states, or even conflict prevention). Nevertheless, an increasing number of states are advocating for greater consideration of climate threats.[63] Regarding UN peace operations' environmental footprint, the Security Council has been slow in taking the issue on board. As discussed later, some member states have been vocally opposed to stricter policies and environmental standards for peacekeeping operations. As a result, they have included environmental concerns in peace operations' mandates only since 2013 (and still not systematically), starting with MINUSMA. However, aside from member states' support in other arenas – the General Assembly's Special Committee on Peacekeeping Operations (C34), Advisory Committee on Administrative and Budgetary Questions, and Fifth Committee – two recent initiatives in the Security Council also show growing interest in environmental matters. Despite much debate among member states, the Security Council released a press statement on the environmental management of peacekeeping operations in December 2017.[64] Although press statements are not legally binding, they can create incentives and conditions for further discussions. In addition, a "Group of Friends Leading on Environmental Management in the Field," co-chaired by Bangladesh and Italy, has recently been created to advocate for further implementation of DFS's Environment Strategy for UN peace operations.

UN Peace Operations' Environmental Approach

Growing attention to potential environmental damage caused by the UN has led to calls for the conceptualization and implementation of an environmental strategy for UN peace operations. This includes environmental policies and guidelines produced since the late 2000s, DFS's Environment Strategy, training material and staff dedicated to environmental affairs, and small-scale projects that can highlight best practices.

Environmental Policy and Guidelines

On April 25, 2013, in the resolution that established the new peacekeeping operation in Mali (MINUSMA), the UN Security Council called for an assessment of the effects of the mission on the environment, requesting "the Secretary-General to consider the environmental impacts of the operations of MINUSMA when fulfilling its mandated tasks and, in this context, encouraging MINUSMA to manage them, as appropriate."[65] For the first time, a UN peacekeeping operation received a direct mandate to address the environmental consequences of its activities. Since then, the Security Council has also requested four other missions to consider and manage their environmental footprint: UNAMID (in 2013), the UN Support Office in Somalia (UNSOS, in 2015), MONUSCO, and MINUSCA

60 UN Security Council, Statement by the President of the Security Council, UN Doc. S/PRST/2007/22, June 25, 2007.

61 UNEP, Greening the Blue Helmets, pp. 84–99. See also Philippe Le Billon, "Bankrupting Peace Spoilers: Can Peacekeepers Curtail Belligerents' Access to Resource Revenues?," in High-Value Natural Resources and Peacebuilding, Päivi Lujala and Siri Aas Rustad, eds. (London: Earthscan, 2012).

62 UN Security Council, 6982nd Meeting, UN Doc. S/PV.6982, June 19, 2003.

63 UN Security Council Statement S/PRST/2011/15, July 20, 2011. And UN General Assembly Draft Resolution A/63/L.8, 27 Oct 2008. "Security and Climate Change." Armenia, Australia, Austria, Belgium, Bulgaria, Canada, Chile, Cyprus, Czech Republic, Denmark, Estonia, Fiji, Finland, France, Germany, Greece, Hungary, Iceland, Ireland, Israel, Italy, Kiribati, Latvia, Lithuania, Luxembourg, Maldives, Malta, Marshall Islands, Micronesia (Federated States of), Monaco, Nauru, Netherlands, New Zealand, Palau, Papua New Guinea, Philippines, Poland, Portugal, Romania, Samoa, Seychelles, Slovakia, Slovenia, Solomon Islands, Spain, Sweden, Tonga, Turkey, Tuvalu, United Kingdom of Great Britain and Northern Ireland and Vanuatu: draft resolution.

64 This text was initially meant to be a presidential statement, but member states were unable to reach consensus. The text was therefore "downgraded" to a press statement.

65 UN Security Council Resolution 2100 (April 25, 2013), UN Doc. S/RES/2100.

(both in 2017). These mandates came in parallel with a series of measures DPKO and DFS have taken to reduce the environmental impacts of their operations (see Figure 1). In 2009, DPKO and DFS adopted their Environmental Policy for UN Field Missions.[66] Various prior initiatives had prepared them for the adoption of this policy, which was initially drafted with the support of UNEP. According to a former DPKO staff member, one position dedicated to the environment was first created within the Engineering Section at UN headquarters to suggest guidelines and environmental standards.[67] However, standards had yet to be officially institutionalized. He also mentioned a series of interventions from 2004 to 2005 focusing on sanitary conditions and the treatment of wastewater in field missions. In line with the Secretary-General's push toward a climate-neutral UN, a first draft of the Environmental Policy was sent to all DPKO and DFS senior staff in 2007. It took two years before it was officially adopted, following questions over the legal obligations it would entail for the UN. Concentrating mostly on the practices and behaviors of UN peacekeepers, the 2009 Environmental Policy deals with the following topics: solid and hazardous waste; energy; water and wastewater management; wild animals and plants; and cultural and historic sites. Effective since June 1, 2009, it requires each operation to establish an environmental policy – an environmental baseline study, an environmental action plan, and an emergency preparedness plan, with objectives and control measures – and to appoint an environmental officer. It also requires all employees to follow its recommendations as well as those of the environmental guidelines that accompany it, which are available to UN staff on the DPKO/DFS intranet. According to DPKO and DFS, the policy both aims to reduce environmental impact and to improve the health and safety of UN staff and local communities.

Subsequently, the secretary-general brought up the environmental footprint of peace operations in his 2010 report on the Global Field Support Strategy. On several occasions since 2011, member states in the General Assembly (the Second and Fifth Committees and the C34)[68] and in the Security Council have requested the implementation of sound environmental practices, promoted the mitigation of the environmental impact of UN peacekeeping operations, and mandated missions to strengthen their efforts in these areas.[69] For instance, the Security Council's 2017 press statement on the environmental management of peacekeeping operations states:

> The members of the Security Council were cognizant of the possible environmental impact of peacekeeping operations mandated by the Security Council. They underscored the importance that peacekeeping operations endeavor to minimize their impact on the sustainability of the ecosystems where they are deployed, based on sound consideration of the risks, benefits and costs.

They acknowledged that "the modalities in which peacekeeping operations interact with the environment where they are deployed may contribute to the effective and efficient delivery of their mandates." They also "underlined the importance to address comprehensively the environmental impact of peacekeeping operations, in close coordination with the relevant parties involved," being mindful of the environmental goals set out in global agreements such as the Paris Agreement on climate change.[70] Since 2015, environmental management has become a priority for DFS. That year, it adopted a Waste Management Policy for UN Field Missions. At the beginning of 2016, an Environment Section dedicated to environmental management was created in the Office of the Under-Secretary-General for Field Support. The section developed DFS's Environment Strategy in consultation "with missions, HQ actors and relevant partners."[71] Officially released in November 2016, the strategy is divided into

66 UN DPKO and DFS, Environmental Policy for UN Field Missions, UN Doc. PK/G/2009.06, May 31, 2009.

67 Interview with former DPKO official, New York, February 2013.

68 Support in the Fifth Committee is especially important since its decisions provide the basis for peacekeeping budgets approved in the General Assembly.

69 Maertens, "Quand les Casques bleus passent au vert," p. 66.

70 UN Security Council, Press Statement on Environmental Management of Peacekeeping Operations, UN Doc. SC/13134-ENV/DEV/1830-PKO/700, December 21, 2017.

two phases. The first focuses on setting baseline data for June 2020. The second aspires to the following vision for June 2023: "responsible missions that achieve maximum efficiency in their use of natural resources and operate at a minimum risk to people, societies and ecosystems; contributing to a positive impact on these whenever possible."[72] It provides a precise timetable (see Figure 2) and performance indicators for five pillars: energy, water and wastewater, solid waste, wider impact, and the introduction of an environmental management system.[73]

To implement the Environment Strategy, missions use a standard template to develop their environmental action plan through data collection and budget planning. By November 2017, each mission had a mission-wide environmental action plan for the 2017/2018 budgetary cycle.[74] For the first time, member states also agreed on a set of 14 key performance indicators for all missions, including one indicator on environmental issues. By setting common indicators for all missions, this decision supports the creation of an environmental performance management system. DFS's Environment Section is also developing a methodology to assess the wider environmental impact and is working with missions to monitor waste and collect reliable data on energy and water consumption to provide more accurate baseline data. Environmental management policies are constantly being updated to meet environmental challenges while being disseminated in key documents, such as in specific manuals like the forthcoming revised Liquidation Manual.[75] The Environment Strategy is considered to be "a living document, updated as progress is made and approaches evolve."[76] DFS's Environment Section, current missions, and the UN Global Service Centre in Brindisi are working on its implementation, with DFS recognizing that there is still "a long way to go."[77]

71 UN Field Support, DFS Environment Strategy, "Executive Summary," April 2017, p. 1.
72 Ibid.
73 UN Field Support, DFS Environment Strategy, "Executive Summary," April 2017, p. 1.
74 UN Field Support, Progress So Far: DFS Environment Strategy, November 2017, p. 1, available at https://peacekeeping.un.org/sites/default/files/171116_progress_so_far.pdf.
75 Ibid.
76 UN Field Support, DFS Environment Strategy, "Executive Summary," November 2017, p. 1.
77 UN Field Support, DFS Environment Strategy, "Executive Summary," April 2017, p. 1.

Limits and Constraints

While peace operations have a considerable degree of flexibility, they also face numerous limits and constraints that have been slowing down the process of greening UN peace operations. This is why it took a number of years to define and approve a comprehensive environmental strategy, with almost 10 years between the first draft of the Environmental Policy, finally adopted in 2009, and the launch of DFS's Environment Strategy at the end of 2016.

Peace operations face a number of limits and constraints in implementing environmental policies and strategies. First, these are unevenly implemented from one mission to another due to disparities in terms of staff allocation, budget, equipment, local circumstances, and senior leadership. Second, UN headquarters has had difficulty ensuring oversight of missions and assessing their performance. Third, the UN's organizational culture and member states' preferences restrict the design and operation of missions, particularly in terms of sourcing and procurement.

Uneven Implementation of the Environment Strategy

Missions implement UN environmental policies and guidelines unevenly. The implementation of the Environment Strategy is uneven due to numerous disparities among missions in terms of staff allocation, budget, equipment, local circumstances, and senior leadership. Each mission receives a different budget according to its mandate and tasks, and not every mission has leadership that recognizes the risks of not integrating environmental considerations into daily operations, including the potential for more backlash and higher costs in the long term (e.g., due to compensation claims for environmental damage). Moreover, each operation includes troops from different countries and cultures, who come with materials, equipment, and goods with varying environmental and lifestyle standards. These differences are manifested in each mission's environmental footprint. On the one hand, a UN base deployed by wealthier countries generates a larger long-term environmental footprint than one deployed by less wealthy nations. As wealthier countries bring more equipment and resources into mission areas to support the quality of life of their troops (such as larger and more equipped modular structures for dwelling that require more energy to maintain leisure spaces, gyms, and canteens) and the efficiency of the mission (such as munitions, vehicles, and telecommunications equipment).[78] The differences can be identified in the spatial organization, deployment, and use of land and equipment.[79] On the other hand, wealthier countries can purchase more eco-friendly materials and invest more in improving local capacity.[80] Because of such disparities, models that are successful in one mission cannot be reproduced in all contexts.

Difficulty in Ensuring Oversight from Headquarters

The lack of standardization in the environmental approach also results from difficulty in ensuring oversight inside missions and from UN headquarters, as the oversight system used by headquarters to verify the implementation of its policies at the field level is still incomplete. However, the recent introduction of a performance and risk management framework to report detailed data from each mission should, in the long run, improve this situation, which past audits and evaluations have deemed inadequate. The system is short on automated tools and resources to systematically measure performance. Data on the long-term impact of missions, needed to strengthen efforts to improve environmental sustainability even after their departure, is also missing. Such processes of data collection and verification are indispensable to achieve even implementation of environmental policies across missions.

Despite recent efforts to improve data collection, the challenges facing the oversight system also result from the gap between UN headquarters, which decides on environmental policies, and field missions, which are meant to implement them. Staff members serving in UN peace operations who are already responsible for a large number of tasks might not have internalized these policies, and it is difficult for headquarters to closely supervise their implementation. While the Environmental Policy is compulsory for all missions, there are no penalties for noncompliance, despite the fact that it includes a dedicated section on "standards of conduct for personnel." In other words, it is an ineffective policy without individual accountability for staff members who are not performing.[81]

The oversight system's difficulties also lie in the ambiguous position of environmental issues between substantive and support divisions. While the negative consequences of poor environmental management mostly affect the substantive side of missions – especially since they impact the relationship with local communities, support divisions are in charge of environmental issues as part of their tasks related to equipment and camp management. Shortcomings in the oversight system can lead to "greenwashing": displaying best practices and success stories and using policies to show efforts are being made while hiding or denying mistakes and mismanagement. Indeed, according to several UN officials, information is selectively reported, especially from missions to headquarters. This creates a vicious cycle: by not informing headquarters and member states of their failures for fear of damaging their image and relationship with local actors, mission leaders are unable to obtain approval for the compensation or funding necessary to reduce their environmental impact.

Although it is too early to assess the effectiveness of the new performance management system set up in 2017, recent efforts have aimed to address some of these issues. Through guidelines and training modules on data collection, UN headquarters intends to improve the collection of data related to key performance indicators for the five pillars of the Environment Strategy. Identification of data owners (e.g., staff in charge of monitoring and communicating data)

78 Joel van der Beek, "A Speculative Financial and Socio-economic Model for Evaluating and Enhancing International Peacekeeping Missions," in *BLUE: The Architecture of UN Peacekeeping*, pp. 42–43.
79 Shoshan, *BLUE: The Architecture of UN Peacekeeping*, pp. 6–17.
80 Van der Beek, "A Speculative Financial and Socio-economic Model for Evaluating and Enhancing International Peacekeeping Missions," pp. 42–43.
81 Maertens, "Quand les Casques bleus passent au vert," p. 73.

and accountability for data accuracy should also support systematic monitoring of environmental performance.

Politics of Sourcing and Procurement

The difficulty of reducing peace operations' environmental impact also results from the politics of sourcing and procurement. The UN's organizational culture and member states' preferences shape the way peacekeeping operations are designed and carried out. UN peace operations are planned as short-term operations, although the median duration of peacekeeping missions since 2000 has been 6.5 years, and their mandates are renewed each year.[82] Missions are also carried out on a yearly budget.

This budgetary cycle was among the challenges DFS identified in the implementation of its Environmental Policy, as it encumbers long-term investment, planning, and procurement of materials, particularly since the financial crisis of 2007–2008 increased financial pressure from member states. The brief and urgent timeline of mission deployments, coupled with Security concerns, leads to the implementation of planning procedures that leave many pressing environmental concerns – such as those related to the design of camps' waste management infrastructure – unplanned and unresolved. These procedures are hard to change and continue to be applied, especially for rapid deployments.[83] Besides their initial design, how missions are carried out, especially in terms of procurement and sourcing, affects their environmental impact. UN missions primarily rely on international suppliers and external logistics firms that shape the landscape where missions operate and inflate their environmental footprint.

The fact that the Security Council could only agree on a press statement on the environmental management of peacekeeping operations in December 2017 is a consequence and an illustration of this opposition. Likewise, all mandates for peace operations from the General Assembly and the Security Council refer to "existing rules and regulations" when requesting missions to manage their environmental impact. The 2017 manual on reimbursement for contingent-owned equipment introduced a financial incentive (5%) for troop- and police-contributing countries to deploy with environmentally enhanced accommodations or to replace fuel generators with renewable energy sources.[84] However, no agreement has been reached so far in the Fifth Committee, and debate continues over the appropriate standards.[85] Moreover, in comparison to other violations committed in the context of peace operations, civil society has not been advocating very vocally for greener interventions so far.[86] Without public pressure, member states have managed to slow down the process of mainstreaming environmental policies. It is therefore not surprising that it took 10 years for DFS to formulate its Environment Strategy.

Recommendations

While this overview focuses on UN peace operations' environmental concerns and practices, it does not imply that environmental management is one of their main activities, although, because it is a crosscutting issue, it does touch upon much of what they do. Yet environmental problems echo the "do no harm" principle and deserve greater attention because of their potentially destructive and protracted effects on the environment and people's livelihoods.

Based on this review of environmental concerns and issues at stake, and of the current Environment Strategy and its weaknesses, we have put forward a series of tangible recommendations. Advocating for a better understanding of long-term impacts, we suggest ways to mitigate and reduce UN peace operations' environmental footprint and the environmental pressure they place on local ecosystems and communities.

82 UN Field Support, DFS Environment Strategy, "Executive Summary," November 2017, p. 3.

83 Shoshan and Szita, "Reimagining Peacekeeping Missions."

84 "An environmental enhancement supplement of an additional 5 per cent of the reimbursement rate to the troop/police contributor will be added if the provided tentage is shown to have additional features included which are designed to improve the heating and cooling effectiveness and efficiency of the facility." UN General Assembly, Manual on Policies and Procedures Concerning the Reimbursement and Control of Contingent-Owned Equipment of Troop/Police Contributors Participating in Peacekeeping Missions, UN Doc. A/72/288, August 4, 2017.

85 Ibid.

86 In the case of the cholera outbreak in Haiti, the focus has been on official recognition of the UN's responsibility and compensation packages for the victims.

Short-term Recommendations

These short-term recommendations concern the full implementation of the DFS Environment Strategy and the achievement of its objectives.

1. Increase financial and human resources dedicated to the implementation of the environment strategies and to planning.

Each mission should be given adequate human resources to implement and comply with the Environmental Policy, depending on its characteristics (availability of local infrastructure, deployment in hard-to-reach areas, number of camps, etc.). Member states should allow adequate staff, including environmental officers in missions and in headquarters in charge of facilitating the implementation of the Environmental Policy and guidelines, assessing compliance with them, preventing environmental damage, promoting eco-friendly practices, and systematically collecting lessons learned. Member states and mission leadership should also strengthen human resources in the areas of engineering and urban planning by reviewing terms of reference for positions in mission support and appointing at least one environmental engineer per mission (in addition to the environmental officers in the Office of the Director of Mission Support). Urban planners should also be commissioned to provide preliminary spatial and socioeconomic analyses of the local context to help identify opportunities for collaboration and local sourcing in the short and long term (if assessments indicate this will not have a negative impact on the environment). Moreover, these preliminary analyses and the presence of environmental engineers could be used to train other engineers and UN actors in each mission on a holistic approach to environmental management.

Adequate human and financial resources should also be devoted to planning missions to ensure that infrastructure integrates and strengthens local systems in the short and long term. Member states and DFS should focus on three main areas: a. Energy, by providing funding to focus more on energy efficiency and on renewable energy when feasible; b. Water and wastewater, by financially supporting projects to install and operate all treatment plants without any risk and to monitor groundwater; and c. Solid waste management (an area that so far has no dedicated positions), by appointing waste management officers in engineering sections in charge of designing and managing missions' infrastructure.

2. Implement mandatory training on environmental management for all personnel in missions.

DFS and DPKO should ensure that environmental issues are included in pre-deployment training for all civilians operating in missions. Troop- and police-contributing countries should include environmental management in the pre-deployment training of their troops and police. Drawing on the increase in human resources proposed above, in-mission training on environmental management should also be mandatory for all uniformed personnel. Training modules should seek to raise general awareness of issues related to natural resources and the environment as well as to provide specific technical knowledge. They should also address the specificities of the local context.

3. Systematically collect data on environmental management from all missions and disseminate lessons learned and best practices

In order to assess improvements and set achievable goals in terms of energy efficiency; water, wastewater, and solid waste management; and environmental restoration, DFS should develop consistent methodologies to collect comparable data over time. Member states should mandate each mission to assess its environmental footprint and the potential risks of its presence for the environment and local communities' livelihoods. The environmental assessment should also take into account the long-term effects of both degradation and regeneration of the resources used by the UN.

The UN should also strengthen its capacity to collect and disseminate lessons learned and best practices about environmental management and the reduction of missions' footprints. DFS should be vocal not only about its best practices but also about lessons learned from bad experiences and include them in annual reporting to member states.

4. Use local capacities where feasible

DFS should consider sourcing its maintenance locally where feasible. The most significant contributor to the UN environmental footprint is the transport of people and goods into missions by air, sea, or land. The use of local materials, depending on thorough environmental and economic assessments of the possible medium- and long-term impact, and local expertise can exponentially reduce the cost and environmental footprint of UN missions. Moreover, after the first months of deployment, regulated local production of supplies could provide employment, help build capacity, and sustain environmentally minded growth, which could eventually contribute to sustainable development not only at the local level but also globally. For instance, if food production is sourced locally when feasible, peace operations could reduce the environmental footprint caused by long-distance transportation of produce and support small-scale farmers, agricultural production, food access, and food security.

Medium-term Recommendations

Due to the difficulty of implementation, the following recommendations are considered to be medium-term targets, although they still address very urgent matters.

5. Continue to reinforce oversight by systematically monitoring performance indicators and fostering data ownership and accountability.

UN headquarters should continue to reinforce its capacity to oversee the implementation of its Environment Strategy in two ways. First, it should continue efforts to strengthen reporting between missions and headquarters through both formal mechanisms and informal meetings between DFS's Environment Section and environmental officers in the field. Second, it should regularly audit data supplied by missions. Data ownership should be systematically established and formal mechanisms put in place to hold data owners accountable for the accuracy of the information they supply.

6. Extend DFS's partnership with UNEP.

DFS should extend its partnership with UNEP to offer permanent technical assistance at UN headquarters and in missions. DFS should also seek support from UNEP to advocate for more environmentally responsible peace operations.

7. Advocate for member states to support sustainable environmental management in peace operations.

DFS should seek support from member states, building on the "Group of Friends on Leading on Environmental Management in the Field" and on the 2017 Security Council press statement. While highlighting the long-term benefits of more sustainable interventions, DFS should warn member states of the significant risks and potentially disastrous effects of noncompliance with the Environmental Policy and guidelines and remind the UN of its obligation to apply the "do no harm" principle. DFS should advocate for member states to provide adequate human and financial resources to enable effective compliance with the Environmental Policy and Environment Strategy. DFS should request member states to create legal obligations that would enable liability for noncompliance.

Long-term Recommendation

This last recommendation addresses long-term issues. By focusing on local settings and comprehensive and integrated indicators, it relates to the UN's legacy and accountability even long after the departure of missions.

8. Develop comprehensive indicators and an integrated approach to environmental concerns.

The footprint of UN peace operations should be examined through multidisciplinary and multi-scalar methods by environmental engineers, economists, and urban planners. They should examine the footprint at a variety of levels and in different contexts, from the site to the local region, the country, and the global environment, to identify the negative impact on natural and man-made environments and to prevent misunderstanding of the local context. The footprint of each peacekeeper and physical structure, such as bases, airfields, and headquarters, must also be measured in relation to local circumstances and capacities. By measuring the environmental footprint of peace operations in a more context-specific way, DFS can identify concrete challenges and the potential to foster a positive legacy. As such, each mission should be analyzed from a comprehensive environmental and spatial perspective that takes into account its impact on the local context. Such an approach will necessitate the development of indicators that complement the current Environment Strategy. Such indicators can be developed through collaboration among urban designers, environmental officers, engineers, and local experts. Based on such an analysis, actions can be taken to build capacity and reduce the footprint of UN peace operations from beginning to end.

UNMIL disposal site. Monrovia, 2017.

UN field mission's greenhouse gas emissions in 2016

	Number of Personnel (#)	Total Emissions (tCO2eq)	Per capita Emissions (tCO2eq/ Personnel)	Share of total emissions (%)			Facilities-related Emissions Intensity (kgCO2eq/m2)	Per capita Emissions (tCO2eq/ Malian)	Per capita Emissions (tCO2eq/ Liberia)
				Air Travel	Other Travel	Facilities			
Field Missions	124,683	1,051,771	8.44	32	14	54	377.94	0.17	0.26
UN system	264,221	1,896,199	7.18	42	12	46	104.81		

Source: Field missions refer to peacekeeping operations, special political missions, and support missions. These figures include emissions resulting from the use of armored vehicles. They do not include emissions from freight, but DFS is currently in discussions to see if it will be possible to include contractors' emissions in the future. UNEP, Greening the Blue Report 2017.

Source: Our World in Data. https://ourworldindata.org/co2/country/mali

UN field missions' waste in 2016

	Waste per Capita (Kg/person/ annum)	Reused/ Recycled/ Composted/ Recovered (%)	Incinerated Closed (%)	Incinerated Open (%)	Landfilled (%)	Controlled Disposal (%)	Other (%)	Waste per Capita (Kg/person/ annum)	Per capita Emissions (tCO2eq/ Liberia)
Field Missions	677	25	9	11	9	33	13	237	237*
UN system	554	30	10	7	11	30	12		

Source: This first inventory has been completed without the participation of all missions. Proxies have been used to assess the average waste per capita. Ibid.

Source: 1) World Bank. http://documents1.worldbank.org/curated/en/302341468126264791/pdf/68135-REVISED-What-a-Waste-2012-Final-updated.pdf 2)https://africancleancities. org/data/D2_S3_Jica_Databook.pdf
*Monrovia

UN peace operations and the environment: Stepping stones reports, policies, and SDG13

General
Reports
Policies
UN-wide agenda

COVID-19 response: The current crisis is an opportunity for a profound, systemic shift to a more sustainable economy that works for both people and the planet.

The UN Secretary-General has proposed six climate-positive actions for governments to take once they go about building back their economies and societies:

- Green transition: Investments must accelerate the decarbonization of all aspects of our economy
- Green jobs and sustainable and inclusive growth
- Green economy: making societies and people more resilient through a transition that is fair to all and leaves no one behind
- Invest in sustainable solutions: fossil fuel subsidies must end and polluters must pay for their pollution
- Confront all climate risks
- Cooperation – no country can succeed alone

2019 was the second warmest year on record and the end of the warmest decade (2010-2019) ever recorded

IPCC Climate Report 2018

Carbon dioxide (CO_2) levels and other greenhouse gases in the atmosphere rose to new records in 2019.

SDG Climate Action Goal 13: Take urgent action to combat climate change and its impacts

The Paris Agreement, adopted in 2015, aims to strengthen the global response to the threat of climate change by keeping a global temperature rise this century well below 2 degrees Celsius above pre-industrial levels

The Kyoto Protocol was adopted on 11 Dec 1997 and entered into force on 16 February 2005 to limit and reduce greenhouse gases (GHG) emission

2021

2020

2019

2018

DFS rolls out environmental performance and risk management system to all field missions with process and performance indicators across five pillars: Energy, Water and wastewater, solid waste, wider impacts, env. management

2017

DFS creates Environmental Technical Support Unit to provide technical assistance to field missions in implementing its Environmental Strategy

Security Council releases press statement on the environmental management of peacekeeping operations

General Assembly approves 14 results-based budgeting indicators for missions to report on for 2017/2018, including one on the environment

2016

UN Global Service Centre and UN Environment launch Rapid Env. and Climate Technical Assistance Facility (REACT)

DFS launches its Environmental Strategy

OIOS publishes report on waste management in UNFIL

OIOS publishes report on DFS guidance and oversight of wastewater management in peacekeeping operations

DFS created an Environment Section under the office of the under-secretry-general

OIOS publishes report on waste management in UNFIL

OIOS publishes report on waste management in MONUSCO

OIOS publishes report on waste management in UNOCI

OIOS publishes report on waste management in MINUSTAH

OIOS publishes report on waste management in UNAMID

2015

DPKO/DFS adopt Waste Management Policy for UN Field Missions

2014

MINUSMA is the first UN peacekeeping mission to receive a direct mandate from the Security Council to consider and manage the environmental impact of its operations

2013

OIOS audits waste management in the field, making strong recommendations to address the situation

UN Environment releases its report "Greening the Blue Helmets"

2012

Member states in the C34 stress "the importance for peacekeeping missions to take steps aimed at implementing sound environmental practices"

2011

Cholera breaks out in Haiti

UN-wide "Greening the Blue: campaign is launched

2010

DPKO/DFS adopt Environmental Policy for UN Field Missions

2009

2008

First environmental officer is appointed at DFS

Secretary-General Ban Ki-moon puts climate change as his priority, and Chief Executives Board agrees on "moving towards a climate-neutral United Nations.

2007

2006

2004-2005

First Field evaluations with a focus on sanitary conditions and treatment of wastewater take place

UNMIL's disposal site.
Monrovia, 2017.

Speeding Up the Disposal Record: Disposal Site 2

The UN mandates fragment reason into silos that make very little sense to someone outside the organization.

One of our hosts in Liberia, who managed the logistics aspect of UNMIL's rapid downsizing, had a problem. The UN had invested hundreds of thousands of USD in gym equipment that was spread all over the country. It was an impossible task to find anyone able to disassemble the equipment and transport it to Monrovia. The UN was not allowed to sell it, and the Liberian government could not afford to maintain gyms. As they prepared to govern without the presence of the UN, they had other urgent matters to attend to, such as stark poverty; a lack of basic resources, infrastructure, or a job market; high crime levels, and the immense war trauma. Moreover, the departure of the UN mission coincided with the election of a new government. Ellen Johnson, who had served as a president of the country from 2006 to 2018 was to leave Liberia and clear the way for a new elective representation and a new government to form, a transition that heightened tensions everywhere. At that moment it seemed that the gym equipment, the main concern of our host, was the least of anyone else's worries.

We passed a group of young Liberians at the disposal site, working tirelessly to move as much equipment as possible through a metal shredding machine. Next to them were two stacks: one of computers, hard drives, and other electronics, and another of shredded metal trash, which they quickly stuffed into crates.

This was not the only metal waste on the site. At its edge, we passed large piles of weapons collected by the mission during its time in Liberia. The guns and bullets were sitting in open puddles of chemicals waiting to dissolve.

UNMIL's disposal site. Monrovia, 2017.

UNMIL's chemical pools at the disposal site. Monrovia, 2017.

Disarmament

With the arrival of the UN peacekeepers in Liberia in 2003, a fragile peace agreement was signed between the rebels and the local government, just after Charles Taylor left the country on August 11, 2003. One of the first assignments of the peacekeepers was to disarm the country. Rebels and militias were everywhere; child soldiers were still walking around with guns. In some of the remote areas, fighting was still taking place as the news about the peace agreement had yet to arrive. After so many years of violence, the UN had to be creative about how to disarm about 40,000 members of the armed militias.[87]

Early disarmament attempts were put on hold as "thousands of fighters swamped the peacekeepers demanding payment in return for their guns." When their demands were unanswered, they went on a rampage and several people were killed. This eruption of violence forced the UN to reevaluate their response, knowing that until more guns could be removed from circulation, the potential for renewed violence would remain.[88] Eventually they agreed to pay US$75 up-front to fighters who would relinquish their guns when the disarmament resumed. The tactic could literally backfire because it could actually attract the smuggling of arms into Liberia from the surrounding region.[89]

Disarmament, demobilization and reintegration (DDR) is "a long process of removing weapons from the hands of members of armed groups, taking these combatants out of their groups and helping them to reintegrate as civilians into society."[90] DDR seeks to support ex-combatants and those associated with armed groups so they can become active participants in the peace process. These actions aim to "lay the groundwork for safeguarding and sustaining the communities to which these individuals return, while building capacity for long-term peace, security, and development.

In situations where it is too early or not possible to carry out DDR work, the UN supports Community Violence Reduction program that lead to the right conditions for political processes to progress and armed groups to disband."[91]

In the case of Liberia, children were recruited as soldiers at very young ages. More than 38,000 children are estimated to have taken part in the war as fighters, porters, ammunition carriers, cooks, and sex slaves. They lost their childhoods to the war. After a decade of fighting, they had to restart their lives, deal with the war trauma, and learn basic skills to allow them to integrate back into society.

87 Doyle, Mark, "UN team starts Liberia groundwork", BBC, available at: http://news.bbc.co.uk/2/hi/africa/3406833.stm.

88 Ibid.

89 Doyle, Mark. "UN's Liberia 'honeymoon' to end", BBC, available at: http://news.bbc.co.uk/2/hi/africa/3423215.stm.

90 "DDR is a critical part of efforts to create a secure and stable environment in which the process of recovery can begin. United Nations multidimensional peacekeeping operations are usually mandated to assist in the development and implementation of national DDR programmes. This may entail the provision of technical advice; the securing of disarmament and cantonment sites; and/or the collection and destruction of weapons, ammunition and other material surrendered by the former combatants. Other agencies, working in close coordination with the United Nations peacekeeping operation, are responsible for supporting the critical reintegration process, which aims to provide demobilized former combatants with sustainable livelihoods." Source: UN Principles and Guidelines 2008, available at: https://issuu.com/uniccanberra/docs/capstone_doctrine_eng

91 Ibid.

SGCU 185030 5
22G1
MAX. GR. 30 480 KG
67 200 LB
TARE 2 000 KG
4 410 LB
NET 28 480 KG
62 790 LB
33.1 CU.M
1 170 CU.FT

Zwedru

Zwedru Area

A year after the launch of UNMIL, a contingent of 1,000 Ethiopian peacekeepers set up the first base out of Monrovia in Zwedru, just down the road from the city's Grace Baptist Church. They cleared the bush around an abandoned building and erected military tents.[92] In 2004, the mission in Liberia totaled 15,000 peacekeepers and was considered the largest peace mission in the world. Now, however, operating missions tend to be even bigger. At that time, the government of Liberia and the two rebel movements still occupied the areas they were holding when the peace deal was signed in Accra, and 40,000 Liberian militia members were still in possession of ammunition and had to be disarmed. In Zwedru, the UN troops were sent to set up a presence in the more rural areas and patrol the borders with Sierra Leone, Guinea, and Ivory Coast—a border deep in the jungle that is said to be untraceable and uncontrollable.

92 Doyle, Mark, "UN's Liberia 'honeymoon' to end, BBC, available at: http://news.bbc.co.uk/2/hi/africa/3423215.stm.

In the spring of 2017, we took a flight from the former civilian airport of Monrovia to the airfield in Zwedru, both were UN-controlled. The UN mission operated all flights from Monrovia to Zwedru through a subcontracted South African company. We flew relatively low, and the transition from the densely settled area of Monrovia to the thick leafy jungle was brief. Occasionally, we could make out small villages of relatively low density amid the compact woodlands. Their architecture appeared tribal: clusters of vernacular mud and wood structures. Although Liberia is a small country, spanning 300 km from the ocean shore to its north-east border with Ivory Coast, the poor quality of its transportation infrastructure makes travel challenging and the distance between the urban center and the rural areas even more remote. A one-hour flight would translate into an undetermined amount of driving time, as roads are unreliable, particularly during the rainy season. Aviation capacity across the country is limited too; only a few UN flights, like those in Mali, could allocate a restricted number of seats to local citizens with an urgent need to cross the country.

UN Bases Zwedru Area

NAME	DEPLOYMENT status at the time of the visit	STATE	SIZE	OWNERSHIP
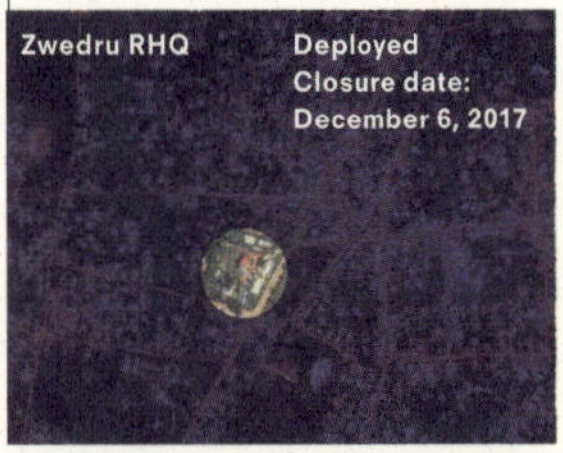 Zwedru RHQ	Deployed Closure date: December 6, 2017	Former municipal 5-story building included offices and a canteen, radio towers, water treatment and energy plants. Large water reserve bags were spread around the backyard.	About 2.6 hectares	Government
 Indian FPU	Decommissioned Closure date: February 14, 2017	The site included around 20 modular structures partly connected by open-air corridors, but somewhat randomly situated on the site. After the UN drawdown, Liberian civil servants (police units) began inhabiting the base with their families.	About 2 hectares	Government
 Logistic base	Decommissioned Closure date: December 6, 2016	The site included several modular structures (office spaces and open-air shaded spaces). Several UN trucks were parked at the entrance to the site. The base has yet to be reused.	2.7 hectares	Government
 China Med, Zwedru Gedeh County	Deployed Closure date: July 4, 2016	Modular structures form a series of small clinics connected with an open-air corridor. The hospital was adjacent to the ground floor of the local UN HQ.	Included within the area of Zwedru HQ	Government
 Zwedru Airfield	Deployed Closure date: July 4, 2017	Zwedru airfield included a small and rundown terminal (waiting room) that was located along an unpaved landing strip. The modest airport was of significant value for this remote region, which that was hard to reach by car or by any other transport means – in particular during the rainy season due to the poor state of the roads.	About 0.4 hectares + landing strip 1700 meters long	Government
 China ENG, Zwedru, Gedeh County (White Stadium)	Decommissioned Closure date: March 24, 2017	This UN site included a soccer field surrounded by a series of UN modular buildings that formed long strips of programs, such as offices, kitchens, lodging and recreational facilities, toilets, and showers. Along one of the edges of the soccer field, around 15 defective UN vehicles – trucks, jeeps and small cranes – were randomly parked. The site used to be Zwedru's soccer stadium.	About 3.5 hectares	Government

ZWEDRU is the capital of Grand Gedeh County, one of the 15 counties in Liberia, with 25,678 residents of mainly Krahn, Mandingo, Fulani, Gio, and Mano tribes. The town is also known as Tchien and is named after the head of a local anteater creek. Its nature is rich in plants, minerals, and all sorts of living species, and its forest is the habitat of rare bird species.

The city is surrounded by rubber plantations, diamond mines, and cattle. Its fertile land is rich in coffee, cocoa, piassava, sugarcane, tobacco, and citrus fruits. Before the war, the city was known for timber production and its wood, leather goods, beverages, paints, soap, and building materials.

Mines, Old Wars and Current Stresses

It is said that Zwedru is "in some ways the place where Liberia's descent into chaos first began," as it is the hometown of Samuel Kanyon Doe, the leader of the first military coup d'état in Liberia.[93] During the civil wars, various militias operated from the jungle, moving along and across the country's borders. The fighting between rebels and the Liberian army left Zwedru and the entire country in ruins.

93 Doyle, Mark, "UN team starts Liberia groundwork," BBC, available at: http://news.bbc.co.uk/2/hi/africa/3406833.stm.

Zwedru is the largest city in the southeast. It is home to about 25,678 residents. The city is landlocked and surrounded by thick woods. It is situated along the intersection of two highways and has a small airport, William D. Coleman Airfield, with a gravel surfaced runway serving only domestic flights. Before the war, it was an important administrative, marketing, and logistic hub, surrounded by rubber plantations and diamond mines. Like the rest of the country, its geology favors the existence of deposits of a wide range of metals and industrial minerals, including gold, iron ore, diamonds, base metals, bauxite, manganese, fluorspar, kyanite, and phosphate. Mines around the city are still active. Although mining is high-risk labor for the locals, it offers a last resort for people who are struggling to make a living otherwise. Today, the unemployment rate is high in the entire region, and so are the levels of malnutrition and general desperation. In interviews conducted in Zwedru, locals mentioned that, although the Liberian government owns the land, the mines are operated by foreign private entities.

During the war, diamonds were continually mined by warlords. Liberia's gems, gold, and diamonds, like the ones from Angola, Ivory Coast, and Sierra Leone, were called blood diamonds. In 2001, civil society pressure was put on the security council to strengthen mining regulations and stop the use of "diamonds and other natural resources to finance armed conflicts in Angola and the Mano River Union states of Liberia, Sierra Leone, and Guinea. Despite improved

Resource flows in new wars by Mary Kaldor.

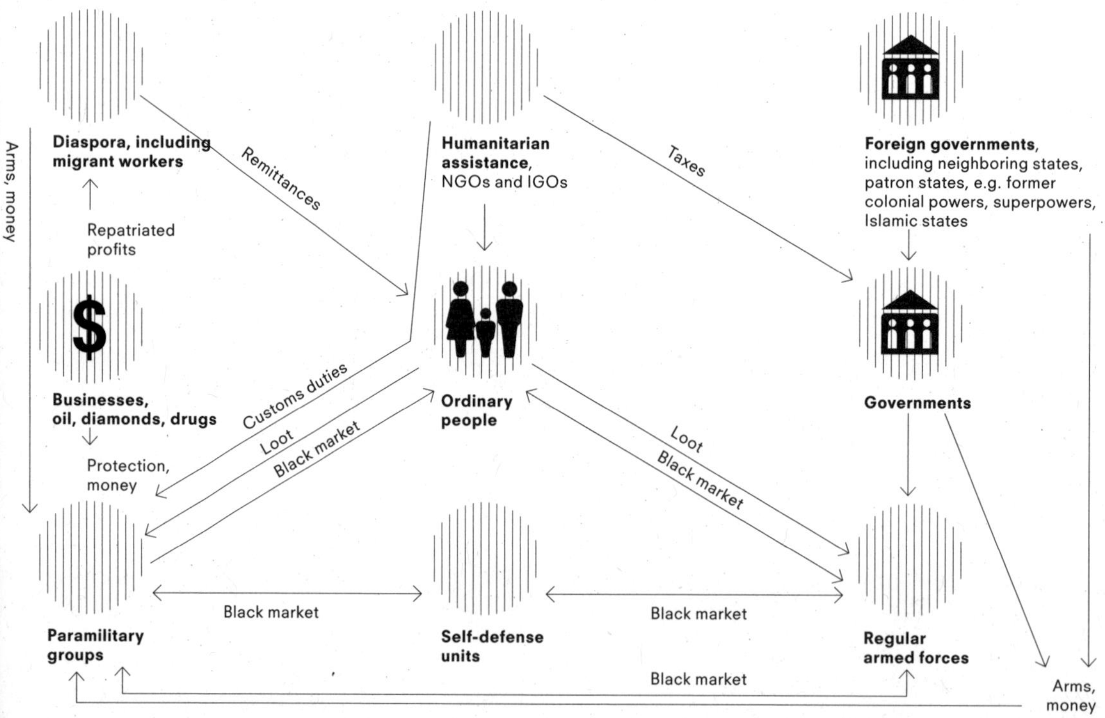

enforcement and monitoring of UN arms and diamond sanctions, reports submitted to the Security Council in October charge that both the Angolan rebel leader, Mr. Jonas Savimbi, and the Liberian government still violate the trade and weapons bans with the help of a global network of arms dealers, diamond merchants, and natural resources companies."[94]

In *New and Old Wars*, Mary Kaldor writes about the difference between the wars of the 20th century and the new wars by analyzing their economic flows. She describes two parallel processes: the first is the erosion, decentralization, and delegitimization of the nation state; and the second is the intervention of external global actors.[95]

> [In the old wars], administration is centralized to increase the efficiency of the war and to maximize revenue to pay for the war...The main aim of the war effort is to maximize the use of force so as to engage and defeat the enemy in battle. The new type of war economy is almost totally the opposite. The new wars are "globalized" wars. They involve the fragmentation and decentralization of the state. Participation is low relative to the population both because of lack of pay and because of lack of legitimacy on the part of the warring parties. There is very little domestic production, so the war effort is heavily dependent on local predation and external support. Battles are rare, most violence is directed against civilians, and cooperation between warring factions is common.[96]

Kaldor illustrates the typical flow of resources in the new wars, where "external support to ordinary people, in the form of remittances and humanitarian assistance, is recycled via various forms of asset transfer and black-market trading into military resources. Direct assistance from foreign governments, protection money from producers of commodities, and assistance from the diaspora enhance the capacity of the various fighting units to extract further resources from ordinary people and thus sustain their military efforts."[97]

Although the UN implemented some measures to restrict the smuggling of gems from conflict-affected regions and war zones, the lax enforcement by member states allowed the continuation of illegal trafficking. During the civil war in Liberia, a former Soviet Air Force officer, Victor Bout, who resided at Hotel Africa, used his network of airfreight companies to trade weapons for gems. During and after the war, the movement of diamonds out of Liberia continued illegally and unofficially through countries like Belgium, the US, and Burkina Faso.[98] In interviews we conducted in Monrovia, we were told, off the record, that during the Ebola pandemic only one airline kept its weekly flight schedule: Brussel Airlines. They suspected it had to do with the movement of gems out of Liberia.

In 2000, southern African diamond-producing countries attempted to curtail the flow of rough diamonds, used by rebels to finance armed conflicts aimed at overthrowing legitimate governments, which had led to the deaths of hundreds of thousands of people and immeasurable human suffering throughout the region. They initiated the Kimberley Process.[99] Among its objectives, it sought to protect the legitimate diamond industry, upon which many countries depended. That process led to the emergence of the Kimberley Process Certification Scheme, an international certification scheme for rough diamonds based primarily on national certification schemes and on internationally agreed minimum standards.

In March 2018, the General Assembly adopted a resolution seeking an alignment of efforts to end the illicit diamond trade with the 2030 Agenda for Sustainable Development.[100]

94 "Conflict Diamonds Evade UN Sanctions", UN, available at: www.un.org/africarenewal/magazine/december-2001/conflict-diamonds-evade-un-sanctions.
95 Kaldor, Mary, New and Old Wars: Organized Violence in a Global Era, Polity Press, 2012.
96 Ibid.
97 Ibid.
98 Fleshman, Michael, "'Conflict diamonds evade UN sanctions", available at: www.un.org/africarenewal/magazine/december-2001/conflict-diamonds-evade-un-sanctions.
99 "The Kimberly Process", available at: www.kimberleyprocess.com.
100 "General Assembly Adopts Resolution Seeking Alignment of Efforts to End Illicit Diamond Trade", Achieve 2030 Agenda for Sustainable Development, available at: www.un.org/press/en/2018/ga12002.doc.htm.

The resolution underscored how the global diamond certification scheme can contribute to international peace and security and sustainable development while also proclaiming 2021–2030 the United Nations' Decade on Ecosystem Restoration. By adopting a resolution on breaking the link between armed conflict and the illicit trade of rough diamonds, the 193-member organization encouraged further strengthening the Kimberley Process and enhancing its effectiveness in addressing challenges posed to the diamond industry and related communities by instability and conflict.[101]

101 "Underlining Critical Role of Diamond Certification to Global Peace, Security, General Assembly Adopts Resolution Urging Strengthening Kimberley Process", available at: www.un.org/press/en/2019/ga12124.doc.htm.

Airfield and surroundings. Zwedru, 2017.

ZWEDRU
AIRFIELD

CENTRAL BANK
OF LIBERIA
ZWEDRU BRANCH

A view from UNMIL HQ, 2017.

UN Bases in Zwedru

Since the beginning of UNMIL, seven UN bases were set up in Zwedru by various TCC. In 2017, UNMIL was in its final liquidation phase. Most of the bases had already been closed and handed over to the Liberian government. Only the mission headquarters remained at minimal occupancy, situated inside an old, repurposed school building on top of a hill with views over the city.

Ideas for Imaginative Uses and Legacy of UNMIL Infrastructure

During the field research in Liberia, we visited multiple bases in Monrovia and Zwedru. The condition of UNMIL sites at the end of missions varies, as evidenced in the descriptions below. While some were reused (or reusable), many were left in a dilapidated state. We found abandoned containers, parts of modular buildings, furniture, broken-down UN vehicles, and all sorts of hardware scattered around most sites. Although the UN liquidation team left behind these "assets" in agreement with Liberia's government agencies, the local government—with low to negative GDP and urgent priorities to address (see Liberia Urban Challenges)—had no resources to maintain these crumbling items.

The research focus on UNMIL aims to investigate the material legacy of the peacekeeping mission in its final stage of transition and liquidation. The following findings were also used to advocate for the UN peacekeeping department to work closely with UN country teams and local agencies to improve plans for the mission's assets to be better repurposed by the local community.

The next section identifies several potential avenues for repurposing the UNMIL bases in ways that can contribute to peacebuilding and local development. This part of the research was presented to UN agencies, their funders, and TCCs at the Secretariat in NYC, along with additional findings and recommendations, during a sequence of formal and informal meetings in 2017 and 2018 with the support of the NYU Center on International Cooperation. While some of the proposals were no longer feasible due to the mission's changing status, they were intended to generate insights and ideas for transitions in broader terms.

Zwedru Area

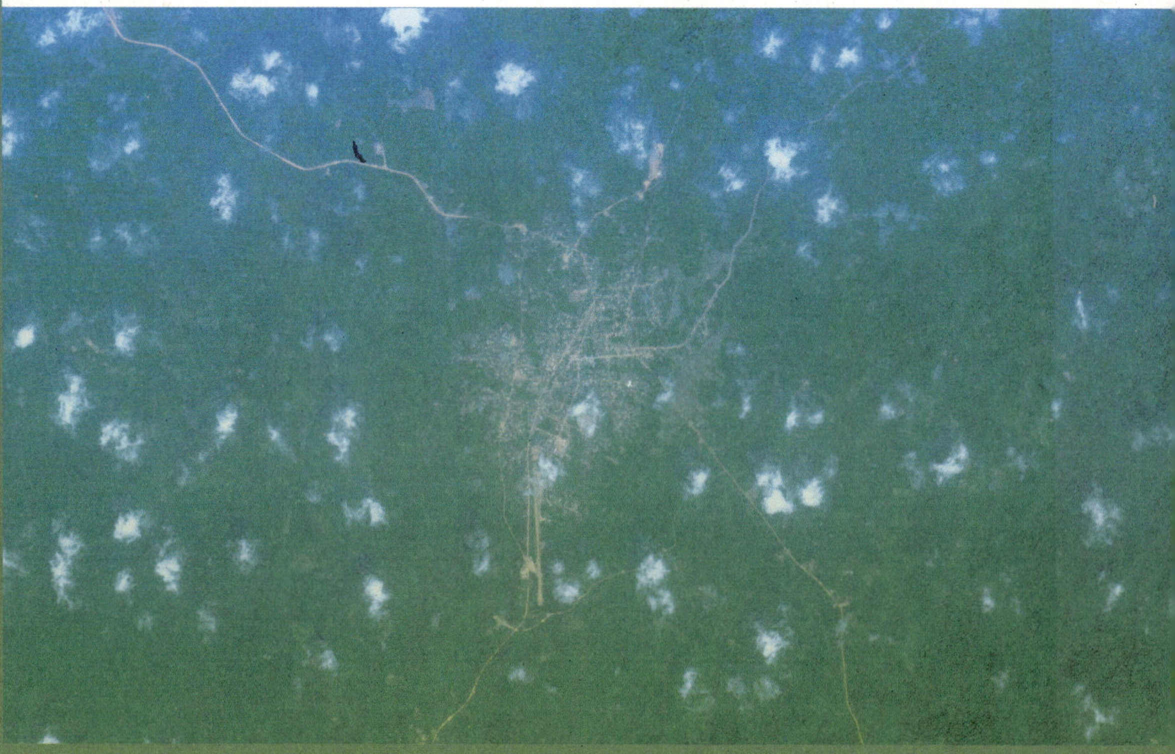

1. UN Health Care Facilities in Relation to their Surroundings

UNMIL Hospital in Monrovia

One of UNMIL's level 3 field hospitals[102] was situated in the Freeport area of Monrovia. The hospital's area totaled roughly 1.41 hectares. It was deployed by the Pakistani contingent and featured several specialized care units: a surgical ward and two operating rooms, as well as a dentist, gynecologist, and other specialized facilities and equipment. The maximum capacity of the hospital was 40 patients per day. As of late 2017, the usage of the hospital stood at 10–15 patients per week. The hospital, as part of the UN operations, was mandated to treat UN personnel exclusively. Although it was surrounded by other UN bases, such as the Star Base and Camp Abuja, the hospital was close to locally inhabited areas. The first populated area was located at a distance of roughly 100 meters from the base and the second was located 600 meters away. The nearest hospital to this area of Monrovia was 6 kilometers away.

Healthcare in Liberia

The civil war in Liberia destroyed the country's healthcare facilities and, to date, most of the population lacks access to adequate medical care and has no access to adequate sanitation facilities. Multiple local and international efforts are taking place to improve the quality of healthcare in Liberia, especially after the Ebola outbreak. Nevertheless, there is a need to continue strengthening Liberia's health system and help prevent similar epidemics from imposing such a devastating human toll.

According to recent statistics:[103]

- Health expenditures: 10% of GDP – US$390 million (2017)
- Physicians density: 1 physician/50,000 population
- 0.02 physicians/1,000 population (2010)
- Hospital bed density: 1 bed/1,250 population
- 0.8 beds/1,000 population (2010)

Opportunities for Engagement, Capacity-Building, and Legacy

As noted above, the hospital in Monrovia has a standing capacity of 40 patients per day yet often sees just 10 patients a week. If transition and legacy considerations are taken into account early in a mission, the reserve capacity of a mission's healthcare could – at no additional cost – be used to build local capacity by allowing unoccupied medical personnel to share know-how with local healthcare providers and/or offer treatments in inhabited areas around the base. Such activities could be organized in collaboration with other UN agencies as well as civil society organizations to increase awareness of health concerns, address medical needs, generate local support for the mission, and identify partners for long-term capacity building by country teams and others during and after the transition process.

102 UN Medical Facilities Levels:

(a) Basic level (first aid): Basic level (first aid) medical services comprise the basic immediate first aid provided to a casualty by the nearest person on site, at the point of injury.

(b) Level 1 medical facilities provide the first level of medical care, i.e., primary health care and immediate lifesaving and resuscitation services. Normally included within basic level 1 capabilities are: routine sick calls and the management of minor sicknesses and injuries among personnel for immediate return to duty; casualty collection from the point of injury/wounding and limited triage; stabilization of casualties; preparation of casualties for evacuation to the next level of medical capability or the appropriate level of medical facility depending on the type and gravity of the injuries; limited inpatient services; and advice on disease prevention, medical risk assessment and force protection within the area of responsibility. A level 1 medical facility is the first level of medical care where a doctor/physician is available.

(c) Level 2 medical facilities provide the next level of medical care and the first level at which basic surgical expertise is available and life support services and hospital and ancillary services are provided within the mission area. A level 2 medical facility provides all level 1 capabilities and, in addition, includes capabilities for emergency surgery, damage control surgery, post-operative services and high-dependency care, intensive care resuscitation and inpatient services, and basic imagistic, laboratory, pharmaceutical, preventive medicine and dental services. Maintenance of patient records and tracking of evacuated patients are also minimum capabilities required for a level 2 medical facility.

(d) Level 3 medical facilities provide the third and highest level of medical care deployed within a mission area. At this level, all capabilities of a level 1 and 2 medical facility are provided, as are capabilities for multidisciplinary surgical services, specialist services and specialist diagnostic services, increased high-dependency care capacity, extended intensive care services and specialist outpatient services.

103 "World Fact Book: Liberia", CIA, available at: www.cia.gov/the-world-factbook/countries/liberia.

UNMIL hospital. Freeport. Monrovia, 2017. Aerial view: Google Earth.

UNMIL hospital. Monrovia, 2017.

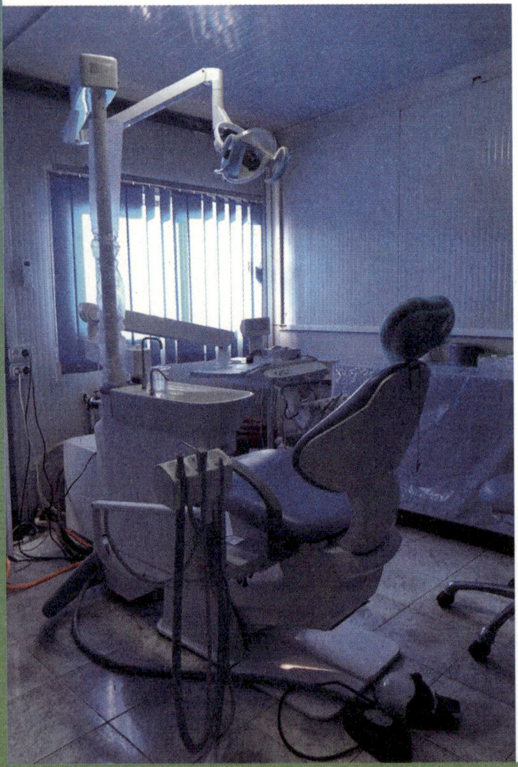

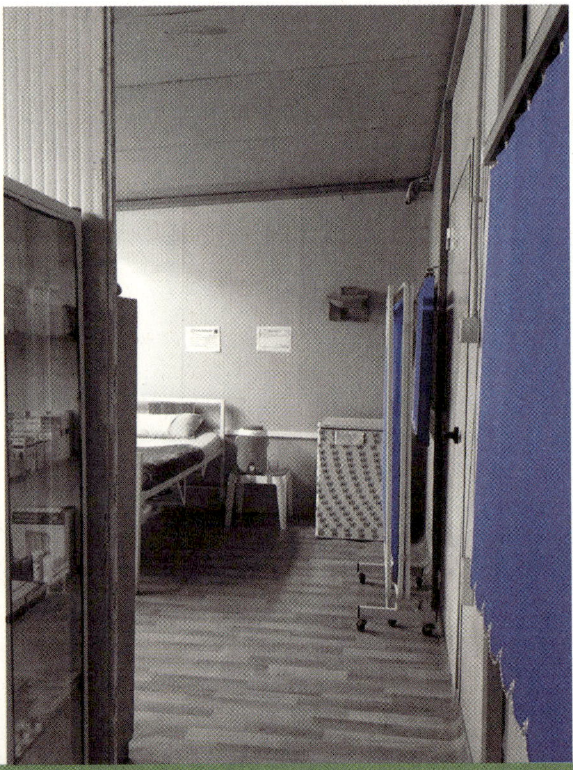

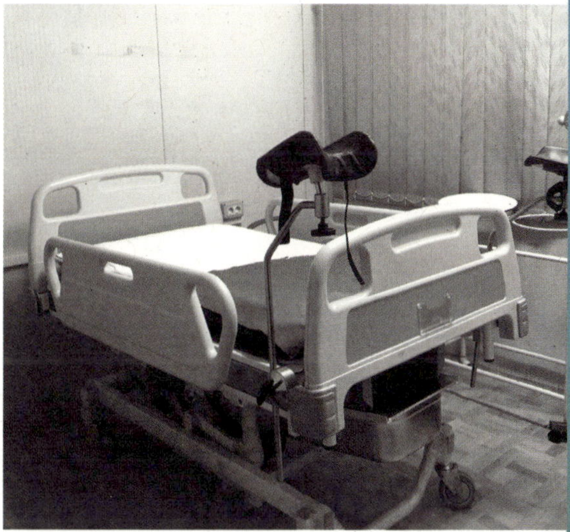

UNMIL hospital. Monrovia, 2017.

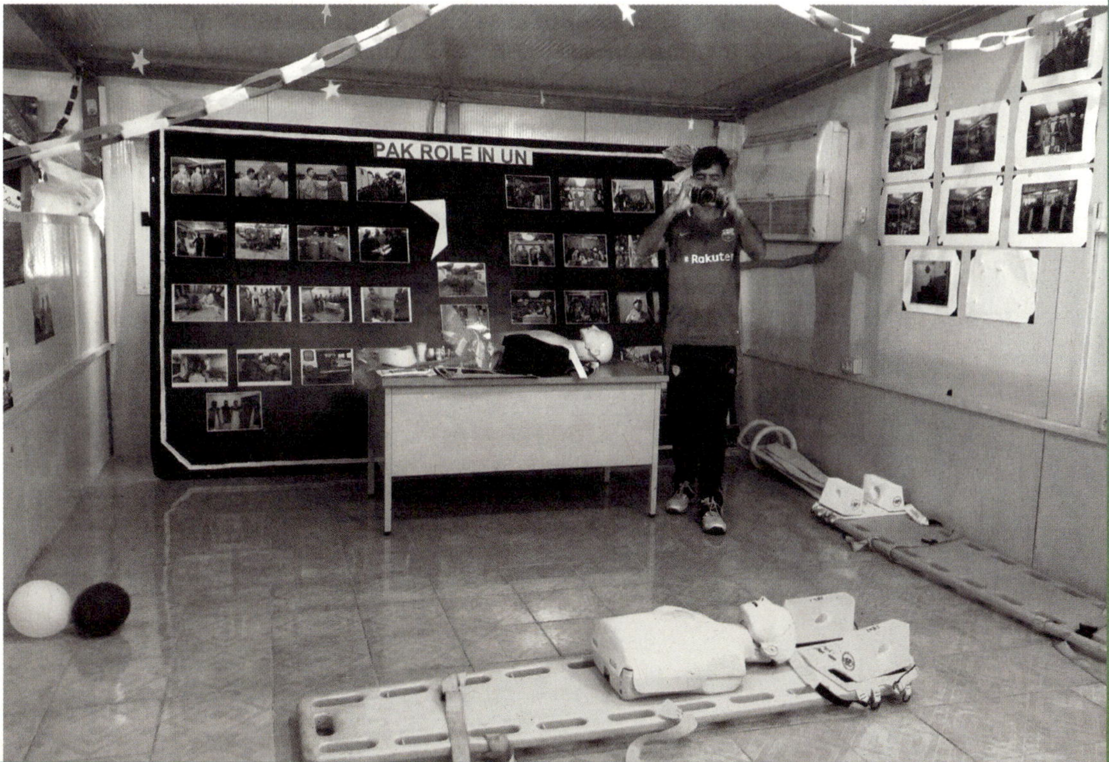

China FPU. Monrovia, 2017. Aerial view: Google Earth.

2. Food Security and Self-Sufficient Deployment at the Chinese Base

The Chinese base was located in the Freeport area, south of Star Base and the Pakistani hospital. It was situated along the Atlantic coast and had direct access to the shoreline and a pier. The base was self-sustained and produced its own food. Two aquaponic greenhouses were maintained by one gardener and could generate enough food for 140 people for three weeks. The produce included cabbage, spinach, pumpkins, beans, eggplants and peppers, as well as a variety of herbs. According to the interviews conducted at the base, the construction cost of the two greenhouses was about US$4,000. The base included a small pig farm, and a fishing area was demarcated in the ocean.

The Chinese peacekeepers experimented with the production of food. In the interview they mentioned that their goal was threefold:

1. to introduce this experiment to other UN missions, because it is a more sustainable practice; 2. to transfer, in particular, the aquaponic gardening know-how to the Liberian Ministry of Agriculture in order to improve local access to fresh produce and food production; and 3. to export this know-how to other African countries that struggle with famine and sustaining food security in the region and the world.

Food Security and Food Access in Liberia

Chronic malnutrition affects almost one-third of the Liberian children under 5 years of age.[104] "The causes include seasonal food deficits, poor dietary diversity, poor infant feeding, a high prevalence of illness, and inadequate access to sanitation, resulting in environmental enteropathy (contamination with fecal bacteria that can impair the body's ability to absorb nutrients)."[105] Most households lack essential food products and are highly dependent on the importation of expensive and low-quality staple foods and casual labor for survival.[106]

Opportunities for Engagement, Capacity-Building, and Legacy

The Chinese base brought forward multiple opportunities to improve the footprint and legacy of UN bases:

- A self-sufficient base reduces the environmental footprint.
- Gardening can offer a therapeutic activity to improve peacekeepers' quality of life.
- Successful practice of food production, with the low use of water and low-tech infrastructure, can be shared with local farmers directly or through a third-party agency (NGOs and/or community representatives).
- Empowering the local population to produce their own food is paramount to sustaining peace and the 2030 Agenda.[107]

104 LISGIS, 2015, "Proposed Food Security Monitoring and Surveillance System", presented on October 8, 2015, the Food Security Cluster Meeting.
105 1) R. Yovsi, K. Samba, B. Bahr, et al. 2010, "A Qualitative Study of Infant and Young Child Feeding Practices in Liberia", UNICEF; 2) Nyepon, Francis. "Liberiaś WASH Crisis: Impact on Water, Sanitation, and Hygiene." The Liberian Dialogue, 2015, available at: http://theliberiandialogue.org/2015/03/14/liberias-wash-crisis-impact-on-water-sanitation-hygiene-2/. 3) Humphrey, J. 2009. "Child Undernutrition, Tropical Enteropathy, Toilets, and Handwashing", The Lancet, Vol. 374, pp. 1032–35.
106 USAID office of food for peace food security desk review for Liberia, 2016, available at: www.usaid.gov/sites/default/files/documents/1866/FFP-Desk-Review-Liberia-Feb2016v2.pdf.
107 The world is not on track to achieve Zero Hunger by 2030. If recent trends continue, the number of people affected by hunger could surpass 840 million by 2030. After decades of steady decline, the number of people who suffer from hunger – as measured by the prevalence of undernourishment – began to slowly increase again in 2015. Current estimates show that nearly 690 million people are hungry, or 8.9% of the world population – up by 10 million people in one year and by nearly 60 million in five years. According to the World Food Programme, 135 million people suffer from acute hunger largely due to man-made conflicts, climate change, and economic downturns. The COVID-19 pandemic could now double that number, putting an additional 130 million people at risk of suffering acute hunger by the end of 2020.

Farming long beans. China FPU. Monrovia, 2017.

Fishing. China FPU. Monrovia, 2017.

Pig farm. China FPU. Monrovia, 2017.

Chinese cabbage and aquaponic farming. China FPU. Monrovia, 2017.

3. Repurposing a Decommissioned UN Base for Community Use

3.1 Gardens at the Indian Formed Police Unit (FPU) in Zwedru

The former UNMIL base was situated within the growing urban fabric of Zwedru, surrounded by local neighborhoods. During the liquidation process of the base, UN officers and local government officials jointly examined the asset. They established what would be removed and what would be left at the site after the drawdown. The base was comprised of modular hard-walled offices, accommodation facilities, and equipment such as, toilets, showers, electrical systems, wiring, lights and light fittings, ceiling fans, air conditioners, perimeter and security lighting, generators and switchboards, in addition to a water supply system, a water treatment plant, water and fuel tanks, communication systems, sea containers, a perimeter fence, signage and security items.[108]

108 See UN bases liquidation list in the appendices.

It was agreed that 21 air conditioning units would be removed by the UN, as well as the submersible water pump, communication equipment, one sea container, all UN signage, seven security lights around the perimeter and the fire extinguishers. Everything else was handed over to the local community. On November 30, 2018, at the time of our site visit, the base resembled a small neighborhood inhabited by local police officers. The modular structures were occupied, filled by domestic furniture, colorful curtains and the space in between the built structures was decorated with well-maintained gardens. The latter had been planted by the Indian peacekeepers.

Opportunities for Engagement, Capacity-Building, and Legacy

Repurposing the Indian FPU brought forward several opportunities:

- The base was well maintained and seemed to have been repurposed by the local police unit rapidly after the UN drawdown.
- The rapid reoccupation of the former UN base by another community prevented its exhaustion during an in-between stage of non-occupancy. The time between the departure of the UN and the reuse of the facility is critical. Bases that were left behind without any specific program looked dilapidated; often doors and windows in the structures remained open, allowing the rain to flow in and destroy what was left. In other cases, after a drawdown, abandoned structures were looted, and pieces of UN equipment were scattered around the area of the base and the nearby neighborhoods.

Views of before and during UNMIL deployment. Indian FPU. Zwedru, 2017. Aerial view: Google Earth.

Blooming gardens after decommissioning. Indian FPU. Zwedru, 2017

3.2 Football Stadium at the China ENG base in Zwedru (Gedeh County)

At the time of the field visit, the site included: UN containers, vehicles in different states and sizes, observation posts, fences, and large modular open roofed structures. The site was reminiscent of its former life as a local soccer stadium, with two netted goal posts situated at the far ends of the playing field and, along its perimeter, a wooden seating area.

The site was located deep within the growing and densifying urban fabric of Zwedru, and its inherent communal value made the space well suited for a youth sports-center, a school, or other public program. At the time of their deployment, the Chinese contingent invested in refurbishing small-scale infrastructure around the base, repairing roads, and introducing a waste collection site in the forest area to help the rapidly growing city to improve its infrastructure and services.[109]

Opportunities for Engagement, Capacity-Building, and Legacy

Due to its size, spatial quality, and location within the city, the base's site could make an attractive place for further development opportunities in Zwedru. For example, in the goals of the UNCT (UN Country Team) and the Liberian Peacebuilding Plan, youth issues are identified as a critical area for support in Liberia and a fundamental factor in Liberia's fragility. There are numerous links between land reform, economic empowerment, and young people. In all relevant strategic frameworks – the AFTII, UNDAF and the Peacebuilding Plan – the empowerment of young people is considered essential for sustainability. Parts of a UN base, such as the large soccer field in Zwedru, can provide the space and opportunity to engage with the local community and particularly its youth. Government and international donors can be brought on board to provide resources to refurbish and reprogram the place, support and enact the Liberian Peacebuilding Plan.[110]

109 1) "Chinese Contingent Inaugurates New Equipment." UNMIL, UNPK. February 2018, available at: https://unmil.unmissions.org/chinese-contingent-inaugurates-new-equipment; and "Chinese Contingent Donates to Zwedru School", UNMIL, UNPK, available at: https://unmil.unmissions.org/chinese-contingent-donates-zwedru-school; and 2) "Chinese Engineers Construct a Road:" UNMIL, UNPK, available at: https://unmil.unmissions.org/chinese-engineers-construct-road-community-college.

110 "Technical and Operational Capacities to Support the UN Commitments", UNMIL, UNPK, 2018, available at: https://unmil.unmissions.org/sites/default/files/unct_capacity_mapping_findings-22may2017_0.pdf.

UNMIL base inside a repurposed community football stadium. Zwedru, 2017.

UN
UN

3.3 Fences between UN Camps and Local Neighborhoods: Camp Abuja in Monrovia

The Nigerian base, Camp Abuja, was located north of the Star Base. It measured almost 10 hectares and consisted of old and dilapidated Liberian buildings of various sizes, in addition to newly installed UN modular structures. The northwest part of the base was adjacent to a small informal Liberian neighborhood.

The proximity between the two communities can be both a challenge and an opportunity. The barbed-wire fence belonging to the base framed the edge of the local neighborhood, located only a couple of meters away from the front doors of its houses. When we visited the neighborhood bordering the base, children and small domesticated animals such as chickens were roaming around the fence. While formally separated, the adjacent realities of the neighborhood and the camp were connected and contingent to one another.

Like many bases, Camp Abuja was built as a fortified island surrounded by walls, barbed wire, watchtowers and trenches. The transition in Liberia presents an opportunity to ensure that such bases are re-imagined as spaces of peace: for instance, by removing the barbed wire and gradually allowing the adjacent communities to access and use the base infrastructure at the end of the mission.

Opportunities for Engagement, Capacity-Building and Legacy

Throughout the mission, and especially during times of transition, UN peacekeeping missions should be able to integrate community outreach programs in collaboration with local governments, NGOs, and UN Country Teams in order to find ways to make feasible plans for a sustainable transition and legacy. If not at the beginning of a mission, then before a liquidation process begins, they should map and assess how the base can be beneficial to adjacent neighborhoods – from providing access to clean water, sewage, and support for small-scale domestic agriculture projects to water harvesting or drainage systems.

Furthermore, such considerations of transition and legacy should be taken into account from the beginning of the mission – that is, during the initial period of assessing the local context.

Camp Abuja. Monrovia Freeport, 2017. Aerial view: Google Earth.

The view of the informal neighborhood from the base. Camp Abuja. Monrovia Freeport, 2017.

Summary of Findings

The following summary highlights the main findings of the UNMIL and MINUSMA research. It is further expanded in the next "Design for Legacy" chapter and its matrix for policymakers on pages 369–381.

1. UN missions bring into fragile contexts an enormous amount of hardware, technology, and resources. Indeed, peacekeeping operations often have budgets and coverage that are unmatched by host governments or by the combined presence of the UN Country Team and nongovernmental organizations. Such vast physical presence creates *responsibilities* as well as *opportunities*.

2. The *urbanization* of peacekeeping presents enormous challenges and opportunities that should be front and center in policy discussions in the UN and at intergovernmental processes. Often, however, the urban fabric in which modern peacekeeping unfolds receive little if any attention. As but one example: the 2015 Report of the High-Level Independent Panel on UN Peace Operations (the HIPPO report) does not mention the word "urban," even as it calls on peacekeepers to engage with local communities and to consider their impact on local economies.

3. Although they are budgeted on a yearly basis, most missions last for years, if not for decades. It is crucial that they be designed with a *long-term, evolutionary perspective* in mind, not only in terms of the software (mandates) of missions, but also their hardware (infrastructure and technology).

4. The footprint of peacekeeping rarely looks the same at the end of a mission as it does at the beginning. Yet, the way bases and super-camps evolve can be more haphazard than planned. The steady introduction of *incremental design changes* can help missions overcome the short-term planning and budgetary constraints they face, enabling missions gradually to attain, and leave behind, a more *sustainable, cost-effective footprint.*

5. It is crucial that transition and legacy planning begin as early as possible, in close collaboration with peacebuilding and development actors such as the Peacebuilding Commission, the Peacebuilding Fund, and the UN Country Team. Planning should be informed by *joint analysis* of the relevant socio-economic, cultural, political, and ecological environment in which UN bases are or will

be situated. Such analysis should be regularly updated and should form the basis for legacy building.

6. With creativity and careful transition planning, and in line with growing calls for coherent, cross-pillar approaches, the infrastructure of peacekeeping can have a *lasting, positive impact on local development* through the following:

a. Designing or transitioning bases and buildings such that they can be repurposed for other uses, including schools, medical clinics, and community centers, after a mission ends
b. Utilizing local sourcing of materials, equipment, and labor, accompanied by robust market analysis to ensure it is sustainable and equitable
c. Shifting gradually toward food self-sufficiency via community gardens, fish farms, and animal husbandry
d. Making strategic use of sunk costs and reserve capacity, such as under-used hospital facilities for local empowerment
e. Adopting low-tech and easily maintained technology, such as rain harvesting techniques, wherever appropriate
f. Seizing opportunities as they arise for legacy and capacity-building pilot projects in the communities surrounding UN bases

Crucially, none of these ideas or proposals require a departure from existing policy frameworks or, indeed, from certain activities already undertaken by (and budgeted for) UN missions. To the contrary, there is by now a robust consensus that peacekeeping, peacebuilding, and development are *complex, nonlinear, co-constitutive processes.*

UN

Camp Abuja. Monrovia, 2017.

Design for Legacy

V. Design for Legacy

Design for Legacy chapter brings forward our findings and recommendations for UN agencies and TCCS It is a design intervention on a policy level that aims to introduce design thinking, including values of responsibility, accountability, and legacy, into the processes of planning, constructing, liquidating, and repurposing UN bases.

UN peacekeeping operations unfold today on a large scale alongside hundreds of inhabited sites in conflict-affected regions. Their bases, camps, super camps, headquarters, logistic hubs, and airfields are designed and built by military engineers to support peacekeepers for the duration of UN missions, providing them not only with safety but with direct access to resources such as water, electricity, food, and medical services. Surrounded by fences and walls, these spaces are designed to operate as self-contained islands, yet they invariably impact their surroundings in long-lasting and harmful ways. The expanding scope of missions, their personnel, material footprints, and dependency on global supply chains contribute to an increase in the UN's environmental impacts and carbon emissions.

Current UN missions are situated in sub-Saharan Africa and the Sahel,[1] areas that are struggling with a harsh daily reality of the climate crisis—desertification, intensifying droughts, mudslides, and floods. At worst, they risk increasing the devastation of lives and resource scarcity, which exacerbates violence, armed conflicts, and wars. With careful planning, however, they have untapped potential. Beyond the mandates, infrastructure, technology, and resources that a UN mission brings to bear, it can open up new opportunities in some of the world's most impoverished and imperiled areas. Growing recognition of the interplay between peace, development, and prevention—coupled with mounting calls within the UN for inclusive, longer-term approaches—has created space for new ways of thinking about the physical and technological footprint of peacekeeping missions. As the UN draws down and closes missions from Liberia to Haiti and develops transition strategies for operations in Mali and the Democratic Republic of the Congo, the question of imaginative uses for this infrastructure takes on a new salience.

The UN itself talks about "guidelines for a cross-pillar integrated approach"[2]—combining peace, development and prevention—with the 2030 Climate Action increasingly weighing in at all levels of UN activities.[3] It is in the material form, the architecture of missions, where legacy is made and where policies, bureaucracies, and financial systems are being materialized and translated into a built environment. Integrated and regenerative design in missions can contribute to, and even steward resilient and equitable environments that systemically combine the needs of society with the integrity of nature.

UN missions should advance community empowerment and environmental awareness in their mandates and help instigate alternative visions for the future of the vulnerable areas they occupy. In the end, the missions will be gone, but their legacy will remain.

1 The Sahel is engulfed by violence. Climate change, food insecurity and extremists are largely to blame. Available at: www.weforum.org/agenda/2019/01/all-the-warning-signs-are-showing-in-the-sahel-we-must-act-now.

2 An integrated and coherent approach among relevant political, security, and development actors – both in and outside the United Nations system – is critical to peacebuilding and sustaining peace. See also peace and security reform: https://reform.un.org/content/peace-and-security-reform.

3 Tackling Climate Change Goal 13 calls for urgent action to combat climate change and its impacts. It is intrinsically linked to all 16 of the other Goals of the 2030 Agenda for Sustainable Development. To address climate change, countries adopted the Paris Agreement to limit global temperature rise to well below 2 degrees Celsius, available at: www.un.org sustainabledevelopment/climate-action.

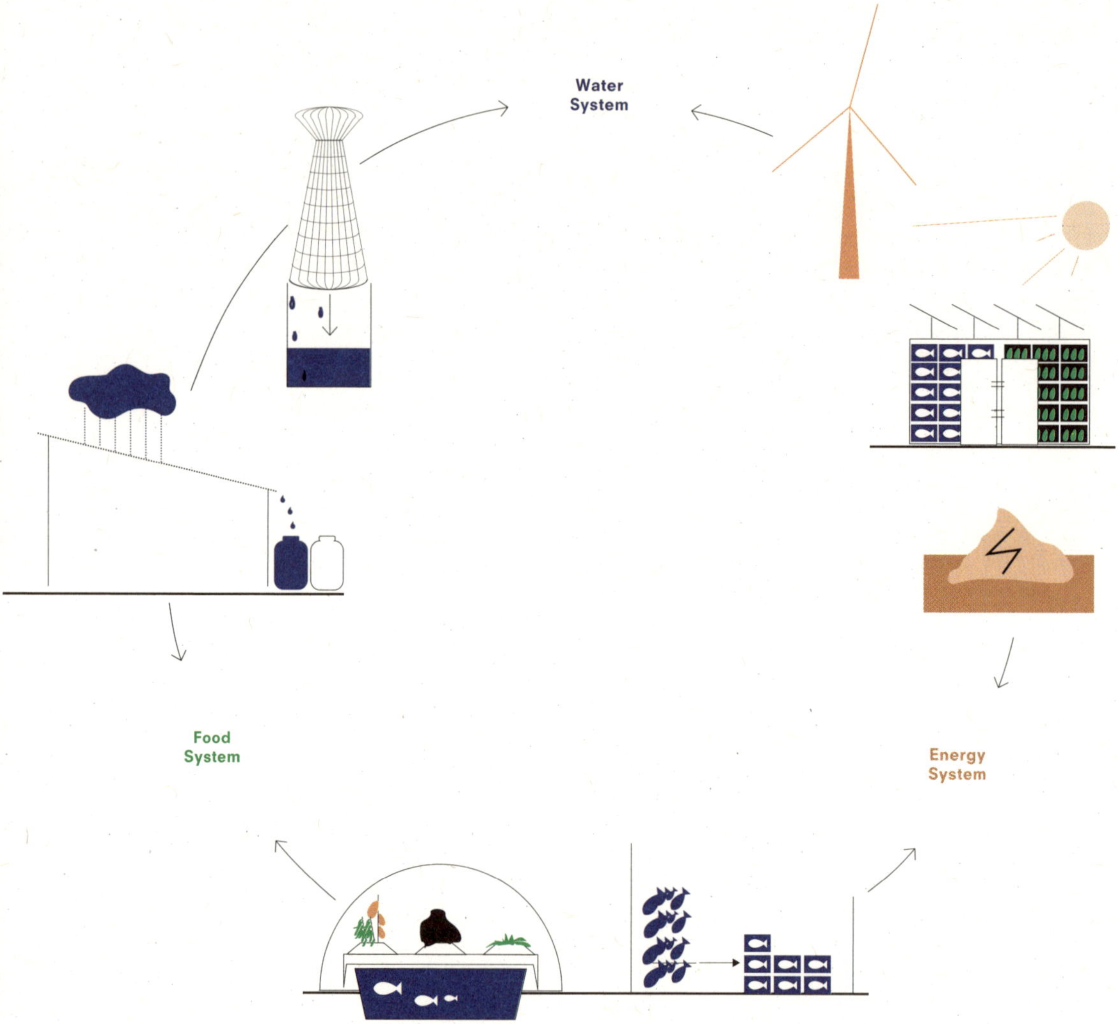

Circular and regenerative resources for UN bases, and communities in time of crisis.

Agendas for Peace

Leah Zamore

The enlarged mandates, growing urbanization, and substantial material imprint of peacekeeping missions has created opportunities as well as challenges. The vast physical presence of peacekeeping missions—which oftentimes far exceeds that of the host government or the UN Country Team—and their proximity to local communities have also created responsibilities.

Bases should be designed in a way that provides space for peace and development, as opposed to hindering it.

Policy processes and reviews related to peacekeeping (such as the HIPPO report[4] and the UN's Environmental Strategy[5]) have repeatedly highlighted the need for missions to:

- Work across pillars (peace and security human rights and development)
- Engage more closely with local communities
- Adopt more people-centered approaches
- Minimize the environmental impact
- Stimulate local economies, where possible
- Enhance national ownership and leadership

The physical footprint of UN bases provides a vital opportunity to realize these commitments. There is now a clear consensus in favor of comprehensive approaches that cut across the three pillars of the UN.

4 Central to the HIPPO report of June 2015 was a strong insistence on escaping the bifurcation in planning, management, and funding between peacekeeping operations and the large field-based special political missions, in favor of what we called a "spectrum of peace operations". This would enable the UN to deliver and adapt more flexibly tailored missions, rather than be constrained by mindsets and bureaucracies inclined to templates, available at: 1) https://theglobalobservatory.org/2020/09/lessons-from-hippo-2015-review-for-future-peace-operations/, and 2) https://peaceoperationsreview.org/wp-content/uploads/2015/08/HIPPO_Report_1_June_2015.pdf.

5 The Environment Strategy of the United Nations Department of Field Support (DFS) came into effect in January 2017. It sets out a vision that DFS will strive to achieve by 2023 in relation to environmental management in peace operations. It also defines phase one objectives up to June 2020 across five pillars. The strategy is a living document, updated as progress is made and approaches evolve. This summary document outlines the analysis and priorities set out in the full document following one year of implementation. See: https://peacekeeping.un.org/sites/default/files/171116_dfs_exec_summary_environment_0.

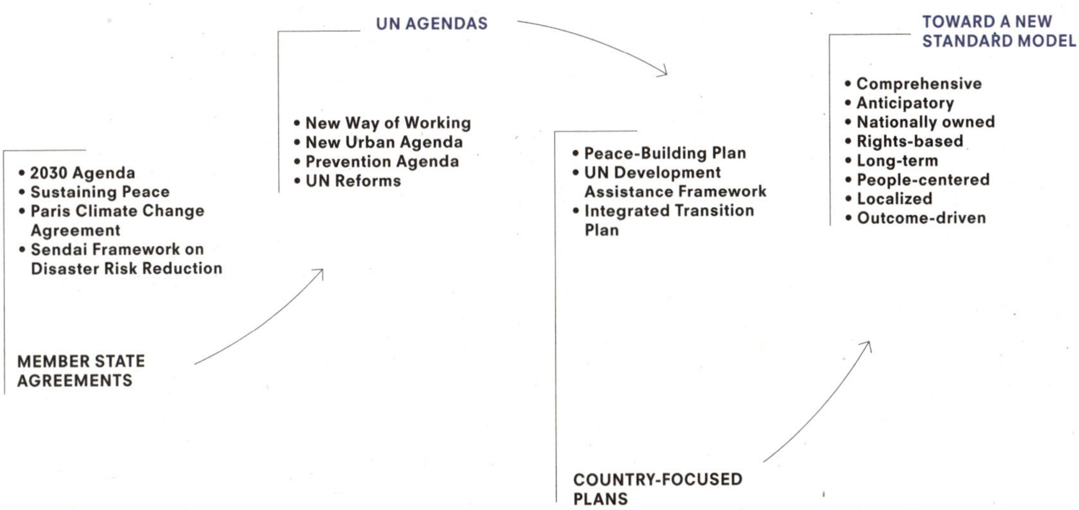

Speculative Financial and Socio-economic Model for Evaluating and Enhancing International Peacekeeping Missions

Joel van der Beek

The UN compound of the future should enable peacekeeping missions to have a more sustainable and beneficial effect on the lives of people of the regions where they operate. In view of this vision, we have developed a speculative model that can be implemented in every peacekeeping mission. In this model, we elaborate on the role that peacekeeping missions could play in the socio-economic sphere. The model draws on three socio-economic elements while respecting the sovereign state: creating opportunities via the market space, ensuring that the trading partners and principles are aligned, and building for the future through sustainable investments and capacity building.

Peacekeeping missions follow periods of severe violent conflict. They arrive at a scene that can be characterized by national instability, a weakened position of national authorities, and having human lives at stake. The nation-state is exhausted by the costs of the conflict and is sinking into regressive relationships with other countries. The peacekeeping missions aim at restoring peace, safety, stability, and basic conditions to rebuild society.

Safety and stability are keywords related to UN missions and humanitarian interventions. These concepts may not only be interpreted in a military sense but can also be applied in a socio-economic sense. "War and famine. Peace and milk," is a Somali proverb that serves Economists for Peace and Security as a motto. It reflects the relations between violent conflict and economics. Although the causal connection between poverty and war remains a question, the combination of the two is of an explosive nature. It is here where the military aspect of the UN intervention needs to be supplemented with economics for rebuilding the sovereign state and avoiding colonialism.[6]

The UN compound can be seen as an abundance of power and possibilities, compared to its poor, destabilized and disintegrated surroundings. In our view, the UN compound of the future might allocate its opportunities already present in the current models, beyond the direct military range of activities. This would be done with the objective to be socially supportive in bringing stabilization, promoting integration and building for the future.

Peacekeeping missions could play a role in the socioeconomic sphere. They offer once-in-a-lifetime opportunities from the local point of view. They involve a substantial influx of investment and activities, often massive in comparison with the local situation, characterized by severe shortages. This unique opportunity should be seized.

Safeguarding the socio-economic conditions might improve the local safety situation and prevent it from slipping deeper down. Although the start of a peacekeeping mission is characterized by urgency and a focus on the military aspects and, although there is support from Civic Military Cooperation (CIMIC), it would pay off to include additional socio-economic elements, including a picture of the local economy and the social structures that were in place before the conflict and of the situation at the time of the intervention and a need assessment. After all, the damage of wars to society is immense and long-lasting.

In situations of shortages, chaos, and insecurity, solutions should be efficient, adequate, and well structured, with regard both to the short and long term. Therefore, it is important to realize that the space for peacekeeping missions is not unlimited. Although the border with humanitarian aid has become blurred, there has to be a clear distinction between peacekeeping missions and the international civic scene. Military organizations are good

6 Economists for Peace and Security is a UN-registered NGO promoting economic analysis and appropriate action for peace, security and the world economy.

for the resolution of violent conflict, whilst the local private and public sector, assisted by international aid is good at restoring a positive socioeconomic reality. There is a great risk when aid becomes an instrument in the military agenda: namely, aid losing its neutrality and its last-resort role.

The model consists of three elements. The key principle is based on how a sustainable transfer of resources, finance, knowledge, and skills can be realized between the peacekeeping mission and the local community, in order for it to be constructive for the community and to induce minimal risk for society to relapse into war.

Element One: The Market Space

It is very valuable to develop the local economy. The peacekeeping mission can help to rebuild the economy and society, with its purchasing power, by having local resources involved in constructing and operating the compound and the mission. As the conflict erodes the local economy, employment falls, entrepreneurship becomes a hardship, the black market boosts prices, and original structures are weak or absent. War has a discouraging effect on investments. The purchasing power of the peacekeeping mission may stimulate the revitalization of the local economy and society. During the operations of the UN mission or humanitarian intervention, a market space could be established to bridge the distance between the UN compound and the local economy. This market space should be located in between the civic and military space. It would allow local involvement to a maximum while keeping the military zone safe and secured. As many of the assets within the compound are, or can be made, mobile, construction, repair, and maintenance could be done in the market space using local capacity. Currently, the exchange of goods and services between the two systems is low due to security issues. The market space could bridge this gap.

Element Two: Financial Ring-fencing

The acquisition of local resources by the peacekeeping mission should be done in a way that it helps instead of further disrupting the local situation. Prices paid and volumes purchased on the local market should keep pace with local conditions. By paying sustainable prices and buying sustainable volumes, the peacekeeping mission will have a constructive influence on the local economy. When hiring local labor, the paying of extraordinary high wages creates unbalance and social tensions and might even have an adverse effect on getting what the mission needs. The same holds for volumes purchased and prices paid for local products and raw materials. Financial ring-fencing as part of the mission would help to prevent a further collapse of the local economy, while identifying a specific type of resources that can be given back to the economy. [7]

The case of the international reaction to the 2010 Haiti earthquake reveals that massive international support entails the risk that, after the aid, the local society may collapse. In the case of Haiti, inhabitants could no longer afford the skyrocketing rents for housing in Port au Prince. The influx of food and medical supplies and staff completely crowded out and crushed what had survived the earthquake. A large part of the local private sector and the local employment did not survive the humanitarian 'tsunami' and pushed Haiti back into a dependency position.

7 Ring fencing is a term used in finance, referring to the separating or walling off of assets in order to protect them from creditors, specific taxation or regulations.

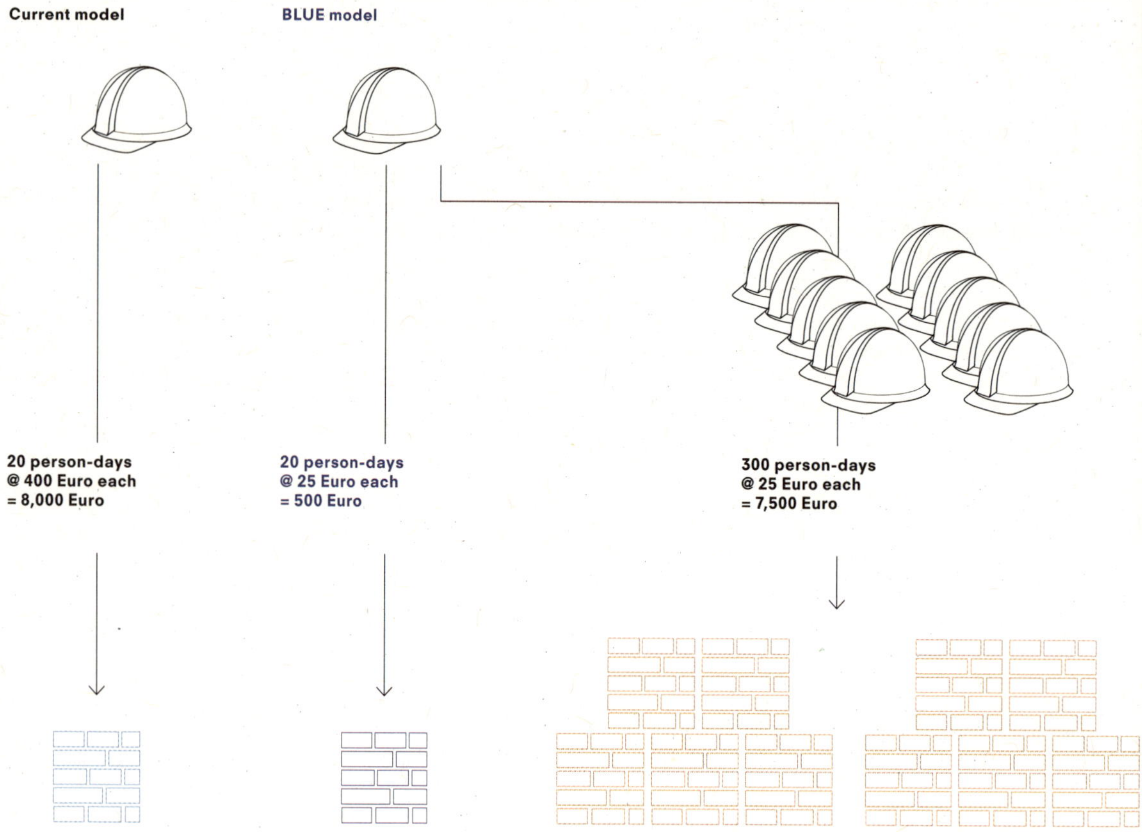

Example diagram for Blue socio-economic model.

Element Three: A Local Development Fund

The market space will allow the peacekeeping mission to increase its local purchases. All over the Sahel region, local purchases and local labor will be at relatively low unit prices, compared to international standards. UN budgets are based on international standards. The difference between the local wage paid to local labor involved in the peacekeeping mission and the international standard should be used to establish a fund. This fund should help to finance building up the local economy and society, create employment, build up capacity, and re-establish entrepreneurship. In this way, the peacekeeping mission can help to rebuild the economy and society by funding local initiatives, both in the private and in the public domain. A part could be used as a revolving fund to stimulate private entrepreneurship through micro-credits; part could be used as grant money for long-term investments in utilities or infrastructures. In this way, the investment gap caused by the war can be compensated partially, and the UN mission can be supportive in setting up a condition for local society to flourish.

Ownership of the fund should be with the peacekeeping mission. A local civic assembly should decide about the allocation of this fund. Investments should be restricted to civic utilities, thereby including adequate reserves for repair and maintenance. The investments should be implemented on short notice, so that staff of the peacekeeping mission can coordinate the implementation and support with equipment. A maximum of local resources would be allocated. Financial control and project management would remain within the staff of the peacekeeping mission. Design, construction works, including labor and building materials, would be paid directly by the project management. An advantage of this "in-kind" character is that it holds a low corruption risk.

A good example would be the establishment of an institute for Technical Vocational Education and Training (TVET). The construction works of the buildings would serve as practicing activities for the students. Conflict creates a defector risk for each individual who collaborates with the peacekeeping mission. This model reduces this risk for the individual local contractor. Also, the investment has a relatively neutral image as the civic assembly and should be such that, apart from serving a military function, it is cost-efficient and its footprint is not negative, but neutral or positive. This condition should be met both during the construction, the operations, and the decommissioning phase of the compound. The three elements of the model could be instrumental in providing the local community with a positive legacy that goes beyond the military interpretation of safety and stability. This speculative evaluation and enhancement model for peacekeeping missions is an invitation for further research on how to improve vulnerable economies.

Designing for Legacy: An Anthropological Perspective

Erella Grassiani

It is important to understand the legacy of peace operations in war-torn countries around the world and how to direct them toward more positive, humanitarian ends. If we hope to influence the legacy of peace operations in the Sahel, critical questions must be asked – questions which raise concerns, open up debates and problematize issues that (mistakenly) are assumed to be simple, straightforward facts.

Issues of Context

One of the central ideas within any anthropological work is the extreme importance of including contexts in our investigations. These contexts can be social, political or historical, for example. Understanding how people perceive their own social reality and the meaning they give to it involves interpreting people's behavior and their words within the different, complex contexts they inhabit. Hence the important question to ask when trying to understand how to 'design for legacy' is to ask about contexts: What is the background and setting (in a broad sense) in which the people involved live and understand their lives? What is the historical context of the place and, for example, the violence people are facing? We should ask the difficult questions about colonial legacies in many countries where peace missions are present today. In order to grasp this multiple contextual setting, I believe deep, ethnographic and historical research is needed. This will help us see and understand if people want to be helped and in what way they will want us to do that. I believe it is then extremely important to involve the people living in places that are touched by the presence of military or peace forces in our efforts to improve their lives.

Complexities of Concepts such as "The Locals"

The most logical thing to do when we want to know what the needs are of the local population is to go and indeed talk to these "locals". However, that is more complicated than it sounds. Related to the former issue of context, we need to understand the complexities of the societies we visit – their power structures, internal conflicts, gender relations to name just a few central issues – in order to start to grasp how these societies work and what their needs are. Coming from the West, we tend to talk to "spokespersons", power-holders or village headmen, but do they really speak for everyone? Are there other voices we should listen to? We should then, whenever possible, pay attention to multiple voices, to power relations and the agendas of the people we speak to. Furthermore, I believe it to be of utmost importance to understand how people feel about the presence of foreign forces near their dwellings. How does it affect them, do they support or criticize the presence, are they afraid of it?

Complexities of Conflict/Post-Conflict

The places where peace operations take place are, by definition, touched by war and violence, and often these wars are accompanied by environmental crises, such as droughts. We often assume that, ideally, when foreign peace missions leave, they leave behind a more peaceful place, a situation of post-conflict perhaps. From an anthropological perspective, concepts of peace, conflict and post-conflict are, however, highly problematic—not because we are pessimists, but because, from our detailed and grounded research, we have learned over the years how misleading these terms can be. 'Peace' seems to mean so many different things to different people, and often we mistake official, formal 'peace' which is based on a paper agreement with signatures of highly placed men and women with the reality 'on the ground.' We should ask ourselves what such 'peace' means for people living in these places, which are now supposedly peaceful or in a state of post-conflict. When looking more closely, we can almost always see that peace agreements practically don't mean anything for the people affected most by war, who live in poverty and have to deal with daily violence. Perhaps the perpetrators are different, but people are still deprived of a real peaceful living environment. People who have faced war and violence, often for decades, will perhaps be afraid of these other foreign uniformed people and this new 'military' camp suddenly arising. We have to consider their ideas, fears, and also their hopes. Importantly, peace is not the complete opposite of war, and we should carefully think about what it means for people themselves. We should keep this in mind when thinking about legacies of peace missions and trying to support people who have experienced war, violence and deprivation.

What we also should consider is the different categorization within the discourse on conflicts and wars. In the public debate, people tend to use essentializing categories such as 'ethnic conflicts' or 'religious violence,' which are very misleading. Such categorizations simplify the experiences of people and the background of violent conflicts. We need to understand that such concepts are constructs and tell a particular story, often one that is far from the truth and one that misses the indispensable contexts in which conflicts, wars, and violence take place.

Development?

Finally, I believe we have to take a critical look at the idea of 'helping' the other, of so-called 'development'. Within anthropology, this term has been used for years, but also heavily scrutinized. Who are we to come and 'help' others, in faraway places? What does development mean, what do we want to develop, and towards what do we want to develop it? One of the most important questions to ask is according to whose standards are we developing in the first place? This brings me to my earlier point of understanding the context in a deep way and understanding what people themselves see as positive developments and needs for their community. We should realize that many of our ideas about welfare, wealth, and happiness are ethnocentric in nature and show a very specific, Western idea of what these concepts mean. We have to be sensitive to the language and concepts used by people themselves and especially to the way they give meaning to their own needs, hopes, and dreams.

Conclusion

We are left with the importance of asking anthropological, critical questions in the context of the Design for Legacy project. With this project, we aim to better and improve the lives of people who are touched by war and violence, but also by the sudden presence of foreign peacekeeping missions, on all kinds of levels. In order to do this in the best, most honorable way, we should gain an in-depth understanding not only of the different contexts of a place and its people but also of who these people or 'locals' are and what the power relations look like within their communities. We need to understand the conflict they are or were part of in-depth and the way they interpret 'peace' or 'post-conflict'. In order to really be able to design for a certain legacy, we should let go of our own ideas about 'development' and 'wellbeing' and learn about the dreams and hopes of people. These hopes and dreams, constructed within their own reality, need to be our starting point when legacies are created.

A Green Strategy for BLUE: Food and Ecological Security through "Deeply Green Urban Agriculture"

Debra Solomon

The Green Strategy of BLUE envisions an approach to greening that simultaneously both nourishes the inhabitants of Gao and Camp Castor as well and their physical environment by designing ecological legacy. The vision is based upon combining the benefits of urban agriculture (UA) in the form of park-like edible landscapes, also known as food forests, with agroecology techniques, already successful at greening formerly desertified regions. The Global Forum for Food and Agriculture (GFFA) Communiqué 2016 emphasizes that food security is 'a prerequisite for political and social stability and crucial for planning and managing the urbanization process successfully, highlighting the capability of agriculture in rural, peri-urban and urban areas not only to supply food but also a wide range of public goods and services', including ecosystem services.[8] Rooting BLUE's Green Strategy in a forest garden format surpasses the notion of the UA 'market garden' to include a densely edible landscape capable of driving positive ecological impacts like water sequestration,

8 Selections from Preamble to the Global Forum for Food and Agriculture (GFFA) Communiqué, January 16, 2016, "How to Feed Our Cities? — Agriculture and Rural Areas in an Era of Urbanisation" www.gffa-berlin.de/wp-content/uploads/2015/10/GFFA_Kommunique_2016_EN.pdf.

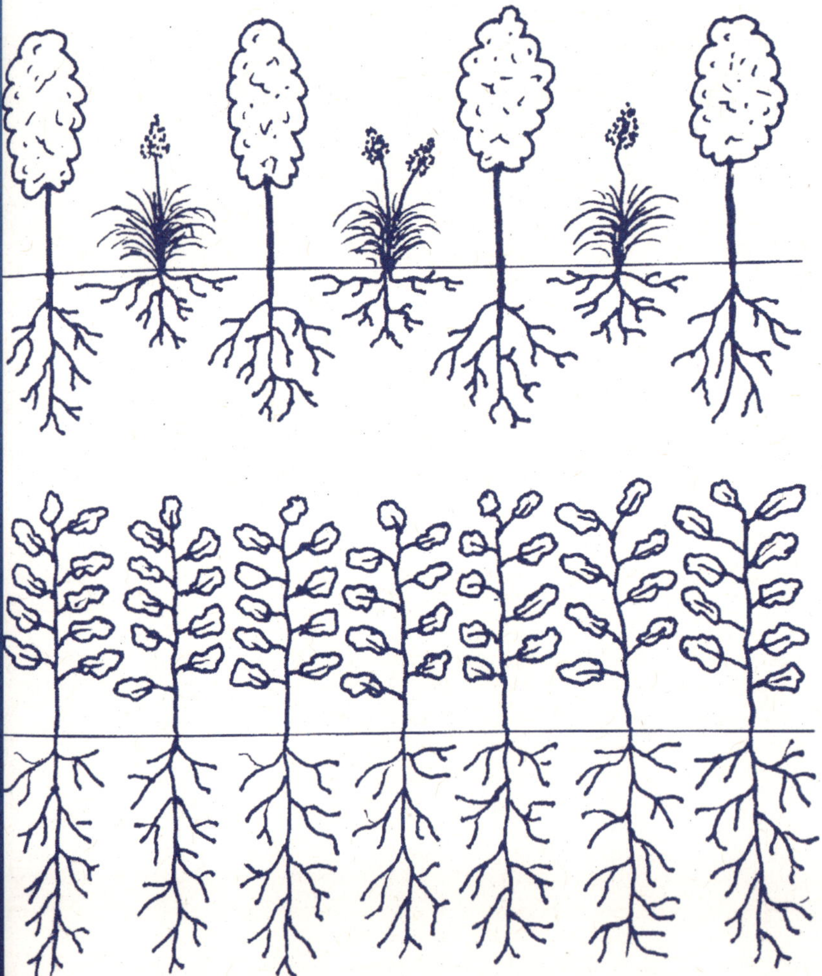

Forms of root separation in an archeology planting. The top drawing shown horizontal stratification, the lower shows vertical root partitioning. Source: P.A.Wojtkowski, Introduction.

preventing urban heat islands, soil regeneration, and the creation of high-value nature,[9] itself a potential source of UA revenue and outputs.

In developing a Green Strategy for Camp Castor and the adjacent city of Gao, any approach, if it is to succeed, will necessarily address social, technological, and ecological factors. Social aspects will acknowledge the multi-stakeholder terrains of the military base, the city, and peri-urban space. Design decisions with regard to the landscape and agroecosystems must be understandable and culturally appropriate for local practitioners of urban agriculture, local market gardening, urban (and peri-urban) conservation agriculture and agroforestry (forest gardening), and pastoralists, and the implemented agrotechnologies should be suitable and appealing to military personnel on and off the base. Technical considerations of the Green Strategy refer to how areas will be designed and built, along with the timeframe, and can concern the use and access to machinery. Ecological aspects describe what local stakeholders deem to be the most pressing priorities concerning the landscape. BLUE's Green Strategy describes a vision that necessarily suits existing social contexts (urban and military, pastoral), technological constraints (timeframe, available resources, and logistics), and ecological improvements and yields.

Design Legacy in Nature

In ecology and agriculture "succession" is the term used to denote the dynamics of legacy. Succession describes the transition between certain crops or plant combinations that, following each other in time, leave behind new conditions in the form of residues and food for future generations of plant, bacterial, and fungal life. This is what is happening when certain plants occupy 'empty' urban plots that, left undisturbed, provide habitats where birds nest and foxes make their homes. Ecological legacy can also be observed underground, where the spaces left over by the roots of one now-dead species provide room for one whose roots will fill the same contours, flourishing on the residues left behind by its predecessor.[10] Planning for ecological succession, i.e., designing an ecological legacy for Camp Castor and the adjacent urban area of Gao, not only entails developing long-term planning that addresses in situ resource building, biodiversity, and the creation of favorable microclimates, it is also about choosing which strategies will be used to achieve these goals. Plant and crop choices are, in fact, the choice for a specific set of plant strategies and form part of a set of useful ecological tools.[11] When we choose distinct plant combinations, we are choosing the notional sum of their survival strategies as our own.

Examples for Camp Castor

In BLUE's Green Strategy, Camp Castor can provide a focal point for ecological security and renewal. The camp complex is a hub of technical resources, labor, and machinery and is capable of embedding ecosystem services to form the foundation of future resources and education. These might include formats that require abundant space, not readily available in the adjacent city of Gao. Plant nurseries combined with agricultural education labs anticipate a future in which the base has been transformed, absorbed into the urban and ecological fabric. The base's peripheral placement in the landscape calls for an easy-to-implement, high-impact greening strategy, strengthened with multi-layered agroforestry at later phases.

Soil grading to create large flat surfaces and providing large uninterrupted areas of paving in Camp Castor (and in urban areas in Gao) work against ecological legacy. A democratic form of ecological legacy design requires assessing all likely forms of 'site disturbance' that may occur during camp design and taking these into account in the design planning of the landscape. In other words, events such as base and road construction, the creation of potentially large

9 Cooper, Tasmin et al. 2007. Final Report for the Study of High Value Nature (HNV), Indicators for Evaluation. Report prepared by the Institute for European Environmental Policy for DG Agriculture.
10 Cardon, Zoe G. and Whitbeck, Julie L., 2007. The Rhizosphere: An Ecological Perspective. p. 131, Figure 6.2. Elsevier Academic Press.
11 Jacke, D. with Toensmeier E., 2005. Edible Forest Gardens, Ecological vision and theory for temperate climate permaculture. p. 241. Chelsea Green Publishing VT.

infrastructures like water storage, imply access to, and the use, of heavy machinery, a disturbance event but also a resource from the perspective of stakeholders keen to source road runoff as an irrigation resource. Large machinery can be used both on and off base to implement land contours, terracing, land swales, and wind belts. Taking an agroecological approach involves, among other things, categorizing levels of land use disturbance to better share their positive effects and resources. Camp Castor is itself a valuable resource of logistics expertise that can aid in programming the 'use' of disturbance events productively.

Some sustainable land management practices that are appropriate for Camp Castor are already in practice in the Sahel and Burkina Faso. These include stone lines,[12] a traditional method for producing soil fertility in desertified areas by capturing silt and organic matter and slowing runoff to create greened areas. Leaving large portions of the base ungraded has advantages for ecological success, and the sloped areas can be transformed through the use of 'fanya juu terraces': self-grading planting zones that increase water retention and mitigate erosion. In general, the spatial planning at Camp Castor should be based upon implementing parkland agroforestry,[13] which, as it sounds, creates park-like zones of productive, high-canopy trees with an equally productive understory, a living landscape, simultaneously food-producing and a nursery for plant and plant knowledge distribution. This resplendent polyculture will ecologically protect the base and adjacent city by transforming a larger landscape into one with a more favorable microclimate. This landscape with requisite biodiversity will, at the same time, produce useful primary and secondary outputs for the adjacent city including beneficial high-value nature in the long term.[14]

12 Jacke, D. with Toensmeier E., 2005. Edible Forest Gardens, Ecological vision and theory for temperate climate permaculture. p. 241. Chelsea Green Publishing VT.
13 Stone Lines – Sustainable Land Management Series (YouTube) last accessed February 16, 2016. www.youtube.com/watch?v=I7lys7uPVP8.
14 Cooper, Tasmin and others. 2007. Final Report for the Study of High Value Nature (HNV), as above.

Though urban agriculture in Africa substantially contributes to providing nutrition through year-round access to fresh food, its practice remains intricately bound up with the use of and competition for the city's resources. A recent recommendation (albeit a study of East African cities) calls for improving urban agricultural systems by focusing on existing low-risk food products (e.g., poultry and mushrooms) and collectively producing high-return products (fruit, and vegetables). These agricultural examples alone are rich in secondary outputs beneficial to urban soil fertility. Well planned and densely planted, a multilayered urban agro-forest brings far more than a year-round source of high-value nutrition. It reduces ecological stress by cooling the city with shade through a multilayered canopy and additionally returns atmospheric carbon to the soil, where it provides fertility. Urban soils improved and remediated through the addition of aforementioned manure and mulch sources have the capability of absorbing and retaining up to 50% more water from seasonal rains, roadside runoff, and even greywater sources. When UA is perceived as food and ecosystem infrastructure, it has the power to cycle urban resources that might otherwise go untapped.

The Green Strategy of BLUE is a vision predicated on combining urban agriculture in the form of park-like edible landscapes and currently practiced agroecology techniques to nourish urban inhabitants whilst greening the physical environment simultaneously. Sustainable agricultural choices use techniques already in practice, prioritizing traditional and local practice. Educational priorities will ideally include urban topsoil production (e.g., vermiculture, composting), in situ soil remediation and erosion prevention, and an awareness of how both above- and below-ground biodiversity impacts ecosystem health, directly connected to overall yield. Successfully applied to both the city of Gao and Camp Castor, BLUE's Green Strategy can produce a democratic, productive landscape, in which both long- and short-term stakeholders drive ecological legacy.

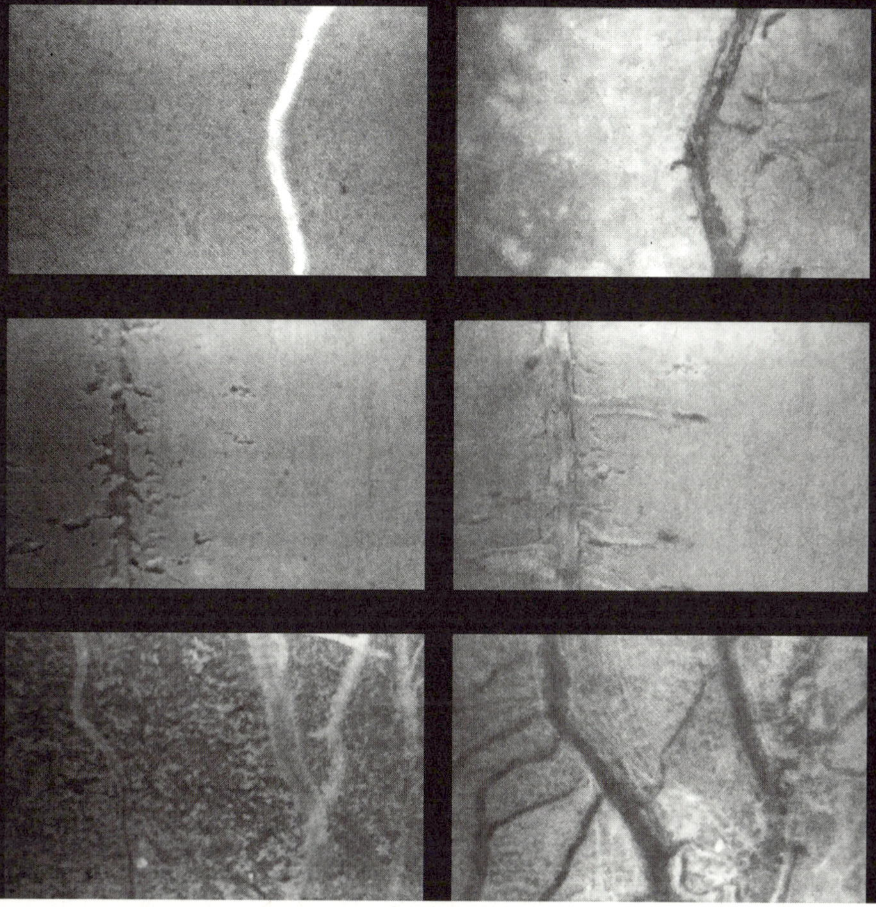

Paired Minirhizotron images showing roots of canola cover crop (left) in compacted plowpan soil (spring) and soy bean roots (right) observed in the same locations in the soil a few months later. The roots can be seen to follow channels made by the preceding canola roots (after S.M. Williams and R.R.Weil, 'Crop cover root channels may alleviate soil compaction effects on soybean crop.' Soil Science Society of America Journal (2006); with permission). Source: Z.g.cardon and J.I. Whitbeck, The Rhizosphere, an ecological perspective, 1st ed. (Amsterdam: elsevier Academic Press, 2007). pp. 131, figure 6.2.

Models and Diagrams

The following models and diagrams aim at visualizing and spatializing the Design for Legacy approach while highlighting opportunities for change and legacy. The proposed processes take into account security and budgetary constraints and offer an environmentally sustainable and socioeconomic mindful approach for the legacy of peacekeeping missions. In these models, the physical organization of the base considers the present fabric of the area surrounding the base and its expected future state to allow for gradual and sustainable handover from both an organizational and a technical point of view. Throughout the mission, the direct interaction between the base and the local population can be carried out in coordination, mediation, and collaboration with the UN Country Teams, which have ongoing relationships with civil society, the local population, and their institutions.

The design approach proposed in the next pages is the result of a long-term project, including field research, workshops, and countless meetings with civil society organizations, local populations, military engineers, urban planners, diplomats, economists, activists, and anthropologists.

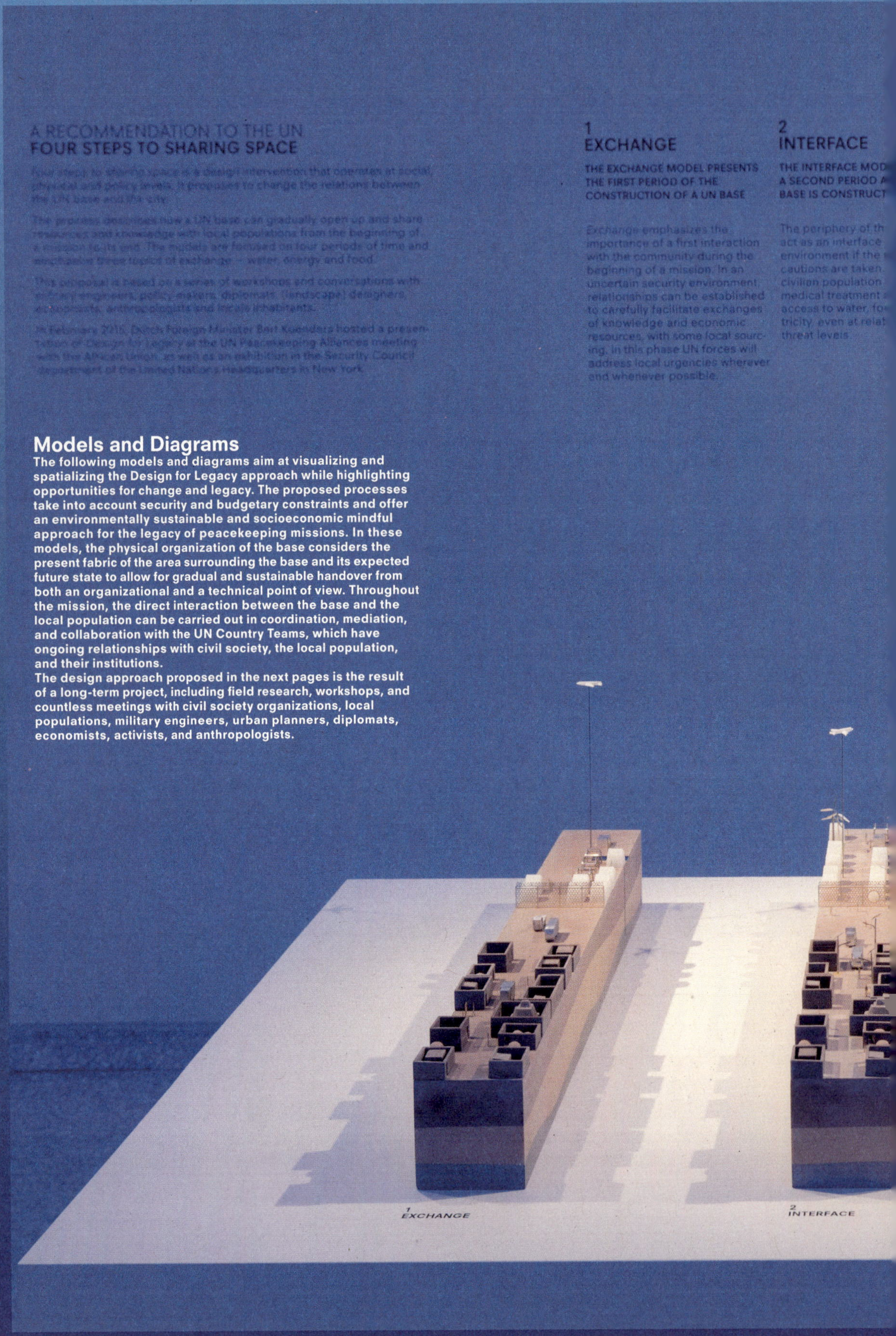

Four steps for sharing space models in the Dutch Pavilion at Venice Architecture Biennale. Photo: Iwan Baan, 2016.

Four Steps to Sharing Space

"Four Steps to Sharing Space" describes a gradual transition process for UN peace mission bases. It shows how resources and knowledge can be shared between the UN and the local population during the lifetime of a peacekeeping mission, with the goal of reducing the environmental footprint and improving local livelihoods.

The four stages are linked to an evolving security situation and to the different periods in a mission's lifespan: beginning, during deployment, handover, and post-mission. During these four periods, various opportunities for local empowerment and capacity building are identified as well as strategies for the reduction of the mission's waste and carbon emissions. The four steps are as follows:

1 Exchange –

The beginning of a mission

A preliminary interaction with the different population groups during the construction phase of the base is important. In an uncertain security environment, relationships should be established to facilitate knowledge exchange and a carefully managed economic exchange, with some local sourcing. During this first exchange, UN forces should address local urgent needs wherever and whenever possible.

2 Interface –

After the construction of a UN base and during deployment at a high-alert level

If the right precautions are taken, the periphery of the base can act as an interface with the local environment, even under relatively high threat levels. Here, in urgent conditions, the civilian population can receive medical treatment and gain access to water, food, and electricity.

Inside the base, regenerative,[15] hybrid low- and high-tech infrastructures such as water, electricity, and sewage should be developed with a legacy in mind.

15 Regenerative design is a process-oriented whole systems approach to design. The term "regenerative" describes processes that restore, renew, or revitalize their own sources of energy and materials. Regenerative design uses whole systems thinking to create resilient and equitable systems that integrate the needs of society with the integrity of nature.

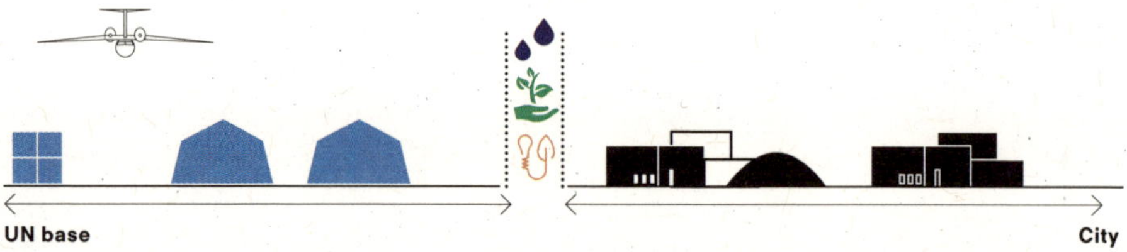

3 Shared Space –

After the construction of a UN base and during its deployment at a lower-alert level

A shared space between the city and the base should be developed in collaboration with UN Country Teams and in cohesion with local institutions and the population living in the vicinity of the base. This shared space can be where UN Country Teams, the peacekeepers and the local community develop and execute projects together. Here, resources, education, trade, employment, and cultural facilities can be designed to build local capacity and empower the local population.

The shared space can be developed gradually. It can contribute to the organization of a safe and secure environment for the local population, as well as for UN troops. In collaboration with the local community, it can become a hub for local development. Through exchanging resources and making knowledge available, local inhabitants can become empowered to develop their environment themselves. Collaborative schools and workshops can experiment with the production of resources by combining low-tech and do-it-yourself solutions with both smaller and larger scale infrastructural production and maintenance. Resources developed in the shared space can be replicated in the city and on the base.

4 Post-mission –

During and after the decommissioning of a UN base

At the end of the mission, elements of the base should be handed over to the local population to become an integral part of the city. Because these parts of bases have been developed with the idea of legacy in mind and have incorporated local techniques, the structures leave behind valuable resources for the city. These opportunities are further detailed in the following models, diagrams, the transition matrix for policy makers, and policy recommendations.

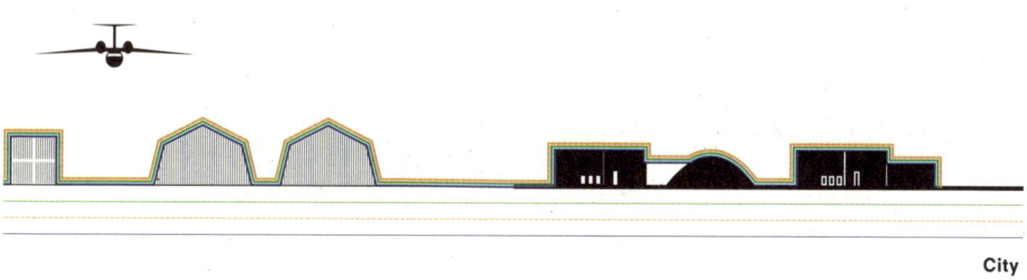

Water

Focus Area: Water

Water is at the core of sustainable development and is critical for socio-economic development, energy and food production, healthy ecosystems and for human survival itself. [16]

UN peacekeeping missions mostly take place in fragile environments prone to droughts and floods, circumstances that are exacerbated by the rising temperatures and climate crisis. During the planning process of a mission, water-related risks should be mapped and accounted for to avoid pollution and the depletion of aquifers and other water sources. UN bases can play an essential role in improving access to clean water. Low-tech decentralized water systems can be embedded in UN bases to provide clean water to the peace-keepers and the local community.

UN Country Teams and civil society organizations can navigate between the peacekeeping mission and the local community so infrastructure and know-how are shared and remain with the local community after the mission has departed. The diagrams on the following pages illustrate how water can become a focal point and a resource to be shared between the UN and the local population throughout the mission.

16 "Goal 6: Ensure availability and sustainable management of water and sanitation for all." available at: https://sustainabledevelopment.un.org/sdg6.

1 **Exchange** – Planning and early deployment phase

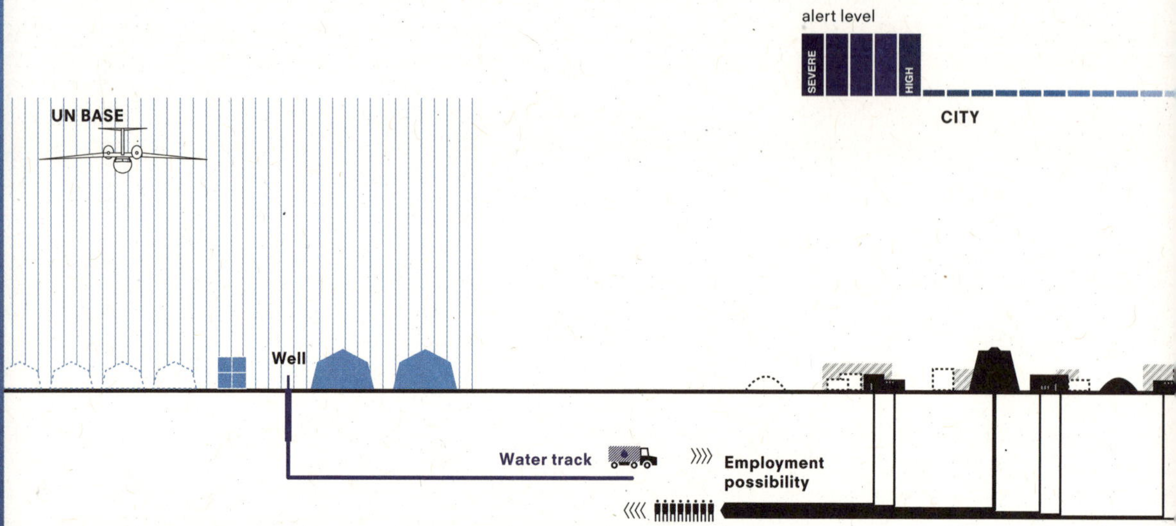

- Assess hydrological conditions, existing water infrastructure, and water access.
- Assess water and wastewater challenges and risks (water scarcity, flooding, contamination).
- Avoid aquifer depletion, run-off, and built infrastructure outside of the floodplain.
- Identify potentials and challenges for water-related legacy based on context.
- Identify low-tech means and methods to supply water for the base and for legacy.
- Identify partners, including local and global knowledge institutions for generating and disseminating water-related know-how.
- Include, in the base, hybrid water infrastructure with low- and high-tech equipment and know-how, rainwater harvesting, and wastewater treatment facilities.

2 **Interface** – After the construction of the camp

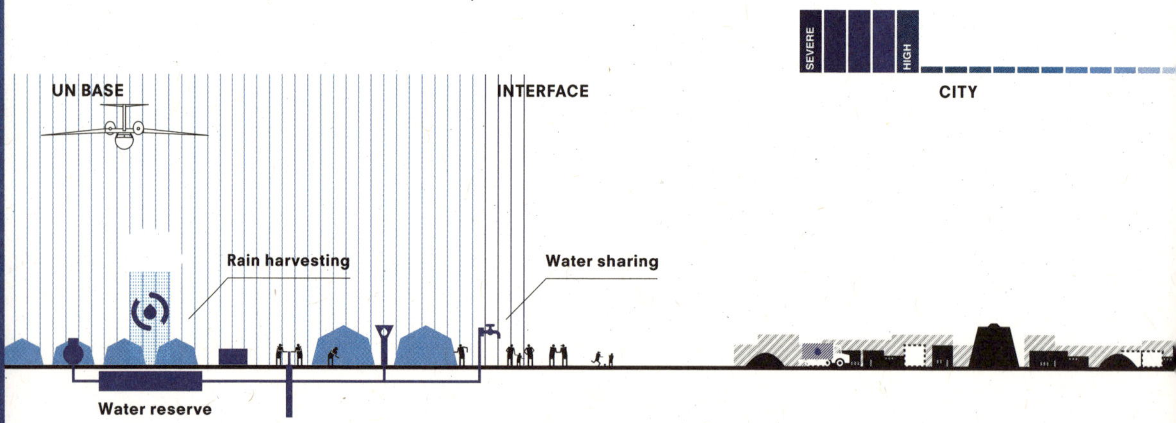

- Respond to water urgencies: water trucks can deliver water in the city.
- Supply water to UN bases through self-sufficient water systems.
- Avoid aquifer depletion—and do recharge, avoid run-off.
- Develop water-related legacy projects in collaboration with the UN Country Team.
- Develop low-tech means and methods to supply water for the base, as well as for legacy.
- Develop pilots and knowledge platform for exchange of water-related know-how.
- Test, improve, and optimize decentralized water systems that fit with the local environments.

3 Shared Space – Mid-mission, when violence abates and the security situation stabilizes

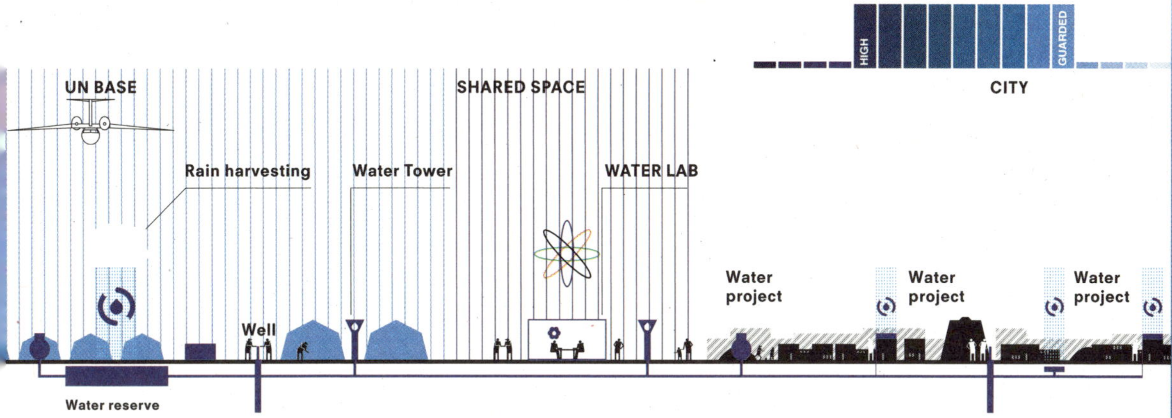

- Use reserve force to build local capacity and distribute water-related knowledge to local institutions such as schools and hospitals.
- Optimize the water system at the base to harvest water, treat wastewater, and re-use.
- Avoid aquifer depletion—and do recharge, avoid run-off.
- Develop and implement water-related legacy projects in collaboration with the UN Country Team.
- Develop low-tech means and methods to supply water for the base and for legacy.
- Develop pilots and knowledge platform for exchange of water-related know-how and establish a "water lab" between the base and the city in collaboration with the UN Country Team, civil society, and local stakeholders.

4 Post-mission – At the end of the mission and after the handover of the camp

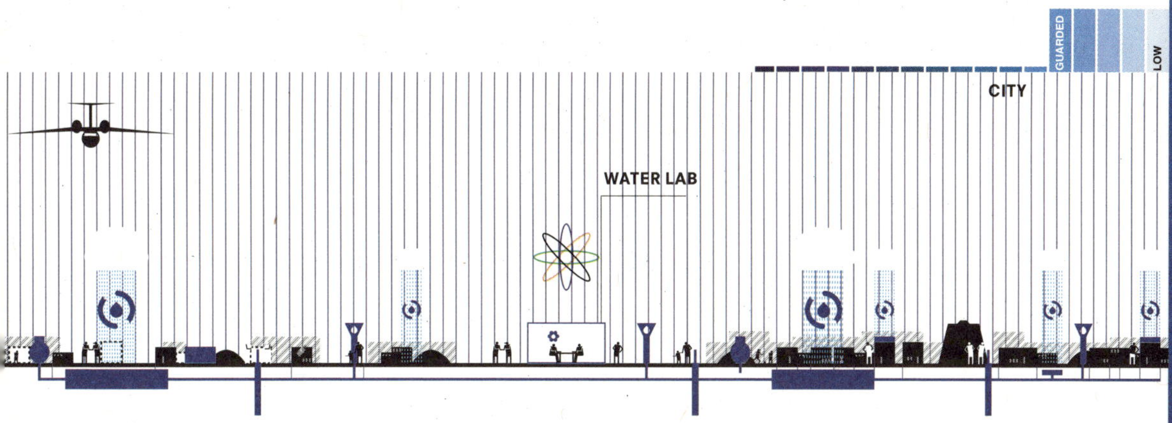

By the end of the mission:

- Transfer knowledge and hand over low-tech equipment to local stakeholders. This process can be supervised and managed by the UN Country Team to allow continuity.
- Ascertain that locals have the capacity to maintain, repurpose, and replicate structures, infrastructure, and know-how in ways that stimulate equitable and sustainable development that empowers the local inhabitants.

Focus Area: Food

End hunger, achieve food security and improved nutrition, and promote sustainable agriculture.[17]

Peacekeeping missions are present in more than 150 inhabited urban and rural areas in Africa, where food insecurity is prevalent. The second SDG calls for integrated investment to increase capacity for agricultural productivity in Africa. Peacekeepers can contribute to this global effort. There are multiple reasons for peacekeepers to reduce food imports and strengthen local food production, from improving peacekeepers' quality of life to reducing the carbon emissions of their operations.

A self-sustained UN base, with carefully managed local sourcing, can contribute to food security in the compound and its surroundings. UN Country Teams and civil society organizations can navigate between the peacekeeping missions and the local community such that food production, processing, and storing know-how is shared and remains with the locals after the mission has left. The diagrams on the next pages demonstrate how food can become a focal point and a resource to share for the benefit of the peacekeepers and the local population.

17 "Goal 2: End hunger, achieve food security and improved nutrition, and promote sustainable agriculture." UN, accessed February 2018: https://sustainabledevelopment.un.org/sdg2.

1 **Exchange** – Planning and early deployment phase

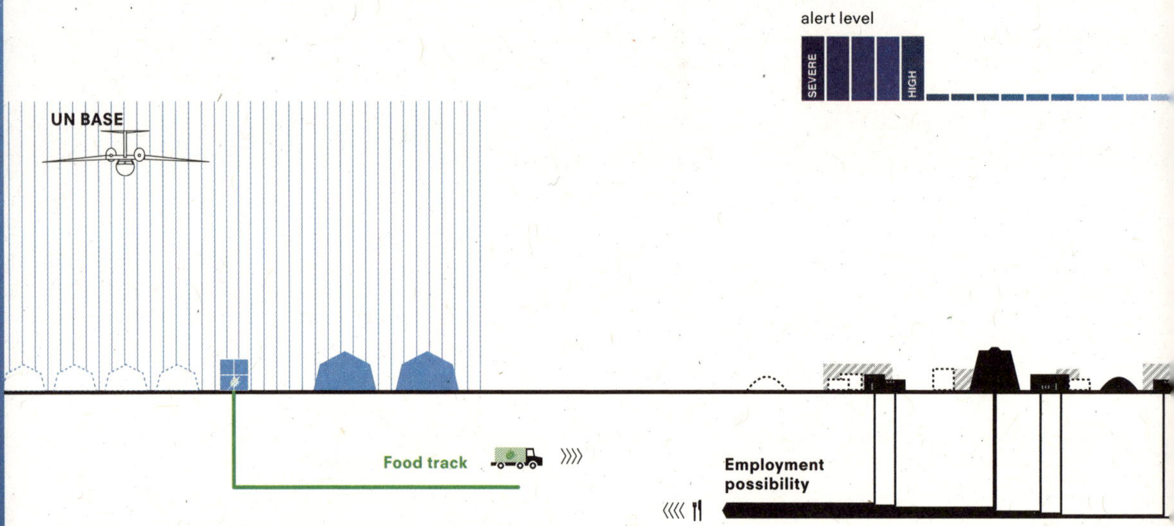

- Assess local food access and food production capacity.
- Assess food-related challenges and risks.
- Identify challenges and potential for food security and related legacy.
- Identify low-tech and environmentally sustainable means and methods to improve food production and access for the base and for legacy such as aquaponic agriculture, fish farming, food processing, and storing.
- Identify local partners for food production know-how transfer.
- Include, in the base, sustainable food production systems.

2 **Interface** – After the construction of the camp

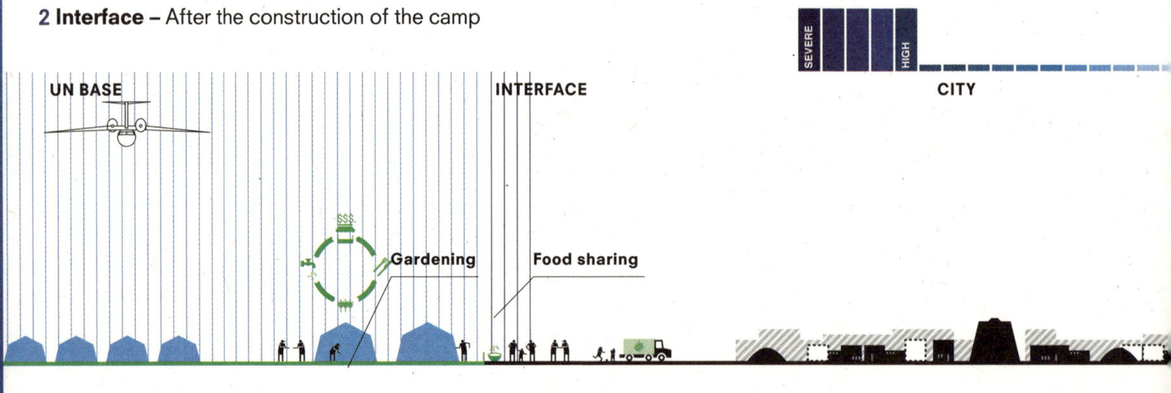

- Respond to urgent food scarcity in collaboration with local and UN food programs.
- Supply food to UN bases through environmentally sustainable food production systems.
- Develop a hybrid system of local sourcing and low-tech food production within the base.
- Prioritize the supply of food to UN bases through local sourcing and on-base food production.
- Share food production knowledge and resources such as sustainable seeds with UN Country Teams, World Food Program, and local actors (farmers, women's collectives, schools, etc.).

3 Shared Space – Mid-mission, when violence abates and the security situation stabilizes

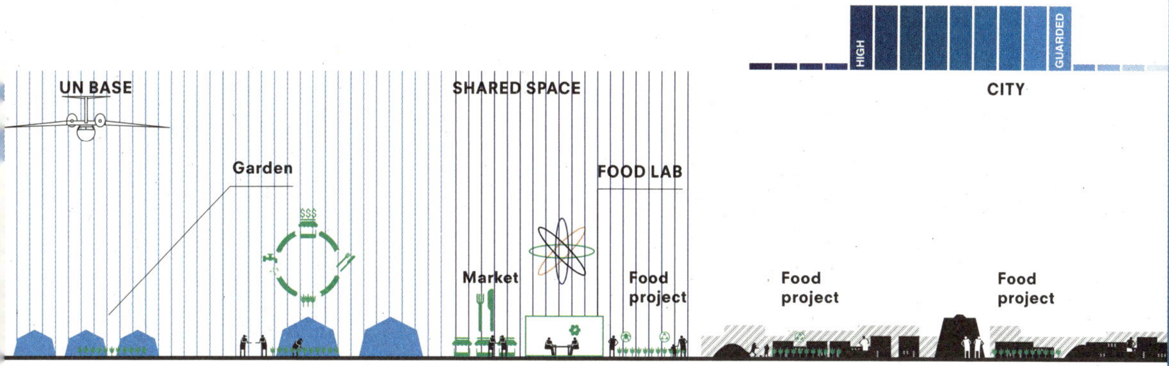

- Establish a food production laboratory in a shared space between the base and the city.
- Optimize food supply to the base through self-sustained, decentralized systems.
- Develop and implement food-related legacy projects in collaboration with the UN Country Team and local stakeholders.
- Develop low-tech means and methods to supply food to the base and for legacy.
- Develop pilots and knowledge platform for exchange of food security know-how
- Test, improve, and optimize decentralized food production, supply, and distribution systems that can be replicated by the locals in the city.

4 Post-mission – At the end of the mission and after the handover of the camp

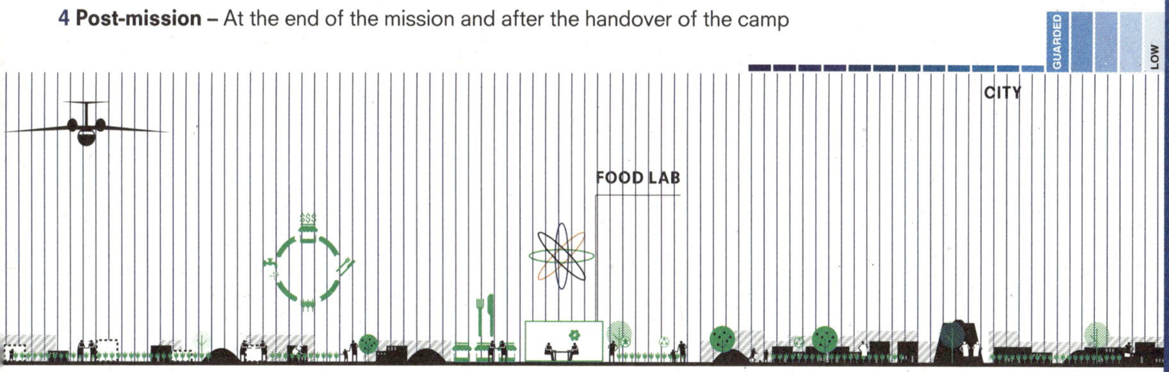

By the end of the mission:

- Transfer knowledge and hand over low-tech equipment to local stakeholders. This process can be supervised and managed by the UN Country Team to allow continuity.
- Ascertain that locals have the capacity to maintain, repurpose, and replicate structures, infrastructure, and know-how in ways that stimulate equitable and sustainable development that empowers the local inhabitants.

Energy

Focus Area: Energy

Ensure access to affordable, reliable, sustainable, and modern energy for all.[1]

Energy scarcity in sub-Saharan Africa is prevalent. About half a billion people still function without electricity. In Liberia, only 19.8 percent of the population has access to electricity. A UN base can contribute to improving access to affordable and renewable energy. As with food and water, UN investment in low-tech, sustainable, regenerative, and renewable energy can be beneficial not only for the peacekeepers but also for the local population and the environment.

UN Country Teams and civil society organizations can navigate between peacekeeping missions and the local community, such that infrastructure and know-how are shared and remain with the locals after the mission has ended. The diagrams on the next pages depict how peacekeeping missions can improve access to electricity in mission areas.

Economists for Peace and Security is a UN-registered NGO promoting economic analysis and appropriate action for peace, security and the world economy.

1 Exchange – Planning and early deployment phase

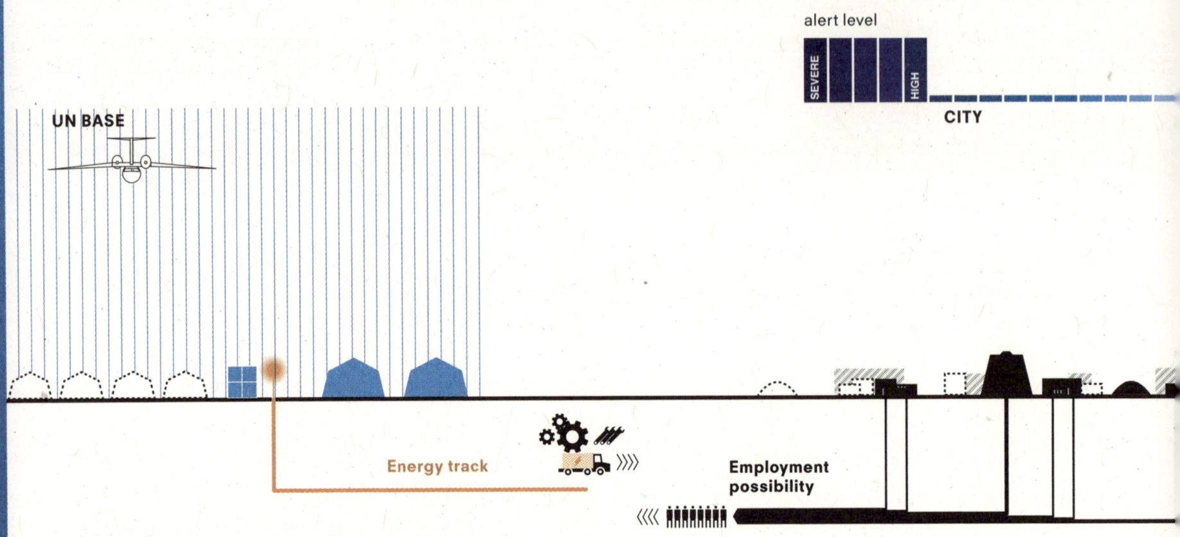

- Assess conditions of existing energy infrastructure.
- Identify low-tech and environmentally sustainable means and methods to improve energy supply for the base and for legacy.
- Identify local partners for energy know-how transfer.
- Repair damaged local infrastructure.
- Include, in the base, sustainable hybrid energy systems (solar, wind, and generators).

2 Interface – After the construction of the camp

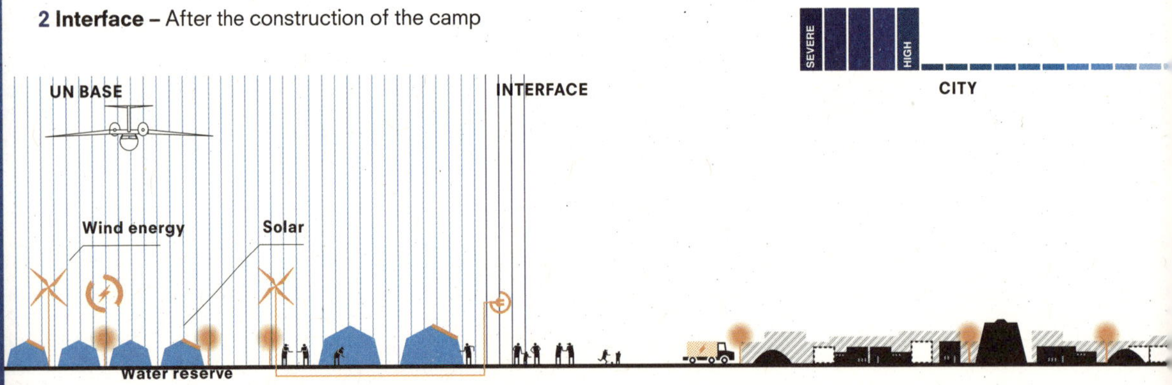

- Respond to urgent energy scarcity in the city through the use of back-up generators.
- Prioritize renewable energy systems.
- Supply and further develop energy to UN bases through renewable low- and high-tech hybrid energy systems.
- Link parts of the energy production systems to the city grid or other important facilities (hospitals, schools, community centers) so it can serve the local community in the present, when needed, and strengthen their energy resources in the future.

3 Shared Space – Mid-mission, when violence abates and the security situation stabilizes

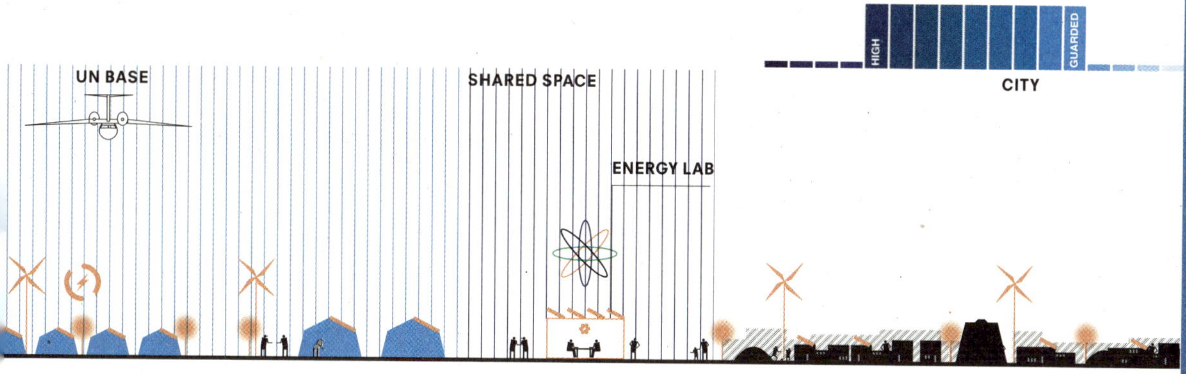

- Establish an energy laboratory in a shared space between the base and the city.
- Optimize energy supply to the base through self-sustained decentralized systems.
- Develop and implement renewable energy-related legacy projects in collaboration with UN Country Teams and local stakeholders.
- Develop low-tech means and methods to supply energy to the base and for legacy.
- Develop pilot programs and a knowledge platform for the exchange of energy production and supply know-how.
- Test, improve, and optimize decentralized renewable energy supply and distribution systems that can be replicated by the locals in the city.

4 Post-mission – At the end of the mission and after the handover of the camp

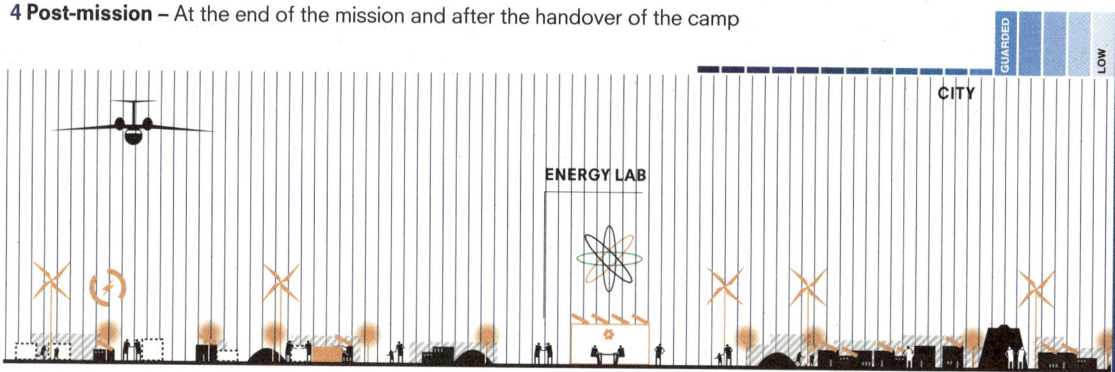

By the end of the mission:

- Transfer knowledge and hand over high- and low-tech equipment to local stakeholders. This process can be supervised and managed by the UN Country Team to allow continuity.
- Ascertain that locals have the capacity to maintain, repurpose, and replicate structures, infrastructure, and know-how in ways that stimulate equitable and sustainable development that empowers the local inhabitants.

Visualizing Legacy Opportunities

Diagrams of regenerative and circular resource systems for UN bases

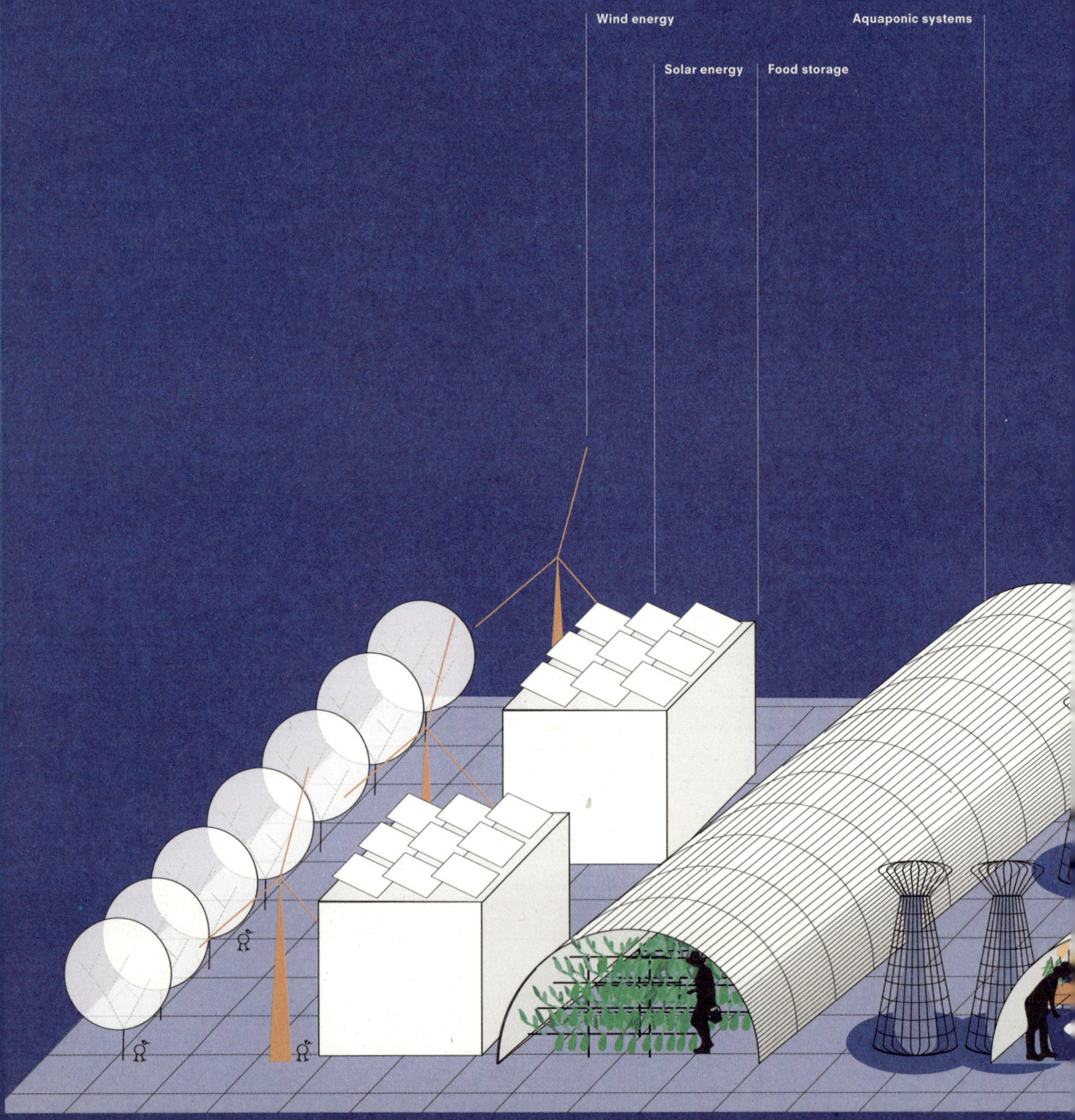

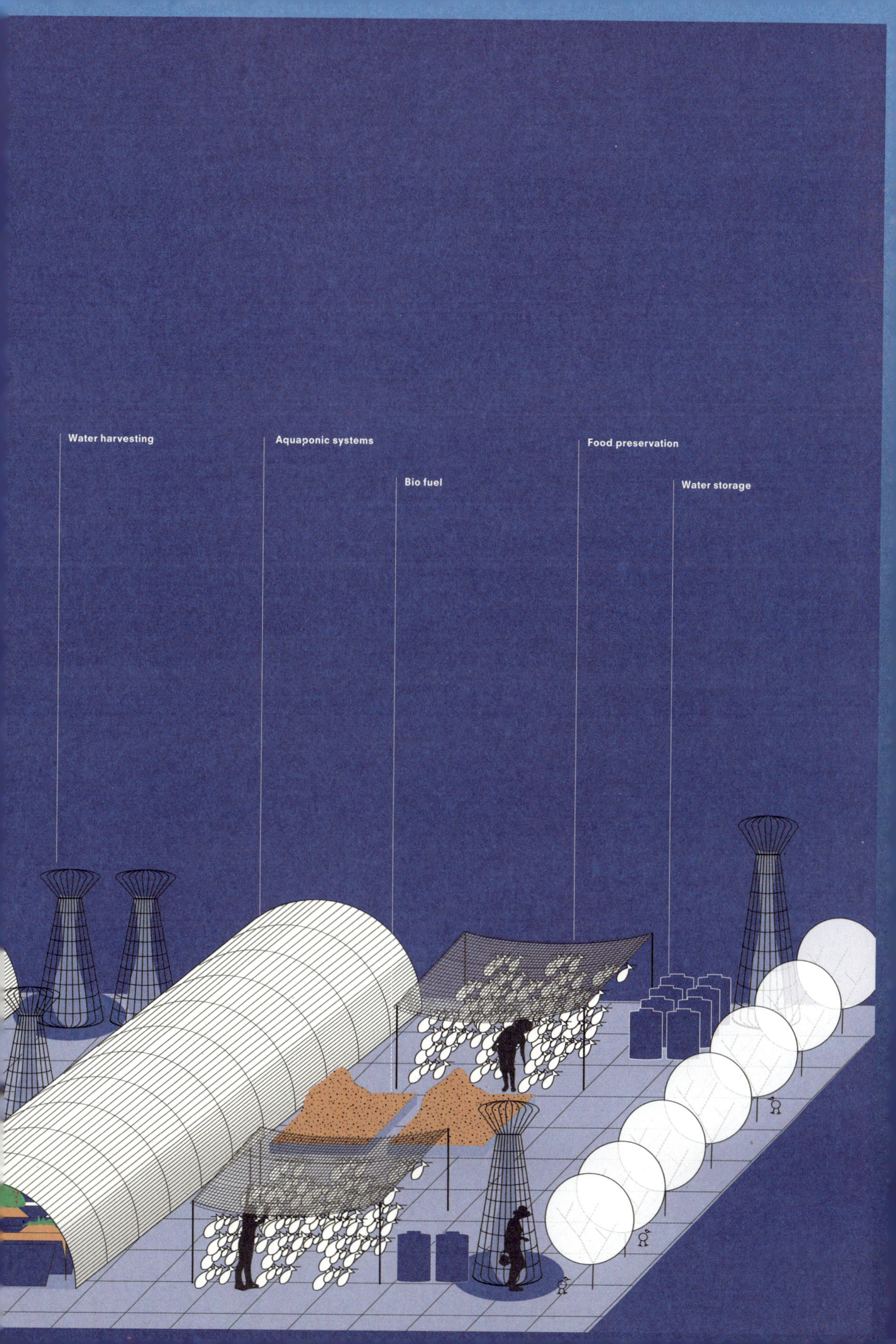

Water harvesting
Aquaponic systems
Bio fuel
Food preservation
Water storage

Legacy Opportunities for Flood-Prone Urban Environments

In fragile urban environments with inadequate or non-existing drainage, waste, or water infrastructure, floods can have a devastating impact on people's livelihoods. For example, floods contaminate water sources, which can result in the outbreak of disease. The diagram to the left illustrates the adverse consequences of flood; the second to the right offers a legacy opportunity while focusing on rainwater harvesting to improve access to clean water in the UN base and its surroundings.

CURRENT WATER FLOW/IMPACT

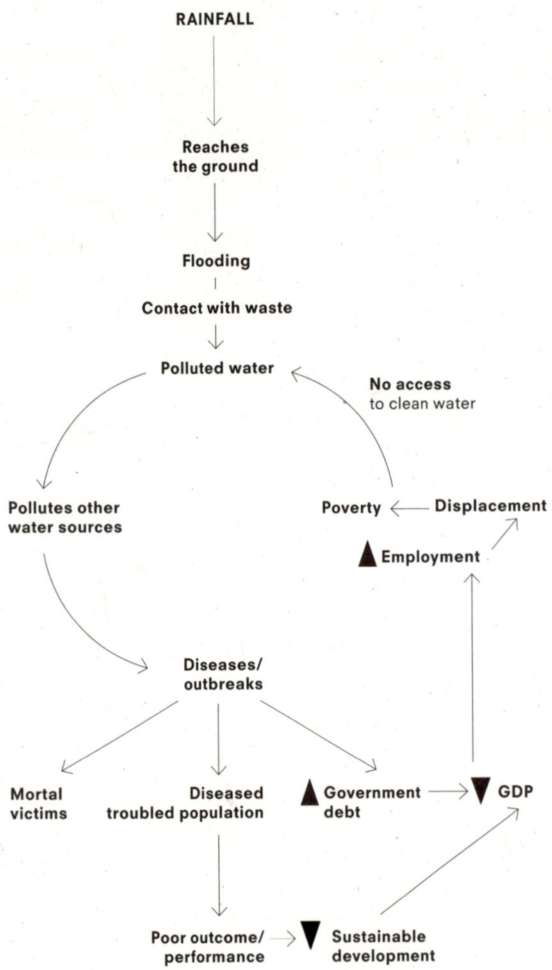

POTENTIAL WATER FLOW/IMPACT

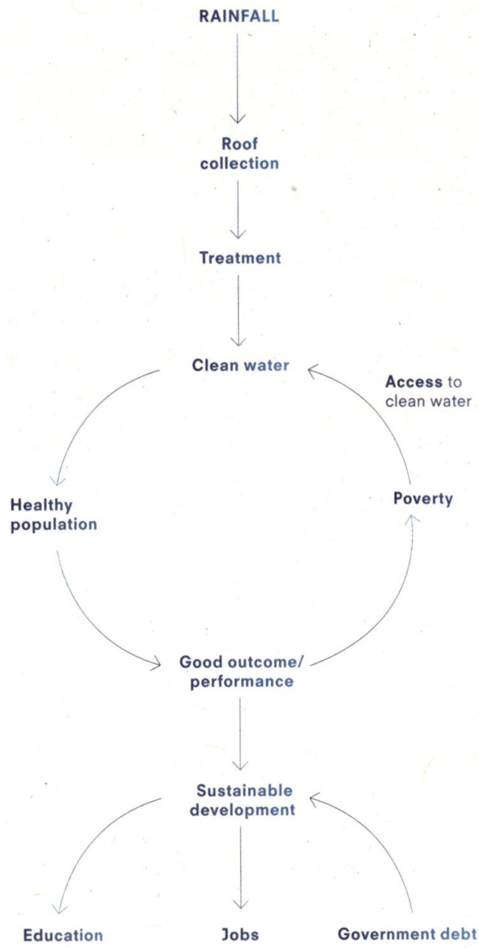

Imaginative Repurposing of a UN Base in Monrovia

The Design for Legacy principles and matrix can be applied to UN bases in various contexts, sites, and scales. For example, this chart visualizes a speculative model for Monrovia. It considers the heavy rainfall and the local population's need for clean water and protein. Both water and food are essential resources for the base and the city's inhabitants. Part of the UN food supply can be produced within the base. For instance, low-tech and decentralized rainwater harvesting systems can be installed to direct water flow from roofs to storage tanks. This infrastructure can be coupled with regenerative food production techniques like fish farming, as shown in the diagram, or small-scale aquaponics, as demonstrated by the Chinese contingent in Monrovia, or food gardens, as shown in the Nepalese base in Gao. This critical know-how can improve access to water and food within the base and can also be shared and further developed with the locals. Rainwater harvesting and regenerative food production systems can be used by the UN Country Team to build local capacity during the mission and resilience to last after its departure.

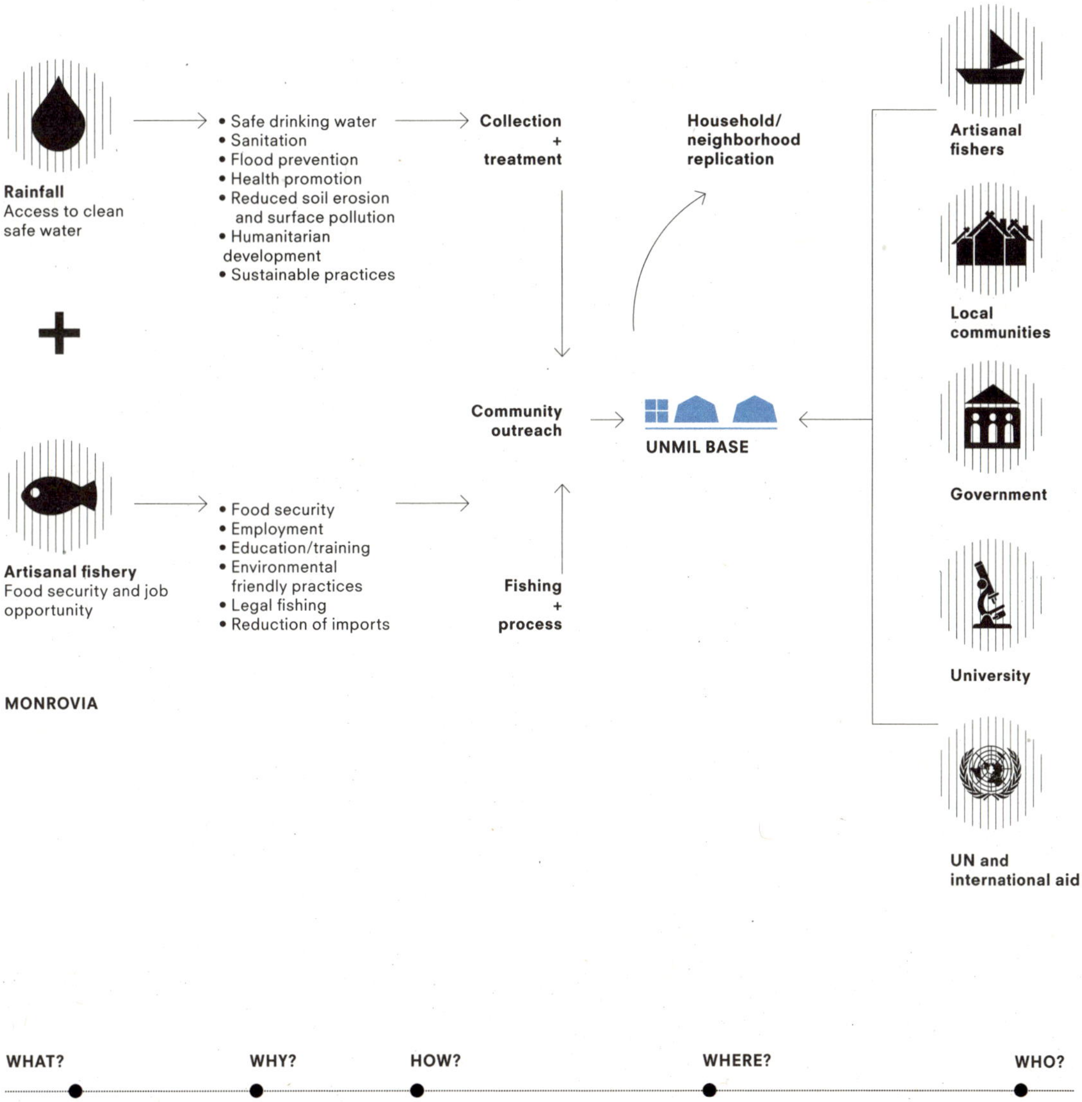

Integrated Design for Rainwater Harvesting at a UN Base and Its Surroundings

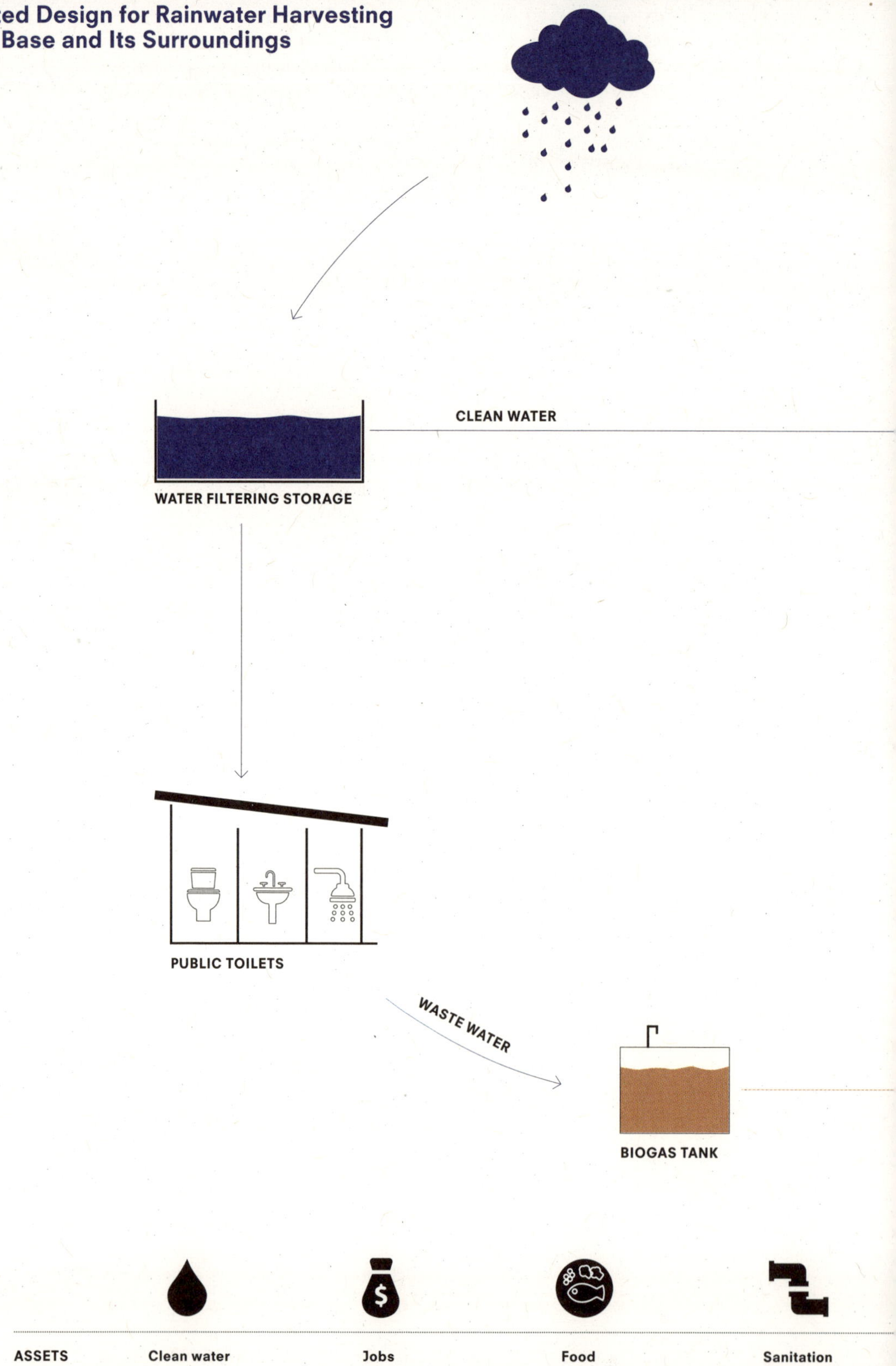

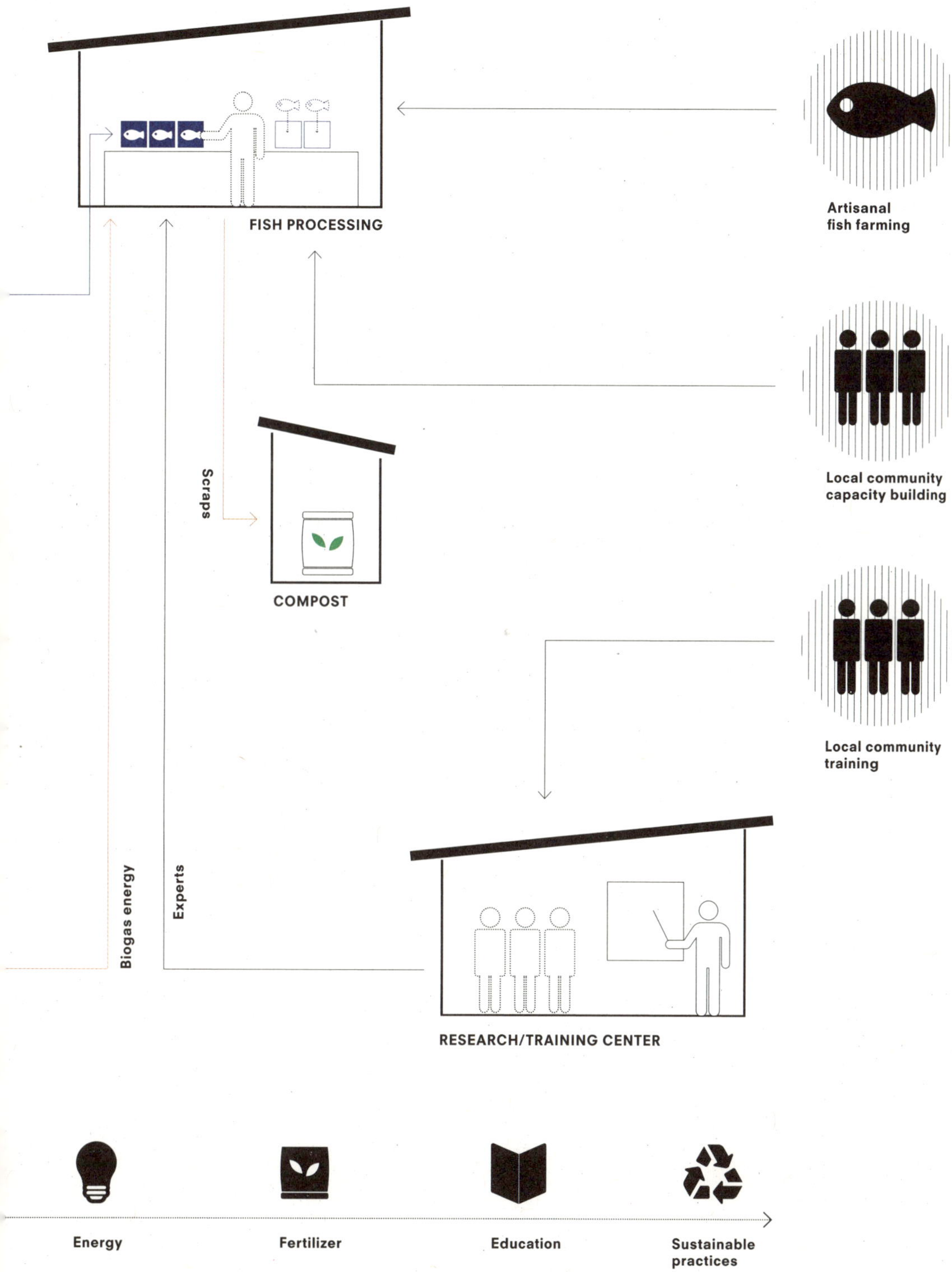
FISH PROCESSING
Artisanal fish farming
Local community capacity building
Scraps
COMPOST
Local community training
Biogas energy
Experts
RESEARCH/TRAINING CENTER
Energy
Fertilizer
Education
Sustainable practices

Imaginative Repurposing of UNMIL Structures for Self-sustained Schools and Community Empowerment Centers

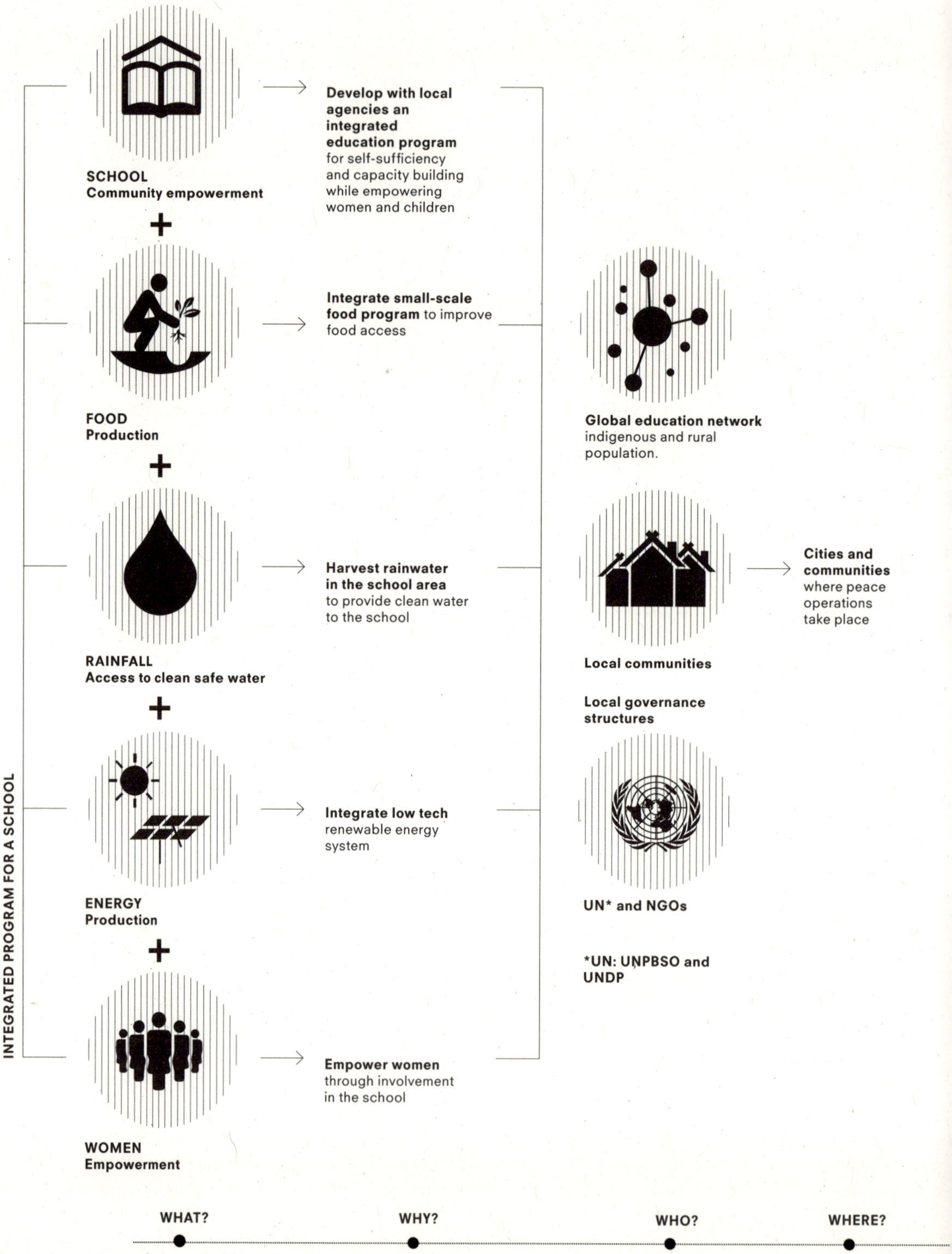

Repurposed UN container as a mobile school.

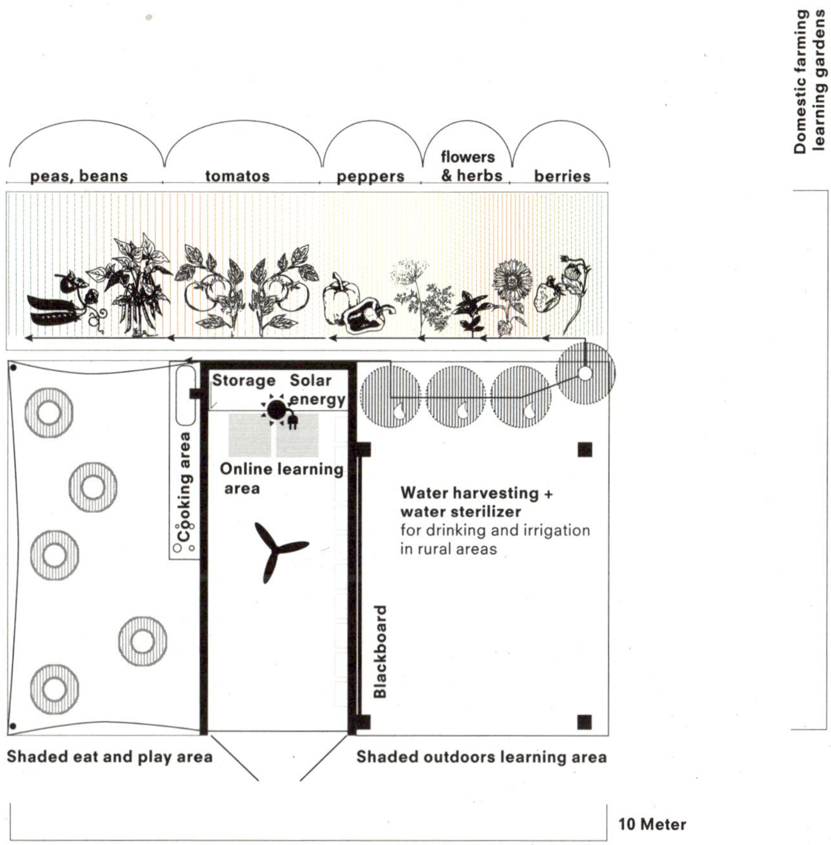

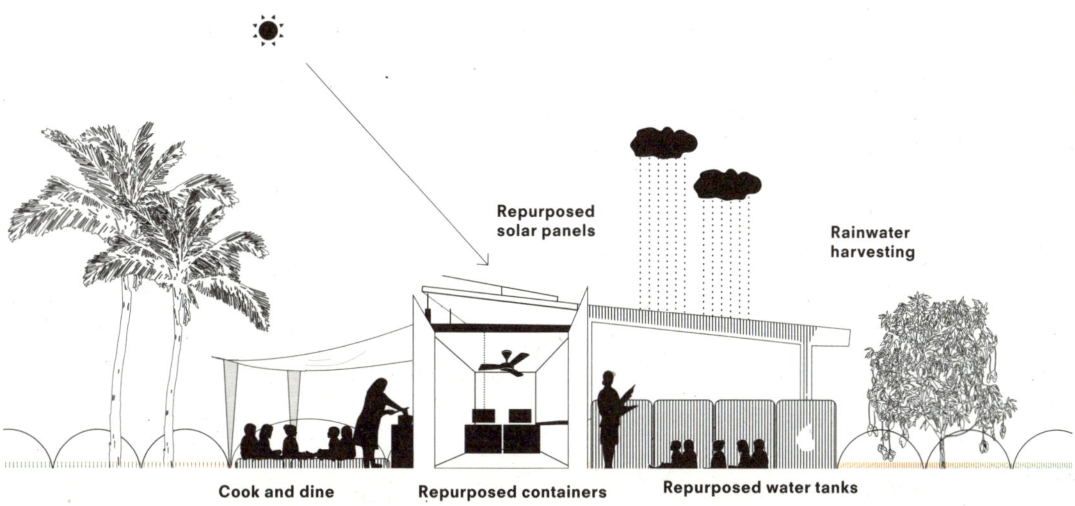

EXAMPLE

Opportunities for the Implementation of Legacy Projects in Monrovia

The map identifies potential sites in and around existing UN bases, public institutions, and communal facilities. See more information in Appendices 5 and 6.

Paved Road
Dirt Roads
Railroad
Waterways

UN Bases
National Police
Jordan FPU Central Prison
School Facilities
Other Educational Facilities
Hospital
Market

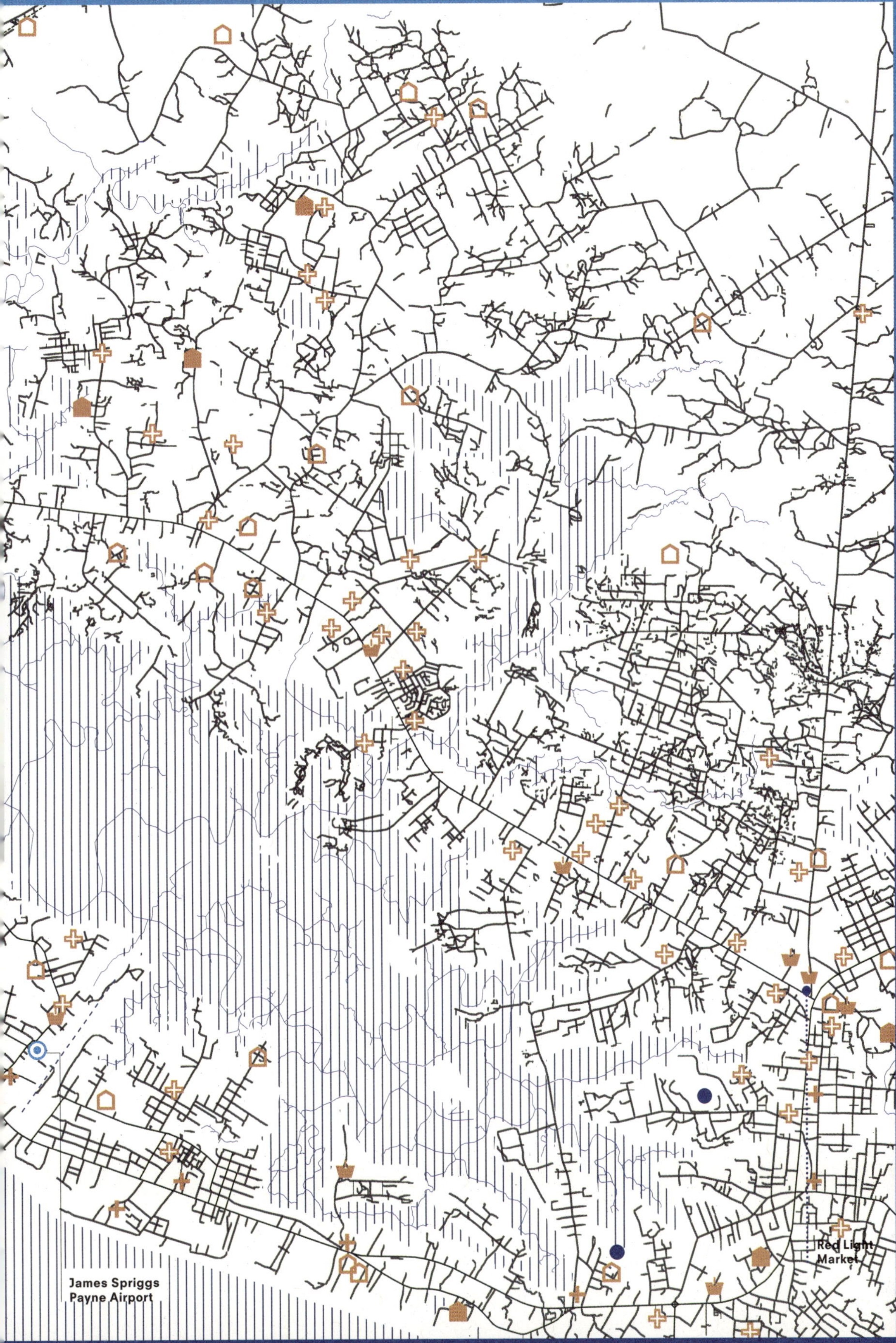
James Spriggs
Payne Airport
Red Light
Market

Legacy Design Matrix for Policymakers

The matrix on the following pages offers an integrated process for policymakers to build legacy. The matrix describes step-by-step activities that should be incorporated throughout the mission to achieve the long-term goals from its initial planning phase to its deployment and its transition to handover.

The matrix was developed with policymakers, diplomats, UN officers, economists, anthropologists, human rights lawyers, activists and military engineers. It builds on findings from field research, spatial analysis, workshops, meetings, and events.

This suggested approach does not necessarily require an increase in funding or personnel. It prioritizes environmentally sustainable and regenerative applications that build capacity and empower the local communities and their institutions. It addresses present and future local, regional, and planetary challenges and considers the interrelated stresses that have a tangible influence on peace and security, including the climate crisis, food insecurity, water, and access to renewable energy sources.

It encourages international institutions to conduct a holistic assessment of the local context and to develop long-term visions for legacy from the beginning of a mission that include and orient its transition design. Because of their exponential footprint, peacekeeping missions must continuously assess and account for their impacts on their complex cultural, socioeconomic, and spatial contexts.

An *environmentally-centered practice* is critical not only to reduce the carbon emissions generated by a mission but to steer the peacekeeping expertise and resources toward *environmental stewardship*. This must become intrinsic to all UN missions and international interventions. The implementation of the matrix may require the set-up of pilot projects to help consolidate the legacy strategy. Because missions are operating within existing inhabited environments, holistic urban methodologies and spatial design are paramount for mitigating short-term actions and constraints by way of long-term visions and strategies for legacy.

The matrix for policymakers in the following pages proposes a process contingent on the lifetime of a mission—from beginning to end. It is divided into the following sections: **1. Overview**, **2. Analysis**, **3. Design** and Implementation as well as three focus areas: **4. Water**, **5. Food**, and **6. Energy**.

Legacy Matrix for Peace Operations 1–6
1 Overview

<table>
<tr><th>PREPARATION/START</th><th>HIGH-SECURITY ALERT SITUATIONS</th><th>LOW-SECURITY ALERT SITUATIONS</th><th>DRAWDOWN/TRANSITION</th></tr>
<tr><td rowspan="7">Begin planning for transitions at the outset of a mission, wherever feasible, including establishing clear processes for engaging relevant UN entities (PBSO, UNDP, UNEP, and others) and local stakeholders for building a shared vision of the (potential) footprint and post-mission life (and use) of the bases.</td><td>Regularly assess risks and opportunities in areas surrounding UN bases, and identify local stakeholders with whom to engage once circumstances allow.</td><td>Continue transition planning and incorporate the views of local stakeholders as extensively as possible.</td><td rowspan="5">Transfer know-how, infrastructure, and equipment according to the early transition strategy, subsequent engagements and lessons-learned, and relevant policies.</td></tr>
<tr><td colspan="2">Communicate risks to local communities and explore how to build resilience.</td></tr>
<tr><td colspan="2">Incentivize pilots and seize opportunities for legacy building as they arise, for instance through the strategic use of QIPs, the Peacebuilding Fund, and the reserve capacity of missions.</td></tr>
<tr><td colspan="2">Gradually phase out unsustainable and ecologically harmful materials and replace them with durable, cost-effective, and environmentally sound structures and technologies that fit the climate and culture.</td></tr>
<tr><td colspan="2">Source locally and build with local techniques and know-how whenever possible to reduce environmental footprint, build capacity, and empower local communities.</td></tr>
<tr><td colspan="3">Work in close collaboration with UN country team, International Financial Institutions, independent experts, and local stakeholders, ensuring that coordination and programming are as inclusive of the local situation as possible.</td></tr>
<tr><td colspan="3">Build local capacity and support local agencies and stakeholders including institutions, civil society, and companies, such as acting as supplier and maintaining the assets now and in the future.</td></tr>
<tr><td colspan="4">Incentivize environmentally sustainable and regenerative mission deployment.</td></tr>
<tr><td colspan="4">Ensure coherence between pillars by continuously i) incorporating development and peacebuilding expertise into the design and management of UN bases, ii) incorporating the future uses of bases into UNCT and peacebuilding programming (e.g., so as to avoid building a school near a base that can shortly be repurposed as a school), and iii) developing a comprehensive environmental management plan with UNEP.</td></tr>
<tr><td colspan="4">Adopt an interdisciplinary, long-term perspective and environmentally sustainable and regenerative practice.</td></tr>
</table>

Local authorities and communities have the capacity to maintain, repurpose, and replicate structures, infrastructure, and know-how in ways that stimulate equitable development, support community cohesion and empowerment, minimize waste, and limit the environmental footprint of missions.

2 **Analysis**

PREPARATION/START	HIGH-SECURITY ALERT SITUATIONS	LOW-SECURITY ALERT SITUATIONS	DRAWDOWN/TRANSITION
	Regularly assess the material impact of the mission on its surroundings, taking into account internal (e.g., the expansion of bases) and external (e.g., population growth around the bases) developments.		
Undertake a shared, multidisciplinary assessment of mission sites, including the local political and socio-economic situation, demographics, community needs and capacities, urban conditions and vulnerabilities, and the natural environment.	nalyze and anticipate natural or man-made events that may require mission assets to be relocated away from vulnerable areas.	Involve local stakeholders in assessments, wherever feasible, both to incorporate their perspectives and to transfer analytical capacity and know-how.	Ensure that the UN country team and local stakeholders have access to analysis, methodologies, and lessons learned.
Carefully analyze of lessons learned throughout the mission.			
Expand indicators to measure the environmental footprint of building systems, such as all materials used for the overall construction of UN bases, their lifespan, sustainability, and decay throughout the mission.			

OUTCOME/POST-MISSION

Local authorities and stakeholders have enhanced capacity to undertake complex planning assessments from a multidisciplinary perspective.

3 Design and Implementation

PREPARATION/START	HIGH-SECURITY ALERT SITUATIONS	LOW-SECURITY ALERT SITUATIONS	DRAWDOWN/TRANSITION

Based on the initial assessment and ongoing analysis, design, manage, and transition sites in ways that i) minimize negative impacts on the built and natural environments, and ii) maximize (future) opportunities for local peacebuilding and sustainable development.

Use a phased approach to the base design, keeping in mind the length of typical missions and the type and extent of infrastructure they traditionally leave behind.

Collaborate closely with development and peacebuilding actors and involve a multidisciplinary group of planners and architects, including local planners, where feasible, in base design.

Gradually replace temporary modular elements with durable, cost-effective, dual-purpose, and regenerative materials that can eventually be used by the UN country team and/or by local stakeholders.

Remove the modular parts of bases for reuse in future UN peacekeeping operations while leaving other elements in as good a condition as possible.

Ensure that base fortifications and scale-ups do not unduly intrude upon the spaces, resources, and standards of living of nearby communities.

Identify excess resources and reserve capacity that can be put to use locally.

Gradually develop the areas outside of bases, for instance, by cultivating community gardens, planting trees, or refurbishing houses.

Design and build a self-sustaining, renewable, and regenerative base, utilizing green building and nature-based solutions that include food, water, energy, waste, and comprehensive environmental management, whenever possible.

Establish a laboratory for knowledge-sharing and transition planning at the edge of the base, in collaboration with the UN country team.

Link the missions' energy, water, and waste collection/treatment systems with the local urban fabric whenever possible.

Use local sourcing and local techniques and expertise wherever possible.

OUTCOME/POST-MISSION

The material legacy of peacekeeping is a positive and long-lasting one, leaving surrounding communities with tools, spaces, and systems that improve their quality of life.

4 Water

<table>
<tr><th>PREPARATION/START</th><th>HIGH-SECURITY ALERT SITUATIONS</th><th>LOW-SECURITY ALERT SITUATIONS</th><th>DRAWDOWN/TRANSITION</th></tr>
<tr><td rowspan="2">Assess hydrological conditions, existing water infrastructure, water affordability and access, (waste-) water challenges and risks (water scarcity, flooding, contamination), and potential opportunities for water-related legacies.</td><td colspan="2">Continuously monitor and assess the impact of conflict and peacekeeping on (waste-)water conditions.</td><td>Transfer knowledge and analyses to local stakeholders or UN country teams.</td></tr>
<tr><td colspan="3">Continuously monitor, assess, and, where feasible, respond to water-related shocks and challenges (drought, floods, etc.).</td></tr>
<tr><td>Build base infrastructure away from floodplains.</td><td colspan="3">Avoid aquifer depletion and capture run-off; avoid impacts downstream.</td></tr>
<tr><td rowspan="2">Identify affordable, sustainable, regenerative, hybrid means and methods, such as rain harvesting and water treatment facilities, to supply water to the base.</td><td colspan="2">Utilize low-tech, sustainable, and regenerative means and methods, such as rain harvesting, to supply water to the base.</td><td rowspan="2">Transition low-tech water solutions and equipment to local stakeholders or UN country teams.</td></tr>
<tr><td colspan="2">Utilize sustainable solutions for water treatment and reuse (for consumption and food production).</td></tr>
<tr><td></td><td></td><td colspan="2">Develop knowledge-sharing platforms (such as water labs) between the base and the city in collaboration with relevant stakeholders.</td></tr>
</table>

OUTCOME/POST-MISSION

Greater and more equitable and sustainable access to safe water, greater water-related know-how, more environmentally sustainable waste management practices, and fewer water-borne illnesses.

5 Food

<table>
<tr><th>PREPARATION/START</th><th>HIGH-SECURITY ALERT SITUATIONS</th><th>LOW-SECURITY ALERT SITUATIONS</th><th>DRAWDOWN/TRANSITION</th></tr>
<tr><td colspan="4">Assess local food access, availability, affordability, food-related challenges and risks, and local food production capacity as well as and level of food insecurity, malnutrition, dependency on food imports, and vulnerability to food price shocks in collaboration with the UN country team and others as appropriate.</td></tr>
<tr><td>Design (and gradually develop) a hybrid system of low-tech food production and sourcing within the base.</td><td colspan="2">Create space in the base for food production, including, gardening, aquaponics, and fish farming.

Identify and seize opportunities for local sourcing of food, paying close attention to the impact on food prices and availability.</td><td>Develop and hand over a hybrid system of food production and local sourcing.</td></tr>
<tr><td colspan="2">Identify opportunities for shared food cultivation.</td><td colspan="2">Transfer excess food capacity and food-related know-how to local stakeholders.

Establish a community garden and/or a food production lab in a shared space between the base and the city.

Refurbish coastal areas or waterways next to a base, where applicable, for fishing and fish farming by UN personnel as well as locals.</td></tr>
</table>

OUTCOME/POST-MISSION

Greater and more equitable access to nutritious food, greater food-related know-how, less dependency on food imports, lower food insecurity, and less malnutrition.

6 **Energy**

PREPARATION/START	HIGH-SECURITY ALERT SITUATIONS	LOW-SECURITY ALERT SITUATIONS	DRAWDOWN/TRANSITION

Assess conditions of existing energy infrastructure, types and amounts of energy used, energy-related risks and challenges, and potential for new sources of energy.

Design (and gradually develop) a hybrid system of low-tech and renewable energy production and sourcing within the base.

Include, in the base, sustainable hybrid energy systems (solar, wind, batteries and generators).

Identify and seize opportunities for local sourcing of food, paying close attention to the impact on food prices and availability.

Develop and hand over a hybrid system of energy production.

Transfer excess energy capacity and energy-related know-how to local stakeholders.

Identify local partners and opportunities to share energy production know-how and infrastructure.

Establish an energy production lab in a shared space between the base and the city.

Develop and implement renewable energy-related legacy projects in collaboration with the UN Team and local stakeholders.

OUTCOME/POST-MISSION

Greater and more equitable access to energy, greater energy-related know-how, better access to affordable, reliable, renewable and sustainable energy in UN mission areas.

Advocacy

Project Timeline

YEAR

2007 — **Field research to Kosovo**

2010 — **Ongoing meetings with policymakers, diplomats from the Dutch Ministries of Foreign Affairs and Defense, and with military mission's engineers**

2011

2012

2013

2014 — **Fellowship Het Nieuwe Instituut**

Apr, 2014. **Workshop. The Future of Compounds**. Het Nieuwe Instituut, Rotterdam, NL

Sep 23. 2015. Seminar. **Drone Salon**. Het Nieuwe Instituut, Rotterdam, NL
May 3, 2015. Exhibition. 2014–1914 **The View from Above**. Het Nieuwe Instituut, Rotterdam, NL

Jan, 2015. **Workshop. Reimagining the peacekeeping mission: Legacy scenarios for Camp Castor in Mali**. Het Nieuwe Instituut, Rotterdam, NL

Oct 23, 2014. Lecture. **Warfare and Welfare**. Forms of Legacy. SUPERSTADT! Art University of Linz

Nov 27, 2014. Seminar. **Missions & Missionaries**. Het Nieuwe Instituut

May 22, 2015. **Crisis Design. Design for Legacy**. The Metropolitan Solution conference, Berlin

2015

Fall Semester, 2015. Studio. **Design for Legacy**. The School of Architecture, Syracuse University

Nov 13, 2015. **Architecture and Conflict.** Institute for Public Knowledge, NYU

2016

Jan 26, 2016–Feb 5, 2016. **Event. Presentation and discussion. BLUE: Islands in Cities**. Hosted by the Dutch Ministry of Foreign Affairs at the UN Secretariat, NYC

Jan 26, 2016. **Exhibition. BLUE: Islands in Cities**. UN Secretariat, NYC

Feb 29, 2016. **Lecture. Architecture and Conflict, BLUE: Islands in Cities**. Harvard GSD

"Legerbasis niet alleen voor leger benutten." van Os, Pieter. NRC. Dec **2015** • "Koenders bezoekt VN in New York." Rijksoverheid. Jan **2016** • "Desert Blues, an interview with curator Malkit Shoshan." Uncube magazine. Mar **2016** • "Defensie en design – de erfenis van Kamp Castor in Mali by Peter Olsthoorn." ArchiNed, Apr **2016** (NL) • "Niederländischer Biennale-Beitrag für Venedig." Baunetz, January **2016** • "Sarà Malkit Shoshan la curatrice del Padiglione Olandese alla Biennale di Architettura di Venezia." Artribune, January **2016** • "An interview with curator Malkit Shoshan." Uncube Magazine. Ampatzidou, Cristina. January **2016** • "Venice Biennale 2016: 4 Remarkable responses to humanitarian crises." Architzer, May **2016** • "Malkit Shoshan on How the City is a Shared Ground for the Instruments of War and Peace." Valencia, Nicolás. ArchDaily, May **2016** • "Malkit Shoshan: La ciudad se convirtió en territorio compartido para la guerra y la paz." Plataforma Arquitecture. May **2016** • "Venice architecture biennale pavilions – a souped-up pre-school playground." The Guardian, May **2016** • "Il meglio della Biennale: i padiglioni selezionati da WOW" WOW, May **2016** • "Timely, Urban, and Contextual: The Venice Architecture Biennale's Most Thought-Provoking Pavilions." Quirk, Vanessa. Metropolis Magazine, May **2016** • "Chief of Defense General Tom Middendorp opens Dutch Pavilion." ArtDaily, May **2016** • Meishar, Naama. "בסיס לשינוי." Haaretz, May **2016** (HE) • "Malkit Shoshan cureert Nederlands paviljoen in Venetië." Architectenkrant, May **2016** • "Aldo und Hanny waren auch schon da." Swiss Architects, May **2016** • "Venice Architecture Biennale Dispatch, Day One." Architectural Record, May **2016** • "Six-Not-to-Miss at the Venice Architecture Biennale 2016." New York Times, May **2016** • "Tra rifugiati e campi profughi, la Biennale cerca soluzioni resilienti." Rinnovabili, May **2016** • "Opening Day for Venice Biennale." Bostoncommons, May **2016** • "Dutch Pavilion at Venice Biennale focuses on the architecture of UN peacekeeping missions." Designboom, May **2016** • "Reporting from the biennale," Dutch Pavilion. The Photo Phore. June **2016** • "The New Home." Times of Malta, Morelli, Naima. July **2016** • "Poverty, Homelessness, and War." Enky. Guggenheim, Lana. July **2016** • "Biennale di architettura, l'Olanda e il futuro del peacekeeping." Il Sole 24 Ore. July **2016** (IT) • "Мы понимаем, что такое архитектура, когда наша жизнь зависит от нее." Colta, June **2016** (RU) • "A Patchwork of Alternatives." Stylepark, Wagner, Thomas. June **2016** • "Olanda: alla Biennale gli accampamenti dell'ONU." Giornale dell'Architettura, Lucia Pierro e Marco Scarpinato. June **2016** • "BLUE: the Netherlands at the Venice Architecture Biennale **2016**." Miatello, Angelo, at al. Inexhibit, Bianchini, Riccardo. June **2016** • "Olanda: L'architettura delle Missioni di Pace dei Caschi Blu." Aida News, June **2016** • Stathaki, Ellie. "World

Mar, 2016. UN Delegation. **Field Research Mali**

Apr, 2016. Lecture. **Reporting from Mali**. Het Nieuwe Instituut. Rotterdam, NL.

2017

May 26, 2016–Nov, 2016. **Exhibition. BLUE: The Architecture of UN Peacekeeping Missions**. Dutch Pavilion. Venice Architecture Biennale

Fall Semester, 2016. **Seminar. Architecture of Peace**. Harvard Graduate School of Design

Nov 27, 2016. **Lecture: Design as Activism. Contested territories and spaces of interventions**. The New School

Feb 9, 2017–Feb 10, 2017. **Workshops: Design for Legacy and Missions in Cities at the Future Force Conference**. The Hague, NL

2018

Nov 6, 2017–Dec 15, 2017. **Exhibition. BLUE: Design for Legacy in Border Ecologies**. Harvard GSD. Cambridge, USA

Oct 14, 2017–Jan 14, 2018. **Exhibition. BLUE: Design for Legacy in Change Makers**. Museum Boijmans Van Beuningen, Rotterdam, NL

Jan. 14–15 2018. **Keynote lecture and workshop. Building peace? The fragile side of architecture**. The Basel Peace Forum. Basel, Switzerland.

Apr 18, 2018. **Event. The Environmental Impact of UN Peace Operations**. Hosted by the International Peace Institute

Apr 18, 2018. **Policy Report. Greening Peacekeeping: The Environmental Impact of UN Peace Operations**. Published by the International Peace Institute

Apr. 30, 2018. **Workshop. Peacekeeping, and Sustaining Peace, through the lens of Urban Planning and Development**. FAST, NYU-CIC, NYU-IPK, UN Agencies

2019

Nov 30, 2018. **Event. UN Secretariat, NYC. UN Peacekeeping Missions in Urban Environments and the Legacy of UNMIL**. hosted by the Permanent Mission of the UK, Australia and Liberia to the UN

Feb, 2019. Event hosted by the Permanent Mission of Australia to UN. **Peacekeeping Missions in Urban Environments. The Legacy of UNMIL**

Sep 10, 2019. **Event. The Legacy of UN Peace Operations**. Sep, 2019. **Discussion. Pilots for Transition and Sustaining Peace. Focus area: MINUSMA. UNPB, UNPO, UNDFS, Permanent Missions of Australia, Mali and UK to the UN.**

Nov, 2019. **Publication. Peacekeeping Missions in Urban Environments. The Legacy of UNMIL**. By FAST with CIC-NYU

2020

Jun, 2020. **Essay. Hotel Africa and the Crumbling of Modernity. Malkit Shoshan visits a Dom-Ino House, a UN Base, and an Irish Bar**. Canadian Center for Architecture

Dec, 2020. **Essay. Architecture After Conflict. In the book Architects After Architecture. Alternative Pathways for Practice**

Collaborative research with policy institutes with the support of UN TCCs and funders.

tour: the 2016 Venice Architecture Biennale's national participation." Wallpaper Magazine, June **2016** • "BLUE: Architecture of UN Peacekeeping Missions: Inside the Netherlands' Pavilion at the 2016 Venice Biennale." ArchDaily, June **2016** • "2016 Venice Biennale: Dutch Pavilion, "BLUE: Architecture of UN Peacekeeping Missions." Architectmagazine, June **2016** • "Top 9 Picks from the Venice Architecture Biennale." Artnet News, June **2016** • "Malkit Shoshan on the architecture of diplomacy." Casale, Rockey. Wong, Karen. Surface Magazine. July **2016** • Merin, Gilli. "For Centuries Maps Have Been Used As Tools Of Control." Mark Magazine, July **2016** • "Blueprint reviews architecture venice biennale." Design Curial, August **2016** • "23 Landmarks books about cities every architect should read." UIC. Barcelona. September **2016** • "Designing homes to welcome refugees." The Lancet, September 2016 • "Malkit Shoshan curator Biënnale van Venetië." Het Parool, December 2015 (NL)"Nederlands biënnalepaviljoen Venetië in teken van BLUE." Architectenweb. December **2015** (NL) • "Defensie en Design." Archined, April 2016 (NL) • "BLUE: Architectuur van VN Vredesmissies." ArchitectuurNL, May **2016** (NL) • "Middendorp opent Nederlands paviljoen." Bouwformatie, May **2016** (NL) • "Hoogste militair opent Nederlands Paviljoen Venetië."Nieuwsbericht 26-05-2016. Avrm, May **2016** (NL) • "Opening BLUE op Architectuurbiënnale Venetië." Knudsen, Jacqueline. ArchitectuurNL, May **2016** (NL) • "De Smaak van... Malkit Shoshan." Koelewijn, Rinskje. NRC Handelsblad, May **2016** (NL) • "Deze architecte wil letterlijk aan de vrede bouwen." Leclaire, Annemiek. Vrij Nederland, May 2016 (NL) • "Nederlands Paviljoen in Venetië kleur blauw." Trouw, May **2016** (NL) • "Goed ontwerp." FD, May **2016** (NL) • "Nederlands paviljoen Biënnale Venetië kleurt blauw van de camouflagenetten." Witman, Bob. Volkskrant, May **2016** (NL) • "Vredesmissie heeft meer design nodig," May **2016** • "Nederland Biënnale paviljoen officieel geopend." Het Parool, May **2016** (NL) • "Bouwen met modder, bamboe en afval." De Lange, Henny. Trouw. June **2016** (NL) • "Architectuurbiënnale Venetië: ingebedde architecten." Archined. June **2016** (NL) • "Dipinto di blu." NIW. July 2016 (IT) • "De metropool wordt overschat." Het Parool. July **2016** (NL) • "The World in Our Eyes. A discussion with Stefano Boeri and Malkit Shoshan." FIG Projects. Form of Form. Lars Muller Publishers, **2016** • "Sustaining Peace in an Urban World" Terreform. Dec, **2016** • "Inteview with Malkit Shoshan" in Change Makers. (pp 95–111). van Kersteren, Annemartine. Museum van Boijmans Beuningen, **2018** • "The Environmental Impact of UN Peace Operations." Jake Sherman. IPI, **2018** • "EVENT SUMMARY: Launch of UN Peacekeeping Missions in Urban Environments: The Legacy of UNMIL" CIC-NYU. Leah Zamore. Feb, **2019**

BLUE: Architecture of UN Peacekeeping Missions Exhibition at The Dutch Pavilion.
2016 Venice Architecture Biennale. Photos: Iwan Baan.

BLUE: Architecture of UN Peacekeeping Missions at the Dutch Pavilion. 2016 Venice Architecture Biennale. Photos: Iwan Baan.

USCITA DI SICUREZZA

BLUE: Architecture of UN Peacekeeping Missions Exhibition at the Dutch Pavilion.
2016 Venice Architecture Biennale. Photos: Iwan Baan.

The opening of the exhibition BLUE:
Architecture of UN Peacekeeping Missions. The Dutch Pavilion for the 2016 Venice Architecture Biennale.
Guus Beumer, director Het Nieuwe Instituut, Rotterdam.

Malkit Shoshan. Founding director Foundation for Achieving Seamless Territory.

Marjan Hammersma, NL Director General Media and Culture.

Tom Middendorp. Chief of Defense of the Armed forces of the Netherlands.

Photos: Simone Ferraro

Dutch Military Delegation. BLUE. Venice, 2016.

Galedou Master Soumy. Malian artist and rapper. BLUE. Venice, 2016.

Photo: Simone Ferraro

Koenders visits the United Nations Headquarters in New York

Report by The Dutch Ministry of Foreign Affairs, January 25, 2016

Foreign minister Bert Koenders will visit UN Headquarters in New York on Monday and Tuesday. During his visit, he will meet with UN Secretary-General Ban Ki-moon and various UN envoys. The minister will also deliver a speech on the Middle East to the UN Security Council.

Mr Koenders and Mr Ban will meet on Tuesday to discuss the approach to a number of urgent problems, including the migration crisis and terrorism. 'Migration and international security are priorities of the Dutch EU Presidency,' said Mr Koenders. 'It is useful to work with other international forums to find ways to strengthen each other's work on these pressing issues.' Some of the topics Mr Koenders will discuss with UN envoys include Syria and the fight against ISIS.

While in New York, the minister will also take part in a counterterrorism meeting, where he will speak about the outcomes of the recent anti-terrorism conference held in The Hague. Mr Koenders will call on the meeting's participants to put the agreements made in The Hague – on issues like information sharing, for instance – into practice as soon as possible.

The minister will also highlight the outcomes of the Planetary Security Conference. The conference, held late last year in The Hague, brought together security and climate change experts for the first time. 'We can't keep treating climate change and security as separate issues,' remarked the minister. 'And I'm going to stress this point in New York.'

Mr Koenders will also open an exhibition entitled 'Blue: Islands in Cities' at UN Headquarters. It charts the research by Dutch-Israeli architect Malkit Shoshan on how UN peace mission bases can be used by local communities both during and after a mission.

Mr Koenders will also speak about the Kingdom of the Netherlands' bid for a seat on the UN Security Council for the 2017–2018 term. 'We want to shoulder our share of international responsibility and make a meaningful contribution towards a safer, fairer and more prosperous world,' commented Mr Koenders. The elections will be held in June.

Presentation of BLUE: Island in Cities at the UN Secretariat in NYC hosted by Bert Koenders, the Dutch Minister of Foreign Affairs, 2016.

United Nations Headquarters, NYC

Future Force Conference, The Hague

Future Force Conference 2017 Peacekeeping missions in cities and design for legacy

Report by the Dutch Ministry of Defence, February, 2017

Participants: Malkit Shoshan (Founder of the architectural think tank FAST. The Foundation for Achieving Seamless Territory), Joel van der Beek (Economist, Director Econovision), Erella Grassiani (Anthropologist, University of Amsterdam), Puck van Dijk (Philosophical Moderator), Floris Alkemade (Chief Government Architect, Chairman of the Board of Government Advisors), Debra Solomon (Founder of Urbaniahoeve, social design lab for urban agriculture), Erwin Marx (Senior Staff Officer for Infrastructure & EP at Directorate of Operations), Renilda Steeghs (Ambassador for Cultural Cooperation, Dutch Ministry of Foreign Affairs)

Which key themes and trends were discussed?

- How to integrate local community needs into the needs of the military base to improve peace-making efforts.
  Which challenges and issues were identified?
- How to solve the time gap: referring to combining all different perspectives in practice.
- Anthropological view: how to combine local and 'Western' perspectives? First, cooperate with the locals. Second: who are the locals? What are their views, ideas, feelings and so on? Understand them in all different ways.
  What were possible solutions offered?
- Combine all different kinds of expertise. This is a theoretical solution; in practice, it appears that we have not yet reached this stage.
- Broaden the 3D-perspective: defence, diplomacy, and development.

Best practices/lessons learned

- Make a concrete link between Western ambitions and local reality.

Which recommendations/ideas emerged during the sessions?

- Integration of a wide range of sectors, both governmental and non-governmental, when planning a mission. This to create unified goals and positive outcomes for all actors involved (e.g. local communities, military, government).
- Tailor-made approach: by taking into account the local level, perspective, ideas, wishes and culture.
- Be aware of your impact abroad. Be aware of possible (negative) influence in the surrounding area. Merely being present will influence the population one way or another.

Quotes

- From a designer perspective: 'If you have a hammer, every problem looks like a nail'. (Floris Alkemade)
- Use bases as food for the next generation. (Floris Alkemade)
- Conflicts cannot be solved in isolation. (Malkit Shoshan)
- Crises have a circular effect that needs to be taken into account. (Malkit Shoshan)

The Environmental Impact of UN Peace Operations

Report by the International Peace Institute
April 18, 2018

In recent years, United Nations peace operations have increasingly begun addressing environmental challenges related to their own impact and the conditions in which they operate. Missions, particularly large deployments in arid, land-locked countries, have considerable resource requirements and can cause significant, if unintended, environmental damage to countries the UN is seeking to assist.

To discuss this impact and the UN response, IPI launched a new report at an April 18th policy forum with the Permanent Missions of the People's Republic of Bangladesh, Italy, and Finland. The report, Greening Peacekeeping: The Environmental Impact of UN Peace Operations, assesses the challenges that the Department of Field Support (DFS) faces in implementing its environment strategy. Looking at the UN policies, guidelines, and training material, it also provides recommendations for improving local environmental sustainability and building resilience.

In opening remarks, Kai Sauer, Permanent Representative of Finland to the UN, signaled that environmental challenges actually offer an opportunity for peacekeepers to engage more deeply with the populations they serve. "We can have a positive impact on the local communities by sharing our knowledge and culture on environmental sustainability and solutions," he said. So, beyond their traditional role, peacekeepers "can also be building up the local capacity in environmental questions."

Sebastiano Cardi, Permanent Representative of Italy to the UN, highlighted the new formation of a Group of Friends between Italy, Bangladesh, and Finland as leaders on environmental management in the field. Bangladesh and Italy, in particular, are large contributors to peacekeeping operations, ranked second and twentieth out of all troop and police-contributing countries, as of March 31. As such, he said, they have a pressing obligation to respond immediately to the environmental damage caused by missions.

In 2017, the UN Department of Field Support launched an environmental strategy to guide its field missions. Mr. Cardi said that a challenge to implementing new environmental initiatives is finding the balance between respecting a host country's sovereignty and achieving the mandated goals of a mission.

As the UN is a field-oriented organization, he said, "It is therefore important that we get it right in terms of doing no harm to the territories and the people where the organization operates." In addition, he made a call to action for peacekeeping missions to "leave whenever possible, a positive trace of the presence of the UN, not only in an environmental field, but, of course, in all other fields as well."

Atul Khare, Under-Secretary-General of the UN Department of Field Support, affirmed the value of holding a discussion with civil society on environmental management in peace operations. "It is very great that, for the first time, we are discussing a report on this issue by an entity external to the UN, that is, the IPI," he said. "This, to my mind, bodes very well for greater interest in civil society for this issue."

Member state contributions need not be technologically complex or expensive, he pointed out. "We think of solutions to environmental problems as engineering solutions...but sometimes even low-tech solutions are as good or perhaps better in dealing with environmental management than high-tech solutions," he said.

Asked why environmental management was important, he answered, "Good environmental management actually contributes to peace and security."

"If we do not do good environmental management, the chance of environmentally related crisis in the future in a country cannot be ruled out," he said. "In order to avoid our inheritors, our children of today, blaming us for not having exercised due diligence, let us do it now."

Lucile Maertens, who co-authored the report with Malkit Shoshan, is a lecturer at the University of Lausanne in Switzerland. "Environmental consequences can extend long after the mission is gone and can be irreversible," she said. She urged that the environment "should not be considered as a secondary issue, but should be taken into account from the start while designing and deploying a mission."

This is also a matter of accountability for the UN and its "legitimacy and credibility," she added. For reform to be effective, policy and regulatory initiatives should not come solely from UN headquarters, but should rely mostly on local input, she said.

Ms. Shoshan, director of an architectural think tank, the Foundation for Achieving Seamless Territory (FAST), emphasized four main points from the publication. They were the spatial manifestation and footprint of peace operations, the role of global logistic chains in the politics of sourcing and procurement, the challenges and opportunities for the local community, and the value of an integrated approach, including the development of comprehensive indicators to insure a sustainable legacy with environmental concerns.

Atul Khare, UN Under-Secretary-General, Department of Field Support.

Malkit Shoshan, Director, Foundation for Achieving Seamless Territory.

Kai Sauer, Permanent Representative of Finland to the UN.

Sebastiano Cardur, Permanent Representative of Italy to the UN.

Jake Sherman, IPI Director of the Brian Urquhart Center for Peace Operations Below: **Lucile Maertens, Lecturer, University of Lausanne, Switzerland.**

Annica Waleij, Senior Analyst, Swedish Defence Research Agency Below: **Tareq Md. Artiful Islam, Deputy Permanent Representative of the People's of Bangaladesh to the UN.**

INSTITUTE
IPI
KHARE
MAERTENS
SHERMAN
WALEIJ

In 2016, she said, field missions were responsible for half of the greenhouse gas emissions of the entire UN system. The discrepancy between considering peace operations as short term activities and the time the missions truly last, she said, leads to an "extensive wasteful practice that has a protracted impact on the environment."

In 2009, the global flow of commodities and expertise to peace operations grew exponentially. The scale and new basis in missions such as that in Mali, she explained, resulted in "excessive, wasteful practices that increase and solidify the inequality between the local situation and the global presence."

Citing research from the report, she noted that scarcity and vulnerability often lie at the center of the conflict that the UN is there to resolve. Peacekeeping missions often enter complex and fragile ecosystems, where resources are scarce and the government is not responsive to the needs of its people. Pressures intensify as a result of climate change and population growth, and deployment of UN peace operations can add stress to ecosystems.

Peacekeepers are not trained in environmental and urban management, but through small-scale and "head-on" projects, they can identify opportunities to help provide access to clean water, food, and reduce their global footprint gradually, she said. And by locally sourcing both high and low-tech technologies, they can empower the populations of individual locations.

Annica Waleij, Senior Analyst at the Swedish Defence Research Agency, remarked that reform will not happen immediately. "I commend [the report] for not shying away from acknowledging the fact that you have an organization with a lot of member states," she said. "There's a lot of different perspectives and interest, and it's sometimes very hard to reach consensus. So naturally it takes time. You have to be very persistent."

Tareq Md. Ariful Islam, Deputy Permanent Representative of Bangladesh to the UN, reflected on the obstacles to environmental reform in closing remarks. "The question of enhancing human and financial resources for implementing the environmental strategy would perhaps be the most challenging part," he said. For these recommendations to succeed, he said, "Environmental management...has to get the political support that it needs." Jake Sherman, IPI Director of the Brian Urquhart Center on Peace Operations, moderated.

Event Summary: Launch of UN Peacekeeping Missions in Urban Environments: The Legacy of UNMIL

Report by Leah Zamore and Shavon Bell, the NYU Center on International Cooperation, February 7, 2019

The infrastructure, technology, and resources that a United Nations peacekeeping operation brings can open up new opportunities in key conflict-affected areas of the world.

United Nations (UN) peacekeeping operations unfold today in hundreds of cities and towns in conflict-affected regions. Designed as fortified, self-contained islands, their bases, super-camps, logistical hubs, and airfields invariably impact their surroundings, often in long-lasting, unintended, and sometimes challenging ways. With careful planning, the large-scale physical footprint of peacekeeping missions also has enormous potential. In addition to its mandate, the infrastructure, technology, and resources that a UN mission brings can open up new opportunities in key conflict-affected areas of the world.

This finding is the subject of an ongoing, multidisciplinary project spearheaded by Malkit Shoshan of the Foundation for Achieving Seamless Territory (FAST), with Leah Zamore at the NYU Center on International Cooperation (CIC). The project has thus far focused on the evolution and drawdown of the UN Mission in Liberia (UNMIL).

Recommendations emerging from the research include:

- Paying closer attention to the urbanization of peacekeeping
- Taking a longer-term, evolutionary perspective in the design of mission architecture
- Planning for transitions and drawdowns at the outset of a mission such that bases and buildings can be repurposed for other uses, such as schools, health clinics, and community centers
- Utilizing local sourcing of materials, equipment, and labor
- Shifting gradually toward food self-sufficiency via community gardens, fish farms, and animal husbandry
- Making strategic use of sunk costs and reserve capacity, such as under-used hospital facilities
- Adopting low-tech and easily maintained technology such as rain-harvesting techniques
- Seizing opportunities as they arise for community engagement
- These findings were officially launched in the book UN Peacekeeping Missions in Urban Environments: The Legacy of UNMIL

The launch event, co-hosted by the Missions of Australia, Liberia, and the United Kingdom and held at the UN headquarters on November 30, 2018, featured a presentation of the project by Ms. Shoshan and a spirited discussion with Deputy Permanent Representative **Israel Chocko Davies** of the Permanent Mission of Liberia, Rania Dagash of the Department of Peacekeeping Operations (DPKO), **Henk-Jan Brinkman** of the Peacebuilding Support Office (PBSO), **David Yardley** from the Permanent Mission of Australia, **Ellen Kang** from the Permanent Mission of the Republic of Korea, and **Sam Grout-Smith** from the Permanent Mission of the United Kingdom, with CIC Deputy Director **Paige Arthur** serving as moderator. Together, the speakers addressed the project from their own vantage points, bringing in factors relevant to physical infrastructure such as human behavior, societal dynamics, local perceptions of the UN, community ownership, long-established UN procedures, and multilayered conflict.

To open the session, Mr. Yardley of Australia emphasized the alignment of this project with the UN's commitment to sustaining peace, a key part of the secretary-general's reform agenda. Following this, Arthur discussed themes that would become thematic threads throughout the afternoon's discussion, such as the need for national ownership, participatory approaches, and practicality. From her perspective, member states, UN agencies, and other peacebuilding partners needed to "manage missions in a way that supports host countries to build peace after a mission departs." Following this introduction, Shoshan applied these concepts as well as those from architecture and urban planning as the points of departure for her analysis. She explained that UN mission sites traditionally function as islands, designed by engineers who are largely concerned with security for the mission personnel. They are frequently surrounded by fences and other barriers which not only physically divide mission staff from the local community, but also serve as a symbol of the social and economic divide between UN staff and locals. In addition, they disrupt the daily lives of the local population, who need to navigate their way around bases and security corridors that prioritize the safety and movement of UN sites, vehicles, and personnel. Considering the $550 million spent on the facilities and infrastructure of these missions, and given that they are increasingly placed in urban settings, their careful construction is critical, and their potential to bring positive change is significant. The central

AUSTRALIA
FAST
NYU-CIC

ENGLISH

ITED KINGDOM

(L–R): **Malkit Shoshan, Foundation for Achieving Seamless Territory; Gizem Sucuoglu, UN Peacebuilding Support Office; Rania Dagash, Department of Peacekeeping Operations; David Yardley, Permanent Mission of Australia; Israel Chocko Davis, Permanent Mission of Liberia; Paige Arthur, NYU Center on International Cooperation; Sam Grout-Smith, Permanent Mission of the United Kingdom; Ellen Kang, Permanent Mission of the Republic of Korea.**

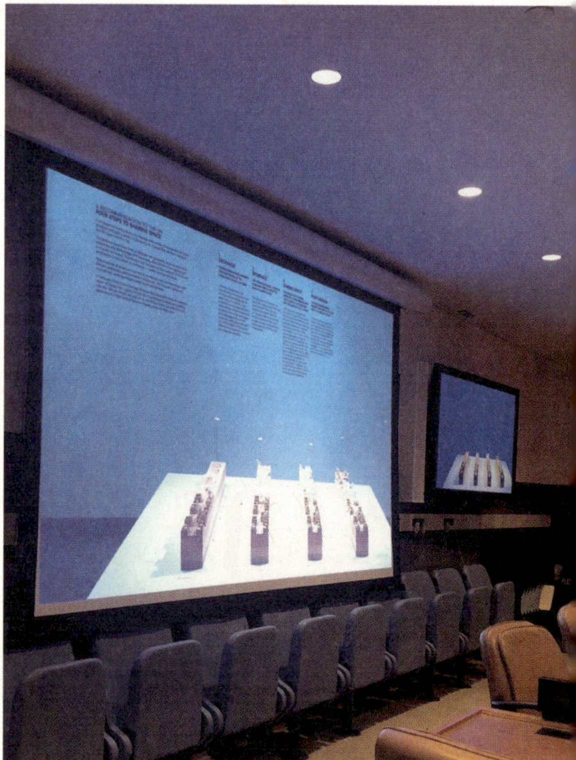

consideration, in Shoshan's view, was "how UN bases can be designed in a way that opens up, and does not hinder, space for peace and development."

In fact, UNMIL was one of the first of these integrated missions, for which Deputy Permanent Representative Davies said that he "took pride" because "Liberians themselves played a pivotal role in UNMIL's achievements." Throughout the transition process of this mission, in which facilities changed hands from the UN and other peace partners to the Liberian government, some locations were repurposed to fit the local goals of the surrounding community.

The project centered on an analysis of 13 peacekeeping bases in the country, all managed by the UN or other nations, such as China and Nigeria, and their condition and relation to the local context following the mission drawdown. From this analysis of factors such as fencing and physical barriers, physical integration with the surrounding community, food production within a given facility, environmental restrictions, water access, urban expansion of the surrounding community, and unemployment among locals, FAST and CIC issued recommendations based upon lessons learned from failed integration, and shed light on the practical components of successful integration, such as the rapid repurposing of mission spaces, and community involvement throughout the transition process.

UN officials Dagash of DPKO and Brinkman of PBSO responded with significant interest, with Dagash mentioning the necessity of multisectoral approaches and community integration "in contexts that are not just conflict-ridden, but are also the epicenter of multilayered violence." In addition, she mentioned the positive and negative impacts of missions, ranging from the frequent decrease in purchasing power among the local communities, or the increase in job training that often follows a mission's arrival, a point which Brinkman also discussed, expressing the "need to minimize the possibilities for negative impact and maximize the positive impact." Further, Dagash underscored the need for bilateral and triangular partnerships as well as engagement with local communities to fulfill this vision. Despite the constraints that DPKO faces, such as tight timelines, limited resources, and security constraints, Dagash described the first steps in rectifying these community integration issues, such as environmental analysis within the Department of Field Support (DFS), a new performance management system, and the sourcing of local vendors. In Brinkman's opinion, UN solutions such as these must be driven by analysis of relevant actors and positive agents of change, who are frequently women and youth. These groups must be empowered to lead their local institutions, he said, adding that mission transition plans "need to have national ownership and involve people in the design," and that military approaches to peacekeeping are insufficient in addressing community integration issues.

The question and answer session following these presentations prompted further exploration of these themes, with questions and comments from the United Kingdom, Brazil, and the Republic of Korea. More specifically, participants asked about the implications of peacekeeping for migration and urbanization, discussed the need for these ideas to be implemented systematically, and the need to bridge the development-peace nexus. Shoshan responded to these questions by describing a need for contextualization and localization of processes, with local actors directly involved, and echoed calls for systematic implementation of the study's recommendations, rather than implementation on an ad hoc basis. Dagash and Brinkman mentioned that planning for a mission exit and transition period must begin from the start of the mission, and that DPKO may not always have the technical expertise to pursue these recommendations, although they are moving in a direction that further prioritizes a focus on community engagement as it relates to infrastructure, as evidenced by the environmentalist section of DFS.

Overall, FAST and CIC highlighted the positive possibilities of UN missions through an imaginative, practical, and multidisciplinary perspective. With the partnership of Liberia, Australia, the United Kingdom, and further collaboration with DPKO and PBSO, there is now a chorus of voices both in and around the UN that recognize the significant potential of this strategy, and that can find the means to bring a more participatory and inclusive vision of peacekeeping infrastructure, as well as peacekeeping impact, to fruition.

BLUE: Architecture of UN Peacekeeping Missions in Border Ecologies Exhbition at Harvard University Graduate School of Design

Photos: Justin Knight, 2017.

FAROUK
DIFFRA
DOKURA
TODACH
CAMP
HIGHWAY
TEJALEI
BANTON
ANTHONY
AGOK

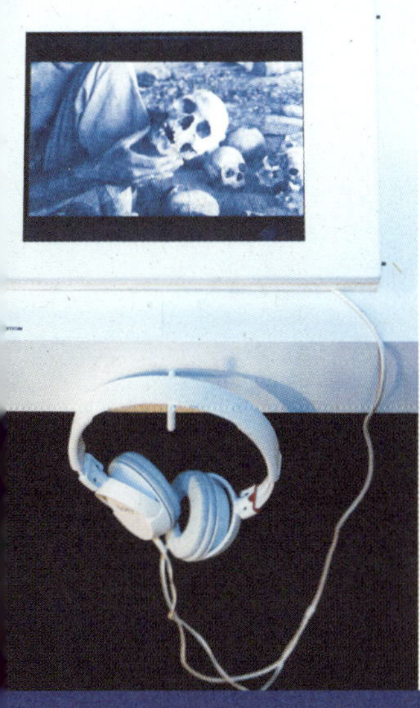

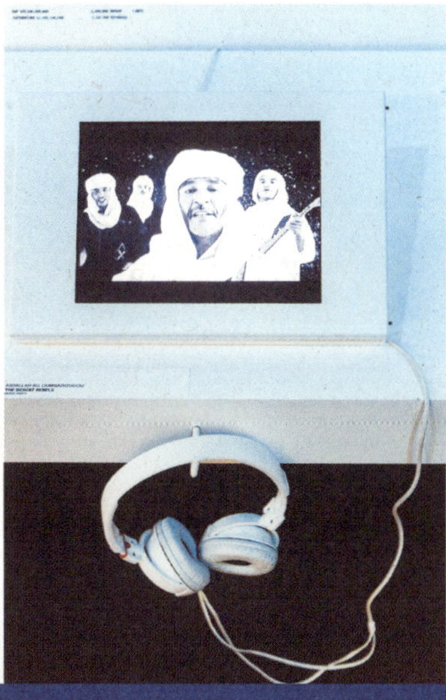

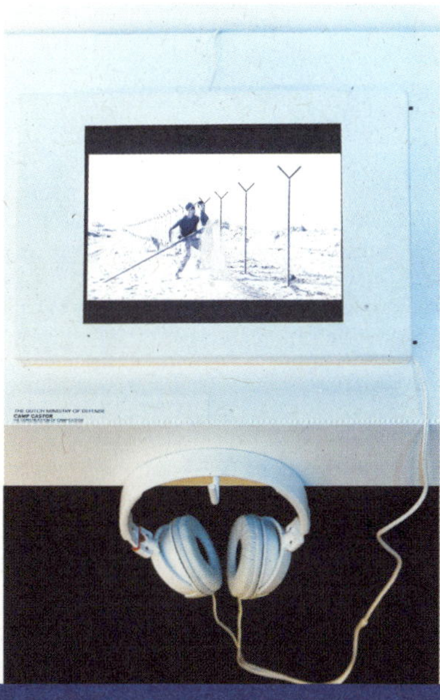

BLUE: Architecture of UN Peacekeeping Missions in Change the System exhibition. Museum Boijmans Van Beuningen, Rotterdam, 2017.

Abbreviations

ACS American Colonization Society
C34 The Special Committee on Peacekeeping Operations (C34) was established in 1965 under the General Assembly Fourth Committee in order to review and provide recommendations on United Nations Peacekeeping Operations. The committee consists of 147 Member States involved in peacekeeping missions and observing members such as the International Criminal Police Organization (Interpol). The Special Committee holds annual substantive debates, at the end of which policy recommendations for the current UN peacekeeping missions are published
CAR Central African Republic
CIC Center on International Cooperation at New York University
DDR Disarmament, Demobilization, and Reintegration
DFS/ DOS Department of Field Support/Department of Operational Support
DPKO/DPO Department of Peacekeeping Operations/ Department of Peace Operations
ECOMOG Economic Community of West African States Monitoring Group
FAST Foundation for Achieving Seamless Territory
Fifth Committee The United Nations General Assembly Fifth Committee (also known as the Administrative and Budgetary Committee or C5) is one of six main committees at the United Nations General Assembly. It deals with internal United Nations administrative and budgetary matters
FPU Formed Police Units
Fractals Infinitely complex patterns that are self-similar across different scales. They are created by repeating a simple process over and over in an ongoing feedback loop. Driven by recursion, fractals are images of dynamic systems – the pictures of Chaos
GAMMA A Dutch Hardware store chain. It started on May 11, 1971 in Breda
GSA General Services Agency
Hesco Concertainer, known colloquially as the HESCO MIL, Hesco barrier, or Hesco bastion, is a modern gabion primarily used for flood control and military fortifications. It is made of a collapsible wire mesh container and heavy duty fabric liner and is used as a temporary to semi-permanent levee or blast wall against small-arms fire and/ or explosives
INPFL Independent National Patriotic Front of Liberia
IPI International Peace Institute
LURD Liberians United for Reconciliation and Democracy
MINUCI United Nations Operation in Côte d'Ivoire
MINURCA United Nations Mission in the Central African Republic
MINURCAT United Nations Mission in the Central African Republic and Chad
MINURSO United Nations Mission for the Referendum in Western Sahara
MINUSCA UN peacekeeping mission in the Central African Republic
MINUSMA United Nations Multidimensional Integrated Stabilization Mission in Mali
MINUSTAH United Nations Stabilization Mission in Haiti
MNLA National Movement for the Liberation of Azawad
MOB Mission Operation Base
MODEL Movement for Democracy in Liberia
MONUA United Nations Observer Mission in Angola.
MONUC United Nations Organization Mission in the Democratic Republic of the Congo
MONUSCO United Nations Organization Stabilization Mission in the Democratic Republic of Congo
MOVOCON Movement Control
NIBATT Nigerian Battalion
NPFL National Patriotic Front of Liberia
OIOS Office of Internal Oversight Services
ONUB United Nations Operation in Burundi
ONUC United Nations Operation in the Congo
OUMOZ United Nations Operation in Mozambique
PB Peacebuilding
PK Peacekeeping
PRC People's Redemption Council
QIP Quick Impact Projects, designed to build confidence in the mission, its mandate and the peace process
RHQ Regional Headquarters
Super camp Large UN peacekeeping base with presence of multiple TCCs and UN agencies
TCC Troop-Contributing Countries
TVET Technical and Vocational Education and Training
UN United Nations
UN CHARTER The Charter of the United Nations is the founding document of the United Nations. It was signed on June 26, 1945 in San Francisco at the conclusion of the United Nations Conference on International Organization and came into force on October 24, 1945
UNCT UN Country Team exists in 131 countries, covering all of the 162 countries where there are United Nations programs. The UNCT includes all the UN entities working on sustainable development, emergency, recovery and transition in program countries
UNAMID United Nations – African Union Hybrid Operation in Darfur
UNAMIR United Nations Assistance Mission for Rwanda
UNAMSIL United Nations Mission in Sierra Leone
UNASOG United Nations Aouzou Strip Observer Group
UNEP United Nations Environment Program
UNGM United Nations Global Marketplace
UNHCR UN Refugee Agency
UNMEE UN Mission in Ethiopia and Eritrea
UNMIK UN Mission in Kosovo
UNMIL UN Mission in Liberia
UNMIS United Nations Mission in Sudan
UNMISS United Nations Mission in South Sudan
UNOCI United Nations Operation in Côte d'Ivoire
UNOMIL United Nations Observer Mission in Liberia
UNOMSIL United Nations Observer Mission in Sierra Leone.
UNOMUR United Nations Observer Mission Uganda–Rwanda
UNOSOM United Nations Operation in Somalia

Appendix 1: Timeline · Selection of Key Events in the History of Eurpean Colonization of Africa

1342–1700

- Site of colonial expedition
- Company and trade
- Christian Mission
- Fort
- Explorer
- Other event

Canary Islands 1342
Francesco Desvalers

Cape Bojador 1343
Francesco Desvalers

Cape Blanco 1441
Portuguese

Fortress 1443
Island of Arguin
Trading European wheat and cloth for African gold and slaves

Senegal, Gambia, Guinea 1447
Portuguese

Senegal, Gambia River 1455
Antoniotto Usodimare
Francesco Desvalers

Bijagós Islands, Cape Verde Archipelago 1455
Diego Gomes
Antonio de Nol

Bissau Islands 1462
Serra Leoa

Serra Leoa 1471
Ghana, Gold Coast
Almina Fort
Fernao Gomes

Cameroon 1472
Sao Tome Base
(safe Haven for criminals and expelled)

Rivers and Kingdom of Ko

Kingdom of Benin 1485
João Afonso d'Aveiros
Martin of Behaim

Cape of Good Hope
Bartolomeu Dias

Slave Trade

Cape of Storms 1488
Vasco da Gama

Quelimane (Mozambi
Mombasa, Malindi (K

Calicut, India

Congo 1495

Age of Discovery — 1400 — 1500

Madagascar* 1513

*** One of the ships under command of Diogo Dias arrived at an island east of Africa that bore the name Madagascar. But only a century later, between 1613 and 1619, the Portuguese explored the island. They signed treaties with local chiefs and sent the first missionaries, who found it impossible to make locals believe in Hell, and were eventually expelled.**
Source: Wikipedia

Cape of Good Hope 1581
(En) Francis Drake

Zanzibar 1583
Swahili coast
Portuguese

Senegal 1626
Island of Arguin
(Fr) Compagnie de l'Occident

(NL) The West India Company conquered Elmina 1637
Island of Arguin

(NL) East Indies Company: Indian Ocean

The Dutch built 16 forts including Gorée in Senegal, partly overtaking Portugal as the main slave-trading power. The Dutch Gold Coast and Dutch Slave Trade.

Fort Dauphin 1642
Madagascar
French East India Company
History of the Great Island of Madagascar and Relations (Book)

Swedish Gold Coast 1650
Swedish Africa Company

(En) Jacob Fort 1651
St. Andrew's Island Colony
Fort Jillifree
St. Mary Island

(Sw) Fort Carlsborg 1652

(Sw) Fort Carlsborg 1652
Cape Town
Founded by Jan van Riebeeck

Danish Gold Coast 1658
Danish West India-Guinea Company 54–55

Atlas Maior 1662–1672

Gross Friederichsburg Fort 1677
Fort of Arguin restoration 1677

1600

1700

Timeline · Selection of Key Events in the History of Eurpean Colonization of Africa

1700–1945

■ Gross Friederichsburg Fort
■ Fort of Arguin **restoration are sold to the Netherlands** 1720

X **Treaty of San Ildefonso**
Islands of Annobón, Fernando Poo in waters of the Gulf of Guinea, the Guinean coast between the Niger River and the Ogooué River are given to Spain (1777)

⬢ **(En) of The Association for Promoting the Discovery of the Interior Parts of Africa** 1788

Discovery of the origin and course of the Niger River and the location of Timbuktu, the "lost city" of gold

(En) Cape Town English Colony 1814

Ottoman and Egyptian rule over Sudan (1820)

French Occupation of Algier 1830

Egyptian rule over Zanzibar 1840–1848

+ **Multiple Protestant Missions Guinea Coast, South Africa, Zanzibar**

+ **Missionaries visited little-known regions and peoples, and in many instances became explorers and pioneers of trade and empire.**

• **David Livingstone, a Scotti missionary discovered: Orange River, Kalahari Des Lake Ngami, Zambezi River Victoria Falls, Bie, Angola**

+ **Route: Benguella to the mo of the Rovuma, Lake Tanga Lake Victoria;**

+ **Route: South Morocco-Sah Sudan, Gabon Region, Gorilla existence**

X 1870: **10% of Africa under form European control**

British South Africa Company looked for minerals and ways to improve river navigation in the central and southern Africa region.
Copper rapidly became the primary export of Central Africa and it remains essential to the economy even today.

Age of Discovery

1800

1900

X **Berlin (Congo/West Africa) Conference** 1884

Spheres of Influence

Principle of Effective Occupation

(Belgium) International Congo Society

1· Congo Free State by Belgium
2· Brazzaville, Congo as French Colony
3· Portugal Kongo Empire

France takes over Tunisia, Congo, Guinea

England takes over Ethiopia, Nile, Suez Canal, Egypt

French West Africa
French Equatorial Africa
1895–1960

German East Africa
1885–1919

(Belguium) Congo Free State
1885–1908

X 1914: **90% of Africa under formal European control with only Ethiopia and Liberia remaining independent**

X 1914–1918 **World War I**

X 1920 **League of Nations**

X 1939–1945 **World War II**

X **October 24**, 1945
United Nations came into existance

Appendix 2: UN Bases in Liberia and Their Closure Date

List of bases: Sites Closed in FY 2015/2016

No - Camp - Field Office - Final Inspection Dates

1. UNMIL Field Office Cestos City, Rivercess Co. July 1, 2015

2. NIBATT Military Camp, Pleebo, Maryland Co. July 9, 2015

3. NIBATT Camp, Cheesman Avenue, Monrovia July 31, 2015

4. BAN-ENG Camp, Saclepea, Nimba Co. August 19, 2015

5. BAN-MED, CARI Complex, Bong Co. August 28, 2015

6. PAKRAM Asphalt Plant, Schieffelin. September 16, 2015

7. NIBATT Camp at Executive Mansion. October 29, 2015

8. Barclayville Camp, Grand Kru Co. December 8, 2015

9 Jordan FPU at Monrovia Central Prison December 22, 2015

10. NIBATT Camp, 24 Street, Sinkor. December 22, 2015

11. Indian FPU National Correction Palace. December 29, 2015

12. Robert Sport Field Office, Cape Mount Co. January 15, 2016

13. GHANBATT 21 Camp, Voinjama, Lofa Co. January 22, 2016

14. Ghanbatt HQ Camp, Cari, Bong. January 24, 2016

15. GHANBATT Camp LPRC, Monrovia. January 27, 2016

16. Bopolu UNMIL Consolidated Compound. January 28, 2016

17. GHANBATT Alpha Camp, Zorzor, Lofa Co. January 29, 2016

18. Ganbatt 21 Camp, Sanniquelie, Nimba Co. February 5, 2016

19. Ghanbatt 21 Camp, Ganta, Nimba Co. February 16, 2016

20. Nigerian FPU LPMC, Gbarnga, Bong Co. March 18, 2016

21. Indian FPU Camp, Congo Town Monrovia March 29, 2016

22. Jordan FPU Camp Voinjama, Lofa Co. April 15, 2016

23. Nepal FPU Tubmanburg, Bomi Co. April 18, 2016

24. NIBATT 36 Tappita, Nimba Co. April 28, 2016

25. NIBATT 36 Fishtown, River Gee Co. April 25, 2016

26. NIBATT 36 Zwedru, Grand Gedeh County May 3, 2016

27. NIBATT 36 Harper, Maryland Co. May 5, 2016

28. Tubmanburg Field Office, Bomi County May 10, 2016

29. BAN-ENG Ganta, Nimba Co. May 12, 2016

30. Buchanan Field Office, Grand Bassa County. May 13, 2016

31. National Policy Academy. May 13, 2016

32. Kakata Field Office, Margibi Co. May 17, 2016

33. Fuel Cell Harper Port. June 7, 2016

34. BAN-ENG Gbarnga, Bong County. June 21, 2016

35. China Med, Zwedru, Gd. Gedeh County. July 4, 2016

36. China ENG, Zwedru, Gd. Gedeh County. July 4, 2016

37. Water Plant, Harper Maryland County. July 5, 2016

38. Ban-ENG, BD Den, Monrovia. July 15, 2016

39. NIBATT 37, SKD Camp at Monrovia, Montsrrado County. August 9, 2016

40. Sector B4 Harper, TPT Workshop. September 21, 2016

41. Sector B4 Harper, Air Field. September 21, 2016

42. Sector B4 Harper, Light House. September 21, 2016

43. Sector B4 Harper, Field Office. September 21, 2016

44. Sector A4 Greenville, Filed Office. September 30, 2016

45. Sector A4 Greenville, Air Field. September 30, 2016

46. Sector A4 Greenville, Fuel Station. September 30, 2016

48. NIBATT 37, Vatican Compound. October 11, 2016

49. PAKRAM Camp – RIA, Margibi County. December 9, 2016

50. Transit Camp3 – RIA, Margibi County. December 9, 2016

51. UNMIL/ZWEDRU/INDIAN FPU. February 14, 2017

52. UNPOL Liberian Police HQ Monrovia. February 24, 2017

53. UNMIL/GBARNGA/NIG FPU-2. February 27, 2017

53. UNPOL Team Site - RIA Margibi County. March 3, 2017

54. UNPOL Liberian Police HQ Monrovia. March 17, 2017

55. UNMIL/MONROVIA/CHINTPT. March 22, 2017

57. UNMIL/MONROVIA/CAMP CLARA. March 24, 2017

58. UNMIL/MONROVIA/ MOVCON FREEPORT. March 28, 2017

59. UNMIL/MONROVIA/TC2. April 21, 2017

60. Spriggs Air Field (former NIBATT 38 Site). June 1, 2017

61. UNMIL/GBARNGA/AIRFIELD-FUEL STATION. June 15, 2017

62. UNMIL/GBARNGA/RHQ CARI. June 16, 2017

63. UNMIL/MONROVIA/UNV TRANSIT HOUSE. June 29, 2017

64. B3 Zwedru. UNMIL/ZWEDRU/ AIRFIELD. 6-Dec-17

65. B3 Zwedru UNMIL/ZWEDRU/ LOG BASE. 6-Dec-17

66. B3 Zwedru UNMIL/ZWEDRU/ RHQ. 6-Dec-17

67. B1 Voinjama UNMIL/ VOINJAMA/RHQ. 12-Dec-17

68. B1 Voinjama UNMIL/ VOINJAMA/LOGBASE. 12-Dec-17

69. B1 Voinjama UNMIL/ VOINJAMA/STAFF WELFARE CENTER. 12-Dec-17

70. B1 Voinjama UNMIL/ VOINJAMA/HELIPAD. 12-Dec-17

71. B2 Gbarnga UNMIL/ GBARNGA/NIG FPU-2. 19-Dec-17

72. A2 Monrovia. UNMIL/ MONROVIA/CAMP LAGOS. 11-Jan-18

73. A2 Monrovia. UNMIL/ MONROVIA/RIA (UAU). 30-Jan-18

74. A2 Monrovia. UNMIL/ MONROVIA/CAMP ABUJA. 31-Jan-18

75. A2 Monrovia. UNMIL/ MONROVIA/CHINFPU FREEPORT. 15-Feb-18

76. A2 Monrovia. UNMIL/ MONROVIA/LNP HQ. 21-Mar-18

77. A2 Monrovia UNMIL/ MONROVIA/GERMAN EMBASSY. 17-Apr-18

78. A2. Monrovia. UNMIL/ MONROVIA/SPA. 26-Apr-18

79. A2. Monrovia. UNMIL/ MONROVIA/PAP including Annex. 30-Apr-18

80. A2 Monrovia. UNMIL/ MONROVIA/STAR BASE29-Jun-18

The Spatial Distribution of UN Bases in Liberia

2017

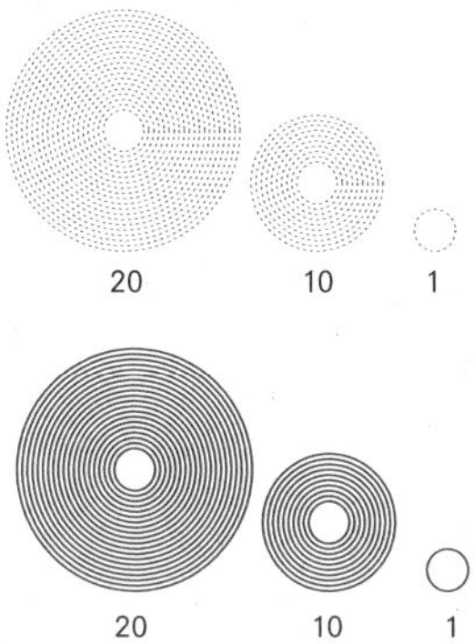

Operating bases and units: 8
Number of personnel: 209
Ceased bases and units: 71

Appendix 3: Approximated Environmental Impact of UNMIL Based on Data Collected by various TCC and UN Agencies

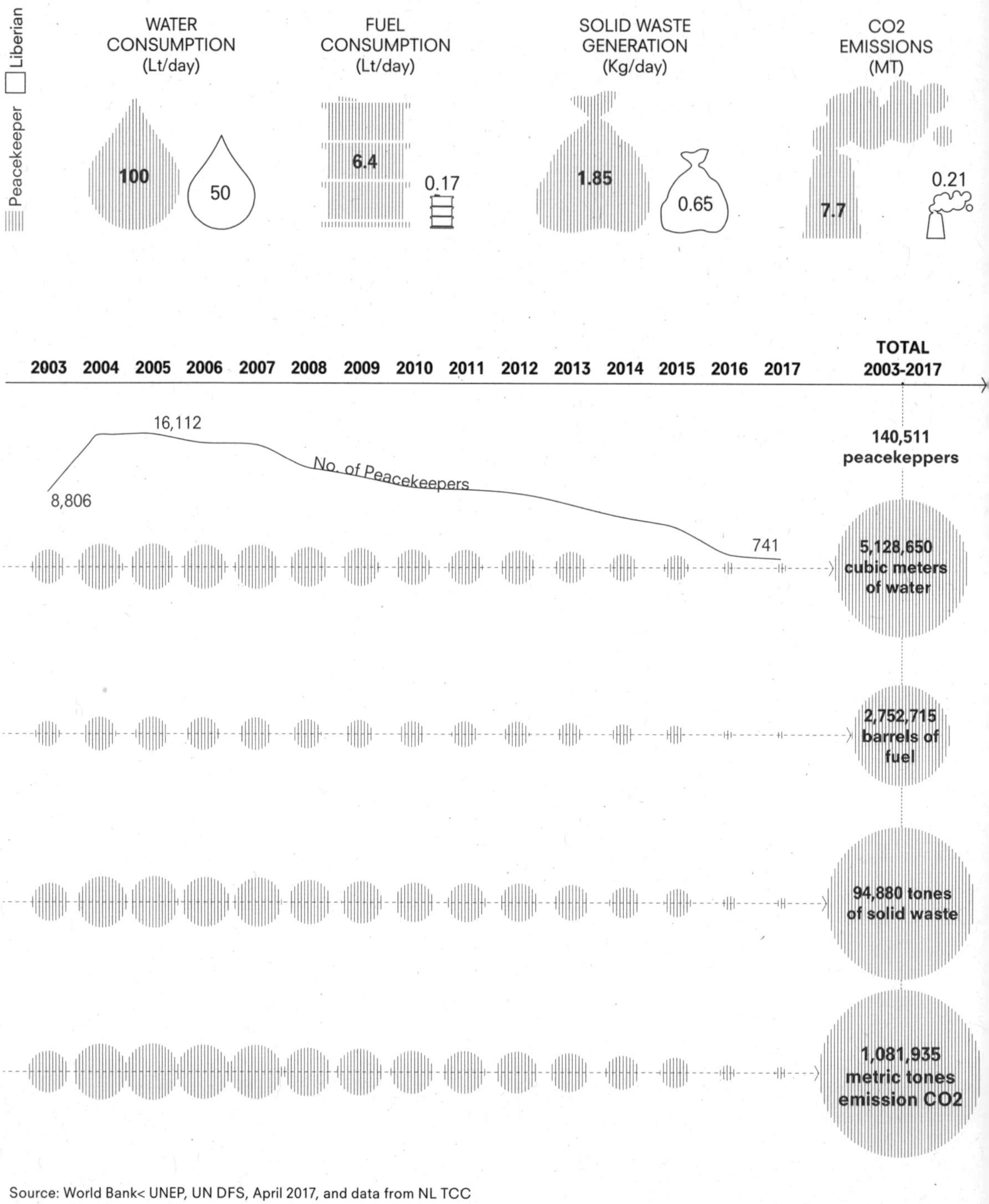

Source: World Bank< UNEP, UN DFS, April 2017, and data from NL TCC

Appendix 4: Liberia Food Insecurity, Natural Resources and UN Bases

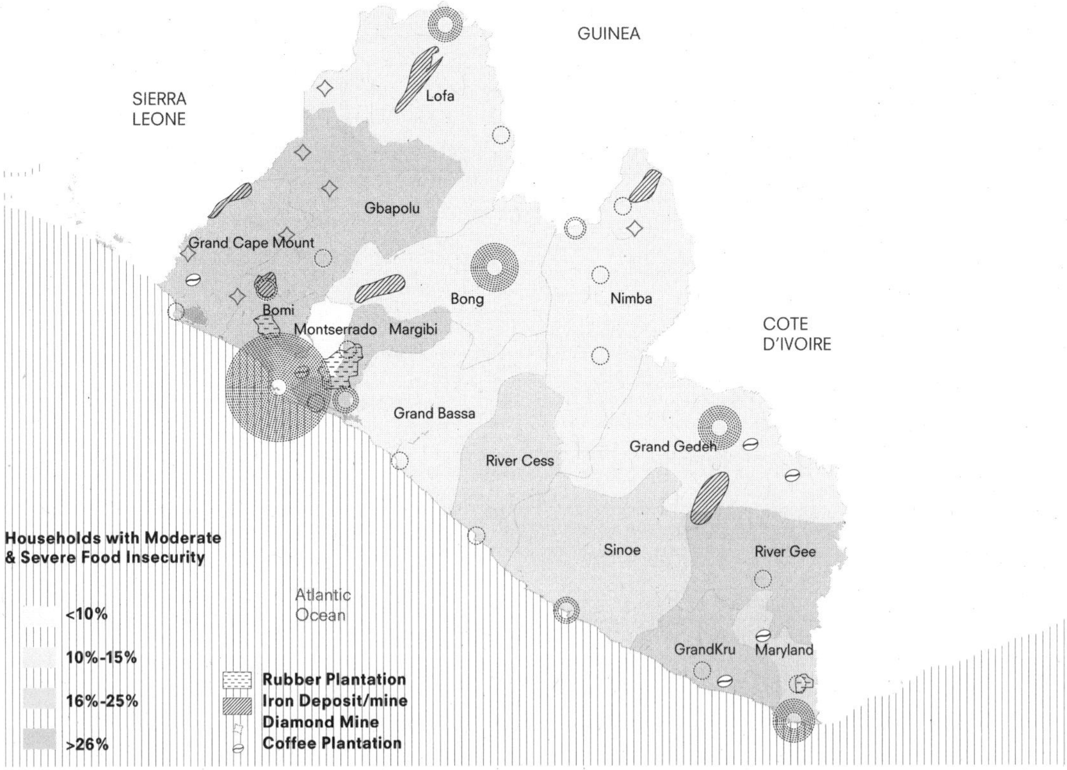

Liberia poverty, displacement and UN peacekeeping presence

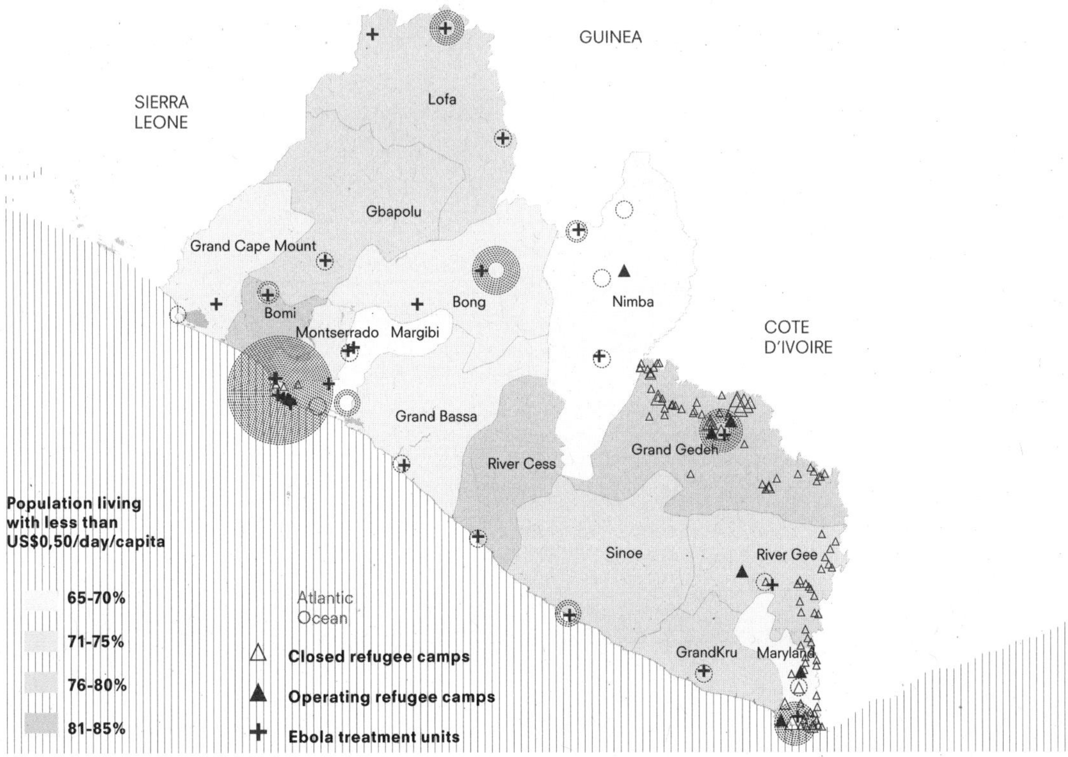

Appendix 5: Natural Resources and Trade

Main exportation products

US$383M
Passenger and cargo ships

US$215M
Iron ore

US$102M
Rubber

US$39.7M
Rough wood

(Low-employment industries)

The Liberian-flag fleet is the second-largest in the world, only after Panama.

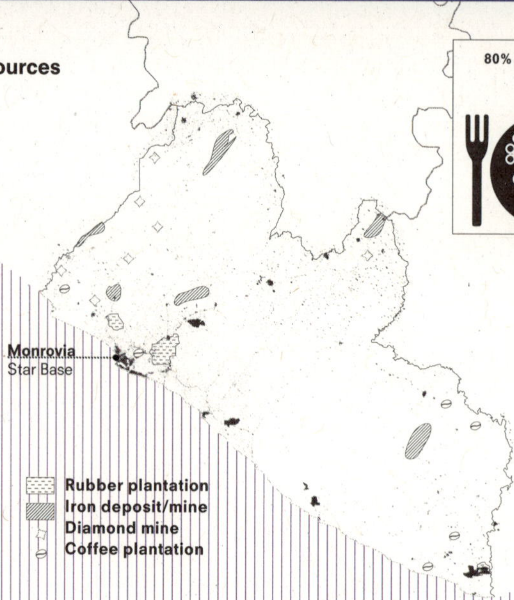

Rubber plantation
Iron deposit/mine
Diamond mine
Coffee plantation

80% importation

"Over 20% of food consumption is from national production. This share is higher in rural areas (36%) compared to urban areas (10%). In Montserrado, less than 2% comes from Liberian production"
(LISGIS. Household Income and Expenditure Survey 2014)

2015 main export destinations	2015 main import origins
$280M Poland	**$1.36B China**
$152M China	$1.32B S. Korea
$76.5M India	$862M Japan
$44.5M US	$565M Philippines
$39.2M Greece	$336M Germany
$32.8M France	$289M Poland
$19.9M Spain	$159M India
$15M Germany	$140M US

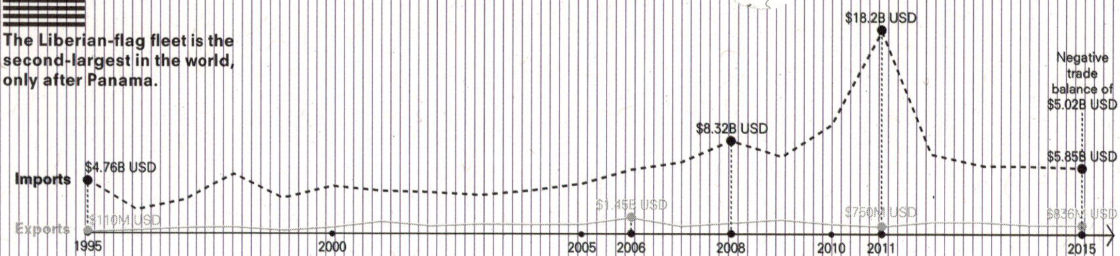

Monrovia and UN bases

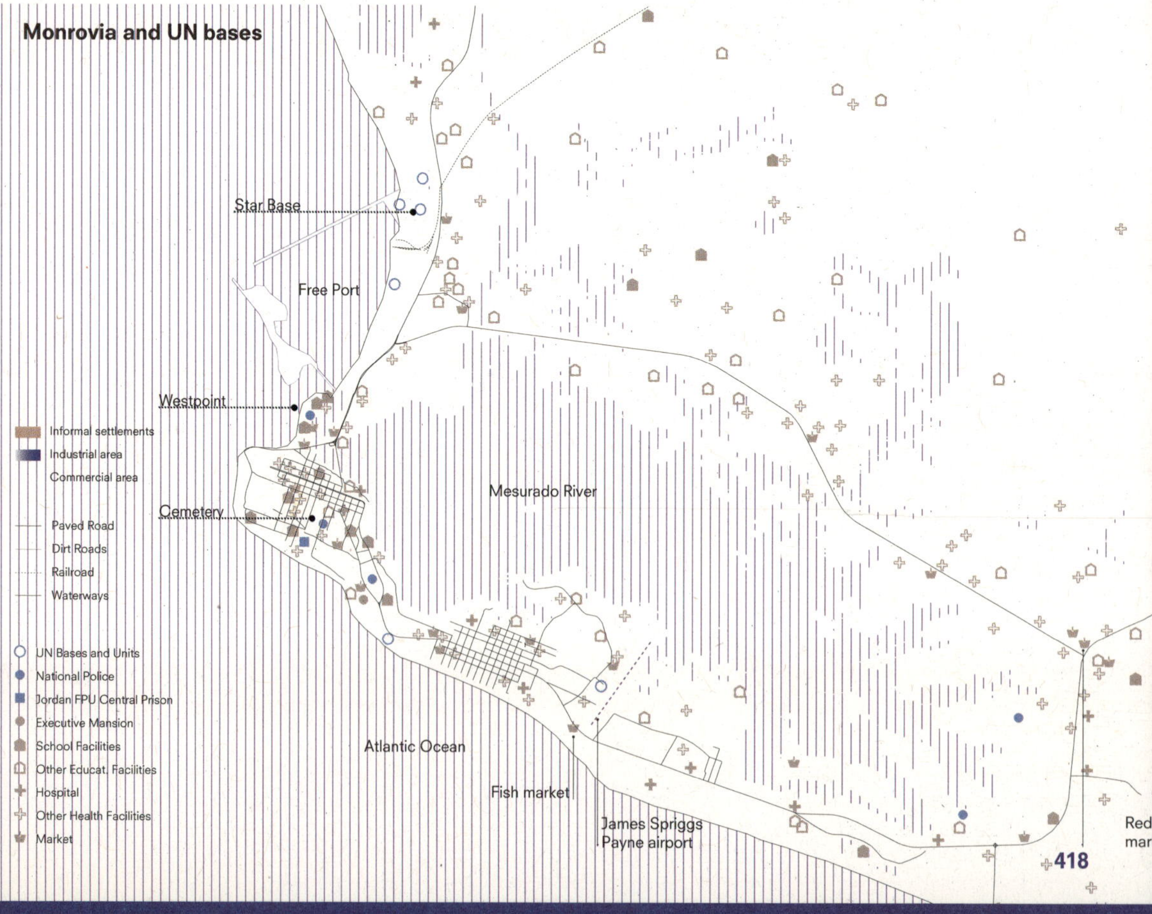

Appendix 6: A Detailed Plan of the Star Base, UNMIL HQ, in Monrovia Freeport

Appendix 7: UNMIL Assets in Situ

Examples of UNMIL bases characteristics and equipments

VOINJAMA, D2 CAMP

UNMIL, GHANBATT D2 CAMP, VOINJAMA

GHANBATT D2 Camp | Voinjama | Lofa | Liberia

CHARACTERISTIC

- Prefabs Units
- Chain link fence
- Security lightings
- Water Treatment Plant
- Water Storage
- Toilet
- Kitchen
- Fuel Tanks

General Description

The camp is suited for military camp or police quarter. It may be also considered as long-training site for military or civilians that require accommodation and feeding. On the other hand the facilities may be converted to GoL offices.

United Nations Mission in Liberia (UNMIL)

CONTACTS:

UNMIL HQ
Pan African Plaza
Tubman Boulevard, 1st Street
Your Monrovia, Liberia

Phone: 770-31-4032/4000/6000
Fax: 1-212-963-9924
www.unmil.org

Assets to leave in situ

All assets are currently in use. If well maintained they can serve GoL for another few years.

Barcode	Generic Description	Commnets
MIL 20938	Fuel Storage	Round Fuel Storage Tank
MIL 20267	Fuel Storage	Round Fuel Storage Tank
MIL 23003	AMA Storage Tank 1000 ltr	Transportable Fuel Tank
MIL 23026	AMA Storage Tank 2500 ltr	Transportable Fuel Tank
MIL 23019	AMA Storage Tank 1000 ltr	Transportable Fuel Tank
MIL MIL 20462, MIL 20677	HARZ Fuel Tank	Round Storage Tank with pump
MIL 22936	18X6 Mod Prefab	
MIL 22927	18X6 Mod Prefab	
MIL 22926	18X6 Mod Prefab	
MIL 21813	18X6 Mod Prefab	
MIL 21543	18X6 Mod Prefab	
MIL 21818	18X6 Mod Prefab	
MIL 22924	18X6 Mod Prefab	
MIL 21544	18X6 Mod Prefab	
MIL 21552	18X6 Mod Prefab	
MIL 21819	18X6 Mod Prefab	
MIL 21814	18X6 Mod Prefab	
MIL 22925	18X6 Mod Prefab	
MIL 22840	18X6 Mod Prefab	
MIL 22933	18X6 Mod Prefab	
MIL 21551	18X6 Mod Prefab	
MIL 22948	18X6 Mod Prefab	
MIL22947	18X6 Mod Prefab	
MIL 22899	3X3 Mod Prefab	
MIL 22923	3X3 Mod Prefab	
MIL 22922	3X3 Mod Prefab	
MIL 22058	11 X Single Mod Prefab	
MIL 21976	11 X Single Mod Prefab	
MIL 21978	11 X Single Mod Prefab	
MIL 21980	11 X Single Mod Prefab	
MIL 22027	11 X Single Mod Prefab	
MIL 21935	11 X Single Mod Prefab	
SDS-Y-00877	11 X Single Mod Prefab	
MIL 21936	11 X Single Mod Prefab	
MIL 21934	11 X Single Mod Prefab	
MIL 21917	11 X Single Mod Prefab	
MIL 22918	11 X Single Mod Prefab	

MIL 22243	5 X 20FT Containerized Ablution	Toilet
MIL 22229	5 X 20FT Containerized Ablution	Toilet
MIL 22757	5 X 20FT Containerized Ablution	Toilet
MIL 22756	5 X 20FT Containerized Ablution	Toilet
MIL 22761	5 X 20FT Containerized Ablution	Toilet
MIL 23116	5 X 8FT Containerized Ablution	Toilet
MIL 23132	5 X 8FT Containerized Ablution	Toilet
MIL 23124	5 X 8FT Containerized Ablution	Toilet
MIL 23119	5 X 8FT Containerized Ablution	Toilet
MIL 23120	5 X 8FT Containerized Ablution	Toilet
MIL 22772	WTP	Water Treatment Plant
MIL 22782	WTP	Water Treatment Plant
MIL 22394	WTP	Water Treatment Plant
MIL 19122	6 X Water Storage	Flexible Bladder for Water Storage
MIL 37638	6 X Water Storage	Flexible Bladder for Water Storage
MIL 37646	6 X Water Storage	Flexible Bladder for Water Storage
MIL 37392	6 X Water Storage	Flexible Bladder for Water Storage
MIL 37637	6 X Water Storage	Flexible Bladder for Water Storage

ZWEDRU, INFPU NCP

UNMIL, INFPU NCP CAMP, ZWEDRU

InFPU NCP Camp | Zwedru | Grand Gedeh | Liberia

CHARACTERISTIC

- Prefabs Units
- Toilet
- Kitchen
- Tents
- Communication Tower
- Water tanks
- Shower and Laundry
- Security Fence
- Entrance Gate
- Security lightings
- Security Observation Towers
- Security Observation Spots
- Water Storage
- Generator Shed

General Description

The camp is attached to the Central Prison in Zwedru. It may be used to accommodate Liberian military, police, or Corrections Officers.

United Nations Mission in Liberia (UNMIL)

CONTACTS:

UNMIL HQ
Pan African Plaza
Tubman Boulevard, 1st Street
Your Monrovia, Liberia

Phone: 770-31-4032/4000/6000
Fax: 1-212-963-9924
www.unmil.org

Assets to leave in situ

All assets are currently in use. If well maintained they can serve GoL for another few years.

Barcode	Generic Description	Comments
MIL 16611	Prefabs 1X3 mod	
MIL 21418	Prefabs 1X3 mod	
MIL 19140	Tent	Soft walls UN Tent
MIL 19371	Tent	Soft walls UN Tent
SIL 17591	1 X 8 ft. Containerized Field Ablution	Toiled
MIL 22205	1 X 20 ft. Containerized Field Ablution	Toiled
N/A	1 x 50ft Mash Antenna	Communication Tower
N/A	2 x Concrete field toilets	Toiled
N/A	1 x Field shower/laundry area	Shower and Laundry
N/A	3 x polytanks (500lit/cap to 3000lit/cap)	Plastic water tanks
N/A	1 x field kitchen & mess (collapsible)	Kitchen facilities
N/A	2 x wooden shed (collapsible)	Shed for Generator
N/A	4 x Elevated Observation Post	Security Observation Towers
N/A	4 x ground observatin post	Security Observation spots
N/A	1 x set of perimeter fence & gate	Security Fence and Entrance Gate
N/A	11 x security/perimeter lights	Security Lights

SCHEFFLIN, MONROVIA

21 April 2017

UNMIL FIELD OFFICE, SCHEFFLIN TRANSIT CAMP 2

UNMIL Coumpound | Monrovia | Mont Serado | Liberia

MAIN ASSETS

Prefab	12
Containerized Kitchens	14
Ablutions, Showers	6
Cook House	1
Generators	4
Refrigerated Container	1
Air Conditioners	5
Security lights	28
Water Purification	1
Waste Water Treatment	2
Water Tanks (storage)	34
Water Bor Well	1
Water Tower	1
Coms Tower	1

General Description

The Transit Camp 2 is the remaining part of Pakistani Asphalt Plant handed over to Armed Forces of Liberia (AFL) in 2015. The two camps facilities, bitumen, and all gifted assets are to be used by AFL to process the asphalt which will be used for numerous road projects the AFL is undertaking.

United Nations Mission in Liberia (UNMIL)

CONTACTS:

UNMIL HQ
Pan African Plaza
Tubman Boulevard, 1st Street
Your Monrovia, Liberia

Phone: 770-31-4032/4000/6000
Fax: 1-212-963-9924
www.unmil.org

Assets to leave in situ

All assets are currently in use. If well maintained they can serve GoL for another few years.

Generic Description	Comments
10 x 6 Modular prefab buildings	
5 x3 Modular Prefab buildings	
1 x 1 Modular Prefab buildings	
8 x 25 Men Containerized kitchens	
2 x 250 Men Containerized kitchens	
4 x 20' Ablutions	
2 x 20' Prefab Ablutions, Shower and WC	
4 x 20' Prefab Ablutions, WC	
1 x Prefab Soft Walls, 4.8M x 7.2M	
1 x Field ablution (Toilets & Bathrooms)	
3 x Septic Tanks	
1 x Field cook house	
Walk ways (concrete and cement)	
1 x canopy	Constructed with timber and GI sheets for all prefabs
3 x hard wall buildings	
3 x Generator Set	75KVA, 50KVA, 2.5KVA
1 x 20' Refrigerated container	
2 x 125KVA Generator Set	
1 x Electrical Panel, Switch Board Main	
2 x Electrical Panels, Distribution Panels	
1 x Armored Cable	Connected from generator to main switch board).
5 x Split & 4 x Window Ale's	Air conditioners
28 x Security lights	
1 x Generator shed	Constructed with wood & GI sheets
4 x Electrical Panels & 1 x Changeover Switch	
1 x Water Purification	Purification Sterilization, Filtration & Reverse OSMOSIS
2 x 20,000 Ltr Water storage bladders	
3 x 20,000 Ltr water storage Soft	
2 x Waste Water Treatment	Standalone Complete Septic Module
29 x Poly Tanks	Water Tanks, (3,000Ltrs, 2,000Ltrs & 1,000ltrs)
1 x deep well & 1 x bore well	
1 x submersible water pump	
1 x water Tower	
1 x Metal Tank	
1 x CISCO NETWORK SWITCH	

1 x Communications Equipment Shelter	
1 x Terminal Multi-Channel Digital Radio	
1 x 120' Tower	
10 x Sea containers	
2 x Freezer containers	
2 x LPG Cylinders	
44 x Stackable chairs	
65 x Stackable chairs	
45 x standing fans	
14 x standing fans	Damaged
10 x garbage bins	
156 x single beds	
156 x stackable chairs	gray +blue
9 x folding tables	brown
10 x folding tables	(gray
3 x folding tables	Gray damaged
359 x mattresses	
2 x office desk	

Appendix 8: The Liquidation of Camp Clara (in the site of former Hotel Africa)

Example of a decommissioning inspection report

Annex B

UNITED NATIONS — NATIONS UNIES

UNMIL

United Nations Mission in Liberia

UNMIL Control Number: **MSOC/SECA2/10/2017**

LAND AND / OR PROPERTY INSPECTION REPORT

1. Inspection Type: Initial/**Final**/Other

2. Facility Location and Description: **NIBAT 38 – Camp Clara, Montserrado County**

3. Date of Inspection: **24th March, 2017**

4. Intent of Inspection:

   a. **To identify actions to be taken by all Parties for the successful and consenting hand-over of NIBATT 38-Cam Clara County Compound to the Government of Liberia (GoL)**
   b. **Hand/Take Over of UN-owned assets to GoL in full compliance with the UN rules and regulations, in particular the Financial Rule 105.22 (e).**

5. **Members of the Joint Inspection Team represented**:

   i. Florence F. Brandy, Superintendent, Mont. Co.
   ii. Musu K. Tompson, President Governor Council
   iii. Sylvester S. Lama, Dev. Supt. Mont. Co.
   iv. Edwin P. Kezele, Inspector, EPA
   v. Shohan Fernando, MSOC/UNMIL
   vi. Robert Gimeh, MSOC/UNMIL
   vii. Joyce Mulinde, EU/UNMIL
   viii. Paul G Sayeweh, Claims-PMS/UNMIL
   ix. Oppong Danso, AMU/UNMIL
   x. Nisar Ahmad, Eng. UNMIL
   xi. Abdelrahman Khalil, PDU, UNMIL
   xii. Roger Yantani, Eng. UNMIL
   xiii. Simeon Ajiboye, FST, UNMIL
   xiv. Susanna Alvoni, Security, UNMIL
   xv. Mohammed Swaray, PDU/PMS, UNMIL
   xvi. Charles Atebawone, MSOC, UNMIL
   xvii. Sylvain K. Kpindy, PCIU, UNMIL
   xviii. Sgt. Hassan Yusuf, NIBATT 38
   xix. Domingos Natividade, Life Support/UNMIL
   xx. Stephen Wafula, GITTS
   xxi. Young Siah Goh (Thomas), GITTS

Prepared by MSOC

Page 1

xxii. Gautam Pandey, Engineering
xxiii. Sam Kargbo, MSOC/UNMIL

The **Joint UNMIL/GoL Initial Inspection** for the handing over of **the NIBAT 38- Camp Clara, Montserrado** County has been conducted on **24th March, 2017**. The team conducted physical verification and inspection of all the structures, plus the expendable and non-expendable UN assets and agreed on the actions below.

6. **Description of agreed upon actions:**
(To include descriptions and details of any landlord-owned structure remains any existing UN equipment to be removed, UN-owned equipment to be left in situ, and repair or refurbishments to be completed before hand over)

a. Prefabs Accommodations/Hard Walls/Field Kitchen/Field Toilets & Showers:

I. There are 6 x 6 modular prefab buildings in good condition (MIL-22932, 22934, 22935, 22938, 22941 & 22944),As per request of GoL representatives and recommendation of MSOC, Engineering Section and RAO, the prefab buildings with all the lighting and fittings will be left in situ 'as is'.
II. There are 3 x 20' Containerized accommodations in good condition in the camp, 2 x without barcode and 1 x with bar code SDS-Z-01459. As per request of GoL representatives and recommendation of MSOC, Engineering Section and RAO, the containerized buildings will be left in situ 'as is'.
III. There are 5 x 20' containerized ablution buildings shower & WC MODULE with SOLAR water heating system (MIL- 51395, 51398, 51401, 51402, 51403). As per recommendation of MSOC, Engineering Section and RAO, the ablutions will be retrieved for use in other Mission's facilities
IV. There is 1 x 20' containerized ablution buildings shower & WC MODULE with SOLAR water heating system (MIL- 51258). As per request of GoL representatives and recommendation of MSOC, Engineering Section and RAO, the ablutions will be left in situ 'as is'.
V. There are 6 x 20'containerized ablutions (MIL-20437, 23157, 23161, 23162, 23165 & 23167). As per request of GoL representatives and recommendation of MSOC, Engineering Section and RAO, the ablutions will be left in situ 'as is'.
VI. There is 1 x 20'prefab ablution building WC MODULE (MIL- 23163). As per request of GoL representatives and recommendation of MSOC, Engineering section and RAO, the ablution building will be left in situ 'as is '.
VII. There are 4 x Rub Hall with barcodes (MIL 23153, MIL 23216, MIL 23217 and MIL 23218). As per request of GoL representatives and recommendation of MSOC, Engineering Section and RAO, the Rubb Halls will be left in situ 'as is'.
VIII. There are 2 x garbage collection sheds in the camp. As per request of GoL representatives and recommendation of MSOC, Engineering Section and RAO, the garbage collection shed will be cleaned and left in situ 'as is'.
IX. There are 2 x concrete platforms for fuel tanks. As per request of GoL representatives and recommendation of MSOC, Engineering Section and RAO, the concrete platforms will be left in situ 'as is'.

X. There are 2 x Field laundry in the camp. As per request of GoL representatives and recommendation of MSOC, Engineering Section and RAO, the field laundry will be left in situ 'as is'.

XI. There are 7 x Field ablutions (Toilets & bathrooms). As per request of GoL representatives and recommendation of MSOC, Engineering Section and RAO, the field ablutions will be left in situ 'as is'.

XII. There is 1 x Field cook house & 1 x Field dinning. (Constructed with timber and GI sheets). As per request of GoL representatives and recommendation of MSOC, Engineering Section and RAO, the field cook house and field dinning will be left in situ 'as is'.

XIII. There are 9 x TPT workshops/parking sheds (constructed with Timber, cement & GI sheets). As per request of GoL representatives and recommendation of MSOC, Engineering Section and RAO, the TPT workshops/parking sheds will be left in situ 'as is'.

XIV. There are 4 x Sheds for WTPs (constructed with Timber, cement and GI sheets). As per request of GoL representatives and recommendation of MSOC, Engineering Section and RAO, the sheds for WTPs will be left in situ 'as is'.

XV. There is 1 x Solid wall building for storage (constructed with sliding panels). As per request of GoL representatives and recommendation of MSOC, Engineering Section and RAO, this building will be left in situ 'as is'.

XVI. There is 1 x workshop (constructed with Timber & GI sheets). As per request of GoL representatives and recommendation of MSOC, Engineering Section and RAO, the workshop will be left in situ 'as is'.

XVII. There are 6 x sea side palava huts, 1 x basketball yard, & 1 x Military parade shed. As per request of GoL representatives and recommendation of MSOC, Engineering Section and RAO, these structures will be left in situ 'as is'.

XVIII. All walk ways with overhead shed (constructed with concrete, timber & GI sheets). As per request of GoL representatives and recommendation of MSOC, Engineering Section and RAO, these walk ways will be left in situ 'as is'.

XIX. There are 2 x soft wall tents partially damaged. As per request of GoL representatives and recommendation of MSOC, Engineering Section and RAO, the soft wall tents will be left in situ 'as is'.

XX. There is 1 x Field washroom & ablution point & 1 x Field kitchen (constructed with timber & GI sheets). As per request of GoL representatives and recommendation of MSOC, Engineering Section and RAO, the field wash room & field kitchen will be left in situ 'as is'.

XXI. There are 23 x hard wall buildings (pre-constructed, old & collapse). As per request of GoL representatives and recommendation of MSOC, Engineering Section and RAO, the hard wall buildings will be left in situ 'as is'.

XXII. There are 27 x hard wall buildings (pre – constructed). As per request of GoL representatives and recommendation of MSOC, Engineering Section and RAO, the hard wall buildings will be left in situ 'as is'.

XXIII. There is 1 x Prefab structure (written off). As per request of GoL representatives and recommendation of MSOC, Engineering Section and RAO, the prefab structure will be left in situ 'as is'.

b. **Electrical Systems: Wiring/Lights and Light Fittings/Ceiling Fans/Air-conditioners/Generators/ Switch Boards:**

i. There is 1 x Electrical control panel (FOD-06378) & 6 x Electrical Panel, Distribution panel (MCT-A- 03359, SIL- 22425, 22861, 22867, MIL- 17994 & MIK-42892). As per request of GoL representatives and recommendation of Engineering Section, MSOC and RAO, the control panel & distribution panels will be left in situ 'as is'.

ii. There are 28 x Electrical panels old COE. As per request of GoL representatives and recommendation of MSOC, Engineering section and RAO, the old panels will be left in situ 'as is'.

iii. There are 2 x Electric water heaters & 1 x Electric cable roll. As per request of GoL representatives and recommendation of MSOC, Engineering section and RAO, the water heaters and cable roll will be left in situ 'as is'.

iv. There is 1 x Switch high voltage, Change over switch (MIL-17380). As per request of GoL representatives and recommendation of Engineering Section, MSOC and RAO, the high voltage switch & change over switch will be left in situ 'as is'.

v. There are 9 x changeover switch (big & small). As per request of GoL representatives and recommendation of MSOC, Engineering Section and RAO, the changeover switches will be left in situ 'as is'.

vi. There is 1 x Armord Cable (connected from Generator to main switch board). As per request of GoL representatives and recommendation of MSOC, Engineering section and RAO, the Armord cable will be left in situ 'as is'.

vii. There are 39 x Split Units A/C's & 56 x window type A/C's in the camp. As per request of GoL representatives and recommendation of MSOC, Engineering Section and RAO, the 39 splits & 56 window AC Units will be left in situ 'as is'.

viii. There are 3 x generator sheds constructed with wood and GI sheets. As per request of GoL representatives and recommendation of MSOC, Engineering Section and RAO, the Sheds will be left in situ 'as is'.

c. **Water Supply System/ WTP/ Connections/Water Tanks & Water Bladders/Fuel Tank**

i. There are 2 x Fuel storage Tank, 5,000 Liters (MIL-23085) & 1,000 liters (MIL-23021). As per LIFE support Section, MSOC and RAO, the fuel tanks will be left in situ 'as is'.

ii. There are 4 x Water Purification-Sterilization, Water Filtration and Reverse OSMOSIS (MIL-22399, 22402, 22716, & 22718). As per recommendation of MSOC, RAO and Engineering Section, the water purification equipment will be retrieved for use in other Mission's facilities.

iii. There are 4 x Water Purification- Sterilization, Water Desalination Unit (MIL- 23469, 23470, 23471 & 23901). As per recommendation of MSOC, RAO and Engineering Section, the water desalination units will be retrieved for use in other Mission's facilities.

iv. There are 2 x Water Purification-Sterilization, Basic water treatment Plant (MIL- 23474 & 23900). As per recommendation of MSOC, RAO and Engineering Section, the basic water plant will be retrieved for use in other Mission's facilities.

v. There is 1 x Water Purification-Sterilization, Water quality Parameters LAB, Critical Parameters (MIL- 49435). As per recommendation of MSOC, RAO and Engineering Section, the water quality parameter LAB will be retrieved for use in other Mission's facilities.

vi. There is 1 x Water treatment plant (23144). As per recommendation of MSOC, RAO and Engineering Section, the water treatment plant will be retrieved for use in other Mission's facilities.

vii. There are 3 x 10,000Ltr Water storage bladders (MIL- 35757, 35764 & 35765). As per recommendation of MSOC, RAO and Engineering Section, the water storage bladders will be retrieved for use in other Mission's facilities.

viii. There are 6 x 40,000ltr water storage bladders. 3 x water bladders with bar codes (MIL-37623, 22728 & 19335) & 3 x without bar codes. As per recommendation of MSOC, RAO and Engineering Section, the water storage bladders will be retrieved for use in other Mission's facilities.

ix. There are 3 x 12,000ltrs water storage bladders (MIL- 22719, 22720 & 22721). As per recommendation of MSOC, RAO and Engineering Section, the water storage bladders will be retrieved for use in other Mission's facilities.

x. There is 1 x 20,000 Water storage bladders (MIL- 22726). As per recommendation of MSOC, RAO and Engineering Section, the water storage bladder will be retrieved for use in other Mission's facilities.

xi. There are 4 x Sewage Systems 20', Sewage T.P Plant (125 MAN) (MIL-23144, 23160, 23155 & 23164). As per request of GoL representatives and recommendation of MSOC, Engineering Section and RAO, the Sewage systems TP Plants will be left in situ 'as is'.

xii. There is 1 x Swage System, 20' Sewage T.P Plant (300MAN) (MIL- 23152). As per request of GoL representatives and recommendation of MSOC, Engineering Section and RAO, the Sewage systems TP Plant will be left in situ 'as is'.

xiii. There are 2 x Pressure Pumps, High Pressure Pump (MIL 19152 and one with no barcode). As per request of GoL representatives and recommendation of MSOC, Engineering Section and RAO, the pressure pumps will be left in situ 'as is'.

xiv. There is 1 x Submersible water pump (no bar code). As per request of GoL representatives and recommendation of MSOC, Engineering Section and RAO, the Submersible pump will be left in situ 'as is'.

xv. There are 44 x 3,000ltr Poly tanks. As per request of GoL representatives and recommendation of MSOC, Engineering Section and RAO, the poly tanks will be left in situ 'as is'.

xvi. There are 13 x 1,000 Ltr & 2,000 Ltr combined Poly tanks in the Camp. As per request of GoL representatives and recommendation of MSOC, Engineering Section and RAO, the poly tanks will be left in situ 'as is'.

xvii. There are 17 x damaged poly tanks (Various). As per request of GoL representatives and recommendation of MSOC, Engineering Section and RAO, the poly tanks will be retrieved to dispose in Log base.

xviii. There are 3 x Water pressure tanks & 2 x bore holes. As per request of GoL representatives and recommendation of MSOC, Engineering Section and RAO, the water pressure tanks & 2 bore holes will be left in situ 'as is'.

xix. There are 3 x HICLEAR Septic system (5 Cubic meter cap) & 5 x Septic tanks (constructed with cement and blocks). As per request of GoL representatives and recommendation of MSOC, Engineering Section and RAO, the HICLEAR septic tank & 5 septic tanks will be left in situ 'as is'.

d. Communications Equipment and systems:

i. There are 2 x CISCO NETWORK SWITCHES (MIL-54289 & 42706). As per recommendation of MSOC, RAO and GITTS Section, the SISCO SWITCH will be retrieved for use in other Mission's facilities.

ii. There is 1 x APRISA RADIO (MIL- 55795). As per recommendation of MSOC, RAO and GITTS Section, the APRISA RADIO will be retrieved for use in other Mission's facilities.

iii. There is 1 x 80' Tower, Rohn 25 (no barcode). As per request of GoL representatives and recommendation of MSOC, GITTS Section and RAO, the Tower will be left in situ 'as is'.

e. Sea Containers:

I. There are 9 x Sea containers in the camp, (MCT-Z-03175, MIL-23169, SDS-Z- 01002, SDS-Z- 01258, MIL- 21690, SIL- 42495, MIL- 51022, MIL 51021 & MIL 23787). The containers will be retrieved for use in other Mission's facilities.

II. There are 11 x Sea containers in the camp, (no barcode) SR# 100108, (SDS-Z- 00071, MIL- 51197, MIL 51191, MIL 23372, SDS-Z- 01246, MIL-22711, MIL 23769, MIL 23673, MIL 23648 and MIL

23667). As per recommendation of MSOC, RAO and LIFE Support Section, the Sea containers will be retrieved for use in other Mission's facilities.

iii. There is 1 x Sea Container at Security Guard Post (MIL22848), as per request of GoL representatives and recommendation of MSOC, LS Section and RAO, the Sea Container will be left in situ 'as is'.

f. Supply items and furniture

i. None

g. Aviation Assets

i. None.

h. Yard and Car Park

I. The yard will be handed over to GoL 'as is'.

i. Perimeter Fence/ Concertina Wires:

1. There is 1 x PAKQRF Fencing Wire Chain Link MON/MIL/CCL/L01/i002 (1600000863). As per request of GoL representative and recommendation of RAO and UNMIL Engineering Section the wire Chain Link fence will be left in situ 'as is'.

j. Signage:

i. All signage representing the UNMIL and the Contingent will be removed or painted over by the Contingent before the closing date of the compound.

k. Security items/ Security Observation Post/Gabion Baskets/Fire Extinguishers:

I. There is 1 x Security guard post at entrance gate. As per request of GoL representatives and recommendation of MSOC, RAO and Engineering section the security guard post will be left in situ "as is".

II. There are also Security street lights in the camp. As per request of GoL representatives and recommendation of MSOC, RAO and Engineering Section the street lights will be left in situ "as is".

III. There are 8 x Security Flood lights located inside the camp. As per request of GoL representatives and recommendation of Engineering Section, MSOC and RAO, they flood lights will be left in situ 'as is'.

IV. There is 1 x Iron Gate at the entrance in the camp. As per request of GoL representatives and recommendation of MSOC, RAO and Engineering Section the Iron Gate will be left in situ "as is".

V. There are 9 x watch towers in the camp. As per request of GoL representatives and recommendation of MSOC, RAO and Engineering Section the towers will be left in situ "as is".

l. Other services such as security, cleaning services, etc.

i. Security and cleaning services currently conducted by UNMIL will be discontinued upon handover of the camp to GoL.

ii. All metal, plastic and wooden junks and old vehicle tires within the camp shall be removed and disposed appropriately.

iii. All septic tanks within the camp shall be emptied and cleaned as requested by EPA representative and recommended by UNMIL Environmental Section, all septic tanks will be left in situ "as is".

List of UN-owned equipment to be left *in situ*, as it is agreed by the both sides:

i. 6 x 6 modular prefab buildings in good condition (MIL-22932, 22934, 22935, 22938, 22941 & 22944).
ii. 3 x 20' Containerized accommodations in good condition in the camp, 2 x without barcode and 1 x with bar code SDS-Z-01459.
iii. 1 x 20' containerized ablution buildings shower & WC MODULE with SOLAR water heating system (MIL- 51258).
iv. 6 x 20'containerized ablutions (MIL-20437, 23157, 23161, 23162, 23165 & 23167)
v. 1 x 20'prefab ablution building WC MODULE (MIL- 23163).
vi. 4 x Rubb Halls (MIL 23153, MIL 23216, MIL 23217 and MIL 23218).
vii. 2 x garbage collections shed in the camp.
viii. 2 x concrete platforms for fuel tanks.
ix. 2 x Field laundry in the camp.
x. 7 x Field ablutions (Toilets & bathrooms).
xi. 1 x Field cook house & 1 x Field dinning. (Constructed with timber and GI sheets).
xii. 9 x TPT workshops/parking shed (constructed with Timber, cement & GI sheets).
xiii. 4 x Sheds for WTPs (constructed with Timber, cement and GI sheets).
xiv. 1 x Solid wall building for storage (constructed with sliding panels).
xv. 1 x workshop (constructed with Timber & GI sheets).
xvi. 6 x sea side palava huts, 1 x basketball yard, & 1 x Military parade shed.
xvii. All walk ways with overhead shed (constructed with concrete, timber & GI sheets.
xviii. 2 x soft wall tents partially damaged.
xix. 1 x Field washroom & ablution point & 1 x Field kitchen (constructed with timber & GI sheets).
xx. 23 x hard wall buildings (pre-constructed, old & collapse).
xxi. 27 x hard wall buildings (pre – constructed).
xxii. There is 1 x Prefab structure (written off).
xxiii. 1 x Electrical panel, control panel (FOD-06378) & 6 x Electrical Panel, Distribution panel (MCT- A- 03359, SIL- 22425, 22861, 22867, MIL- 17994 & MIK-42892).
xxiv. 28 x old COE, Electrical panels.
xxv. 2 x Electric water heaters & 1 x Electric cable roll.
xxvi. 1 x Switches high voltage, Change over switch (MIL-17380).
xxvii. 9 x changeover switch (big & small).
xxviii. 1 x Armord Cable (connected from Generator to main switch board).
xxix. 39 x Split Units A/C's & 56 x window type A/C's in the camp.
xxx. 3 x generator sheds constructed with wood and GI sheets.
xxxi. 2 x Fuel storage Tank2, 5,000 Liters (MIL-23085) & 1,000 liters (MIL-23021).
xxxii. 4 x Sewage Systems 20', Sewage T.P Plant (125 MAN) (MIL-23144, 23160, 23155 & 23164).
xxxiii. 1 x Swage System, 20' Sewage T.P Plant (300MAN) (MIL- 23152).
xxxiv. 2 x Pressure Pumps, High Pressure Pump (MIL 19152 and one no barcode).
xxxv. 1 x Submersible water pumps (no bar code).
xxxvi. 44 x 3,000ltr Poly tanks.
xxxvii. 13 x 1,000 Ltr & 2,000 Ltr combined Poly tanks.
xxxviii. 3 x Water pressure tanks & 2 x bore holes.
xxxix. 3 x HICLEAR Septic system (5 Cubic meter cap) & 5 x Septic tanks (constructed with cement and blocks).
xl. 1 x 80' Tower, Rohn 25 (no barcode).
xli. 1 x Sea Container (Security Post) MIL 22848.
xlii. 1 x PAKQRF Fencing Wire Chain Link MON/MIL/CCL/L01/i002 (1600000863).
xliii. Security Street lights in the camp.
xliv. 8 x Security Flood lights located inside the camp.
xlv. 1 x Iron gate at the entrance in the camp.

xlvi. 9 x watch towers in the camp.
xlvii. 1 x Security guard post at entrance gate

List of UN-owned Equipment to be removed:

i. 5 x 20' containerized ablution buildings shower & WC MODULE with SOLAR water heating system (MIL- 51395, 51398, 51401, 51402 & 51403).
ii. 4 x Water Purification-Sterilization, Water Filtration and Reverse OSMOSIS (MIL- 22399, 22402, 22716, & 22718).
iii. 4 x Water Purification- Sterilization, Water Desalination Unit (MIL- 23469, 23470, 23471 & 23901).
iv. 2 x Water Purification-Sterilization, Basic water treatment Plant (MIL- 23474 & 23900).
v. 1 x Water Purification-Sterilization, Water quality Parameters LAB, Critical Parameters (MIL- 49435).
vi. 1 x Water treatment plant (23144).
vii. 3 x 10,000Ltr Water storage bladders (MIL- 35757, 35764 & 35765).
viii. 6 x 40,000ltr water storage bladders. 3 x water bladders with bar codes (MIL-37623, 22728 & 19335) & 3 x without barcodes.
ix. 3 x 12,000ltrs water storage bladders (MIL- 22719, 22720 & 22721).
x. 1 x 20,000 Water storage bladder (MIL- 22726).
xi. 17 x damaged poly tanks (Various).
xii. 2 x CISCO NETWORK SWITCH (MIL-54289 & 42706).
xiii. 1 x APRISA RADIO (MIL- 55795).
xiv. 11 x Sea containers in the camp, (no barcode) SR# 100108, (SDS-Z- 00071, MIL- 51197, MIL 51191, MIL 23372, SDS-Z- 01246, MIL-22711, MIL 23769, MIL 23673, MIL 23648 and MIL 23667).
xv. 9 x Sea containers in the camp, (MCT-Z-03175, MIL-23169, SDS-Z- 01002, 01258, MIL-21690, SIL- 42495, MIL- 51022, MIL 51021 and MIL 23787).

7. Final Inspection and hand over **24th March 2017**

By signing the present report, the Parties hereby agree that this report contains all of the actions to be taken by the Parties, in connection with the agreement of the hand-over of the premises.

UNMIL Representative: Shohan Fernando Logistic Assistant
(Name and Title)

Signature: [signature] Date: 24/03/2017

UNMIL Witness: Rkcorob Civa Coordination Officer

(Name and Title)

Signature: [signature] Date: 03/24/17

GoL County Superintendent: SYLVESTER S. LAMA / ASSistant Superintendent. Dev.

(Name and Title)

Signature: S.S. Lama Date: March 24, 2017

GoL/Witness: J. Michael Williams – Clerk (Commissioner's Office TOV)

(Name and Title)

Signature: [signature] Date: 24/03/17

Prepared by MSOC

Page 10

Bibliography

Allan Yarema, The American Colonization Society: An Avenue to Freedom?. Lanham, MD: University Press of America, 2006. p. 38.

Amin, Ash. "Spatialities of Globalisation" Environment and Planning A: Economy and Space, vol. 34, no. 3, Mar. 2002, pp. 385–399.

An Editorial. Journal of Peace Research, 1964, Vol. 1, No. 1. 1964, pp. 1–4.

Anna Tsing, Heather Swanson, Elaine Gan, Nils Bubandt (eds.), Arts of Living on a Damaged Planet: Ghosts and Monsters of the Anthropocene. Minneapolis: University of Minnesota Press, 2017, p. G2.

Barreto, Luis Filipe. The Down of a new age. The UNESCO Courier: a window open on the world, XLII, 4, p. 4–7.

Bazzano, Alessandra N et al. "Qualitative Studies of Infant and Young Child Feeding in Lower-Income Countries: A Systematic Review and Synthesis of Dietary Patterns." Nutrients vol. 9,10 1140. 18 Oct. 2017.

Beckles, Hilary McD. Slave voyages: the transatlantic trade in enslaved Africans. Norwegian Agency for Development Cooperation. Availabe at: www.slavevoyages.org.

Betts, Raymond F. "Decolonization: A Brief History of the Word." Beyond Empire and Nation: The Decolonization of African and Asian Societies, 1930s–1970s, edited by ELS BOGAERTS and Remco Raben, Brill, 2012, pp. 23–38, www.jstor.org/stable/10.1163/j.ctt1w8h2zm.5.

Boutros Boutros-Ghali. "An Agenda for Peace: Preventive Diplomacy, Peace-making and Peace-keeping", available at: https://digitallibrary.un.org/record/145749?ln=en.

Brahimi Report. Report of the Panel on United Nations Peace Operations (2000). A/55/305–S/2000/809. Distr.: General 21 August 2000.

Brown, Adrienne M. Emergent Strategy: Shaping Change, Changing Worlds. Chico, CA: AK Press, 2017.

Budget Framework Paper 2017/18. Presented to the National Legislature of the Republic of Liberia on 30th April 2017 at the Capitol Hill, Monrovia, Liberia, available at: www.cabri-sbo.org/uploads/bia/liberia_2017_formulation_external_budget_framework_ministry_of_finance_ecowas_english_.pdf.

Budget Framework Paper FY 2017/18. Presented to the National Legislature of the Republic of Liberia on 30th April 2017 at the Capitol Hill, Monrovia, Liberia, available at: www.cabri-sbo.org/uploads/files/Documents/liberia_2017_formulation_external_budget_framework_ministry_of_finance_ecowas_english_1.pdf.

Capstone Doctrine. "United Nations Peacekeeping Operations Principles and Guide-lines," available at: www.un.org/ruleoflaw/blog/document/united-nations-peacekeeping-operations-principles-and-guidelines-the-capstone-doctrine.

Cardon, Zoe G. and Whitbeck, Julie L., 2007. The Rhizosphere: An Ecological Perspective. p. 131, Figure 6.2. Elsevier Academic Press.

Carse, Ashley. "Dredge." Anthropocene Unseen: A Lexicon, edited by Cymene Howe and Anand Pandian, Punctum Books, 2020, pp. 121–125.

Charles E. Nowell and Felipe Fernandez-Armesto. Henry the Navigator. Encyclopædia Britannica, available at: www.britannica.com/biography/Henry-the-Navigator.

Churchill, Carl. Heyduk, Trent. "Mapping The Tuareg Rebellion", available at: www.arcgis.com/apps/Cascade/index.

CIA World Factbook, "Liberia" available at: www.cia.gov/library/Publications/the-world-factbook/geos/li.html.

CIA World Factbook, "Mali", available at: www.cia.gov/library/publications/the-world-factbook/geos/ml.html.

CLUVA, "Climate Change and Urban Vulnerability in Africa," available at: www.cluva.eu.

Cooper, Helene. The House at Sugar Beach. Prince Frederick, MD: Recorded Books, 2008.

d'Entreves, Maurizio Passerin, "Hannah Arendt", The Stanford Encyclopedia of Philosophy (Fall 2019 Edition), Edward N. Zalta (ed.), available at: https://plato.stanford.edu/archives/fall2019/entries/arendt/.

Decolonization, United Nations, available at: www.un.org/en/sections/issues-depth/decolonization.

DFS Environment Strategy, "Executive Summary," UN Field Support, November 2017, p. 3.

Doyle, Mark, "UN team starts Liberia groundwork," BBC, available at: http://news.bbc.co.uk/2/hi/africa/3406833.stm.

Doyle, Mark, "UN's Liberia 'honeymoon' to end, BBC, available at: http://news.bbc.co.uk/2/hi/africa/3423215.stm.

Doyle, Mark. "UN's Liberia 'honeymoon' to end", BBC, available at: http://news.bbc.co.uk/2/hi/africa/3423215.stm.

Easterling, Keller, Extrastatecraft: The Power of Infrastructure Space, London: Verso Books, 2016.

Ecolog International. "Integrated Service Solutions," 2017, available at: https://ecolog-international.com/en.

Ecolog, available at: https://ecolog-international.com.

Elmina Castle. Wikipedia, available at: en.wikipedia.org/wiki/Elmina_Castle.

Environmental Risk and Performance-Management," available at: https://peacekeeping.un.org/en/environmental-risk-and-performance-management.

Farvacque-Vitkovic, Catherine, Alicia Casalis, Mahine Diop, and Christian Eghoff, "Development of the Cities of Mali – Challenges and Priorities," Humanitarian Library, September 2007, available at: www.humanitarianlibrary.org/sites/default/files/2013/07/wp104_english.pdf.

Fleshman, Michael, "'Conflict diamonds evade UN sanctions", available at: www.un.org/africarenewal/magazine/december-2001/conflict-diamonds-evade-un-sanctions.

Future Force Conference. 2017, available at: www.futureforce conference.com.

Gautam, R, BR Sthapit, PK Shrestha (eds.), "Home Gardens" in "Enhancing the contribution of home garden to on-farm management of plant genetic resources and to improve the livelihoods of Nepalese farmers: Lessons learned and policy implications", 2004, Pokhara, Nepal. LI-BIRD, Bioversity International and SDC.

Ghana. "History – Early Contact", available at: https://GlobalSecurity.org.

Geospatial, location information for a better world. UN. Available at: www.un.org/geospatial.

Gladstone, Rick. "Cholera 'Forever Destroyed' U.N.'s Image in Haiti, Ban Ki-moon Says", NY Times. www.nytimes.com/2021/06/06/world/americas/cholera-haiti-ban-ki-moon-memoir.html.

Global Footprint Network, available at http://data.foot-print-network.org/#/compareCountries?

Global Forum Food and Agriculture. "How to Feed Our Cities? – Agriculture and Rural Areas in an Era of Urbanisation", available at: www.gffa-berlin.de/wp-content/uploads/2015/10/GFFA_Kommunique_2016_EN.pdf.

Griaule, Marcel. Conversations with Ogotemmêli: An Introduction to Dogon Religious Ideas. London: Published for the International African Institute by the Oxford University Press, 1970. Print.

Hair, P. E. H., "Was Columbus' First Very Long Voyage a Voyage from Guinea?" History in Africa, vol. 22, 1995, pp. 223–237.

Henry the Navigator, "Lisbon Portugal Guide," available at: http://lisbonlisboaportugal.com/Lisbon-information/Henry_Navigator.html.

Herscher, Andrew. Violence Taking Place: The Architecture of the Kosovo Conflict. Stanford Univ. Press, 2010.

Hibbs, Mark. "Uranium in Sahara Sand," Carnegie Endowment for International Peace, available at: https://carnegieendowment.org/2013/01/22/uranium-in-saharan-sands-pub-50707.

Hollander, Craig. "Navigating Slavery: Robert F. Stockton and the Limits of Antislavery Thought", available at: https://slavery.princeton.edu/stories/navigating-slavery.

Human Rights Watch. "Charles Taylor", available at: www.hrw.org/topic/international-justice/charles-taylor.

Humphrey, J. 2009. "Child Under-nutrition, Tropical Enteropathy, Toilets, and Handwashing." The Lancet. Vol. 374, pp. 1032–1035.

International Crisis Group, "A Tale of Two Councils: Strengthening AU-UN Cooperation", available at: www.crisisgroup.org/africa/279-tale-two-councils-strengthening-au-un-cooperation.

Iris & B. Gerald Cantor Center for Visual Arts at Stanford University. "Art of Being Tuareg. Sahara Nomads in a Modern World," available at: africa.si.edu/exhibits/tuareg/who.html.

Jacke, D. with Toensmeier E., 2005. Edible Forest Gardens, Ecological vision and theory for temperate climate permaculture. p. 241. Chelsea Green Publishing VT.

van der Beek, Joel. "A Speculative Financial and Socio-economic Model for Evaluating and Enhancing International Peacekeeping Missions," in BLUE: The Architecture of UN Peace-keeping, pp. 42–43.

Johan Galtung. "Violence, Peace, and Peace Research". Journal of Peace Research, 1969, Vol. 6, No. 3 (1969), pp. 167–191.

Kaldor, Mary, New and Old Wars: Organized Violence in a Global Era, Polity Press, 2012.

Kant, Immanuel. Perpetual Peace: A Philosophical Sketch, 1795. London: S. Sonnenschein, 1903.

Kemp, Martin. "Simon Stevin and Pieter Saenredam: A Study of Mathematics and Vision in Dutch Science and Art." The Art Bulletin, vol. 68, no. 2, 1986, pp. 237–252.

Kenkel, Kai, Michael, "Five Generations of Peace Operations: From the 'Thin Blue Line' to 'Painting a Country Blue'", In Revista Brasileira de Política International 56, no. 1 (2013), pp. 122–143.

Klein, Naomi. The Shock Doctrine. Penguin Books, 2008.

Koenders visits UN in New York. Government of the Netherlands. 25-01-2016, 13:45, available at: www.government.nl/latest/news/2016/01/26/koenders-visits-un-in-new-york.

Koenders, Bert. "Speech Koenders at 'What Design can Do'." Government of the Netherlands, available at: government.nl/documents/speeches/2016/07/01/speech-koenders-at-what-design-can-do, and "Koenders visits UN in New York."

Le, Corbusier, and Frederick Etchells. "Towards a New Architecture." New York: Dover Publications, 1986, p. 11.

Left, Sarah. "War in Liberia". The Guardian. London. Retrieved January 18, 2008.

Liberia Comprehensive Peace Agreement, available at: www.usip.org/sites/default/files/file/resources/collections/peace_agreements/liberia_08182003.pdf.

Library of Congress. "From Colony to Republic. 1820 to 1847", available at: www.loc.gov/collections/maps-of-liberia-1830-to-1870/articles-and-essays/history-of-liberia/1820-to-1847.

LISGIS, 2015, "Proposed Food Security Monitoring and Surveillance System", presented on October 8, 2015, the Food Security Cluster Meeting.

Lourenço, Eduardo. The Lusiads: from national epic to universal myth. Albuquerque, Luis de. The UNESCO Courier: a window open on the world, XLII, 4, 2009, pp. 10–13.

Lucile Maertens and Malkit Shoshan, "Greening Peacekeeping: The Environmental Impact of UN Peace Operations," New York: International Peace Institute, April 2018.

Lucile Maertens, "Le HCR et l'appropriation progressive de l'agenda environnemental," in Mobilité humaine et environne-ment: Du global au local, Christel Cournil and Chloé Vlassopoulos, eds.

MacLennan, Michael. "A New Urban Paradigm: Pathways to Sustainable Development," UN Development Programme, Policy in Focus 13, no. 3, available at: https://ipcig.org/pub/eng/PIF37_A_new_urban_paradigm_pathways_to_sustainable_development.pdf.

María, Puig de la Bellacasa. Matters of Care: Speculative Ethics in More than Human Worlds. University of Minnesota Press, 2017, p18.

Martin, Ian. „Lessons From the High-Level Panel's 2015 Review for the Future of Peace Operations", available at: https://theglobalobservatory.org/2020/09/lessons-from-hippo-2015-review-for-future-peace-operations.

Massing, Andreas. "Mapping the Malagueta Coast: A history of the Lower Guinea Coast, 1460–1510 through Portuguese maps and accounts." History in Africa, vol. 36, 2009, pp. 331–365.

MINUSMA. „Background – United Nations Multidimensional Integrated Stabilization Mission in Mali," 2017, available at: www.un.org/en/peacekeeping/missions/minusma/background.

MINUSMA. „Fact Sheet," UN Peacekeeping, 2017, available at: https://peacekeeping.un.org/en/mission/minusma.

MNLA. „The National Movement for the Liberation of Azawad," available at https://www.mnlamov.net.

MONUSCO. „Facts Sheet," available at: peacekeeping.un.org/en/mission/monusco.

Muggah, Rubert. „The Sahel is engulfed by violence. Climate change, food insecurity and extremists are largely to blame." Available at: www.weforum.org/agenda/2019/01/all-the-warning-signs-are-showing-in-the-sahel-we-must-act-now.

Muspelheim, Norse mythology, Encyclopedia Britannica, available at: www.britannica.com/topic/Muspelheim.

N.C. Roberts, „Spanning „bleeding" boundaries: humanitarianism, NGOs, and the civilian-military nexus in the Post-Cold war era," Public Administration Review, March/April 2010, pp. 212–222, available at: http://hdl.handle.net/10945/40808.

Nepal Army. „Nepal to deploy 140 soldiers to Mali for peacekeeping", available at: https://kathmandupost.com/valley/2014/01/29/na-to-deploy-140-soldiers-to-mali-for-peacekeeping.

Newitt, Malyn, ed., The Portuguese In West Africa, Cambridge University Press, 1950, p. 93.

Nyepon, Francis. „Liberia's WASH Crisis: Impact on Water, Sanitation, and Hygiene." The Liberian Dialogue, available at: https://theliberiandialogue.org/2015/03/14/liberias-wash-crisis-impact-on-water-sanitation-hygiene..

Nyepon, Francis. „Liberiaís WASH Crisis: Impact on Water, Sanitation, and Hygiene." The Liberian Dialogue, 2015, available at: https://theliberiandialogue.org/2015/03/14/liberias-wash-crisis-impact-on-water-sanitation-hygiene.

O'Farrell, Michael. „Dispatch from Camp Clara." NewsScoops.Org – Irish News-paper Investigations, available at: www.newsscoops.org/?p=443.

OIOS. „Liquidation", Office of Internal Oversight Services International Audit Division Report 2018/067, UN, available at: https://casquebleu.org/index.php?title=Liquidation.

PBS. „The Lone Star: The Story of Liberia", available at: www.pbs.org/wgbh/globalconnections/liberia/essays/history.

Philippe Le Billon, „Bankrupting Peace Spoilers: Can Peacekeepers Curtail Belligerents' Access to Resource Revenues?," in High-Value Natural Resources and Peacebuilding, Päivi Lujala and Siri Aas Rustad, eds. London: Earthscan, 2012.

Power-Greene, Ousmane. „'One of the Wildest Projects Ever': Abolitionists and the Anticolonizationist Impulse, 1830–1840." In Against Wind and Tide: The African American Struggle against the Colonization Movement. NYU Press, 2014. p. 46.

QIPs. „Quick Impact Projects (QIPs) explained," United Nations, available at: https://peacekeeping.un.org/en/quick-impact-projects-communities.

ReliefWeb, „Event Summary: Launch of UN Peacekeeping Missions in Urban Environments: The Legacy of UNMIL – Liberia. 2019." available at: https://reliefweb.int/report/liberia/event-summary-launch-un-peacekeeping-missions-urban-environments-legacy-unmil.

Reychler and A. Langer (eds.), „Luc Reychler: A Pioneer in Sustainable Peacebuilding Architecture" in Pioneers in Arts, Humanities, Science, Engineering, Practice 24. 2020, pp 271–299.

Rogoff, Irit. 2018. „Becoming Research" in: Choi Jina and Helen Jungyeon Ku, eds. The Curatorial in Parallax. Seoul, Republic of Korea: National Museum of Modern and Contemporary Art, Korea, pp. 39–52.

Secretary-General. „Good Environmental Steward-ship Integral to Peace-building, Secretary-General Says in Message for International Day" SG/SM/16316-OBV/1396. NOVEMBER 4 2014, available at: www.un.org/press/en/2014/sgsm16316.doc.htm.

Security Council. „Climate Change' Biggest Threat Modern Humans Have Ever Faced', World-Renowned Naturalist Tells Security Council, Calls for Greater Global Cooperation," SC/14445 FEBRUARY 23 2021, available at: www.un.org/press/en/2021/sc14445.doc.htm.

Security Council. „Fifth Committee Approves $6.51 Billion for 13 Peacekeeping Operations in 2019/20, Joint Management of Active Missions' Cash Balances, as Resumed Session Ends," available at: un.org/press/en/2019/gaab4328.doc.htm „Fifth Committee Recommends $5.4 Billion Budget for 2018-2019 Biennium as It Concludes Main Part of Seventy-Second Session," available at: un.org/press/en/2017/gaab4270.doc.htm.

Sérgio Vieira de Mello (Under-Secretary-General for Humanitarian Affairs and Emergency Relief Coordinator), United Nations. Security Council, S/PV.3968. January 21, 1999.

Shoshan, M. „The Architecture of UN Peacekeeping." In BLUE. Archis, 2016, pp. 6–19.

Shoshan, Malkit (Ed.). BLUE. Architecture of UN. Peacekeeping Missions. Volume 48. Archis, 2016, pp. 1–48.

Shoshan, Malkit and Szita, Jane. „Reimagining the Peace-keeping Mission: Legacy Scenarios for Camp Castor," Het Nieuwe Instituut, January 2015, available at: https://drones-honeycombs.hetnieuweinstituut.nl/sites/default/files/workshop_report._gao_legacy.pdf.

Shoshan, Malkit. „BLUE: Islands in Cities." available at: https://blue.hetnieuweinstituut.nl/en/blue-islands-cities-26-january-2016-new-york.

Shoshan, Malkit. „From an Island to a Catalyst." BLUE: Architecture of UN Peacekeeping Missions. Archis, 2016, p. 8.

Shoshan, Malkit. „BLUE: Architecture of UN Peacekeeping Missions," Dutch entry at the

15th International Architecture Exhibition, available at: https://blue.hetnieuweinstituut.nl/en.

Siahyonkron Nyanseor, Elder. Kpanneh, Doe J. „Justice at last?" The Economist. May 31, 2007. Retrieved August 5, 2007, available at: www.theperspective.org/2018/0410201803.php.

Sousa, Agnieszka, „Poor Nations Need Farm Investment or Face Importing More Food," Bloomberg.com, October 9, 2017, available at: www.bloomberg.com/news/articles/2017-10-09/poor-nations-need-farm-investment-or-face-importing-more-food-j8jssozu.

Stevin, Simon. „Weapon and Warefare,", available at: https://weaponsandwarfare.com/2019/03/23/simon-stevin-c-1548-1620.

Stone Lines – Sustainable Land Management Series (YouTube) last accessed February 16, 2016. www.youtube.com/watch?v=I7lys7uPVP8.

Taylor, Peter J., „Places, Spaces, and Macy's: Place Space Tensions in the Political Geographies of Modernities", Progress in Human Geography 23 (1), pp. 7–26.

The Congrès internationaux d'architecture moderne (CIAM), available at: www.hisour.com/congres-internationaux-darchitecture-moderne-28191.

The Guardian. „How a tyrant's ‚logs of war' bring terror to West Africa." May 27, 2001, available at: www.theguardian.com/world/2001/may/27/theobserver.

The Kimberly Process, available at: www.kimberleyprocess.com.

Tsing, Anna, et al., editors. Arts of Living on a Damaged Planet: Ghosts and Monsters of the Anthropocene. University of Minnesota Press, 2017.

U.S. Government Accountability Office, „UN Peacekeeping: Cost Estimate for Hypothetical U.S. Operation Exceeds Actual Costs for Comparable UN Operation," available at: https://www.gao.gov/assets/690/689900.pdf.

Ugochukwu, Nnaemeka. „Regenerative Sustainability: The New Frontier in the Sustainability Movement „, available at: https://ecowarriorprincess.net/2020/05/regenerative-sustainability-new-frontier-sustainability-movement/.

Ulrike Gehring and Peter Weibel (Eds.) Mapping Spaces. Networks of Knowledge in 17th Century Landscape Painting.

UN Climate Change. „Climate Change Is an Increasing Threat to Africa," United Nations Climate Change, available at: https://unfccc.int/news/climate-change-is-an-increasing-threat-to-africa.

UN."Data," available at: https://peacekeeping.un.org/en/data.

UN Department of Field Support, Cartographic Section and online data. UN Geospatial Information Section website, available at: www.un.org/Depts/Cartographic/english/htmain.htm.

UN DPKO and DFS, Environ-mental Policy for UN Field Missions, UN Doc. PK/G/2009.06, May 31, 2009.

UN Educational, Scientific and Cultural Organization. Convention Concerning the Protection of The World Cultural and Natural Heritage. World Heritage Committee Forty-third session Baku, Republic of Azerbaijan June 30 – July 10 2019, available at: https://whc.unesco.org/archive/2019/whc19-43com-7A-en.pdf.

UN General Assembly Resolution 66/288, The Future We Want (July 27, 2012), UN Doc. A/RES/66/288, September 11, 2012, para. 96.

UN General Assembly, Manual on Policies and Procedures Concerning the Reimbursement and Control of Contingent-Owned Equipment of Troop/Police Contributors Participating in Peacekeeping Missions, UN Doc. A/72/288, August 4, 2017.

UN Member States, „UN Membership and Member States," available at: un.org/en/member-states.

UN News. „Mali: UN officials welcome accord between Government and Tuareg rebels." UN, June 2013, available at: https://news.un.org/en/story/2013/06/442632.

UN News. „Peace and Security reform", available at: https://reform.un.org/content/peace-and-security-reform.

UN News. „Climate Change' Biggest Threat Modern Humans Have Ever Faced', World-Renowned Naturalist Tells Security Council, Calls for Greater Global Cooperation", available at: www.un.org/press/en/2021/sc14445.doc.htm.

UN News. „Climate Change Is an Increasing Threat to Africa", available at; https://unfccc.int/news/climate-change-is-an-increasing-threat-to-africa.

UN News. „General Assembly Adopts Resolution Seeking Alignment of Efforts to End Illicit Diamond Trade" Achieve 2030 Agenda for Sustainable Development, available at: www.un.org/press/en/2018/ga12002.doc.htm.

UN News. „Report of The Independent Panel on the Safety and Security of UN Personnel in Iraq, October 20, 2003", available at: www.un.org/News/dh/iraq/ safety-security-un-personnel-iraq.pdf.

UN News. „The United Nations mission in Mali has received allegations of serious misconduct by its peacekeeping troops last week, including an alleged incident of sexual abuse", available at: https://news.un.org/en/story/2013/09/449892.

UN News. „Underlining Critical Role of Diamond Certification to Global Peace, Security, General Assembly Adopts Resolution Urging Strengthening Kimberley Process", available at: www.un.org/press/en/2019/ga12124.doc.htm.

UN OCHA. „Environmental Emergencies", available at: www.unocha.org/themes/environmental-emergencies.

UN OCHA. „Joint UNEP/OCHA Environment Unit, Environment and Humanitarian Action: Increasing Effectiveness, Sustainability and Accountability, August 2014", available at www.unocha.org/sites/unocha/files/EHA%20Study%20webfinal_1.pdf.

UN Peacekeeping, „'MINUSCA FACT SHEET", available at: https://peacekeeping.un.org/en/mission/minusca.

UN Peacekeeping, „'MINUSMA FACT SHEET," available at: https://peacekeeping.un.org/en/mission/minusma.

UN Peacekeeping, „Environmental Impact and sustainability", available at: https://peacekeeping.un.org/en/environmental-impact-and sustainability.

UN Peacekeeping, „Our History" accessed May 2018: https://peacekeeping.un.org/en/our-history.

UN Peacekeeping, „Peacekeeping Operations Fact Sheet," 2017, available at: peacekeeping.un.org/sites/default/files/pk_fact_sheet_dec_17.pdf.

UN Peacekeeping, „United Nations Peacekeeping Missions Military Engineer Unit Manual, September 2015", available at: http://3.230.11.73/wp-content/uploads/2020/07/UN-PK-Military-Engineers-Manual.pdf.

UN Peacekeeping, „What is peacekeeping?", available at: https://peacekeeping.un.org/en/what-is-peacekeeping.

UN Principles and Guidelines 2008, available at: https://issuu.com/uniccanberra/docs/capstone_doctrine_eng.

UN Procurement Division, „Statistics," accessed January 2018: https://www.un.org/Depts/ptd/statistics/2016.

UN Security Council Resolution 1343 (March 7 2001), UN Doc. S/RES/1343.

UN Security Council Resolution 1625 (September 14, 2005), UN Doc. S/RES/1625.

UN Security Council Resolution 2100 (April 25, 2013), UN Doc. S/RES/2100.

UN Security Council Statement S/PRST/2011/15, July 20, 2011. And UN General Assembly Draft Resolution A/63/L.8, October 27 2008. „Security and Climate Change." Armenia, Australia, Austria, Belgium, Bulgaria, Canada, Chile, Cyprus, Czech Republic, Denmark, Estonia, Fiji, Finland, France, Germany, Greece, Hungary, Iceland, Ireland, Israel, Italy, Kiribati, Latvia, Lithuania, Luxembourg, Maldives, Malta, Marshall Islands, Micronesia (Federated States of), Monaco, Nauru, Netherlands, New Zealand, Palau, Papua New Guinea, Philippines, Poland, Portugal, Romania, Samoa, Seychelles, Slovakia, Slovenia, Solomon Islands, Spain, Sweden, Tonga, Turkey, Tuvalu, United Kingdom of Great Britain and Northern Ireland and Vanuatu: draft resolution.

UN Security Council, 6982nd Meeting, UN Doc. S/PV.6982, June 19, 2003.

UN Security Council, Press Statement on Environmental Management of Peacekeeping Operations, UN Doc. SC/13134-ENV/DEV/1830-PKO/700, December 21, 2017.

UN Security Council, Statement by the President of the Security Council, UN Doc. S/PRST/2007/22, June 25, 2007.

UN."'List of peacekeeping operations," available at: https://peacekeeping.un.org/sites/default/files/180413_unpeacekeeping-operationlist_2.pdf.

UNCT, „How we work?", available at: https://unsdg.un.org/about/how-we-work.

UNEMG, available at: http://unemg.org.

UNEP, „Greening the Blue Helmets. Environment, Natural Resources and UN Peacekeeping Operations." 2012. available at: https://wedocs.unep.org/bitstream/handle/20.500.11822/8840/UNEP_greening_blue_helmets.

UNEP, Greening the Blue Report 2017: The UN System's Environmental Footprint and Efforts to Reduce It, 2017, available at: www.greeningtheblue.org/resources/climate-neutrality.

UNEP. „Greening the Blue Report

2016. The UN system's environmental footprint and efforts to reduce it," available at: www.greeningtheblue.org.

UNGA. „Manual on Policies and Procedures concerning the Reimbursement and Control of Contingent-Owned Equipment of Troop/Police Contributors Participating in Peacekeeping Missions." A/72/288. August 2017.

United Nations Global Marketplace, available at: www.ungm.org.

UNMIL "Documents", available at: https://unmil.unmissions.org/Documents and www.cabri-sbo.org/uploads/files/Documents/liberia_2017_formulation_external_budget_framework_ministry_of_finance_ecowas_english_1.pdf

UNMIL, UNPK, "Chinese Contingent Donates to Zwedru School", available at: https://unmil.unmissions.org/chinese-contingent-donates-zwedru-school.

UNMIL, UNPK, "Chinese Engineers Construct a Road:" available at: https://unmil.unmissions.org/chinese-engineers-construct-road-community-college.

UNMIL, UNPK, „Technical and Operational Capacities to Support the UN Commitments", 2018, available at: https://unmil.unmissions.org/sites/default/files/unct_capacity_mapping_findings-22may2017_0.pdf.

UNMIL, UNPK. „Chinese Contingent Inaugurates New Equipment." February 2018, available at: https://unmil.unmissions.org/chinese-contingent-inaugurates-new-equipment.

UNMIL, UNPK. „Technical and Operational Capacities to Support the UN Commitments." Available at: https://unmil.unmissions.org/sites/default/files/unct_capacity_mapping_findings-22may2017_0.pdf.

UNMIL. „Factsheet." UN, available at: https://peacekeeping.un.org/en/mission/unmil.

UNMISS, „Fact Sheet", UN Peacekeeping, available at: https://peacekeeping.un.org/en/mission/minusca.

UNPK. „Environmental Impact and sustainability", available at: https://peacekeeping.un.org/en/environmental-impact-and-sustainability.

UNSDGs. „End hunger, achieve food Security and improved nutrition and promote sustainable agriculture." UN, available at: https://sustainabledevelopment.un.org/sdg2.

UNSDGs. Goal 6, „Ensure availability and sustainable management of water and sanitation for all." UN, available at: https://sustainabledevelopment.un.org/sdg6.

UNSDGs. Goal 7. „Ensure access to affordable, reliable, sustainable and modern energy for all" UN, available at: https://sustainabledevelopment.un.org/sdg7.

UNSDGs. Goal 13, available at: www.un.org sustainabledevelopment/climate-action.

UNSDGs. „The New Urban Agenda: Key Commitments," United Nations, October 20, 2016, available at: www.un.org/sustainabledevelopment/blog/2016/10/newurbanagenda.

USAID Office of Food for Peace, Food Security Desk Review for Liberia, 2016, available at: www.usaid.gov/sites/default/files/documents/1866/FFP-Desk-Review-Liberia-Feb2016v2.pdf.

Wada, Kayomi, „El Mina São Jorge da Mina", BlackPast. January 11, 2010.

Wells, Jeremias. „Henry the Navigator Inaugurates the Age of Discovery," available at: https://nobility.org/2012/11/12/henry-discovery.

Westendorf, Jasmine. „Sexual abuse by UN peacekeepers is shocking and shameful. Why does it persist?", see: www.abc.net.au/news/2020-06-15/united-nations-un-peacekeeping-sexual-exploitation-abuse/12286664.

Williams, Andrew J. "'Reconstruction' before the Marshall Plan." Review of International Studies, vol. 31, no. 3, Cambridge University Press, 2005, pp. 541–58.

World Bank, „After Ebola," available at: www.worldbank.org/en/news/feature/2017/06/07/after-ebola-liberias-health-system-on-path-to-recovery.

World Meteorological Organization, „State of the Climate in Africa, 2019." available at: https://library.wmo.int/doc_num.php?explnum_id=10421.

Yovsi, R.; Samba, K.; Bahr, B. et al. A Qualitative Study of Infant and Young Child Feeding Practices in Liberia. UNICEF, 2010.

UN Peacekeeping. „The Story of UNMIL. United Nations in Liberia," available at: https://unmil.unmissions.org/sites/default/files/the_story_of_unmil.pdf.

Maps and Diagrams Data Sources

ClimaTemp, "Rainfall Precipitation in Monrovia, Liberia", December 2017, available: www.Liberia.climatemps.com/precipitation.php.

Dutch Ministry of Defence Archive.

Geospatial, location information for a better world. UN. Available at: https://www.un.org/geospatial.

International Federation of Red Cross, available at: www.ifrc.org.

Kumpel, Emily et al. "Urban Water Services in Fragile States: An Analysis of Drinking Water Sources and Quality in Port Harcourt, Nigeria, and Monrovia, Liberia." The American Journal of Tropical Medicine and Hygiene 95.1 (2016):, pp. 229–238. PMC. Web. 21 May 2018; World Bank and UHL & Associates study, 2011.

Liberia. Agricultural Sectors, available at: www.export.gov/article?id=Liberia-Agricultural-Sectors.

Trading Economics, "Liberia GDP", available at: https://tradingeconomics.com/liberia/gdp.

Liberia Demographic and Health Survey (2013), available at: www.lisgis.net/pg_img/Liberia%202013%20DHS%20Final%20Report_Partial.pdf.

The World Fact Book, CIA. "Liberia", February, 2017, available at: www.cia.gov/library/Publications/the-world-factbook/geos/li.html.

Liberia Water and Sanitation and Education photographs by UNICEF, available at: www.unicef.org.

NASA. "Earth at Night", available at: www.nasa.gov/topics/earth/earthday/gall_earth_night.html.

OECD Library. "An Atlas of the Sahara-Sahel Geography, Economics and Security Sahel and West Africa Club", available at: www.oecd-ilibrary.org.

Open Street Map, available at: www.openstreetmap.org.

Ordaz-Németh I, Arandjelovic M, Boesch L, Gatiso T, Grimes T, Kuehl HS, et al. (2017) The socio-economic drivers of bushmeat consumption during the West African Ebola crisis. PLoS Negl Trop Dis 11(3): e0005450. https://doi.org/10.1371/journal.pntd.0005450.

"Small flame but no fire: Wood fuel in the (Intended) Nationally Determined Contributions of countries in Sub-Saharan Africa", available at: www.cifor.org/library/6651/small-flame-but-no-fire-wood-fuel-in-the-intended-nationally-determined-contributions-of-countries-in-sub-saharan-africa.

Trading Economics, available at: https://tradingeconomics.com/liberia/gdp.

UN Audiovisual Library, available at: www.unmultimedia.org/avlibrary.

United Nations Archives and Records Management Section, Department of Operational Support (DOS), UN Headquarters in New York.

UN Department of Field Support. United Nations, available at: www.un.org/Depts/Cartographic/english/htmain.htm.

UNMIL. "Progress Report," available at: https://unmil.unmissions.org/documents.

USAID, Liberia. SITUATIONAL ANALYSIS REPORT LIBERIA MUNICIPAL WATER PROJECT, available at: www.usaid.gov/sites/default/files/documents/1860/2012-11%20LMWP%20SA%20Report.pdf.

USAID office of food for peace food Security desk review for liberia, 2016–2020, available at: www.usaid.gov/sites/default/files/documents/1866/FFP-Desk-Review-Liberia-Feb2016v2.pdf.

Water Aid, available at: www.wateraid.org/where-we-work/page/liberia.

"Water Catchment Calculator", available at: www.rhinotanks.com.au/catchment_calculator/do_calculate.

World Captial Cities, available at: worldcapitalcities.com.

World Health Organization, The Global Health Observatory, available at: www.who.int/data/gho/data/themes/mortality-and-global-health-estimates.

Urnam Expansio. Background map USGS Earth Explorer. Landsat 8, Feb-16. West Africa: Land Use and Land Cover Dynamics. Case Study: Urban growth in Liberia's only metropolis: Monrovia, available at: https://eros.usgs.gov/westafrica/case-study/urban-growth-liberias-only-metropolis-monrovia.

Years of Civil Conflict in Liberia Create Waste Mismanagement and Health and Environmental Degradatio, available at: www.worldbank.org/en/news/feature/2010/05/12/years-of-civil-conflict-in-liberia-create-waste-mismanagement-and-health-and-environmental-degradation.

Photographs

Dutch Ministry of Defense

Flickr

Foundation Dogon Education

Iwan Baan (the Venice Architecture Biennale opening)

Justin Knight (Border Ecologies exhibition at Harvard GSD)

Malkit Shoshan (Mali/MINUSMA and Liberia/UNMIL)

Moussa Ag Assarid and Studio Jonas Staal

Rob Gijsbers (the Venice Architecture Biennale models),

Stadsarchief Amsterdam

Simone Ferraro (the Venice Architecture Biennale)

Videos

Overview Construction Camp Castor, Mediacenter Ministry of Defense. 2014

Special Forces Mali, Mediacenter Ministry of Defense, 2014

Desert Rebel. Abdallah Oumbadougou. Directed by François Bergeron. 2009

The TELLEM-Expedition, Herman Haan/NCRV, 1964

Index

Published by
Actar Publishers,
New York, Barcelona
www.actar.com

Photographs
Dutch Ministry of Defense, Foundation Dogon Education, Flickr, Iwan Baan (the Venice Architecture Biennale opening), Justin Knight (Harvard GSD exhibition), Malkit Shoshan (Mali/MINUSMA and Liberia/UNMIL), Moussa Ag Assarid, Rob Gijsbers (the Venice Architecture Biennale models), Simone Ferraro (the Venice Architecture Biennale opening), Stadsarchief Amsterdam.

Videos
Camp Castor Livable, Mediacenter Ministry of Defense. 2014.
Overview Construction Camp Castor, Mediacenter Ministry of Defense. 2014.
Special Forces Mali, Mediacenter Ministry of Defense, 2014.
Desert Rebel Abdallah Oumbadougou, directed by François Bergeron. 2009.
The TELLEM-Expedition, Herman Haan/NCRV, 1964.

Distribution
Actar D, Inc. New York, Barcelona.

New York
440 Park Avenue South, 17th Floor
New York, NY 10016, USA

ISBN: 9781948765824
ISBN-10: 1948765829

Colophon

BLUE: Architecture of UN Peacekeeping Missions

Author
Malkit Shoshan

Additional Essays
Arnon Grunberg, Debra Solomon, Erella Grassiani, Joel van der Beek Marcel Rot, Marion de Vos

Interviews
Moussa Ag Assarid (Representative of the MNLA: The Movement for the Liberation of Azawad), Rob de Vos (Former Consul General of the Netherlands in NY and the first Dutch ambassador in Mali)

Book Design
Irma Boom and Julia Neller

Illustrations, Maps, and Diagrams
Malkit Shoshan with Isabel Carrasco (UNMIL section), Laura van Santen (MINUSMA imageries), and Julia Neller

Models Design
Malkit Shoshan

Models Production
Rob Gijsbers, Studio Roel Huisman

Copy-Editing
Angela Kay Bunning

This book is made possible thanks to the generous support of the Netherlands Creative Industries Fund.

Mali Research and Findings
Led by FAST:Malkit Shoshan with contribution by Debra Solomon, Erella Grassiani, Joel van der Beek, Jonas Staal, LEVS Architecten, Moussa Ag Assarid, Marion de Vos, Peter Chilson, Rob de Vos, and support of the Dutch Ministry of Foreign Affairs: Charlotte van Baak, Eran Nagan, Marleen Monster, Mirjam Tjassing, Renilde Steeghs; Dutch Ministry of Defense: Lt. Col. Alex Jansen, Maj. Erwin Marx, Col. Kees Matthijssen, Col. Norbert Moerkens, Maj. Marcel Rot, Cpt. Thomas Boonen, Cpt. Wouter Eidhof

Photographs Mali Field Research 2016
Malkit Shoshan

This research is made possible thanks to the Netherlands Creative Industries Fund and Het Nieuwe Instituut.

Liberia Research and Findings
Led by FAST: Malkit Shoshan with Isabel Carrasco, and with the support of NYU Center on International Cooperation: Paige Arthur, Leah Zamore, and Sarah Cliffe; Permanent Mission of Australia to the UN: David Yardley; Permanent Mission of the United Kingdom to the UN: Stephen Hickey, Thomas Wheeler, Samuel Grout-Smith; and in conversation with the UN Peacebuilding Support Office: Henk-Jan Brinkman (Chief of Policy, Planning, and Application), Margherita Capellino (Coordination Officer), Gizem Sucuoglu (Regional Program Specialist); UN Department of Peacekeeping Operations: Bibi Eng (Chief of Staff UNMIL), Rania Dagash (Chief of the Policy and Best Practices Services, Division for Policy, Evaluation, and Training), David Penklis (Director, Mission Support, United Nations Mission in Liberia), Joanna Harvey (Senior Environmental Affairs Officer at United Nations), Loudres Kondrk (Logistics Officer, UNMIL), Sophie Ravier (Chief, Environment and Culture Unit); Permanent Mission of Liberia to the United Nations: Israel Choko Davies.
The West Africa Network for Peace-building (WANEP) Liberia: Philip M. Collie, West Point Women for Health and Development, Women's NGO Secretariat of Liberia

Photographs Liberia Field Research 2017
Malkit Shoshan with Isabel Carrasco

This research was made possible thanks to the support of The Australian Mission to the United Nations and The United Kingdom Mission to the UN.

Elements of UN Peacekeeping Missions and the Environment were first published in a report for the International Peace Institute (IPI), authored by Lucile Maertens and Malkit Shoshan with the support of Alexandra Novosseloff, Arthur Boutellis, and the Environment Section at the UN Department of Operational Support.

Design for Legacy
Research and design project led by FAST with contributions to the research, workshops and events by Debra Solomon/URBANIAHOEVE, Erella Grassiani/University of Amsterdam, Henk Ovink, Joel van der Beek/Econo-vision and Economists for Peace and Security, Malkit Shoshan/FAST, Robert Kluijver, Samir Bantal, Dutch Ministry of Foreign Affairs: Charlotte van Baak, Eran Nagan, Marleen Monster, Renilde Steeghs; Dutch Ministry of Defense: Lt. Col. Alex Jansen, Maj. Erwin Marx, Col. Kees Matthijssen, Col. Norbert Moerkens, Maj. Marcel Rot, Cpt. Thomas Boonen, Cpt. Wouter Eidhof, NYU Center on International Cooperation: Leah Zamore and Paige Arthur

With additional thanks to
Matthijs Bouw, Guus Beumer, Sandra Kassenaar, Master Soumy, Jane Szita, and Deen Sharp and the NYU Institute for Public Knowledge